# Anywhere Working and the Future of Work

Yvette Blount
*Macquarie University, Australia*

Marianne Gloet
*University of Melbourne, Australia*

A volume in the Advances in Human Resources Management and Organizational Development (AHRMOD) Book Series

IGI Global
PUBLISHER of TIMELY KNOWLEDGE

Published in the United States of America by
IGI Global
Business Science Reference (an imprint of IGI Global)
701 E. Chocolate Avenue
Hershey PA, USA 17033
Tel: 717-533-8845
Fax: 717-533-8661
E-mail: cust@igi-global.com
Web site: http://www.igi-global.com



Library of Congress Cataloging-in-Publication Data

Names: Blount, Yvette, 1963- editor. | Gloet, Marianne, editor.
Title: Anywhere working and the future of work / Yvette Blount, Marianne Gloet, editors.
Description: Hershey, PA : Business Science Reference, [2021] | Includes bibliographical references and index. | Summary: "This book examines the trends, issues, and limitations of the future of anywhere working"-- Provided by publisher.
Identifiers: LCCN 2020009101 (print) | LCCN 2020009102 (ebook) | ISBN 9781799841593 (hardcover) | ISBN 9781799855620 (paperback) | ISBN 9781799841609 (ebook)
Subjects: LCSH: Telecommuting. | Virtual work teams. | Labor--Forecasting.
Classification: LCC HD2336.3 .A58 2020 (print) | LCC HD2336.3 (ebook) | DDC 331.25/68--dc23
LC record available at https://lccn.loc.gov/2020009101
LC ebook record available at https://lccn.loc.gov/2020009102

This book is published in the IGI Global book series Advances in Human Resources Management and Organizational Development (AHRMOD) (ISSN: 2327-3372; eISSN: 2327-3380)

British Cataloguing in Publication Data
A Cataloguing in Publication record for this book is available from the British Library.

All work contributed to this book is new, previously-unpublished material.
The views expressed in this book are those of the authors, but not necessarily of the publisher.

For electronic access to this publication, please contact: eresources@igi-global.com.

# Advances in Human Resources Management and Organizational Development (AHRMOD) Book Series

ISSN:2327-3372
EISSN:2327-3380

Editor-in-Chief: Patricia Ordóñez de Pablos, Universidad de Oviedo, Spain

**MISSION**

A solid foundation is essential to the development and success of any organization and can be accomplished through the effective and careful management of an organization's human capital. Research in human resources management and organizational development is necessary in providing business leaders with the tools and methodologies which will assist in the development and maintenance of their organizational structure.

The **Advances in Human Resources Management and Organizational Development (AHRMOD) Book Series** aims to publish the latest research on all aspects of human resources as well as the latest methodologies, tools, and theories regarding organizational development and sustainability. The **AHRMOD Book Series** intends to provide business professionals, managers, researchers, and students with the necessary resources to effectively develop and implement organizational strategies.

**COVERAGE**

- Diversity in the Workplace
- Disputes Resolution
- Process Improvement
- Personnel Retention
- Change Management
- Coaching and Mentoring
- Talent Identification and Management
- Entrepreneurialism
- Collaborative Method
- Employee Evaluation

IGI Global is currently accepting manuscripts for publication within this series. To submit a proposal for a volume in this series, please contact our Acquisition Editors at Acquisitions@igi-global.com or visit: http://www.igi-global.com/publish/.

The Advances in Human Resources Management and Organizational Development (AHRMOD) Book Series (ISSN 2327-3372) is published by IGI Global, 701 E. Chocolate Avenue, Hershey, PA 17033-1240, USA, www.igi-global.com. This series is composed of titles available for purchase individually; each title is edited to be contextually exclusive from any other title within the series. For pricing and ordering information please visit http://www.igi-global.com/book-series/advances-human-resources-management-organizational/73670. Postmaster: Send all address changes to above address. 

## Titles in this Series

*For a list of additional titles in this series, please visit:*
http://www.igi-global.com/book-series/advances-human-resources-management-organizational/73670

***Effective Strategies for Communicating Insights in Business***
Ross Jackson (Wittenberg University, USA) and Amanda Reboulet (Air Force Civilian Service, USA)
Business Science Reference • © 2021 • 330pp • H/C (ISBN: 9781799839644) • US $195.00

***Implementation Strategies for Improving Diversity in Organizations***
Claretha Hughes (University of Arkansas, USA)
Business Science Reference • © 2021 • 451pp • H/C (ISBN: 9781799847458) • US $195.00

***Principles of Islamic Ethics for Contemporary Workplaces***
Abdus Sattar Abbasi (COMSATS University Islamabad, Lahore Campus, Pakistan) and Razaq Raj (Leeds Beckett University, UK)
Business Science Reference • © 2021 • 275pp • H/C (ISBN: 9781799852957) • US $215.00

***Impact of Human Resource Management Practices and Interventions in SMEs***
Jayaranjani Sutha (Eastern University, Sri Lanka)
Business Science Reference • © 2020 • 300pp • H/C (ISBN: 9781799848028) • US $195.00

***Impact of Age, Gender, and Technology on Modern Unemployment***
Ali Eren Alper (Niğde Ömer Halisdemir University, Turkey) Mehmet Sedat Uğur (Çankırı Karatekin University, Turkey) and Aleksandra Katarzyna Górecka (Warsaw University of Life Sciences, Poland)
Business Science Reference • © 2020 • 300pp • H/C (ISBN: 9781799850564) • US $195.00

***Contemporary Global Issues in Human Resource Management***
Mehmet Ali Turkmenoglu (Mus Alparslan University, Turkey) and Berat Cicek (Mus Alparslan University, Turkey)
Business Science Reference • © 2020 • 300pp • H/C (ISBN: 9781799831914) • US $215.00

*For an entire list of titles in this series, please visit:*
http://www.igi-global.com/book-series/advances-human-resources-management-organizational/73670

IGI Global
PUBLISHER of TIMELY KNOWLEDGE

701 East Chocolate Avenue, Hershey, PA 17033, USA
Tel: 717-533-8845 x100 • Fax: 717-533-8661
E-Mail: cust@igi-global.com • www.igi-global.com

# Editorial Advisory Board

# Table of Contents

# Detailed Table of Contents



This chapter examines the literature relating to information and communications technology (ICT) and opportunities and barriers relating to anywhere working. The workforce is becoming more global, and workers can work from anywhere and still be connected with colleagues and collaborators. Although ICT is an enabler of anywhere working, sustainable anywhere working requires specific management skills and capabilities. Globalization of work requires organizations to manage workers ranging from full-time employees through to freelancers working in different locations including a central office, co-working center, from home, and other flexible options. The chapter concludes by proposing a research agenda and conceptual framework to identify the management skills and capabilities required to successfully manage anywhere working (other terms include telework and telecommuting). The proposed conceptual framework will inform researchers and managers on best practice for adopting sustainable anywhere working to achieve strategic business objectives.



Western ideas about work have developed as macro and micro level changes continue to shape the social relations of work. As anywhere working developed as an alternative to traditional work arrangements in the 1990s, a system of checks and balances ensured the work practice delivered customer service and product quality. Western low-context work cultures situated the work practice as a logical development in the chronology of the social relations of work. With its tipping-point in the West reached, anywhere working received less attention in high-context work cultures. Specifically, this chapter investigates how the concept of "national culture" impacts thinking about anywhere working. In the high-context work cultures of East and South East Asia, employers, employees, and the stakeholders of organizations and governments have divergent views about the legitimacy of this work practice. The chapter discusses the influence of national culture on thinking about anywhere working in high-context work cultures, drawing on current data concerning anywhere working in selected Asian economies.



Advanced technologies including artificial intelligence, robotics, and machine learning (smart machines) impact understandings about the nature of work. For professionals, semi-professionals, and ancillary workers supplying healthcare and legal services, for example, smart machines change the social relations of work and subvert notions of status and hierarchy that come with occupational groups such as doctors or lawyers. As smart machines continue to disrupt employment, job advertisement might soon carry the warning that humans need not apply. Under the prospect of a new world of work, people require additional knowledge, skills, and attitudes to cope with a future where smart machines radically alter the nature of work in settings where some people work anywhere and anytime while others work nowhere. In any future, people require skills and attitudes to cope with uncertainty. Ideas about multiple intelligences, emotional intelligence, critical thinking, creativity, and problem-solving will help employees cope with any of the futures of work predicted in the literature.



Clinicians (general practitioners, specialists, allied health professionals) are experts in medicine, not technology. The delivery of healthcare using technology includes changes to the way the clinician works; in effect, they work from anywhere. This study examined telehealth adoption from the perspective of clinicians. Data was

social isolation misconceptions, insufficient flexible work opportunities, and inadequate management knowledge of IT support and reasonable adjustment for people with disabilities. Management issues involve cultural intolerance towards diversity and disability in general, as well as lack of policies and processes that create a supportive environment for people with disabilities who wish to engage in flexible working arrangements.

**Section 3**
**Design and Context of Anywhere Working**



The paradigm shift in work dynamics in the digital age leads the evolution of how and where people work. Knowledge workers adopt more flexible working styles: they connect to their laptops and work anywhere. The main disadvantage of this way of working is social isolation. Creative industries often require interdisciplinary interaction and collaboration. Coworking spaces have emerged in order to remove this isolation and create a third place apart from home and office. These spaces have been studied by disciplines such as economics, work psychology, and geography but studies on their spatial characteristics are limited. The aim of the chapter is to propose a conceptual framework to identify design implications for the coworking spaces in terms of spatial preferences of users. Accordingly, literature related to changing work dynamics and workplaces, rise of coworking spaces, and coworking space typology are discussed. The conclusion of the chapter is to propose design implications, which will inform designers, researchers, and managers on best practice for coworking space design.



Workspaces and workplaces have changed significantly over the last decade. Facilitated by networking and collaboration tools, there has been a steady concentration of inner-city coworking spaces providing many opportunities for new flexible work arrangements. Driven by sustainability and creative entrepreneurship, coworking

# Foreword

The key terms in the title of this book, 'Anywhere Working' and 'the Future of Work', much like their relatives 'teleworking', 'digital disruption' and 'gig economy', are now among the most popular memes across the world, particularly since COVID-19 has been affecting our lives and work. According to the *Encyclopedia Britannica*, a meme is 'an element of a culture or system of behaviour passed from one individual to another by imitation'; memes 'carry information, are replicated, and are transmitted from one person to another' verbally, visually and electronically through conversations or practises, books, television, e-mail and the Internet. Memes can be both harmful and beneficial. Since Richard Dawkins coined the term in his 1976 book *The Selfish Gene*, a whole field of study known as memetics has developed to address this form of transmission and its impact on our thinking, knowledge and beliefs (see Johnson, 2007). The most effective remedy to the virus like spread of memes and the dangers of their simplistic and unthinking replication is quality research and critical analysis.

It therefore gives me great pleasure to introduce this book as an antidote to the memes that help spread superficial accounts of Anywhere Working and the future of work through the news media and related publications. Admittedly, as the editors acknowledge, it 'is a "work in progress", given that the COVID-19 pandemic is still driving many initiatives and practices related to anywhere working'. Yet this starting point is most timely and greatly needed since it provides scholars and employers, managers and employees with a comprehensive and critical entry into what we have begun to refer to as wicked problems. Admittedly, the term and concept of the 'wicked problem' or problems could be said to be yet another meme popular now among academics and policymakers. Nevertheless, the concept of the wicked problem helps us recognise complexity and the difficulty in developing and implementing effective solutions and guidelines to work-related policy, strategy and practical problems and (Head, 2019; Guy Peters, 2017).

Attention to the wicked problems raised by Anywhere Working and the future of work, is not new. If we take into account that it is often rather simplistically used as a synonym for 'working from home' (WFH), then we can trace management and scholarly interest back to the 1990s when higher degree research students and academics began to explore the pros and cons of WFH as part of the growing interest in the need to balance work and family responsibilities. Such issues that remain prominent today during COVID-19 lock downs. Of course, interest subsequently shifted to 'teleworking' before expanding to Anywhere Working in recent years but even in this form take up was limited until recently given the fears over control and quality and quantity of work outcomes, the many headed hydra that has dogged the management of work since the industrial revolution.

However, as the chapters in this book so thoughtfully and pervasively demonstrate, Anywhere Working cannot and should not be reduced to WFH alone. Indeed, the great value of this book lies in its breadth of coverage of complex, open-ended, and intractable issues arising from changes to the organization and conduct of work wherever it is conducted, and the skills needed to manage it effectively, ethically and equitably. In this regard, the attention given to questions of employee productivity, to management skill and style, to trust and, as significantly, to the nature of access to and control over technologies, particularly in the form of IT and ICT, smart machines and AI is profoundly valuable. Concerns regarding both access and accessibility to various technologies and who bears the tangible and intangible costs have been voiced by a multitude of stakeholders, ranging from employees to students and also advocates for those who cannot afford adequate technology.

The attention given in the book to the impact of new forms of Anywhere Working made possible through technology on aged care and health services, as well as working people with disabilities is especially welcome. Indepth scholarly attention to telehealth from the perspective of both service recipients and clinicians is particularly notable at this time given the necessity for and rise of telehealth during the COVID pandemic. Hopefully, the chapters on these subjects will encourage more research and publications on the health service dimensions and implications of Anywhere Working that can improve government policies and resourcing.

Last but certainly not least, is the significant attention given in the book to the design of Anywhere Work in relation to diverse stakeholders located in diverse places. Here we find attention to aspects of the future of work that are becoming especially wicked, notably casual, virtual, freelance and 'gig' work, subject rarely explored in terms of Anywhere Work. Here the book provides a corrective to the extensive ink that has been spilled on the isolation that can accompany Anywhere Work by focusing on a range of social opportunities. At a time when individualism and competition dominate approaches to many approaches to work and other activities, the chapters present readers with new possibilities for co-operative work by highlighting the value of innovative approaches to the organization of physical places for social interaction, knowledge sharing and collaboration that can support the emergence of 'smart cities'. Here, too, attention is given not simply to workplace design and the growth of co-working hubs for entrepreneurs but also their nexus with new forms of technology and specifically new digital manufacturing technologies.

A particularly welcome aspect of the book is its incorporation of both conceptual and theoretical frameworks as well as guidelines for practice, thereby ensuring that the book will be of great value to academics, students and employees, employers and managers interested in looking beyond simplistic memes. This book will provide a basis for informed discussion among those willing to engage in deep thought about the wicked problems of work in the present with an eye to developing more creative and fair policies and approaches for the future of work. I congratulate the editors and authors on their contributions.

*Lucy Taksa*
*Centre for Workforce Futures, Macquarie University Business School, Australia*

## REFERENCES

Dawkins, R. (1976). *The Selfish Gene*. Oxford University Press.

Guy Peters, B. (2017). 'What is so wicked about wicked problems? A conceptual analysis and a research program'. *Policy and Society*, *36*(3), 385–396. doi:10.1080/14494035.2017.1361633

Head, B. W. (2019). 'Forty years of wicked problems literature: Forging closer links to policy studies'. *Policy and Society*, *38*(2), 180–197. doi:10.1080/14494035.2018.1488797

# Preface

Anywhere working, or the ability to work from anywhere facilitated by technology is an area of research that resonates strongly in the context of the current COVID-19 pandemic. The most significant work from home experiences arising from lockdowns across the globe will be a topic for examination from the perspective of both employees and employers over the coming months and years. The uptake of telehealth to deliver health services has transformed the way we access health care and how clinicians interact with patients. Co-working centres that have held so much promise for working anywhere will need to adjust to the post-COVID-19 world. To date, much of the research on anywhere working has revolved around the service sector. However, there may be opportunities we have not considered previously. For example, there may be new opportunities for anywhere working in the manufacturing sector facilitated by technology such as 3D printing. This book addresses some of the issues that have now come into sharper focus during 2020. The chapters in this book provide insights into how we can navigate anywhere, working in a post-COVID-19 world.

## SECTION 1: MANAGEMENT, LEADERSHIP, AND WORK ORGANIZATION

Section 1 focuses on management, leadership and work organization issues related to anywhere working. As organizations continue to grow their technical capability and leverage innovative technology, anywhere working has the power to transform how, where and when people work. That is, anywhere working has the power to transform working relationships significantly – for better or for worse. Given that ICT is a significant enabler of anywhere working, a high level of technological capacity and IT support are required to increase the productivity of individuals and teams. Provided they have appropriate IT tools which allow them to conduct their work seamlessly from virtual work locations workers can be more productive when anywhere working. Indeed, the impact of the COVID-19 pandemic in 2020 has made it necessary for people to engage in anywhere working in order for the government, businesses and services to remain productive (and employed).

However, while technology is a significant enabler of anywhere working, many managers and leaders lack experience, skills and capabilities relating to anywhere working. Despite the promise of virtual and mobile forms of work, there is a widespread discrepancy among managers and leaders about the level of acceptance of anywhere working, and this has been a key barrier faced by employees in the past who wish to engage in this practice. Despite the rapid uptake of anywhere working as a response to COVID-19, it remains to be seen whether anywhere working gains traction and support in the future – it may be only a temporary phenomenon arising from a unique set of circumstances relating to the global pandemic.

In any event, anywhere working requires a different managerial approach and style to more traditional forms of working. Managers need to set clear tasks and articulate outcomes to be achieved by individual workers as well as teams. The changing nature of work in the global context depends heavily on teamwork that extends beyond the normal institutional, geographical and temporal boundaries, which means that anywhere workers need to collaborate across time and space. Trust between managers and anywhere workers is essential to foster a productive working environment, as is regular and effective communication. Managers and leaders of anywhere workers should not be concerned about where work is done, as long as employees are productive and demonstrate that tasks are completed successfully and on time. Managers need to carefully select employees for anywhere working, as the most productive anywhere workers tend to be driven, self-motivated and independent workers who are well organized and can deliver results on time and as expected. Not all roles and tasks are conducive to anywhere working. For instance, some roles requiring a high level of customer contact may not be suitable for anywhere working.

Chapter 1, "Working Anywhere Management Opportunities and Challenges," examines the literature on the implications of ICT for anywhere working, as well as management skills and capabilities relating to anywhere working. Rapid changes in the contemporary landscape, including the forces of globalization, world disasters and emergencies such as the COVID-19 outbreak require organizations to manage workers ranging from full-time employees through to freelancers working in different locations including centralized offices, co-working centres, home and other flexible locations. Globalization and flexible work options, particularly anywhere working, will enhance an organization's productivity and competitive advantage if managers have the skills and capabilities to manage the workforce wherever it is located. Anywhere working relies on ICT for effective collaboration and communication, and the choice of technology for supporting collaboration and connectivity will require rethinking the design and the location of work. The chapter also offers a conceptual framework based on current literature to inform managers and researchers on best practice for adopting sustainable anywhere working and proposes some future research directions, including the need for a better understanding of the dynamic nature of ICT and the implications for human resource management to support and enhance anywhere working.

Chapter 2, "National Culture and the Future of Anywhere Working," explores the idea of anywhere working as a new work practice with distinguishing characteristics from both theoretical and practical perspectives. Anywhere working provides opportunities to utilize non-traditional workspaces and new employment relationships; however, the new employment relationships arising from anywhere working have implications for both employees and employers. The first part of the chapter discusses the images and meanings attached to work through the ages in the context of Western ideas and traditions. The notion of a sociological paradigm frames the discussion and analysis of anywhere working in its broadest context. The second part of the chapter discusses the practical implications of anywhere working, highlighting the areas that require new understandings about work practices from the perspectives of employees, employers and the wider society. The final part discusses the neglected area of the influence of national culture on attitudes toward anywhere working, using examples drawn from non-Western societies in the Asian region. Given its rapid spread, anywhere working may be represented as a watershed in employment relations and work practices. In this light, new ways of thinking about the social relations and the nature of work itself are required.

In Chapter 3, "Humans Need Not Apply: Artificial Intelligence, Robotics, Machine Learning, and the Future of Work," the relationships between the development of technology, its application and rate of uptake are considered fundamental to imagining the future of work in any of its forms. Advanced technologies including artificial intelligence, robotics and machine learning (smart machines) impact understandings about the nature of work. For professionals, semi-professionals and ancillary workers supplying health care and legal services, for example, smart machines change the social relations of work and subvert notions of status and hierarchy that come with occupations like doctors or lawyers. As smart machines continue to disrupt employment, job advertisements might soon carry the warning, 'humans need not apply'. The impact of these new technologies could have a profound impact on the future of anywhere working. Under the prospect of a new world of work, people require additional knowledge, skills and attitudes to cope with a future where smart machines radically alter the nature of work in settings where some people work anywhere and anytime while others work nowhere. In any future, people require skills and attitudes to cope with uncertainty. Ideas about multiple intelligences, emotional intelligence, critical thinking, creativity and problem-solving will help employees cope with any of the futures of work predicted in the literature.

## SECTION 2: TELEHEALTH, DISABILITY, AND INCLUSIVENESS

Section 2 is concerned with the potential of anywhere working for the areas of ICT-enabled telehealth and aged care services, as well as in the context of supporting disability and inclusion. Given the societal trend of aging populations and people living longer in general, health care costs are rapidly increasing. The promise of anywhere working to support telehealth and aged care services is vast: delivering cost savings, time savings, allowing for increased frequency of service to clients; greater flexibility of delivery, streamlining of administrative processes and enhanced client/worker relationships. Similarly, given the increasing prevalence of flexible work, co-working hubs, activity-based workspaces and greater acceptance of diversity in the workplace, anywhere working is seen as a means of making employment more accessible for people with disabilities. While ICT enabled delivery may open up new opportunities for telehealth, aged care and disability and inclusion, its success is heavily dependent not only on the technology but on users of the technology. New challenges concerning anywhere working in these areas arise constantly.

Chapter 4, "A Clinician's Perspective on Anywhere Working and Telehealth," examines the major issues and challenges for workers engaged in telehealth service delivery in Australia. In examining the provision of telehealth service delivery from the clinicians' perspective, the challenging and complex landscape surrounding telehealth is revealed. Issues with technology, funding and incentives, practitioner skills and capabilities as well as business process change all combine to create significant challenges for telehealth practitioners. For telehealth to be sustainable, it must be both effective (clinically appropriate) and efficient (seamless and cost-effective). Health care delivery facilitated by technology is a complex endeavor involving multiple stakeholders and many challenges. Careful consideration of both the choice of technology and technology support that facilitates telehealth for both the patient and the clinician is the first criterion for successful telehealth adoption. The second criterion involves funding incentives for clinicians and appropriate funding for telehealth consultations. Analysis of changes in roles, responsibilities and skills of clinicians adopting telehealth consultations is the third criterion. The fourth criterion is the recognition of the necessary changes in business processes and workflow that result from telehealth adoption.

Chapter 5, "Service Delivery in Aged Care: ICT and Anywhere Working," explores ICT-enabled anywhere working was adopted in a not-for-profit aged care organization in Australia. The aged care and services sector has grown over the last decade, leading to shortages of skilled and experienced workers. At the same time, the sector is dealing with significant changes relating to funding of services, an increase in competition from both not-for-profits and for-profit providers, a rise in demand for services, changes in technology as well as variations in government regulations.

Using ICT to streamline operations as well as communicate and collaborate has become critical for delivering efficient and effective services in both residential aged care and community care sections of the aged care and services sector. This case study of a not-for-profit provider shows how a first mover in ICT adoption and utilizing anywhere working can deliver cost savings, provide the ability to respond to the changing regulatory environment as well as attract, train and retain skilled and experienced workers.

Chapter 6, "Access to Flexible Work Arrangements for People With Disabilities: An Australian Study," is the first exploratory research to investigate the relationship between flexible work and disability in Australia and identifies multiple barriers and issues associated with the uptake of flexible or anywhere working arrangements for people with disabilities. There is a need for management to take responsibility for increasing workforce participation by people with disabilities. This involves changes at both the level of employee and employer – including the cultivation of higher levels of tolerance and acceptance arising from equity policies that support recruitment practices focused on diversity balance. Moreover, job and task structures need to be revisited or redesigned as part of a broader reasonable adjustment strategy to match specific and unique workers with tasks. Anywhere work can bring about advantages for people with disabilities and may reduce social stigma associated with a disability because people are judged more by the work they do, rather than by their disability. Sadly, this study highlights that the worlds of managers and workers with disabilities are not yet adequately aligned or transparent – most managers do not yet fully understand the potential that people with disabilities can bring to the workplace, particularly through anywhere working.

## SECTION 3: DESIGN AND CONTEXT OF ANYWHERE WORKING

Globalization and advances in ICT have changed the dynamics of work and the physical spaces where work is done. This shift is characterized by the emergence of new forms of anywhere working, including multi-locational, distributed, mobile and virtual possibilities. No longer is knowledge work confined to traditional offices and manufacturing to large factory settings. Indeed, workplaces and workspaces have changed significantly over the years, as workers become more mobile and technology to support anywhere working becomes more sophisticated. New work models have become more widespread as worker mobility increases. This has drawn attention to several issues such as the need for new work arrangements, work-life balance, workspace design and a focus on wellbeing for anywhere workers. These new work arrangements are required as a response to the growing number of casual, virtual, freelance and 'gig' workers who populate the landscape of anywhere working. Coworking hubs and co-working spaces offer not only a physical place for anywhere work but allow for social interaction, knowledge sharing and collaboration with other like-minded workers. The increasing sophistication of digital technologies has also had a significant impact on the manufacturing sector. One of those technologies is 3D printing for digital fabrication, which opens up the possibility of distributed manufacturing anytime and anywhere.

Chapter 7, "Design for the Future of Work: A Theoretical Framework for Coworking Space Design," examines the growing trend of coworking spaces that provide anywhere workers with a flexible place to work that is set apart from either home or office. As one of the locations that host these new mobile, virtual and distributed ways of working, coworking spaces are shared workplaces used by knowledge workers who are often freelancers and at different levels of expertise in the vast area of the information industry. Coworking spaces afford anywhere workers a sense of socialization, as well as opportunities for collaboration and networking. Practically conceived as office-renting facilities where workers hire a desk and a Wi-Fi connection, these are places where independent professionals live their daily routines side-by-side with professional peers, often working in related sectors. Beyond a physical space, coworking spaces represent a new type of business organization and lifestyle. Coworking spaces are places where social interactions, close contacts and learning opportunities outside traditional office spaces have emerged. Through undertaking a review of current literature on the topic, this chapter offers new insights into the design of modern coworking spaces according to user preferences. A focus on facilitating technology and activity assisted collaboration is recommended for the design of coworking spaces, and a series of ten design characteristics are suggested for facilitating the design process. The chapter also provides guidelines concerning how current research could be extended to examine future issues relating to how coworking spaces can evolve to meet the needs of anywhere workers.

Chapter 8, "Entrepreneurial Needs for Outer Urban Coworking Hubs: An Exploratory Study of A 'Pop-Up' Co-Working Hub," examines the growing need for outer urban coworking facilities. In the past, coworking spaces or hubs have tended to be located in city centres and close to transport hubs such as major train stations. Since many workers live in outer city areas with limited access to coworking centres, the study focuses on the need to provide such spaces for anywhere workers living in outer urban fringe areas. It provides insights on design needs and user profiles through a study of one such outer urban coworking hub in Australia. The study found that the value of the outer urban co-working hubs was not as a place to work *per se*, but a place to socialise, network, attend pop-up events and workshop sessions allowing workers to market their small businesses products or services, making new business connections and attending or running business workshops. The study highlighted the need for local municipal councils and other stakeholders to be more actively engaged in supporting outer urban anywhere workers, thus fostering and reinforcing a 'live local work local – shop local -collaborate globally philosophy and approach. Implications for theory and practice and suggestions for future research are also addressed.

Chapter 9, "3D Printing Build Farms: The Rise of a Distributed Manufacturing Workforce," investigates the possibilities afforded by new digital manufacturing technologies, specifically 3D printing, which opens up new ways to manufacture and supply products. This, in turn, will have a profound impact on anywhere working since design and manufacturing of products, particularly those in engineering and medical applications, will no longer be confined to dedicated manufacturing facilities or large plants. This shift opens up significant possibilities for anywhere working and distributed manufacturing. 3D printing build farms provide the potential for an individual to work from anywhere around the globe to influence community development, through research that brings together supply chain experts, federal and local government departments, town planners, policymakers, manufacturers, entrepreneurs and academics. Expanding smart city initiatives to encompass distributed, digital manufacturing in wider communities could create new ways of thinking about the future of work, as well as strategies for working anywhere. A significant contribution of this chapter concerns the need to think about manufacturing as well as service industries for developing and supporting anywhere working opportunities into the future.

In many ways, this book is a 'work in progress', given that the COVID-19 pandemic is still driving many initiatives and practices related to anywhere working. What remains to be seen, post-COVID-19 is the extent to which anywhere working will continue to be a feature of work organisation and work practice. The contribution of Anywhere Working and the Future of Work is that the chapters presented in this book provide an overview of knowledge we can use to inform and shape how we can move to a way of working anywhere that is sustainable. The topics range from conceptual and management perspectives, the adoption of telehealth, inclusiveness of workers such as those with disabilities, the role of co-working centres and a possible new way of adopting manufacturing processes remotely. Given the current context, only time will tell how sustainable the concept of anywhere working may be in the future.

*Yvette Blount*
*Macquarie University, Australia*

*Marianne Gloet*
*University of Melbourne, Australia*

# Section 1

# Management, Leadership, and Work Organization

# Chapter 1
# Working Anywhere Management Opportunities and Challenges

**Yvette Blount**
https://orcid.org/0000-0003-0129-7400
*Macquarie University, Australia*

## ABSTRACT

*This chapter examines the literature relating to information and communications technology (ICT) and opportunities and barriers relating to anywhere working. The workforce is becoming more global, and workers can work from anywhere and still be connected with colleagues and collaborators. Although ICT is an enabler of anywhere working, sustainable anywhere working requires specific management skills and capabilities. Globalization of work requires organizations to manage workers ranging from full-time employees through to freelancers working in different locations including a central office, co-working center, from home, and other flexible options. The chapter concludes by proposing a research agenda and conceptual framework to identify the management skills and capabilities required to successfully manage anywhere working (other terms include telework and telecommuting). The proposed conceptual framework will inform researchers and managers on best practice for adopting sustainable anywhere working to achieve strategic business objectives.*

DOI: 10.4018/978-1-7998-4159-3.ch001

## INTRODUCTION

Anywhere working (telework, telecommuting, flexible work, remote work, smart work, distributed work, work shifting) refers to employees who work at a location other than a central office location. Nilles (1975) is credited with coining the terms telework and telecommuting, and since the 1970s, technology has advanced to the point where many work tasks can be completed anywhere at any time. On the one hand, technology can provide the connectivity and tools to work anywhere and on the other hand may lead to workers to feeling socially and professionally isolated and unable to separate work and personal life (Freeland 2019, Taplett, Krentz et al. 2019).

Demographic and socio-economic drivers are changing how and where work is done. A significant driver is the changing work environment and flexible working arrangements (World Economic Forum, 2016). At the same time, workers in emerging economies have similar skills to those residing in developed countries; women are more highly educated, and older workers are staying in work longer (The Economist Intelligence Unit, 2015). As the physical location for many jobs becomes less important, organizations can locate talent anywhere in the world by focusing on the work, not the location. Information and communications technology (ICT) underpin digital businesses and can be used for communication such as discussions, monitoring of employees and information sharing (Beauregard, Basile et al. 2019).

Unexpected issues can arise, including extreme weather events, such as the Australian bush fires in 2019/2020, snowstorms, cyclones and floods that can impact a business's ability to provide services to customers. The novel coronavirus in early 2020 forced the quarantine of thousands of people globally who are either in isolation, unable to travel or in hospital. At the time of writing the World Health Organization (WHO) had declared the coronavirus a global pandemic. Some businesses, particularly in China, had closed for some time, others have asked their workers to telework. Japan was also under considerable pressure to provide support for workers to work at home due to the potential impacts of the virus, mainly as Japan is the 2020 host of the Olympic Games (Uhereczky 2020).

As a response to these trends, organizations are likely to employ a small number of core full-time employees supplemented by colleagues contracting or consulting (freelancing) for specific projects wherever they may reside around the globe (World Economic Forum, 2016). The flexibility of using remote and temporary workers introduces management complexity in two ways. The first is how knowledge can be transferred from temporary workers to the organization. The second is how to develop a corporate culture that keeps workers engaged and productive (The Economist Intelligence Unit, 2015). The management challenge is to be able to exploit cultural differences to gain a competitive advantage while managing conflicts and problems (The Economist Intelligence Unit, 2014). An unresolved problem concerns the skills required for managing workers who work from a location other than a central office. Managers need a clear communication plan when dealing with teams that work from diverse locations as well as an understanding of each team member's motivations and expectations (Blount, 2015).

The objectives of this chapter are twofold. The first objective is to examine the literature on the implications of information and communications technology (ICT) for anywhere working relating to management skills and capabilities. The second objective is to propose a conceptual framework derived from the literature to guide practitioners and researchers on balancing ICT disruption and human resource management practices.

## BACKGROUND

The academic and practitioner literature has been examining anywhere working (other terms include telework, telecommuting, remote working) since the 1970s (Nilles, 1975, Hunton, 2010, Blount, 2015). The earlier literature in the 1970s and 1980s also used terms such as working from home, homework, the electronic cottage, Telecottage and telecenter (Nilles, 1975, Bibby, 1995, Toffler, 1980). More recent literature used terms such as virtual worker, virtual teams (Westfall, 2004), home-anchored worker (Wilks and Billsberry, 2007) and flexible work (Papalexandris & Kramar, 1997).

The many terms used in the literature signal the difficulty of defining anywhere working. One criticism is that definitions are too broad (Huws, 1991). In Nilles's early work, telecommuting was defined as local work centers or decentralized places of work (Nilles, 1975) because the cost of ICT was prohibitive for individuals. The emphasis was the substitution of telecommunications for transportation. As telework evolved, the definitions included information and communications technology (ICT) and moving the work to the workers usually located in a home office (Welz & Wolf, 2010). Today, anywhere working refers to regular work done during the worker's usual work time at a location other than a fixed location (Vilhelmson & Thulin, 2016) facilitated by ICT. Regardless of the term used, the focus is on the work rather than the location.

The most recent statistics on the work-at-home/telework population in the U.S. based on an analysis of 2005-2018 (released in 2019) American Community Survey (U.S. Census Bureau) data conducted by GlobalWorkplaceAnalytics.com show that 4.7 million U.S. employees work from home on a part-time basis (GlobalWorkplaceAnalytics 2019). In a blog post, Simovic (2019) curates statistics from different sources, including Global Workplace Analytics, to understand the current state of remote work. Many organizations across the world, at least 44 per cent, do not allow any form of flexible work. Since 2005, the number of people working from home has increased by 140 per cent, and telecommuting has grown by 115 per cent in the last decade.

A related challenge is determining who qualifies as a teleworker (Bailey & Kurland, 2002). The diversity of work arrangements and employment status may be difficult to determine. For example, should a manager that works one a day at home a week be classified as a teleworker? If a worker is casual and does most of their work at a co-working center, are they classified as a teleworker? The trend of using more freelancers further complicates the ability to classify anywhere workers.

Anywhere working can help employees avoid a long commute, better balance their family and work responsibilities, improve productivity, reduce real estate costs for organizations and attract and retain employees (Bentley et al., 2013). Other benefits include increased flexibility and freedom from interruptions (Vilhelmson & Thulin, 2016). On the other hand, overwork (or workaholism) may be a negative outcome of anywhere working. For those engaged in anywhere working, physical and temporal boundaries are more fluid than they are for workers who attend an office (Olson-Buchanan and Boswell, 2006). Overwork may harm workers, families and ultimately, the economy because teleworkers may use technologies in ways that intrude into family life and leisure time (Golden, 2009). Working from a home office has been found to increase the feelings of exhaustion and stress when work and family conflicts are challenging to balance (Golden, 2012). Well-documented limitations of anywhere working also include social and professional isolation (Bailey & Kurland, 2002).

Leading global employers have identified the trend for flexible work arrangements as a significant driver for workplaces of the future. Flexible work arrangements such as telecommuting, co-working spaces, virtual teams, freelancing and online talent platforms are transcending the physical location of the office (World Economic Forum, 2016). The challenge for management is to understand future trends relating to the location of work which is increasingly being disrupted by ICT. How will these trends impact on the management skills and capabilities necessary to be able to manage this workforce effectively?

The take-up rate for anywhere work has not been as high as expected (Huws, 1991, Da Silva, 2010, Hynes, 2014) even though the predicted future of work in the 1970s and 1980s included telework (Stonier, 1980, Toffler, 1980). One caveat to note is that bearing in mind the issues with definitions and classification of teleworkers, accurate estimates of anywhere work take-up are difficult to ascertain. The degree of teleworking in national and international contexts, including international cross-national comparisons, is difficult to determine (Welz &Wolf, 2010). This difficulty leads to issues with identifying the benefits and limitations of anywhere working.

## METHODOLOGY

Library databases were searched using the Multisearch tool. Multisearch provides a way of searching the library's resources, including books (as well as eBooks), articles, journals and other resources. The library's main subscription databases included EBSCOhost, CSA, Ovid, Informit, Thomson Gale, Web of Knowledge, FirstSearch, and Proquest. Previous research in this area guided the keyword searches (Blount, 2015).

The initial searches were carried out between April 2013 and April 2014. Subsequent searches were undertaken regularly (once a month) to ensure the currency of the literature. The literature was added to Endnote. Relevant literature was discovered through literature searches via Multisearch, the Social Science Research Network (SSRN), the Association for Information Systems (AIS), Harvard Business Review and the Association for Computing Machinery (ACM) regular notifications of articles. The purpose was to include high-quality articles with access to the full text that had been through a rigorous peer-review process before publication.

The two major themes that emerged were information and communications technology (ICT)and Management (Blount 2015). The following section summarizes the literature from each of these themes.

## INFORMATION AND COMMUNICATIONS TECHNOLOGY AND MANAGEMENT

### Information and Communication Technology (ICT)

Information and communication technology (ICT) facilitates the ability of workers to work from anywhere. Ubiquitous high-speed broadband, bring your own device (BYOD), smartphones, tablets, cloud-based applications and tools for collaboration and meetings as well as the internet of things (IoT) are technology trends that continue to disrupt work, including the way work is managed. The BYOD trend has seen workers who use their own personal devices and applications also use them for business purposes. For example, workers may use the Cloud to share documents (iCloud, Dropbox), use the phone camera, and location-based mapping applications for work purposes (Vandelannoitte 2015). Although essential, ICT is only the enabler of anywhere working (Vilhelmson & Thulin, 2016, Blount, 2015).

ICT enables work to be done at the location of the worker when the co-location of labor and capital is unnecessary (Jussawalla et al., 1992, Nilles & Mokhtarian, 1998). Knowledge workers (people who have the skills to extract and manage information) that have a hybrid telework arrangement (where employees work some of the time from home) have been found to contribute to significant productivity improvements (Bentley et al., 2013). On the other hand, in 2013, Yahoo and H.P. either banned or significantly limited the ability of their employees to work from home (Matos, 2013, Cairns, 2013). The stated reasons were that working away from the office is not conducive to teamwork, collaboration and employee engagement.

ICT enables organizations and freelancers to connect and collaborate. Technology platforms such as Elance, Guru, Toptal, Freelancer and others provide opportunities for organizations to find workers with specific skills for a project wherever they are in the world (The Economist Intelligence Unit, 2015). This has led to the development of co-working hubs or third spaces (other terms in the literature include urban centers and work hubs). These workspaces provide freelancers, SMEs, entrepreneurs and government employees with space away from a central office to work. The purpose of the co-working hub is to provide spaces to work, collaborate and communicate. Some commentators argue that we are currently in a 'third wave' of work where virtual co-workers use ICT to simulate a shared work environment (Johns & Gratton, 2013).

Cross et al. (2016) argue that although connectivity and collaboration are essential for knowledge work and teamwork, too much collaboration can lead to lower productivity, bottlenecks, and burnout. The time spent by managers and workers on collaborative work has increased significantly over the last two decades. This has led to more meetings, answering email and responding to other colleagues' requests. Although tools such as Basecamp, Slack, and social media are used to collaborate, the more critical component for effective collaboration and use of tools is the enabling conditions, mapping supply, and demand and distributing the work appropriately (Cross et al., 2016, Bjorn et al., 2014).

Access to digital infrastructure such as broadband and wireless is a pre-requisite for anywhere working but not a driving force (Haddon, 2005). Scandinavian countries have had governments that have invested and heavily promoted broadband and wireless (Warf, 2011). In the U.K., recent government policy stipulated that broadband would be universally available to rural England before 2015; however, this date was revised to 2017 (Baker et al., 2015). The extent to which more ubiquitous broadband will impact the uptake of telework is unknown (Moseley & Owen, 2008).

In Australia, and to a lesser extent New Zealand, the technology-related difficulties for ubiquitous fast broadband relate to a relatively small population and a vast continent. The governments of both Australia and New Zealand have developed national broadband strategies that are currently being rolled out (Beltrán, 2014).

In less developed countries, access to telecommunication systems (and in some cases electricity) to support anywhere working is either exorbitantly expensive or extremely limited. In other countries, a lack of investment in digital infrastructure has delayed telework adoption. For example, in Malaysia, the ICT infrastructure was insufficient for the adoption of telework in Malaysian local organizations but not multinational organizations (Ndubisi & Kahraman, 2005). In emerging economies, the mobile internet has the potential to connect people and work for the first time (World Economic Forum, 2016).

## ICT and Management

Management should be aware of issues relating to ICT and anywhere working. The first is the management of employee availability expectations. There should be clear communication policies that explicitly outline the expectation of a worker's availability on their mobiles and email, particularly after hours. This is particularly important for organizations that supply ICT (such as laptops, mobiles, tablets) to their employees (Richardson & Benbunan-Fich, 2011). Texting, Skype, and other applications are becoming more prevalent in business with the acceleration of technological change and younger workers familiar with communication and collaboration technologies. Email is an example of a technology that can be overwhelming, particularly if workers have email notifications turned on. Is there an expectation to respond immediately? Should emails be checked on weekends and after hours? What are the responsibilities of managers to ensure that technologies such as email are used appropriately?

Some organizations are setting policies for email use in the workplace. For example, Volkswagen and Atos have policies on email expectations. In 2012, for some workers in Germany, Volkswagen stopped its Blackberry servers 30 minutes after an employee's shift and restarted them again 30 minutes before the employee's shift (BBC, 2012). In 2011, Thierry Breton, the CEO of Atos (a French-based technology company) embarked on a 'zero email' policy strategy. The reason was that email was causing a loss of productivity and worker dissatisfaction. For example, analysis of email use found that managers on average were spending between 5 and 20 hours a week reading and writing emails. Instead of email, Atos acquired a startup company blueKiwi, an Enterprise Social Network (ESN), to better manage internal collaboration and communication (Silic et al., 2015). France is considering a regulation that would give employees the right to ignore professional emails and other messages when outside the office (McAuley, 2016).

Employees need to have the technological capability to deal with workplace issues, problems and projects quickly as change occurs (Bennett et al., 2010). Intranets and email are not sufficient and can hinder rather than enhance productivity. Communication tools and processes to effectively and efficiently communicate with teleworkers and non-teleworking colleagues are essential for mitigating social and professional isolation experienced by anywhere workers (Bayrak, 2012).

On the one hand, teleworkers use communication technologies to maintain connections with others strategically while at the same time, sustaining a sense of distance to protect their autonomy and flexibility. On the other hand, communication technologies, particularly email, instant messaging and video conferencing caused interruptions leading to increased stress (Fonner & Roloff, 2012).

The richness of online media, particularly social media, is essential for both collaborations and as tools for work-related social connections, exchanges and learning (Baker et al., 2013, Lee et al., 2007). Social media use by employees (and other workers) is subject to workplace policies both inside and outside the physical workspace and working hours. Misuse of social media can lead to damaged relationships with employers, customers, and other stakeholders.

Being connected 'anytime, anywhere' can be detrimental to work-life balance. Workers working from home try to distinguish between home and work by allocating specific times to work activity and a separate area for work (Lal & Dwivedi, 2010). Bring your own device (BYOD) environments where workers use their own technology to access organizational databases, and email raises some organizational policy issues. Policy issues include privacy (who can access data on the smartphone/tablet/laptop) and how much access the I.T. department has or should have to personal devices. For example, does the I.T. department have access/authority to monitor communications and wipe the phone/tablet if it is lost or stolen (Ackerman, 2013)?

## Management Skills and Capabilities

In Australia, organizations including PricewaterhouseCoopers, Telstra, the Australian Stock Exchange, ANZ and Westpac banks have introduced flexible work policies that effectively allow workers to choose where and how they work (Smith 2015). These organizations have introduced policies that in effect, mandate flexible work arrangements, thereby removing discretion from individual managers for rejecting a worker's request for a flexible work arrangement. The manager should find a way to integrate flexible working arrangements into their business.

Mandating flexibility is a significant trend because the relevant legislation in Australia, the Fair Work Act (2009) provides managers with the power to refuse a flexible work request on reasonable business grounds. That is, there is a great deal of discretion for managers to refuse a request for flexible work if they can cite reasonable business grounds. Examples of business grounds include that the arrangement is too costly, other employees arrangements cannot be changed to accommodate the request, it is impractical to change other employees' working arrangements or hire new employees to accommodate the request, the request would result in a significant loss of productivity or have a significant negative impact on customer service (Hegewisch 2009).

ICT has provided the flexibility and freedom to work anywhere by facilitating communication and collaboration with colleagues, managers, and clients. Once the technology issues are resolved, the non-technical issues need to be managed for anywhere working to gain traction (Nilles 1998). Anywhere working needs to be integrated into the business strategy to be successful. Ultimately, the adoption of anywhere working is a senior management decision (Lafferty 2000) because ideally anywhere working should enhance an organization's competitive advantage.

Human resource management practices and policies are essential for the successful management of workers regardless of the work location and the location of the customer (Blount 2011). Specifically, job design, individual characteristics, and management of anywhere work, work/life balance, aging workforce/disabilities and productivity underpin successful anywhere work practices. Job design is an essential component for anywhere work.

One of the most critical components of job design is the level of job autonomy, the freedom to make decisions about work. If job autonomy is high, employees experience a higher level of job satisfaction. Lopes, Lagoa et al. (2014) found that a high level of job autonomy is associated with enhanced worker wellbeing, including improved vitality, psychological flexibility, and self-realization. Jobs with tasks that interlink with other team members may not be suitable for anywhere working or at least not all the time. For example, Turetken, Jain et al. (2011) found that low task interdependence significantly affects telecommuter productivity. Job design should include consideration of job tasks, the level of autonomy of a job, the skills required, workload, career progression and performance management, the cultural context as well as individual characteristics.

Researchers have developed job design characteristics of teleworkers over the last forty years to guide the design of anywhere work (Pratt 1984, Weijers, Meijer et al. 1992). There are two distinct groups of teleworkers. The first is well-educated professionals (e.g. managers, consultants, systems analysts), often working in large organizations such as IBM, Microsoft, and Cisco that have had telework programs in place for decades. The second group of workers include the not so well educated such as data entry and call center workers for whom telework seemed to be a step away from unemployment (Weijers, Meijer et al. 1992).

Managers should not make assumptions that all workers want to work anywhere because this is not the case (Blount 2015). Even if the option to telework is available, workers may not necessarily take advantage of this way of working. Mokhtarian and Salomon (1996) found in their research that there was a wide gap between employees who would like to telework (88%) and those that telework (13%). This may be because workers with small children or other caring responsibilities may be less productive working at home because of interruptions. It may be because workers feel socially and professionally isolated working away from a central office. Even if a job is deemed to be flexible or 'teleworkable,' the worker may not find telework a good person-environment 'fit' (Baker, Bricout et al. 2013). For example, not all workers have a workspace or environment at home to work. For many workers, a separate home office may not be possible (Lee and Hong 2011). Pratt (1984) found that there were some categories of workers that either returned to the office after attempting a telework arrangement or rejected telework altogether.

Mitigation of social and professional isolation and employee engagement may be resolved by offering workers two or three days of home-based telework a week rather than full-time telework (Bentley, McLeod et al. 2013). Alternatively, co-working hubs may be an option for some organizations and workers. A caveat here is that work involving confidential or otherwise sensitive information (for example, dealing with medical records) may not be suitable for co-working environments.

Management of anywhere work becomes more complex as workers have more flexibility to work in multiple locations. Managers need to recognize, understand and be sensitive to different cultures, particularly as more workers freelance and work flexibly. This is particularly relevant in multinationals and mergers. Top manager and line manager attitudes and behaviors to anywhere working are essential for the successful adoption of anywhere work (Peters 2009b). Managers may be constrained by pressures such as work intensification and stringent performance targets. They may find agreeing to anywhere working arrangements difficult if they cannot see the business benefit (Hegewisch 2009).

Research shows that there are still many employers/managers who are not providing the flexibility required for workers because they remain committed to workplace norms such as presenteeism and long hours (particularly in industries such as banking and finance). Presenteeism has several different definitions in the literature (Johns 2010, Ferreira, Martinez et al. 2015). The literature has two distinct meanings, both of which are relevant for anywhere working. The first definition relates to working more hours than one should, putting in 'face time' that does not necessarily increase productivity. Managers may use long hours and being 'present' to rank employees as more productive than their colleagues, particularly workers who take on extra work or commit more time (Golden 2009). That is flexible work arrangements and not being 'seen' can have severe career implications, reduce opportunities for training, promotion and associated benefits such as increased pay (Wheatley 2012b). The second definition relates to attending the workplace when sick or otherwise unhealthy (Hemp 2004, Johns 2010). Unwell workers may not attend the office but may work from home instead. This may not be in the worker's or employer's best interests. If a worker is unwell, it is unlikely that they will be effective or efficient. This is particularly relevant with the novel coronavirus that at the time of writing was sweeping the globe (Uhereczky 2020).

Overwork may be a consequence of anywhere working, particularly if employees work from a home office because the physical and temporal boundaries of working in a central office are removed (Olson-Buchanan and Boswell 2006). Overwork may harm workers, families and ultimately, the economy (Golden 2009). Management has a significant role to play in ensuring that there are policies in place for shutting down the technology or following a strict routine to manage tendencies for overwork (Fonner and Stache 2012).

Fear (2011) used the term' polluted time' to refer to periods or moments where work pressures or commitments prevent someone from making the most of their nonwork time. When working at home is a requirement or a constraint on workers, it does not necessarily contribute to work-life balance. That is, anywhere working may only support work-life balance if anywhere working is offered as a choice (Felstead, Jewson et al. 2002).

Anywhere working has the potential to accommodate the aging workforce, workers with disabilities and other workers who may not be able to attend an office regularly. As the population ages and workers work for longer, employers will likely need to accommodate more flexible work options. To successfully attract and retain older workers, some form of flexibility, such as anywhere working, will need to be considered (Johnson 2011).

The actual benefits of telework may be difficult to ascertain (Ruth and Chaudhry 2008). There are several reasons for this. One reason may be that not all hidden costs are taken into account when measuring benefits. Another reason is that measuring the productivity of teleworkers is problematic. It may be that the employees with an anywhere working arrangement may already be motivated and productive. Many studies have reported that increased productivity because of fewer distractions and flexibility (autonomy) is a driving factor in adopting anywhere working programs. The reasons for this reported increase in productivity may be due to longer work hours (because the employee is using the commute time to work instead of doing something else) and work intensification (Kurkland and Bailey 1999, Montreuil and Lippel 2003). Also, productivity improvements are mostly self-reported, so open to critique. Another reason may be that managers may be more experienced at managing remote workers. Management skill and experience in managing anywhere work is more important as organizations deal with increasing complexity relating to issues such as carbon footprint and business continuity (Golden 2009). Anywhere working can contribute to the continuity of operations and enhance facility management because it can provide cost efficiencies and improve utilization rates leading to the development of sustainable buildings (Gill 2006).

Business continuity management (BCM) is a management process that develops a plan to identify risks and processes for operating after a crisis or incident. Anywhere working is a core driver for effective BCM strategies. From a strategic perspective, adopting anywhere working across the organization can improve emergency response and prevention. Importantly, home-based telework has been used by organizations and governments for continuity of services during disasters and extreme weather events. Examples include the 2001 terrorist attacks in the United States, the earthquake in

Christchurch, New Zealand and potential pandemic diseases (Golden 2009, Donnelly and Proctor-Thomson 2015). Although processes and systems to support anywhere working are essential, what is more important is the line managers skills for successful organizational and worker outcomes (Donnelly and Proctor-Thomson 2015).

The next section explains the conceptual framework for addressing the interrelated and complex issues relating to anywhere working and management skills and capabilities. The two pillars in the conceptual framework are socio-technical theory and media richness theory.

## CONCEPTUAL FRAMEWORK

### Socio-technical Theory

The socio-technical theory is the first pillar of the conceptual framework because we need to understand the interaction between work, ICT, and people. Designing information systems to support anywhere workers requires management insight into how people interact with technology (Cherns 1986, Clegg 2000). Socio-technical theorists argue that managers should design social systems around organizational objectives before considering the technical system. Integration of the activities of the people in the organization using ICT should be a key consideration in technology design (Cherns 1986). Before adopting any new technology, managers should consider how people (workers and other stakeholders) will use the technology and how the technology will support the organization's strategic objectives.

The design of socio-technical systems is rare in practice. In many cases, the design is technology-led, and the social system is designed around the technology. This may lead to inferior technical solutions that may not meet an organization's strategic objectives (Mumford and Beekman 1994). As outlined in a previous section, information systems to support collaboration and connectivity have become more sophisticated. Examples in this regard include the sharing of documents in the Cloud (such as dropbox and google docs) and the ability to simultaneously work on projects and communicate (such as igloo, slack, and ryver).

The socio-technical theory has been criticized as lacking specificity (Lamb and Kling 2003), and its advocates have been charged with not being able to provide successful examples or long term results (Badham, Clegg et al. 2000). Also, the socio-technical approach has been criticized for being simplistic in its universal solution for work design (Badham, Clegg et al. 2000). However, the socio-technical theory explains that technology *per se* is not as important as how the technology is used to support anywhere work.

A proposed multi-level telecommuting framework using the socio-technical framework has been proposed (Bélanger, Watson-Manheim et al. 2012) which shows some of the complexity involved in adopting a telework program. However, as the authors point out, the framework requires evaluation with data from longitudinal studies to establish its usefulness for both researchers and practitioners.

## Media Richness Theory

The second pillar of the conceptual framework is the Media Richness Theory (MRT) developed by Daft & Lengel (1984) who posited that face-to-face contact is the richest of the communication media because of the multitude of cues including body language, facial expression and tone of voice. Research suggests that communication is more complex in teams that are not co-located due to two issues. The first issue is the lack of communication channel richness. The second is the delayed feedback inherent in communication channels (Klitmøller & Lauring, 2013). For example, face-to-face conversations are considered a rich source of media because immediate feedback can enhance understanding and check for misinterpretations. Email, considered lean media, removes the social cues and contextual background that may contribute to misunderstandings of misinterpretations (Klitmøller and Lauring 2013). The underlying assumption is that rich media provides more cues than lean media (Daft & Lengel, 1984, van der Kleij et al., 2009). Therefore, face-to-face communication is richest, followed by video communication; then telephone and lowest on the spectrum is electronic communication such as email and computer documents.

Critics argue that MRT does not sufficiently explain why face-to-face communication is superior to other forms of communication for specific tasks or behaviors. Successful decision-making or negotiation does not necessarily depend on the medium selected, and rich communication is not necessarily dependent on rich media (van der Kleij et al., 2009). Substituting virtual meetings for face-to-face meetings requires an organizational cultural shift. Communication over a new medium can be unfamiliar and relies on the meeting infrastructure (technology that is sufficient for the purpose), organizational culture, employee preferences, attitudes and skills and the external meeting participants (Arnfalk & Kogg, 2003). The socio-technical perspective which emphasizes the interaction of technology and the people that use the technology addresses this limitation.

Globalization and teams working across different time zones and countries hold the promise of greater flexibility and resource utilization (Horwitz, Bravington et al. 2006, Klitmøller and Lauring 2013). The choice of technology for collaboration and communication is key to successful teams that are not co-located. Successful collaboration relies on skills, including conflict resolution, negotiation, knowledge formation, and risk reduction. Richer communication media may lead to more successful anywhere working if the media supports shared meaning (Rhoads, 2010, Turetken et al., 2011). However, the increased use of mobile technologies to communicate and access information has accelerated the blurring of lines between work and nonwork activities (Bélanger et al., 2012).

As outlined above, employee availability expectations are an issue for management. Lean media such as email and an intranet are no longer adequate to support the demands of work in twenty-first-century organizations. Employees require the technological capability to deal with workplace issues, problems, and projects quickly as change occurs (Bennett et al., 2010). Managers may consider a community home space featuring pictures and profiles of team members, a discussion board, a team calendar, or a chat room (Baker et al., 2013). It is unclear whether any technology can replicate the richest media of face-to-face interaction.

*Figure 1. Conceptual Framework: Management Skills and Capabilities*

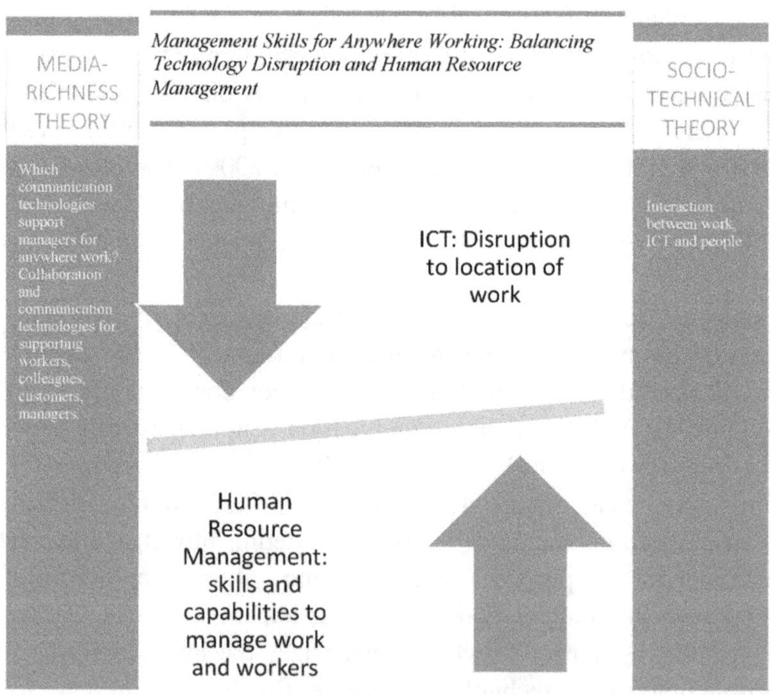


The media richness theory augments the socio-technical theory by addressing the sufficiency of technology choice for communication and collaboration, the two pillars of the conceptual framework. As new technologies disrupt work, human resource management policies and procedures should adjust to the new ways of working. The balance must be recalibrated frequently to ensure that working anywhere continues to provide the organization with a competitive advantage.

## SOLUTIONS AND RECOMMENDATIONS

What are the lessons we can take from these conflicting messages? The workplace of the future will be increasingly globalized and flexible, facilitated by ubiquitous connectivity. There are also unexpected issues that arise, such as the COVID-19 pandemic and extreme weather events (such as the bushfires in the Australian summer) that necessitate organizations to think differently about the location of their workers. Ubiquitous connectivity has the potential to increase work intensification (potentially higher workloads, more work hours). It is also clear that disruptive technologies will continue to change the way we work and live. However, the technology itself is less important than how stakeholders use technology. The technology needs to be sufficient and work as intended. Workers need access to technical support to ensure the technology does not impede productivity.

Management supervision will be outcome-based rather than embedded in the hierarchical structure. The culture will transition to one of presenteeism (spending more hours at work than necessary to be seen and being in the office even if it is not required) to one of being in the right location for the right type of work with the right people.

The type of work will indicate the type of ICT required. For example, knowledge workers have outputs that require working in an environment free from distractions, for example, writing reports. This work is location independent, can be done anywhere and for the most part, does not need the physical presence of team members. There may be a need for collaboration and communication. However, this can easily be accommodated with the sharing of documents. For other types of work, being physically present may be necessary for meetings with clients and staff for collaboration opportunities, performance meetings or building relationships.

Management is responsible for creating opportunities for engagement with the organization to avoid social and professional isolation. This requires careful consideration of job design and communication strategies, including the choice of technology. For example, employees who work from home or a co-working center may be required to attend face-to-face meetings with colleagues and team members regularly. There may be an opportunity for using social media and other tools to engage workers who are unable to attend face-to-face meetings.

Anywhere working is not a 'one size fits all' scenario because many workers still value the routine and socialization aspects of going to a specific office location each day. Some workers may not have an ideal environment from which to work from home due to either accommodation restrictions (unable to have a room as a separate office) or distractions such as small children or eldercare responsibilities. However, there are options such as co-working centers, cafes, libraries and other alternatives that may suit some workers.

Management has a vital role to play in ensuring that there are policies around shutting down the technology or following a strict routine to manage tendencies toward overwork as well as managing employees who do not deliver the agreed outcomes. This is important for the physical and mental wellbeing of workers regardless of where they choose to work. On the one hand, anywhere working provides flexibility to get the work done when it suits the worker. On the other hand, ICT can be intrusive and detrimental to a worker's physical and mental wellbeing.

The conceptual framework using the socio-technical and media richness theories as the two pillars that support ICT and human resource management indicates the balancing act required for successful anywhere working adoption. Organizations need to develop a business case that promotes anywhere working as a source of competitive advantage rather than just a cost-saving mechanism. Attracting and retaining employees with the capabilities and skills to be able to deal with disruptive technologies that are changing the way we live, learn and work will provide organizations with a competitive advantage. Managers need to have the skills to manage the team wherever they are located. The HRM profession should be aware of the future of work trends and develop programs for managers so that they have the skills and capabilities to manage workers anywhere. The skills and capabilities include technology choice and human resource management policies and practices.

## FUTURE RESEARCH DIRECTIONS

Anywhere working success relies on the ability of managers to balance the needs of the workers with organizational objectives effectively. Globalization and flexible work options, particularly anywhere working, are trends that will enhance an organization's competitive advantage if managers have the skills and capabilities to manage the workforce wherever located.

The choice of technology for supporting collaboration and connectivity will require rethinking the design and the location of work. The conceptual model will be further developed to show how the socio-technical theory and media richness theory can be used to understand better the dynamic nature of ICT and the implications for human resource management to support and enhance anywhere working.

## CONCLUSION

Anywhere working relies on ICT to be sufficient for collaboration and communication. The conceptual framework shows that there is a balancing act between ICT and human resource management. As ICT disrupts where work is located and how work is done, managers need to develop and update their skills and capabilities to manage workers to achieve organizational objectives.

Managers and workers should have the skills and capabilities to determine which technology will support the communication and collaboration requirements for anywhere working. Technology choice should consider how the users – workers and other stakeholders – interact with the chosen technology to communicate and collaborate. Consideration should be given to the media richness of the technology. Using rich media communication technologies will not always be necessary or appropriate for certain types of work or interactions. Conversely, lean media may not be a suitable choice for a particular task or interaction.

## REFERENCES

Fair Work Act 2009 No. 28, 2009 as amended.

Badham, Clegg, & Wall. (2000). Sociotechnical Theory. In *Handbook of Ergonomics*. New York: John Wiley.

Baker, P. M. A., Bricout, J. C., Moon, N. W., Coughlan, B., & Pater, J. (2013). Communities of participation: A comparison of disability and aging identified groups on Facebook and LinkedIn. *Telematics and Informatics*, *30*(1), 22–34. doi:10.1016/j.tele.2012.03.004

Beauregard, Basile, & Canonico. (2019). *Telework: outcomes and facilitators for employees*. Academic Press.

Bélanger, F., Watson-Manheim, M. B., & Swan, B. R. (2012). A multi-level socio-technical systems telecommuting framework. *Behaviour & Information Technology*, *32*(12), 1257–1279. doi:10.1080/0144929X.2012.705894

Bentley, T., McLeod, L., Bosua, R., Gloet, M., Teo, S., Rasmussen, E., & Tan, F. (2013). *The Future of Work Program: The Trans-Tasman Telework Survey New Zealand Work Research Institute AUT and IBES (Institute for a Broadband Enabled Society)*. The University of Melbourne.

Blount, Y. (2011). Employee management and service provision: A conceptual framework. *Information Technology & People*, *24*(2), 134–157. doi:10.1108/09593841111137331

Blount, Y. (2015). Pondering the Fault Lines of Anywhere Working (Telework, Telecommuting): A Literature Review. *Foundations and Trends® in Information Systems, 1*(3), 163-276.

Blount, Y. (2015). *Telework: Not Business as Usual. In Business Technologies in Contemporary Organizations: Adoption, Assimilation, and Institutionalization.* IGI Global.

Cherns, A. (1986). Principles of socio-technical design revisited. *Human Relations*, *40*(3), 153–161. doi:10.1177/001872678704000303

Clegg, C. (2000). Socio-technical Principles for System Design. *Applied Ergonomics*, *31*(5), 463–477. doi:10.1016/S0003-6870(00)00009-0 PMID:11059460

Donnelly, N., & Proctor-Thomson, S. B. (2015). Disrupted work: Home-based teleworking (HbTW) in the aftermath of a natural disaster. *New Technology, Work and Employment*, *30*(1), 47–61. doi:10.1111/ntwe.12040

Fear, J. (2011). *Polluted time Blurring the boundaries between work and life*. The Australia Institute.

Felstead, A., Jewson, N., Phizacklea, A., & Walters, S. (2002). Opportunities to work at home in the context of work-life balance. *Human Resource Management Journal*, *12*(1), 54–76. doi:10.1111/j.1748-8583.2002.tb00057.x

Ferreira, A. I., Martinez, L. F., Cooper, C., & Gui, D. M. (2015). LMX as a negative predictor of presenteeism climate: A cross-cultural study in the financial and health sectors. *Journal of Organizational Effectiveness: People and Performance*, *2*(3), 282–302. doi:10.1108/JOEPP-02-2015-0005

Fonner, K. L., & Stache, L. C. (2012). All in a day's work, at home: Teleworkers' management of micro role transitions and the work–home boundary. *New Technology, Work and Employment*, *27*(3), 242–257. doi:10.1111/j.1468-005X.2012.00290.x

Freeland, G. (2019). *If Home Is Where The Heart Is, Work Is Where The WiFi Is*. Retrieved 20 November 2019, from https://www.forbes.com/sites/grantfreeland/2019/11/18/if-home-is-where-the-heart-is-work-is-where-the-wifi-is/#533e54659024

Gill, T. J. (2006). Workplace continuity: How risk and technology will affect facilities strategy. *Journal of Facilities Management*, *4*(2), 110–125. doi:10.1108/14725960610651205

GlobalWorkplaceAnalytics. (2019). *Latest Telecommuting/Mobile Work/Remote Work Statistics*. Retrieved 15 January 2020, from https://globalworkplaceanalytics.com/telecommuting-statistics

Golden, L. (2009). A Brief History of Long Work Time and the Contemporary Sources of Overwork. *Journal of Business Ethics*, *84*(2), 217–227. doi:10.100710551-008-9698-z

Golden, T. D. (2009). Applying technology to work: Toward a better understanding of telework. *Organizational Management Journal*, *6*(4), 241–250. doi:10.1057/omj.2009.33

Hegewisch, A. (2009). Flexible working policies: a comparative review. *Institute for Women's Policy Research, Equality and Human Rights Commission 2009*.

Hemp, P. (2004). Presenteeism: At work-but out of it. *Harvard Business Review*, *82*(10), 49–58. PMID:15559575

Horwitz, F. M., Bravington, D., & Silvis, U. (2006). The promise of virtual teams: Identifying key factors in effectiveness and failure. *Journal of European Industrial Training*, *30*(6), 472–494. doi:10.1108/03090590610688843

Johns, G. (2010). Presenteeism in the workplace: A review and research agenda. *Journal of Organizational Behavior*, *31*(4), 519–542. doi:10.1002/job.630

Johnson, R. W. (2011). Phased Retirement and Workplace Flexibility for Older Adults: Opportunities and Challenges. *The Annals of the American Academy of Political and Social Science*, *638*(1), 68–85. doi:10.1177/0002716211413542

Klitmøller, A., & Lauring, J. (2013). When global virtual teams share knowledge: Media richness, cultural difference and language commonality. *Journal of World Business*, *48*(3), 398–406. doi:10.1016/j.jwb.2012.07.023

Kurkland, N. B., & Bailey, D. E. (1999). The advantages and challenges of working here, there anywhere, and anytime. *Organizational Dynamics*, *28*(2), 53–68. doi:10.1016/S0090-2616(00)80016-9

Lafferty, G. (2000). Telework in Australia: Findings from a National Survey in selected industries. *Australian Bulletin of Labour*, *26*(3), 236–252.

Lamb, R., & Kling, R. (2003). Reconceptualizing Users as Social Actors in Information Systems Research. *Management Information Systems Quarterly*, *27*(2), 197–235. doi:10.2307/30036529

Lee, S.-Y., & Hong, J. H. (2011). Does Family-Friendly Policy Matter? Testing Its Impact on Turnover and Performance. *Public Administration Review*, *71*(6), 870–879. doi:10.1111/j.1540-6210.2011.02416.x

Lopes, H., Lagoa, S., & Calapez, T. (2014). Work autonomy, work pressure, and job satisfaction: An analysis of European Union countries. *Economic and Labour Relations Review*, *25*(2), 306–326. doi:10.1177/1035304614533868

Mokhtarian, P. L., & Salomon, I. (1996). Modeling the choice of telecommuting: 2. A case of the preferred impossible alternative. *Environment & Planning A*, *28*(10), 1859–1876. doi:10.1068/a281859

Montreuil, S., & Lippel, K. (2003). Telework and occupational health: A Quebec empirical study and regulatory implications. *Safety Science*, *41*(4), 339–358. doi:10.1016/S0925-7535(02)00042-5

Mumford, E., & Beekman, G. J. (1994). *Tools for Change and Progress: A Socio-technical Approach to Business Process Re-engineering*. CSG Publications.

Nilles, J. M. (1998). *Managing Telework: Strategies for Managing the Virtual Workforce*. Wiley.

Olson-Buchanan, J. B., & Boswell, W. R. (2006). Blurring boundaries: Correlates of integration and segmentation between work and nonwork. *Journal of Vocational Behavior*, *68*(3), 432–445. doi:10.1016/j.jvb.2005.10.006

Peters, P. B., & Oldenkamp, E. (2009b). Cultural Sources of Variance in Telework Adoption in Two Subsidiaries of and ICT-Multinational. *International Journal of Employment Studies*, *17*(2), 66–101.

Pratt, J. H. (1984). Home teleworking: A study of its pioneers. *Technological Forecasting and Social Change*, *25*(1), 1–14. doi:10.1016/0040-1625(84)90076-3

Ruth, S., & Chaudhry, I. (2008). Telework: A Productivity Paradox? *IEEE Internet Computing*, *12*(6), 87–90. doi:10.1109/MIC.2008.132

Simovic, D. (2019). *The Ultimate List of Remote Work Statistics – 2020 Edition*. Retrieved 15 January 2020, 2019, from https://www.smallbizgenius.net/by-the-numbers/remote-work-statistics/

Smith, F. (2015). *PricewaterhouseCoopers' trusts' staff, makes all roles flexible.* Australian Financial Review, Fairfax Media.

Taplett, F. B., Krentz, M., Garcia-Alonso, J., & Hoteit, L. (2019). *Flex-Work Programs That Actually Work.* Boston Consulting Group.

Turetken, O., Jain, A., Quesenberry, B., & Ngwenyama, O. (2011). An Empirical Investigation of the Impact of Individual and Work Characteristics on Telecommuting Success. *Professional Communication, IEEE Transactions on*, *54*(1), 56–67. doi:10.1109/TPC.2010.2041387

Uhereczky, A. (2020). *Teleworking During The Coronavirus Outbreak - Could It Save Lives?* Retrieved 8 February 2020, from https://www.forbes.com/sites/agnesuhereczky/2020/02/06/teleworking-during-the-coronavirus-outbreak-could-it-save-lives/#76824d237bc2

Vandelannoitte, A. L. (2015). Managing BYOD: How do organizations incorporate user-driven I.T. innovations? *Information Technology & People*, *28*(1), 2–33. doi:10.1108/ITP-11-2012-0129

Weijers, T., Meijer, R., & Spoelman, E. (1992). Telework remains 'made to measure': The large-scale introduction of telework in the Netherlands. *Futures*, *24*(10), 1048–1055. doi:10.1016/0016-3287(92)90136-4

Wheatley, D. (2012b). Work-life balance, travel-to-work, and the dual career household. *Personnel Review*, *41*(6), 813–831. doi:10.1108/00483481211263764

## KEY TERMS AND DEFINITIONS

**Business Continuity Management:** Is defined as the capability of the organization to continue the delivery of products or services at acceptable predefined levels following a disruptive incident (Source: ISO 22301:2012).

**Competitive Advantage:** A term coined by Michael Porter that means an advantage over competitors measured by profits that exceed the average for the industry. This advantage could take the form of a cost advantage (for example, producing goods at a lower cost because of streamlined business processes) or differentiation (for example, excellent customer service).

**Flexible Work:** Arrangements such as telecommuting, co-working spaces, virtual teams, freelancing and online talent platforms are transcending the physical location of the office.

**ICT:** An overarching term that includes communication devices or applications. ICT includes radio, television, mobile phones, computer and network hardware and software and satellite systems. ICT also includes the services and applications such as smart apps and videoconferencing.

**Media Richness Theory:** A framework used to describe a communication media's capacity to reproduce information without loss or distortion. Communication media have varying capacities for resolving ambiguity, negotiating varying interpretations, and facilitating understanding. For example, the online text is less 'rich' than video chat.

**Socio-Technical Systems Theory:** A way of explaining the reciprocal interrelationship or fit between the technical subsystem and the social subsystems in organizations.

**Telework/Telecommuting:** Distant or remote work using information and communications technologies, usually from home or from another location such as a satellite office.

# Chapter 2
# National Culture and the Social Relations of Anywhere Working

**Mike Berrell**
*WADEmatheson, Australia*

## ABSTRACT

*Western ideas about work have developed as macro and micro level changes continue to shape the social relations of work. As anywhere working developed as an alternative to traditional work arrangements in the 1990s, a system of checks and balances ensured the work practice delivered customer service and product quality. Western low-context work cultures situated the work practice as a logical development in the chronology of the social relations of work. With its tipping-point in the West reached, anywhere working received less attention in high-context work cultures. Specifically, this chapter investigates how the concept of "national culture" impacts thinking about anywhere working. In the high-context work cultures of East and South East Asia, employers, employees, and the stakeholders of organizations and governments have divergent views about the legitimacy of this work practice. The chapter discusses the influence of national culture on thinking about anywhere working in high-context work cultures, drawing on current data concerning anywhere working in selected Asian economies.*

DOI: 10.4018/978-1-7998-4159-3.ch002

## INTRODUCTION

This chapter investigates the idea of anywhere working as a new work practice with distinguishing characteristics from both theoretical and practical perspectives. Part One discusses the images and meanings attached to work through the ages in the context of Western ideas and traditions. The notion of a sociological paradigm supplies a framework for the identification and analysis of the salient features of anywhere working in the West.

The second part discusses the practical implications of anywhere working, highlighting areas that require new understandings about the work practice and its ensuing social relations from the perspectives of employees, employers, and the wider society. The notion of most people working anywhere and anytime has momentous implications for a range of stakeholders and their understandings about the social relations of work. While anywhere workers can be employees or self-employed contractors, for the purpose of discussion, this chapter focuses on people in direct employment relationships with a home organization.

The final part discusses the neglected area of national culture's (for example, a Chinese, Japanese, Scandinavian or North American national culture) influence on attitudes to work using examples drawn from non-Western societies in the Asian region. In these countries, high-context cultures dominate social and workplace behavior. The discussion includes the approaches of employers and employees to flexible employment relationships.

## BACKGROUND

From a Western perspective, anywhere working provides opportunities to utilize non-traditional workspaces and new employment relationships in a variety of industrial sectors and organizational types, in both for-profit and not-for-profit settings. Although anywhere working appears ostensibly as a uniform practice, the literature reveals subtle points of difference (Nilles, 1976; Hislop et al., 2015).

Ideas about telework, virtual work, and other forms of anywhere working tracked the rapid advances in 'information, digital and mobile technologies in business and personal communication' [abbreviated as ICT]. Although ICT shape thinking about flexible ways of working, Garrett and Danziger (2007) suggest interpretations should tacitly recognize the legitimacy of traditional understandings about work, workplaces, and organizations as points of comparison.

To this end, the four pillars of anywhere working in the West posit that it:

1. Occurs in places external to an organization's designated workplace.

2. Depends on increasingly sophisticated ICT to facilitate flexible types of work.
3. Reduces the time a person devotes to traditional work within the organization's workplace.
4. Creates numerous types of employment relationships with a range of work options available to employers and employees.

In the West, organizations have management protocols, systems, policies, process, legal edicts, and ethical obligations to bind its employees. These functional elements of traditional work settings are topics canvassed within most textbooks on management and organizations (Samson & Daft, 2015) and human resource management [HRM] (Boxall, Purcell, & Wright, 2008). However, these elements emerge as problematic grey areas when applied to flexible working options.

Anywhere working is a logical outcome of a rapidly expanding and increasingly sophisticated ICT infrastructure (cf. Lin, 2012). As employers (with managers as their proxies) establish bring your own device [BYOD] workspaces and build sophisticated workstations, the potential for people today to work anywhere grows. Mobile technologies make flexible working arrangements [FWAs] an option previously unavailable to most employees (Lake, 2013). Today, working from a home office, work hub, or hot desk is commonplace.

Between 2005 and 2014, the non-self-employed population in the US working from home doubled. As the negative effects of the Global Financial Crisis on economies worldwide diminished and businesses steadily recovered in the early 2010s, the number of employees who engaged in anywhere working increased. Trawling through the United Kingdom's *Labor Force Surveys*, Garner et al. (2016) estimated that approximately one-third of the labor force worked remotely for all or some of the time. As FWAs increase, traditional understandings about the social relations of work and the employment relationship come under pressure.

At a macro-level, anywhere working holds implications for urban planning, population aging, public, fiscal, and monetary policy, and investment in ITC infrastructure. At the micro-level, the work practice has implications for HRM and human resource development [HRD]; for example, this involves determining remuneration, managing relationships, measuring job satisfaction, explaining turnover, measuring customer service satisfaction rates, and designing HRD programs. As FWAs proliferate in the economy, managers must develop a system of checks and balances to ensure this employment option continues to deliver traditional business concerns such as customer service, product quality, employee well-being, and the commercial goals of employers.

The social psychology literature in telecommuting suggests flexible work options have positive and negative effects on employees—in some cases; these effects remain "unknown" (cf. Gajendran & Harrison, 2007). For example, identifying the personal elements of telework in the light of socio-technical theories is a challenging exercise, according to Ruppel, Tworoger, and Tworoger (2012). Recent research into the influences of the connected home and virtual work options on employees and group dynamics includes studies measuring their impact on family relationships (Hill, Ferris, & Martinson, 2003), self-efficacy (Raghuram, Wiesenfeld, & Garud, 2003) and personal health (Brownson, 2004). While much thinking about flexible work options focuses on macro-level issues and micro-level practices, a less canvassed aspect of these working arrangements is the social relations of work that stem from people working anywhere and anytime. Additionally, is there anything unique or intrinsic to flexible work practices that sets them apart from other work practices today?

In the industrial age, Karl Marx (2010), Max Weber (1947), and Emile Durkheim (1964) suggested to varying degrees that a person's relationship to both the physical and social environment of their workplace is an essential factor in understanding the human condition. This elementary relationship had implications for political and social theory. Marx described the looming middle-class workforce spawned by industrial capitalism in England in the 1860s as the "surplus class" of capitalism, consisting of readily identified groups of managers and workers who manipulated symbols of various kinds in their jobs rather than physically transforming raw materials. Nevertheless, they were not anywhere workers as such—the work of the surplus class occurred within well-defined workspaces.

With the emergence of the post-industrial society in the 1950s (Bell, 1975), theories of social class coalesced around the belief that people are more closely connected with others through common elements in their personal, social, and cultural life than by their membership of groups defined by the type of work they performed. From a different standpoint, Ralf Dahrendorf (1959) formed a similar view. Although Marx touched on this revelation in *Grundrisse* and *Theories of Surplus Value II*, Alvin Toffler (1990) aptly captured the full development of these early insights. He sealed the fate of Marx's industrial proletariat concerning the social relations of work: Toffler proposed that the class that once held the key to Marx's alternative future had morphed into a "cognitariat".

In the modern era, studies on the structural elements of the working environment began to identify the influence of workplace organization on the well-being of process workers. In the US, Blauner (1964) observed feelings of alienation as a common affliction among these workers. Other studies of this type explored how work and workplace influenced gender roles, interpersonal relationships, family life, self-efficacy, and depression. From different premises, B.F. Skinner and Sigmund Freud also developed their unique psychological-based models applicable to explaining the social relations of work and a host of other psychologically-induced behaviors.

The extent to which flexible work options alter some of the fundamental beliefs concerning the social relations of work requires in-depth analysis and future research. Marx certainly thought this was the case; he construed class as an outcome of the type of work people performed. Would feelings of alienation also develop among people working in home offices, work hubs, or alone in a remote workspace? Of course, people of all cultural and spiritual persuasions throughout history have continually engaged in pondering answers to questions of similar complexity.

Given the spread of interpretations of the nature and purpose of work, this chapter briefly discusses the chronology of the social relations of work in the West. In this exploration, four different propositions below frame the discussion:

1. Anywhere working is a logical development in the conceptualizations of work and fits within the current theories encompassing the social relations of work and the employment relationship.
2. Anywhere working is a watershed practice and requires new ways of thinking about the social relations of work and the employment relationship.
3. Anywhere working is not actually anything new because it also explains aspects of work in pre-history (clan members engaged in anywhere working to source implements and fashion technology to achieve the goal of the hunt, human survival).

A fourth proposition arises from considering the concept of a national culture:

4. National culture shapes in unique ways how employers and employees think about work and FWAs.

In the light of the fourth proposition, the literature suggests significant differences exist between the values, attitudes, and orientations prevalent in Western cultures (typically referred to as the cultures, social structures and philosophical systems built on North American and Western European traditions) and those in non-Western Eastern cultures (typically referred to as the cultures, social structures and philosophical systems built on East Asian and South-East Asian traditions).

How national culture shapes ideas about anywhere working appears below in a section subtitled 'a different mindset'. The section immediately below presents a cursory review of the images of work from pre-history to the present as a springboard to discussing the social relations of anywhere working today from both Western and non-Western contexts.

## THE MEANING OF WORK THROUGHOUT HISTORY: A WESTERN PERSPECTIVE

Throughout history, people attached different meanings to activities undertaken as work. The section below draws primarily on the works of Adriano Tilgher (1930) and Sabastiano de Grazia (1962). They offer succinct accounts of the meanings and images attached to work by Western societies from antiquity to the modern era.

Ideas about place and time-bounded the concept of manual work, which occurred in specific settings and connected the worker, the activity, and the product. Throughout history, ideas about work always emanated from within the worldviews of societies. For example, the mythic elements of pre-history transformed hunting, the principal form of work, into rituals that supported the embryonic social structures of the time. Campbell's (1988) work of myth aptly portrays transformations of this type.

Emerging from pre-history, in ancient Greece, the idea of an ordered and balanced society meant the absence of intensive forms of manual labor; in essence, the social construction of work portrayed it as a type of affliction arising from the necessity to produce and reproduce material conditions. In this context, Arendt (1958) suggested that slavery in ancient Greece was a mechanism that put manual labor beyond the human condition. In early Christian and Hebrew traditions, the images and meanings attached to work emerged from a worldview, which mediated ideas of work as a form of punishment for original sin (de Grazia, 1962, Mills, 1973).

From the early monastic societies in Christian Europe through to the Middle Ages, similar notions about work held sway. St Augustine's *oeuvre* promoted a belief that people could attain some form of redemption through manual labor. In a similar vein, St. Benedict was clear that while indolence was a sin, work was a requisite activity (de Grazia, 1962); people should endure work and not complain too much about their lot in life. In a Western tradition, this rudimentary image persisted for several centuries, especially as Christianity developed. As de Grazia (1962) emphasizes, the concept of grace meshed with ideas concerning the purpose of work. Moreover, work could simultaneously be the secular expression of devotion, piety, and service (cf. Crowther et al. 1994). This conceptualization continued until the European Renaissance, when society began to view work as an activity with some intrinsic meaning beyond a mundane activity driven by necessity.

With the Renaissance (generally defined as occurring between the 14th and 17th centuries in Europe) and the Reformation, new ideas emerged about work, especially the view that work provided fulfilment beyond the reproduction of material existence. For de Grazia (1962), people worked because it was the right thing to do, with the principle of a "work ethic" developing from this premise (Mills, 1973). Nonetheless, John Calvin's (1509-1564) view that work for work's sake ran a poor second to the notion of religious piety persisted in thinking about work during this time. However, this mindset began to change when ideas about work's multiple dimensions beyond an act of either necessity or piety took hold (Mills, 1951).

Changing ideas about the nature of work grew out of notions about the artisan and artisanship. Principal among these new ideas included the notions that:

- Work was a craft that required unique skills
- Both the process and the product of work had intrinsic qualities beyond an act of necessity
- Work was a way of learning
- Work was a vocation, a pathway
- Work was a means to prosperity (in monetary and personal terms)
- Work provided multiple levels of gratification

Pahl (1988), nevertheless, cautions us about being euphoric concerning these new notions of meaningful work imbued with fulfilment. Whether 14th Century Italian artisans and the rural workers of Britain in the 1700s experienced work with the same sense of accomplishment is problematic. The historical context always shapes understandings about the nature of work.

This brings us to Marx's contributions, a foundation stone for modern interpretations of work relevant to the capacity for people to work anywhere and anytime. Briefly summarized, work offered people a variety of opportunities to engage in meaningful, creative, therapeutic, and emancipating activities. However, for various structural reasons, the capitalist system produced goods (and services) as commodities and created the pre-eminence of exchange values rather than use-values in determining the worth of these products. Thus, the product of work becomes alien to the worker, work becomes meaningless, and alienation ensues. With this sleight of hand, capitalism appropriates the potential of work as a "creative dimension of life"; it is "reduced to a means to life (and) becomes the sole option by which to exist" (Crowther et al., 1994; cf. Eldridge, 1971; Marx, 2010; Nicolaus, 1967).

We arrive back at a conundrum concerning the social relations of work, a subject of deliberation among scholars since antiquity. For example, do those who engage in work—in this case, anywhere working—conceive of and experience work as an act of necessity or an expressive, satisfying, intensely human and liberating activity? Are the practices and accoutrements of anywhere working radically different from other forms of work and work settings? Do the structural elements of anywhere working exert unique social and psychological pressures on workers compared to those exerted on workers in more traditional workspaces?

## A PARADIGM APPROACH TO THE ANALYSIS OF ANYWHERE WORKING

How people view the social relations of anywhere working varies depending upon one's paradigm orientation or their starting point for analysis. Three dominant paradigms supply a superstructure and a springboard to theory development and logical discussions about the social relations of anywhere working.

In the early 1970s, George Ritzer (1975) drew on a variety of seminal sources to develop a paradigm framework as an organizing principle for the social sciences, acknowledging the pioneering ideas of Thomas Kuhn (1970) concerning scientific paradigms. A paradigm's boundary confines critical discussions about social phenomena to a specific set of understandings. Dominant paradigms are shared meanings or distinct ways of thinking about the nature of social phenomena, like anywhere working. However, these meanings are continually changing, represented, and reinforced in the types of resources, approaches and knowledge valued by the anywhere working community. Dominant paradigms exist only because workers adhere to dominant ways of doing and knowing. Scientists once placed the earth at the centre of the universe to create a dominant paradigm about the nature of the cosmos.

Ritzer also implied that a paradigm stands for the broadest consensus about the theories and practices in a field of study. Drawing on the works of Ritzer, the sociological works of Emile Durkheim, Max Weber and the contributions to psychology by B.F Skinner and Sigmund Freud, three paradigms help consolidate thinking about the social relations of anywhere working.

The first paradigm proposes that these relations are consequences of the influence of "social facts" (Durkheim, 1964), the matrix of macro-level social structures, instructions and social constrictions that operate across workplaces. Berger and Luckmann (1967) suggest a matrix of social and psychological filters mediate these facts. Consequently, they appear as "real" for social actors in work settings. The main influences include an organization's systems and structures; for example, organizational charts, job status, rewards, the division of labor and even the use of technology all expose the influence of social facts. Understandings about these elements shape the behavior of all workers.

In the second paradigm, Max Weber's argument for the power of "interpretive understanding" is essential. The ability of people to negotiate the influences of social facts in certain social settings through interpretive understanding is a significant attribute. In other words, understanding the deeper motivations for both rational and non-rational behavior must include the variety of meanings attached to those behaviors by the social actors involved. However, initiative-taking behavior is vital because people must first interpret the environment before acting. Usually, these actions reinforce the patterned nature of social life. Within this paradigm orientation, understanding what motivates people to do what they do is the foundation stone of social analysis, a concept Weber termed *Verstehen*. Anywhere workers continually interpret their immediate environment and the behavior of others as precursors to action.

A third paradigm built on elements of social psychology uncovers the cognitive processes people engage to process social facts and interpretive understandings. While the field is too broad for a consensus of the type described by Ritzer to appear, Skinner and Freud offer points of consensus. Briefly, for Skinner, the contingencies that affect action reveal the deeper meaning attached to work. Examining work practices in the context of external stimuli and the measures of reinforcement is part of what Ritzer sees as a "social definition" paradigm. Skinner sees that anywhere workers act according to the stimulus of the systems and structures that surround them. For Freud, however, it is all a matter of unconscious motivation; clearly, this supplies the rallying point for those committed to a Freudian interpretation of anywhere working.

Ritzer's paradigms emit unique and consistent signals, which help people pinpoint a basic orientation by which to guide their discussions and analyses. Concerning the potential paradigm nature of anywhere working, strong and consistent signals would provide the clues. These signals would include:

- Consensus among the community of practitioners about their focus - what they do and how they do it
- Appropriate exemplars are available to drive theory development and support logical discussion and explanations of the field
- Consistent images of the subject matter
- Distinctive components of the work practice

In the social sciences, the paradigm concept has been valuable in offering explanations for the underlying nature of social phenomena (cf. Berrell & Macpherson, 1995; 1996; Burrell & Morgan, 2005; Gloet & Berrell, 2003; Mackenzie & Knipe, 2006;). Using similar pathways and drawing on Effrat's (1976) review of Ritzer's 1975 book, the following framework supplies the building blocks for a building a sociological paradigm and tracks its theoretical heritage.

Contributions to social psychology also provide cogent and fruitful explanations of the how and why of workplace behavior within the social facts and interpretive understanding paradigms (cf. Argyris, 1967; Argyle, 1992; Bavelas, 1978, Deaux & Snyder, 2012). However, given that systems and structures induce work behaviors, theories such as Marxism, Conflict Theory and Feminist Theory should collapse

*Table 1. Building blocks of a sociological paradigm*

| Paradigm | Focus | Exemplars | Image | Examples of Theories and Orientations |
|---|---|---|---|---|
| Social Facts | Social systems and structures in organizational life and workplace relations | Emile Durkheim | People responding directly to the flux and flow of organizational life and workplace relations | Functionalism<br>Conflict Theory<br>Marxism<br>Critical Theory |
| Social Interpretation | Proactive engagement of workers in negotiating interpreting organizational life and workplace relations; patterned nature of social life | Max Weber | People responding indirectly to the flux and flow of organizational life and workplace relations by interpreting and negotiating the systems and structures and acting accordingly | Phenomenology<br>Hermeneutics<br>Symbolic Interaction<br>Field Theory |
| Psychology of Behaviour - social behaviour following Ritzer | Contingent behaviours and unconscious motivation offer paradigm-type explanations of how people react to organizational life and workplace relations | B.F. Skinner<br>Sigmund Freud | Overt and covert psychological influences at work determine how people interpret and negotiate organizational life and workplace relations | Behavourial Psychology<br>Psychoanalysis<br>Psychodynamics<br>Exchange Theory |

(Source: adapted from Ritzer, 1975)

within a social facts paradigm for researchers wishing to build theories and/or identify the subject matter and images of anywhere working.

## Thinking About Anywhere Working: Some Social and Practical Implications for Western Workplaces

Garner et al. (2016) use three broad organizing themes to frame their discussion about anywhere working. These themes provide anchors for delineating employee-centric, employer-centric, and technology-centric issues. While ideas about the nature of anywhere working crystalized over time, these cornerstone themes are evident in the literature since the mid-1970s (cf. Bentley & Yoong, 2000; Garner et al., 2016; Garrett & Danziger, 2007; Haddon & Silverstone, 1994; Handy & Mokhtarian, 1996; Henson, 1997; Hislop et al., 2015; Jackson & van der Wielen, 2002; Johns & Gratton, 2013; Nilles, 1976, 1998; Wiberg & Ljungberg, 2001).

The table below set out these recurring themes and associated issues. Granted, comparable themes also appear in discussions about other non-traditional work practices. However, in the case of anywhere working, issues have quite different ramifications when employees pursue their vocation in workspaces external to an organization's home site. This external attribute changes the traditional understanding of the employment relationship. At this conjuncture, the themes and issues below are interdependent elements of anywhere working, expressed as impartial constructs with neither positive nor negative connotations.

*Table 2. Some dominant themes and issues in anywhere working in a Western context*

| Employee Centric | Employer Centric | Technology Centric |
|---|---|---|
| • Flexible working arrangements<br>• Well-being<br>• Trust and control<br>• Work-life balance<br>• Morale<br>• Creativity<br>• Reduced travel time<br>• Connections to and relationships with work colleagues<br>• Connections to and relationships with work teams<br>• Connections to and relationships with line manager<br>• Connections to corporate culture<br>• Need for structure in the work environment<br>• Collaboration opportunities | • Cost effectiveness and Return on Investment<br>• Distributed supervisory structures<br>• Management control<br>• Multitude of employment contracts<br>• Multitude of employment relationships<br>• Productivity<br>• Occupational Health and Safety [OH&S] issues<br>• Ensuring appropriate management styles<br>• Investment and maintenance of physical, mobile and digital resources<br>• Human Resource Management [HRM] and Human Resource Development [HRD]<br>• Monitoring the "come and go" nature of work hubs<br>• Confidentiality<br>• Intellectual Property Rights [IPR] | • BYOD infrastructure<br>• Current ICT and keeping abreast of current and future developments<br>• Capacity for increased productivity<br>• More hours available for "work"<br>• Anywhere working is increasingly a viable work option<br>• ICT conducive to working in Smart Hubs<br>• Internet and Intranet - ICT platforms and capabilities |

(adapted from Garner et al., 2016)

The impartiality of the themes and issues suggested in the segregation above evaporates in decision-making in anywhere working contexts. This is because stakeholders view anywhere working from different and often mutually exclusive paradigms or vantage points. Throwing national culture into the mix accentuates these differences. In most cases, people filter their understandings about the themes and issues above through social assumptions, mediated in part by the influences of social facts and interpretive understanding about anywhere working. More comprehensive research would also determine the paradigm orientations impelling these understandings.

# DISCUSSION

Focusing on Western societies, the discussion below explores issues relevant to employers and employees concerning anywhere work. The discussion focusses on people working under FWAs where a formal agreement governs the employment relationship. In this context, FWAs apply to work performed for an employer in a variety of non-traditional settings.

## Employee Centric Themes and Issues

Flexible work opportunities include interpretative understandings about the positive outcomes that flow from FWAs. Clark and Holdsworth's (2017: 28-32) research found positive outcomes related to personal and team effectiveness, citizenship behavior, and personal well-being. Flexibility also offers employees opportunities to arrange their work hours to accommodate personal and family needs, which promotes healthier interpersonal and family relationships, beneficial work-life balance, and a propensity for creative collaborations. From an interpretive understanding viewpoint, self-esteem, motivation, productivity, and collaboration all increase (Garner et al., 2016). The economic benefits for employees include reduced costs for travel, vehicle maintenance, insurance, food, and even dry cleaning (DAE, 2011: 29).

However, although the literature suggests employees experience a drop in stress levels due to a better work-life balance, if workloads are not responsibly managed, these outcomes may be fleeting. For example, Montreuil and Lippel (2003) showed that while "home-based telework" has a positive effect on one's personal health, potential health problems arise when workstations or home offices are poorly designed and/or people work long and unmonitored hours. The long-term psychological effects on individuals working in isolation under FWAs are undetermined. In this context, work hubs might help alleviate this potential downside of FWAs performed in seclusion.

Working in isolation has implications for employers and employees alike. In addressing the issue of "teleworking-enabled stress", Weinert, Maier and Laumer (2015: 1407-1408) describe "telework-exhaustion" and identify factors contributing to this condition. For remote workers, access to relevant information and clear job specifications are essential for achieving cost-effective outcomes. A worker's capacity to manage their workload in autonomous environments also influences productivity. The potential of social and psychological issues that accompany working in isolation also contributes to telework-exhaustion.

Through interpretive understanding, anywhere workers are predisposed to conceive of their workplace as their immediate organizational environment, even though it is quite remote from their organization's physical footprint. However, these employees also lean towards experiencing work hubs as an unrestrained setting, free of the home organization's sanctions. This is particularly the case with the home office. In both cases, in FWAs settings, the responsibility of ensuring the workplace is conducive to producing quality, and timely outcomes in a stress-free environment are effectively shifted from the employer to the employee, which stands our traditional understanding about work on its head. In this case, the anywhere worker needs to address employment relationship issues in complex areas like insurance, workers compensation, personal taxation, and other legal liabilities.

The social psychology of employees might predispose certain types of workers to seek out highly structured workplaces, braced by robust inter-personal relationships. In these circumstances, relationships fashioned in cyberspace are daunting prospects for employees who prefer working in a social setting. FWAs are not the first employment choice for everyone. Importantly, from an employer's perspective, the allocation of assignments to employees working remotely requires a reciprocal and comprehensive negotiation process, which accounts for the predispositions of employees and the needs of employers. Both employers and employees need to be flexible in these discussions.

Recent research (DAE, 2011: 20-32; see Clark & Holdsworth, 2017; Garner et al., 2016) suggests that FWAs deliver wide-ranging benefits to employers, which include improved outcomes in recruitment and retention, reduced absenteeism, and business resilience. Concerning the latter, the COVID-19 pandemic of early 2020 demonstrates the role of FWAs in helping businesses survive in periods of severe economic and social turmoil. Other benefits of FWAs include increased productivity and a decrease in office politics.

On the financial side, DAE (2011) posited that employers accrue cost savings on office space, lower utility expense, and "office decentralization". This later strategy involves "relocating the office to a less central location as there is no longer the same need to be located in a transport hub for easy access by workers".

However, when employers assess the benefits of FWAs, the inclination is to gloss over the advantages of the employment relationship as seen through the eyes of the employee and focus on the 'social facts' or the direct concerns of employers. For example, FWAs raises issues about the supervisory and management structures required to ensure effective control over employees, work processes, productivity, and quality. Also, while inclusive leadership and management styles suit FWAs, highly controlling managers, predisposed to micro-managing their teams, see flexible working as anathema. More likely, traditional concerns about management control will filter through the 'systems and structures' lens of many managers. In this context, the 'come and go' nature of those engaged in FWAs rubs against the deep-seated belief that a manager must exert firm control as a function of their responsibilities. Senior management needs to tread carefully in this aspect of HRM.

In a manager's world, developing and implementing HRM and HRD systems, processes, and strategies sympathetic to FWAs are critical tasks. However, until quite recently, textbooks and other literature in this field paid scant attention to the implications of anywhere working for employers. Most textbooks from the 1980s through to the mid-1990s paid cursory attention to FWAs because of their embryonic stage of development. Nevertheless, such writings guide the approach of the managers in managing Generations X and Y employees and today's Millennials. The implementation of HRM and HRD policies and procedures to remote workspaces presents new challenges for all employers. For example, is it possible for employers to craft one set of policies and procedures applicable to traditional and non-traditional workspaces? Moreover, if line managers view remote workspaces as just an extension of the social facts of their home organization, dysfunction between managers at the home base and employees working remotely is inevitable. Management development and executive education programs will be critical in the coming decades to alleviate such complications.

## Technology Centric Theses and Issues

Considering the return on investment in ICT engages thinking within a systems and structures standpoint. This entails decision-making about sourcing inputs, distributing throughputs, and measuring outputs. Budgets and increased shareholder value dictate the utility of the ICT infrastructure, and these data might usurp data gained through interpretive understandings. However, for employees, interpretive understandings hold sway. Anywhere workers are likely to appraise the utility of ITC through improvements to their immediate workplace – for example, increasing their capacity to access and process data efficiently, undertake market intelligence and communicate expeditiously across remote sites. These outcomes increase productivity and reduce stress in everyday work.

Mobile devices offer employers opportunities to become more productive. Liang et al. (2007) report that the right fit of mobile technologies in an organization increases productivity and profitability (see Lam & Shiu, 2010). However, while ICT provides easy access to an organization's Intranet from internal and remote locations, managers view technologies of this type with trepidation. In their mind, risks abound in environments where mobile ICT is omnipresent. Issues of data security and the theft of intellectual property loom large in the manager's worldview, overly concerned with ensuring robust and secure systems and structures.

Studies also suggest differences in how anywhere workers (including managers working anywhere) perceive ICT. Such differences arise because of age, prior experience of BYOD environments, abilities with digital technology and experience with an ICT infrastructure at an organization-wide level (Garner et al., 2016). Even so, the pervasiveness of ICT and mobile devices today suggests these differences will be short-lived.

## The Social Benefits of FWAs

The more FWAs, the less road traffic and congestion. In Australia, for example, less road traffic resulted in a savings of $470 million annually from congestion costs; in the UK, road congestion costs the economy £20 billion annually (DAE, 2011). Regional development also benefits from FWAs, which help bring jobs to regional areas.

In Australia, a highly urbanized country, FWAs helped stem the flow of people and jobs from regional areas to the large capital cities (DES, 2011). Other benefits to society and the economy include a "reduced carbon footprint (with reductions) in "electricity consumption in the commercial office and from less use of motor vehicles for commuting to work; these outcomes contribute to a "lowering of greenhouse gas emissions" (DAE, 2011).

## Developing a Corporate Culture Relevant to FWAs

Practicing the corporate culture of an organization is a significant challenge for both employees and even employers, especially those working under FWAs. Corporate culture performs a mediating role within an organization by producing exemplars as model behaviors. Its reach is significant and extends to social judgments about the appropriateness of an individual's behavior beyond the workplace. The media are quick to report the shenanigans at an organization's weekend team-building retreat or out of character behaviors observed during a recreational trip (Aston & Corbett, 2016).

For anywhere working, corporate culture is a critical but neglected factor. Lou Gerstner (2002), the one-time head of IMB, discusses how he rescued the lumbering giant from the brink of extinction and posits that corporate culture is not just part of the game - *it is the game*! This proposition elevates the concept to a preeminent level in thinking about its role in anywhere working. The shared assumptions about behavior inside and beyond organizational boundaries and workspaces lay at the heart of corporate culture. This embeddedness consciously and unconsciously influences all work behaviors (Ravasi & Schultz, 2006). In this light, can a corporate culture develop to bind anywhere workers and home-based employees equally? Opinions are divided on answers to this question.

Flexible working creates a paradox because managers can also work flexibly. In some cases, managers thinking from a systems standpoint hold the view that "working remotely all the time" is no way to grow a company (because) personal connections are necessary to cement team working" and presumably, cultivate a corporate culture (Garner et al., 2016). However, in other cases, few of the managers who are also flexible workers feel any disconnect with their work team. Moreover, as a group, "mobile workers establish a variety of personalized boundary management practices to match their particular situations".

This mindset suggests that corporate culture may be a moveable feast of sorts, taking its time to develop fully and become relevant in shaping how anywhere workers experience and practice their home organization's corporate culture. The evolution of a consistent corporate culture might also begin with anywhere workers developing a sub-culture within the broader corporate culture of the home organizations to a point where similarity become the norm. With the emergence of a consistent and indistinguishable corporate culture between home employers and those at remote sites, anywhere working enters its mature stage of development.

## Some Basic Principles for Developing Best Practice in Flexible Working

In the contested space of anywhere working and FWAs, Clark and Holdsworth (2017: 33-34) offer five organizing principles for ensuring effective management and outcomes when employers use these work options:

1. Ensure communications to stakeholders are clear and unambiguous, set work boundaries, and implement systems to manage the expectations of managers and employees
2. Institute formal arrangements concerning the expected effort of work needed to produce agreed-to outcomes
3. Establish and implement consistent practices across all members of a team working under FWAs; this includes recommending approaches to decision-making and implementing equitable HRM and HRD policies across the organization
4. Consider requests to work flexibly on a case-by-case basis, pay attention to the maturity of the applicant, and assess their capacity to work unsupervised; focus on project outcomes and productivity rather than on 'hours worked'
5. Recognize that managers overseeing FWAs can also work themselves flexibly; managers with direct experience of anywhere working and flexible work interact positively with workers under FWAs

## A DIFFERENT MINDSET

Western contexts fixed the discussion above concerning FWAs and anywhere working. However, Wojcik and Barath (2017) show that even within Western workplaces, national culture shapes quite different attitudes to teleworking, FWAs, and anywhere working. In countries across Europe, different modes of thinking appear. Might similar differences also exist in how Western and Eastern societies approach to FWAs?

The scope of this chapter limits the amount of discussion regarding (i) paradigms as they apply to Eastern work cultures, (ii) the issues for anywhere working canvassed above in Table 2, and (iii) the consistent signals emitted that reveal a paradigm orientation. Therefore, the discussion below occurs at a level of generality; a brief example of how researchers might utilize the paradigm concept in the context of Eastern work cultures, occurs at the end of the section.

By the early 1960s, ideas about national culture and its influence on shaping ideas about work and society began to populate the literature (cf. Kroeber & Kluckhohn, 1963). In the 1990s, interpretations of culture *per se*, such as Hofstede's (1994, 2011), offered refreshing viewpoints. Hofstede saw culture as a cognitive system, a set of implicit and explicit behaviors that 'collectively programmed the mind'. A computer screenshot is also a programmed representation, the coming together of intricate lines of code via thousands of electronic connections to produce an image on the screen. Similarly, at the surface level of a workplace, various screenshots inform employers and employees alike about appropriate social relationships, who is the boss, how to communicate correctly, behave appropriately in given situations, and so forth. However, like a computer, workplaces have a complex deep structure of codes—a string of axial principles, where self-evident truths hold sway.

In the view of anthropologist Claude Levi-Strauss (1969, 1979), this array of deep and complex information mediates surface-level ideas about the world of work as timeless truths, transmuting bits and pieces of information into a "grand narrative" or a self-corroborating hierarchy of knowledge (Lyotard, 1986). In effect, this knowledge is a Handbook on Workplace Etiquette. The handbook substantiates a person's unique relationships to their working environment, managers, and co-workers, entirely independent of any objective reality.

During the 1990s, the management and organization literature became germane to exploring more in-depth cross-cultural perspectives in the social relations of work (Adler & Gunderson, 2008; Hall, 1992; Inkpen & Beamish, 1997). From the literature of this type, a view coalesced that culture works at such an embedded level that employers and employees alike are routinely unaware of its influence on themselves or others (Triandis, 1983). Like an "invisible jet stream", national culture registers as unconscious motivation (Hall, 1976).

Studies suggest these deep-seated axial principles subtly influence thinking about FWAs and the opportunities these work options offer. In a large international organization with a significant global footprint, Hofstede (1994; cf. 2011) observed and recorded the comparative attitudes of employees across four cardinal dimensions of organizational life, which he defined as "Power-Distance [PD], Individualism-Collectivism, Masculinity-Femininity and Uncertainty Avoidance". Later studies added the dimensions of "Long-term versus short-term orientation" and "Indulgence versus restraint". From these data, he assembled country scores (the countries fitted loosely within the notion of Western and non-Western work cultures), which allowed for cultural comparisons using an index for each dimension. He concluded that national cultures differed along these dimensions. For example, cultures with a high PD rating would accept and expect that "power is distributed unequally compared to those with lower ratings.

Kluckhohn and Strodtbeck's (1961) work posited that different monocultural groups have distinct ideas concerning the building blocks that brace their socially constructed world. They revealed the locus of big picture thinking and suggested how cultures differed in their approach to universal problems and the anxieties that came with the human condition. These problems and anxieties included the nature and purpose of work, exhibiting appropriate types of behavior in social and interpersonal exchanges, the nature and purpose of human engagement with the natural environment, understanding the temporal focus of daily life, the key features of cosmology, the flow of time, and causation (cf. Hickson & Pugh, 1995). In these quests, axial principles played a decisive role.

Fusing Hofstede's (1994) "dimensions" of cultural difference, Kluckhohn and Strodtbeck's (1961) "values orientation", and Levi-Strauss' (1969, 1979) thoughts on structural oppositions creates a compelling heuristic for dissecting the social relations of work. This melding of groundbreaking ideas reveals how the manifested behaviors of dissimilar national cultures shape attitudes to FWAs and anywhere working and their potential as genuine employment relationships in the Asian region.

In non-Western settings, the dominant themes in anywhere working set out in Table 2 are like those in the West. Both employers and employees enter situations where these themes and issues infiltrate the decision-making process. However, the degree of similarity between the decision outcomes of the two groups is contingent on the subtle influences of national culture. Given the paucity of specific studies into the attitudes of non-Western managers and workers to FWAs and anywhere working limit the scope and depth of the discussion below.

## Employee Centric Themes and Issues: A Non-Western Perspective

In high-context workplaces, the influence of national culture shapes how people think about anywhere working. Most Asian work cultures (judged to be high-context in nature) feature elevated levels of implicit communication and reliance on contextual factors as cues to expected behaviors and responses to issues. For example, concerning Hofstede's PD measure, workers in high-context national cultures rate higher on this dimension that their Western counterparts. In other words, workers are prone to accept higher degrees of managerial authority and power relationships—these are simply the realities of the workplace. In this setting, workers accept the managerial divide with little questioning or criticism. Workers with lower attainments in formal education are also likely to be more comfortable when managed through dyadic, face-to-face relationships. In this sense, high-context workers under FWAs in remote sites might feel cut adrift from the safety of their home base.

The social psychology of high-context workers engenders these workers to seek out highly structured workplaces, where inter-personal and collective relationships dominate. Low tolerance for ambiguous situations among these workers also generates a preference for recurring patterns of management behavior, reinforced through the collective knowledge and support from the workgroup. In critical times, high-context workers are likely to seek out solutions by referring to some "absolute knowledge" to substantiate a proposed course of action and/or legitimize their thoughts, especially in high-reliability work settings. During a crisis, high-context anywhere workers might feel lost without this extensive support network that exists in traditional work settings. While the high-context worker under an FWA can achieve a degree of freedom from management's direct oversight, this freedom creates levels of uncertainty for those who favour performing their duties in settings where face-to-face affiliations abound.

Although advice about human resource related policies and procedures exists in cyberspace, in the dissemination of this knowledge, high-context workers favor learning through direct face-to-face contact with their in-group colleagues. Studies report that managers and workers alike in international joint ventures in Asia often downplay non-personal communications like emails and often avoid online training courses, even those presented with 'live' trainers through Zoom or other learning platforms. This preference is an obstacle for FWAs in remote sites, where ICT is at the heart of the communication process. However, the uptake of social media in the countries of East and South-East Asia [ESEA] suggests this obstacle will soon diminish, bolstering the potential for FWAs and anywhere working among high-context workers.

## Employer Centric Themes and Issues: A Non-Western Perspective

From a non-Western standpoint, holding an executive or a management position implies that person exercises direct control over the activities of their workers and resources in the workplace. Certainly, paternalistic styles of management proliferate among management structures in high-context workplaces, where business plans, priorities, and decisions arrive in a top-down manner. The PD factor means that few workers openly challenge management decisions, bolstering the status of the manager. In an anywhere working context, both managers and workers face the conundrum of how to report unwelcome business news, if at all.

While ESEA management systems are moving closer in style to those in the West, specific people-based characteristics appear immutable (Warner, 2013). These include the under-representation of women in management and the hierarchical traditional family structures that influence management styles. Likely, the first wave of workers using FWAs in ESEA are women, managed by men. This imbalance is highly problematic. In these circumstances, high-context male managers will continue their reign and exercise high control over workers even though women workers require different management styles, especially in cultures where masculinity rules. For women engaged in FWAs, issues of empowerment and equality loom large. Time will tell whether traditional high-context managers continue to be part of the problem or part of the solution.

The influence of social networks like *guanxi*, within China and across the Chinese diaspora, are integral aspects of Chinese business practices. Similar patronage networks exist in other business cultures in ESEA and elsewhere. The tendency to achieve in-group harmony also rebounds on the uptake of FWAs in the region. Access to social networks requires immediacy. However, workers under FWAs often execute their jobs in isolation from face-to-face communications with either their in-group or key players in their patronage networks. Nevertheless, communication technologies Skype, WhatsApp, and FaceTime are slowly changing this preference. Even so, studies report that in crises, high-context workers cherish the direct links with these networks as they exist in traditional workplaces.

The prevalence of group-think and the determining role of seniority in tenure and reward systems for managers in ESEA continues to wield a good measure of influence on managerial behaviors and expectations. In traditional workplaces, overt signs of achievement and/or status include new or enhanced executive titles, more opulent offices, improved resources, new influential members of the patronage network and new business clothes and other accoutrements. Traditional workers gain prestige from these outward displays of status. Such displays, however, are outside the purview of remote workers in ESEA.

For the high-context manager, foregoing direct control of their workers is the most significant shift in mindset required to insert FWAs into the employment relationship. Moving away from a centralized to a decentralized management structure is also a necessary step in managing flexible working.

## Technology Centric Themes and Issues: A Non-Western Perspective

Employers and employees in the region readily adopt the latest forms of ICT, which is positive for implementing FWAs. However, cultural factors continue to wield their influence in work settings. In the individualist cultures of the West, employees tend to search for information independently by tapping into a combination of direct and indirect sources. In collectivist cultures, workers prefer to rely on their subjective assessment of new processes or ideas derived from the opinions of in-group colleagues (Lee et al., 2013). Nevertheless, the knowledge gained through the latter method is biased. The over-reliance on the confirmations of like-minded individuals limits the possibility that decision-making uses a range of relevant input data. Even though mobile technologies offer advantages for high-context remote workers to access information, when workers derive this information primarily from the in-group, problems ensue. Cognizant managers must address this issue.

## Developing a Corporate Culture in Anywhere Working: A Non-Western Perspective

In both Western and Eastern organizations, significant challenges exist for both managers and workers under FWAs concerning how they practice the corporate culture of their organization. Building a corporate culture involves considering a wide range of factors, which together mediate the corporate culture - from styles of leadership, decision making, and communication to mission statements and organizational design. For workers outside the home base, organizational culture appears as a vacuous concept.

Leaving aside the generic factors that contribute to the makings of corporate culture (for example how to inculcate shared assumptions, model behaviors, combat feelings of isolation, and counter the belief that "working remotely ... is no way to grow a company"), the dislocation of direct personal communication between in-group colleagues and patrons are among the challenges faced by organizations in ESEA when developing a corporate culture.

Studies suggest the highly significant role national culture plays in building and supporting a corporate culture (Tayeb, 1995). The sheer number of culturally-driven manifested behaviors, which cross-cut an organization, makes the practice of corporate culture particularly challenging for employees working anywhere. This addition of national culture to the corporate culture mix increases the level of complexity in an already complicated situation. It presents as a Wicked Problem in the context of working in off-site locations (Churchman, 1967). It is difficult for any corporate culture to mediate exemplar behaviors as desirable against a national culture's relentless and subtle drive to reinforce its axial principles.

## The Uptake of FWAs in East and South-East Asia

The potential for FWAs to become the norm in employment in ESEA is promising. In 2007, Karin Anell and Danielle Hartmann reported on this potential. Their extensive study of leading regional companies at the time revealed significant growth in the number of FWAs. Nevertheless, the influence of national culture was steadfast, creating a barrier to change. Japanese and Chinese cultural values worked against implementing FWAs. One crucial concern of Anell and Hartmann was how to overcome the resistance level – in other words, the extent to which a company's corporate culture can supersede the influence of national culture when implementing fully-fledged FWAs. They also identified facilitating factors in the implementation of FWAs. Importantly, as an employment strategy for equal opportunity, FWAs enable women to increase their participation rates in the workforce by combining work and family duties.

The current situation in ESEA reveals different issues and factors affecting the level of acceptance of FWAs. In Malaysia, for example, Asmawi and Othman (2018) highlighted that FWAs are compatible with the demands of an emergent digital economy. However, although the demand for FWAs is increasing, their implementation by employers falls below expectations. In Singapore, the mood for FWAs is more upbeat. Khidhir (2018) expects that "greater levels of flexible working will save businesses money, reduce operating costs and boost productivity, ultimately causing a ripple effect across the economy from core businesses through to supply chains".

A recent report on the push for work flexibility (canvassing the of view of workers from a wide range of industries in China, Hong Kong, Japan and Singapore) established positive attitudes to FWAs among both male and female employees (in *Asia Research*, 2018). However, the willingness of employers to meet this demand is low. However, companies that ignored the trend to FWAs did so "at their peril". The report suggests that employers believed that exemplars of the traditional workspace in ESEA constituted tried and tested work arrangements. For these employers, the traditional way is a rational way of working, which puts management in firm control. Traditional work practices tether the power of in-groups while tightly managing working hours, rosters, rewards, and pay scales. Stringent management controls avoid crossed lines of communication in a workplace where everyone knows their job. For example, in 2018, 78% of employers in Vietnam expected "their staff to stay in the office all the time" (An, 2019).

These deep-seated beliefs motivate employers to overlook the positive benefits of FWAs, which include higher levels of trust and improved staff morale that counter the rigidity found in traditional workspaces. Agnes Chan of EY believes young workers in the new gig economy favor FWAs over full-time work commitments (in *Asia Research*, 2018). Importantly, all genders across ESEA also favour flexible work options because of the increased opportunities to improve their work-life balance. The key findings of the *Hayes 2017 Gender Diversity Report* (Hayes, 2017) reveals employees with young children approve of and seek out FWAs - for example, 37% of workers in China, 34% in Malaysia, 29% in Japan and 26% in Hong Kong sought a flexible work option. The potential for FWAs to break down gender stereotypes in ESEA is considerable.

If ideas about flexible working can overcome unconscious gender biases and attitudes to the social relations of work prevalent in certain national cultures, FWAs will emerge as a preferred employment relationship. While employees view the opportunities of a flexible working future with enthusiasm and clarity, employers have concerns about its longevity. Nevertheless, the Hayes Report also suggests that employees might temper open displays of interest in FWAs because this enthusiasm stifles their career prospects. The most promising factor influencing the uptake of FWAs by employers and employees in ESEA is the ubiquitous digital technology, a powerful driver of work flexibility. Companies harnessing this resource will be ahead of the game by meeting the growing demand among employees for flexible employment options.

Workforces in ESEA are unlikely to buck the global trend toward anywhere working. Polycom (2018) suggests that the move toward flexible work is universal. The number of professional employees in ESEA performing at least part of their work remotely increased dramatically in the last decade; from 14% of employees in May 2012 to just under 66% in 2020. With the life and work choices of millennials and improvements in digital technology driving this remarkable uptake, the demographic indicators suggest FWAs may become the preeminent employment relationship.

Drawing reliable data from ESEA countries is always a thorny issue. In the three Asian countries included in Polycom's international sample, there are upsides and downsides concerning the uptake of FWAs. The responses of regional governments also vary with significant gaps between policy and practice. Consider the following country data gleaned from a recent international survey (Polycom, 2018):

- In Japan, 35% of companies offer workers FWA options (5% work this way "often" and a further 12% "sometime" work this way)

- In China, 75% of companies profess to offer FWA options (29% often work this way and a further 32% sometimes work this way)
- In Singapore, 85% of companies have FWA options (19% often work this way and a further 31% sometimes work this way)

The reasons provided by the remaining workers for not taking up the option in companies that had FWAs included:

- The company turned down my request
- Prefer to work in an office
- Must be on-site to perform my work
- I think it will harm my career
- The company does not supply the necessary ICT for me to work effectively and productively

National culture also influences these explanations. For example, Indian workers suggest that FWAs are for "less hardworking" employees. In Japan, *karōshi* (literally "overwork death") is "occupational sudden mortality" brought about by stress and poor diet through work. This is a common syndrome in other ESEA countries. Even workers under FWAs must overcome this deadly practice.

Whereas the trend for FWAs is accelerating worldwide and particularly so in ESEA where it is beginning to redefine the notion of work (PersolKelly, 2018), Serrano (2016) highlights the dark side of these flexible work practices. Using examples from Indonesia, Malaysia, the Philippines, Singapore, Thailand, and Vietnam, Serrano suggests that the contractual element of FWA contracts offer workers little legal protection. Furthermore, they provide employers with opportunities to adapt or dispose of workers legally. This is undoubtedly a red flag to workers on or seeking a flexible work contract.

Even though Serrano reported that "good practices" in FWAs are capable of reconciling the needs of the workforce with the need of employers in the ASEAN region, across the six countries studied she found few had the robust legal infrastructure necessary to deal effectively with the contractual elements of FWAs. Although the legal statutes in most countries apply to employees on an FWA contract, given the multifaceted nature and the number of clauses in a generic work contract, the level of protection offered ranged from high to minimal (Serrano, 2016: 170-174). The self-employed anywhere worker also faced the vagaries of contract law in their respective countries.

Mobile technology in ESEA allows work to occur anywhere and anytime; the only fixed element is the outcome. While a range of workplaces now accommodate workers under FWAs, estimating the number of these workplaces in ESEA is difficult.

However, a surrogate measure is the level of corporate financial investment in these workplaces, which is growing rapidly. The data below attest to the strength of this type of property investment in ESEA and India (Colliers International, 2019; *Statista*, 2020) from both a supply and demand perspective:

- The Asian Pacific region accounts for 35% of coworking spaces globally
- Bangalore and Chennai had 29% and 27% growth rates respectively in 2018
- In Shanghai, forecast revenue from coworking spaces is 4.3bn RMN in 2021
- Hong Kong set a record of 900,000 sq. ft of new flexible space in 2018, increasing space by 35%
- Singapore registered a record number of take-ups of coworking spaces in 2019
- Flexible office space will remain an important demand driver in the office space market
- In Chengdu in 2018, flexible workspaces expand and changed the landscape for traditional offices
- In Manila, a mobile workforce and multinationals looking to reduce their operating costs have accelerated the rise of flexible workspaces
- In Jakarta, 2018 was another record year for flexible workspaces
- In New Delhi, the demand from corporation and start-ups for flexible workspaces will grow rapidly in the next three years
- In 2019, New Delhi had the highest growth in the number of coworking spaces globally
- In Seoul, demand from flexible workspace operators continues to increase
- In Taipei, property owners must become more accommodating in their office leasing arrangements to cater for the increased demand from anywhere workers

Expectedly, FWAs remained problematic in Japan with national culture casting its omnipresent influence. In Tokyo during 2018, Colliers International saw flexible workspace operators battling for the "limited available opportunities". The gist of a recent editorial piece by Yoko Ishikura (2019), Professor Emeritus of Hitotsubashi University, encapsulates the issues facing the implementation of FWAs in Japan. Barriers to change include an entrenched national culture and lethargy on the part of both corporations and governments. The barriers ranged from the work style of the Japanese, the lack of empowerment of women and the deep-seated perception that a woman's place is in the home to a shortage of "freelancers" and the number of workers engaged in the "traditional pursuit of a full-time job".

While Japan has few startups and a "relatively negative view" of this business model, the new Fukuoka startup city as an innovation hub in 2012 is highly favourable for FWAs and the idea of anywhere working. Professor Ishikura concludes on a positive note:

*The world is changing rapidly, and we cannot continue the same approach as before, and people's work style and career needs are diverse and changing. There is no single right approach or one-size-fits-all solution to accommodating the differences and resolve the complex problem of work styles.*

Time will tell if Professor Ishimura's vision materializes and overcomes the push of the 'invisible jet stream' driving Japan's national culture.

## The Future of FWAs and Anywhere Working in ESEA

The notions of paradigm orientations and national culture help expand the boundaries of research into the most likely future of FWAs and anywhere working in ESEA. Although Eastern and Western employers and employees think differently about the nature of work, workplaces, FWAs, and anywhere working, these differences unfold according to deep level axial principles.

While each national culture thinks differently about the nature of work, they arrive at a similar destination. However, when flexibility becomes the yardstick for determining the nature of an employment relationship that delivers benefits for employers and employees alike, pragmatism may temper or even trump national culture in the employment game. The social and economic benefits for ESEA will be significant so long as regional governments come to the table with supportive legislation to protect workers under FWAs.

While work practices generally change slowly, it is prudent to recognize that Black Swan events have the potential to alter political, economic, social, and technological thinking radically and rapidly (Taleb, 2007). The impact of the coronavirus COVID-19 pandemic in early 2020 thrust FWAs into media headlines around the globe. Although the pandemic was not a true Black Swan in Taleb's estimation (he views it as a White Swan because pandemics are likely and foreseeable events), the subtitle of his book, *the impact of the highly improbable* seems to capture the unpreparedness of governments of any country to respond the pandemic. With infections rising quickly and death tolls at a frightening rate in advanced countries like Italy, Spain, the UK and the US, governments around the world ordered people to "work from home" to stem the community transmission of the virus. This was a whole new ball game for many employers and employees, especially in national cultures adverse to the idea of FWAs or anywhere working.

In Japan, for example, attitudes to FWAs changed almost overnight. According to Osaki (2020), "commuting on packed trains and spending hours in a confined office space are akin to a nightmare in the age of the COVID-19 pandemic". In response to the pandemic, "firms nationwide have been scrambling to enable them to work remotely" with many large corporations quickly implementing telework and other flexible options. CNA (2020) also reports that COVID-19 is a game-changer, which "breaks the mould for telework in office-bound Japan". It is a strange world, indeed when it takes the threat of disease and death to make the benefits of teleworking obvious.

## Next Steps and Future Research in FWAs and Anywhere Working in ESEA

In an environment sceptical of the benefits of anywhere working and FWAs, knowledge is a powerful agent of change. While FWAs face challenges in ESEA, a range of organizations in the region have experienced the positive outcomes of these work options. Professional associations, management development educators, universities, and other stakeholder need to engage in activities that broadcast this success proactively. Newsletters, conferences, and articles in the popular press could disseminate this positive news.

According to Anell and Hartmann (2007: 57), FWAs have helped regional companies to:

- Attract and retain capable workers
- Increase employee engagement, morale, loyalty, and health
- Demonstrate they subscribe to a caring company culture
- Increase diversity in the workplace
- Protect the environment

Paraphrased below are some of Anell and Hartmann's key suppositions and imperatives concerning the future development of FWAs in ESEA:

*They suggest that increasing economic development results in more women entering the workforce, dual-earning couples becoming the employment norm, and a scarcity of human resource talent. In this light, FWAs offer companies a new work arrangement to meet these challenges. FWAs also support the greater engagement of women in the workforce and make it easy for cross-border employees to compare work-life policies and work arrangements within a single company. Before companies introduce flexible working options, a thorough investigation of the country's national culture, as well as its social, economic, and political environment, are mandatory. Companies should also note the prevailing attitudes toward work, the family unit, and a country's work ethic to estimate how FWAs would impact the work environment.*

*While values will vary between counties and across industry types, a company must examine its own corporate culture before thinking about how to implement FWAs. For example, companies must gauge the extent to which FWAs are consistent with existing company policies, determine the level of support among Board members or Directors for FWAs, and assess the strength of the corporate culture's belief in flexibility. In addition, which aspects of a national culture support or inhibit the implementation of FWAs. In ESEA, salary still ranks high on the strategies for the recruitment and retention of employees, especially in India and China. However, as economies develop and change, attitudes toward work and rewards will also change as workers increasingly participate in the global economy and work 24/7 in an environment where the ICT blurs the boundaries of work and life beyond work. In this setting, the demand for FWAs will surely increase (Anell & Hartmann, 2007: 58).*

To support efforts to promote flexible work options as genuine alternatives to traditional forms of work across ESEA, additional research in the four priority areas below would bolster this goal:

1. Variances in the attitudes of employers and employees toward FWAs by country and industry
2. Strategies that promote an organization's corporate culture among employees engaged in anywhere working
3. The role of trust in the cementing positive employment relationships between managers and anywhere workers by country and industry
4. A comparative analysis of the management challenges arising from the use of FWAs

More generally, a longitudinal study of the impact of COVID-19 on global work practices would enrich the literature on FWAs and anywhere working.

## CONCLUSION

Returning to the four propositions concerning anywhere working discussed above, while gaps appear in understandings about the nature of anywhere working, the literature recognizes FWAs as alternative work choices, where the notion of flexibility and choice become the norm in the employment relationship. Addressing the conundrum of anywhere working as a fulfilling, emancipating and human experience, the literature suggests that for employees, FWAs offer higher levels of freedom, achievement, well-being, and fulfilment compared to the experience of workers tied to traditional workplaces. This interpretation requires new understandings to explain how flexible work alters the social relations of work.

The notion of anywhere working particularly has fractured ideas about social class – the activities and products of anywhere workers are too broad to present any unifying theme for defining social class relevant to the anywhere working world. Moreover, if FWAs become the norm, as suggested by Garner et al. (2016), these workers might emerge as a social class of their own. However, determining the political allegiances and economic aspirations of such a diverse group lay well beyond the current environment. Nevertheless, what is certain is that FWAs and anywhere working in a few short years grew from obscurity to prominence among the work choices available to employees and employers in contemporary society.

Concerning the fourth proposition: "national culture influences thinking about anywhere working and FWAs in the high-context work cultures of ESEA", as flexible work options continue their march into the employment relationships and work practices of ESEA, new ways of thinking about the social relations of work will appear with a distinct high-context Eastern flavor. In Western contexts, thinking infuses flexible work options with a low-context flavor. However, whether these two flavors mix to produce a uniform global worldview about FWAs and anywhere working is uncertain.

## REFERENCES

Adler, N., & Gunderson, A. (2008). International dimensions of organizational behavior (5th ed.). Mason: South-Western College Publishing, International Thomson Publishing.

An, M. (2019, August 9). Vietnamese workers are more productive with flexible working hours. *Hanoi Times*. Retrieved from http://hanoitimes.vn/vietnamese-workers-are-more-productive-with-flexible-working-hours-45588.html

Anell, K., & Hartmann, D. (2007). *Flexible Work Arrangement in Asia, what companies are doing, why they are doing it and what lies ahead.* A Report Prepared for the Members of the Global Workforce Roundtable, Boston College Center for Work & Family.

Arendt, H. (1958). *The Human Condition*. University of Chicago Press.

Argyle, M. (1992). *The Social Psychology of Everyday Life*. Routledge.

Argyris, C. (1967). *Personality and Organization: The Conflict between System and Individual*. Harper Collins.

Asia Research. (2018). *The push for flexible working in Asia.* Retrieved from https://asia-research.net/push-flexible-working-asia/

Asmawi, A., & Othman, N. (2018). Barriers to Flexible Work Arrangements (FWA) in Malaysian Knowledge-based Industries. *2018 IEEE International Conference on Industrial Engineering and Engineering Management (IEEM).* 10.1109/IEEM.2018.8607349

Aston, J., & Cornett, B. (2016, July 12). Michael Page staff in ski scandal. *The Australian Financial Review*, 35.

Bavelas, J. (1978). *Personality: Current Theory and Research.* Brooks/Cole.

Bentley, K., & Yoong, P. (2000). Knowledge work and telework: An exploratory study. *Internet Research, 10*(4), 346–356. doi:10.1108/10662240010342658

Berger, P., & Luckmann, T. (1967). *The Social Construction of Reality.* Penguin.

Berrell, M. (1994). The nature of work: An introduction. In F. Crowther, B. Caldwell, J. Chapman, G. Lakomski, & D. Ogilvie (Eds.), *The Workplace in Education: Australian Perspectives. Yearbook of the Australian Council for Educational Administration, 1.* Edward Arnold.

Berrell, M., & Macpherson, R. (1995). Educational sociology and educational administration: Problems with paradigms, epistemology, research, and theory. *Journal of Educational Administration and Foundations, 10*(1), 9–32.

Blauner, R. (1964). *Alienation and Freedom: The Factory Worker and His Industry. Chicago.* University of Chicago Press.

Boxall, P., Purcell, J., & Wright, P. (Eds.). (2008). *The Oxford Handbook on Human Resource Management.* Oxford University Press.

Brownson, K. (2004). The benefits of a work-at-home program. *The Health Care Manager, 23*(2), 141–144. doi:10.1097/00126450-200404000-00007 PMID:15192994

Burrell, G., & Morgan, G. (2005). *Sociological Paradigms and Organizational Analysis: Elements of the Sociology of Corporate Life.* Ashgate.

Channel News Asia (CNA). (2020). Virus breaks the mold for telework in office-bound Japan. *CNA International Edition.* Retrieved from https://www.channelnewsasia.com/news/asia/coronavirus-covid-19-japan-work-from-home-12592548

Churchman, C. (1967). Wicked Problems. *Management Science, 14*(4), B-141–B-146.

Clark, S., & Holdsworth, L. (2017). *Flexibility in the Workplace: Implications of flexible work arrangements for individuals, teams, and organizations*. Alliance Manchester Business School, University of Manchester, for the Advisory, Conciliation and Arbitration Service UK. www.acas.org.uk

Colliers International. (2019). *The Flexible Workspace Outlook Report: APAC*. Colliers International. Retrieved from http://flexiblespace.colliers.com/

Crowther, F., Caldwell, B., Chapman, J., Lakomski, G., & Ogilvie, D. (Eds.). (1994). *The Workplace in Education, Australian Perspectives, 1*. Edward Arnold.

Dahrendorf, R. (1959). *Class and Class Conflict in Industrial Society*. Stanford University Press.

de Grazia, S. (1962). *Of Time, Work and Leisure*. Krauss Reprint Co.

Deaux, K., & Snyder, M. (Eds.). (2012). *The Oxford Handbook of Personality and Social Psychology*. Oxford University Press. doi:10.1093/oxfordhb/9780195398991.001.0001

Department of Sustainability, Environment, Water, Population and Communities (DES). (2011). Sustainable Australia - Sustainable Communities: A sustainable population strategy for Australia, Canberra.

Dunbar, R. (2016). Do online social media cut through the constraints that limit the size of offline social networks? *Royal Society Open Science*. Retrieved from http://rsos.royalsocietypublishing.org/content/3/1/150292

Durkheim, E. (1964). *The Rules of Sociological Method*. The Free Press.

Economics, D. A. (2011). *Next Generation Telework: A Literature Review*. Department of Broadband, Communications, and the Digital Economy. Retrieved from https://melbourneinstitute.unimelb.edu.au/assets/documents/hilda-bibliography/other-publications/2011/Next_Generation_Telework-A_Literature_Review-July_2011.pdf

Effrat, A. (1976). Book Review, *Sociology, A Multiple Paradigm Science* by George Ritzer. *American Journal of Sociology, 81*(6), 1512–1514. doi:10.1086/226243

Eldridge, J. (1971). *The Sociology of Industrial Life*. Nelson.

Gajendran, R., & Harrison, D. (2007). The Good, the Bad, and the Unknown about Teleworking: Meta-Analysis of Psychological Mediators and Individual Consequences. *The Journal of Applied Psychology, 92*(6), 1524–1541. doi:10.1037/0021-9010.92.6.1524 PMID:18020794

Garner, C., Forbes, P., Sheldon, H., Shoesmith, D., & Ternouth, P. (2016). *Working Anywhere, A Winning Formula for Good Work?* The Work Foundation (Lancaster University), The Work Foundation Alliance Limited. Retrieved from http://www.theworkfoundation.com/Reports/398/Working-Anywhere

Garrett, R., & Danziger, J. (2007). Which Telework? Defining and Testing a Taxonomy of Technology-Mediated Work at a Distance. *Social Science Computer Review*, *25*(1), 27–47. doi:10.1177/0894439306293819

Gerstner, L. (2002). *Who Says Elephants Can't Dance? Leading a Great Enterprise through Dramatic Change*. Harper Business.

Gloet, M., & Berrell, M. (2003). The dual paradigm nature of knowledge management: Implications for achieving quality outcomes in human resource management. *Journal of Knowledge Management*, *7*(1), 78–89. doi:10.1108/13673270310463635

Habermas, J. (1971). *Knowledge and Human Interests*. Beacon Hill.

Haddon, L., & Silverstone, R. (1994). Telework and the Changing Relationship of Home and Work. In R. Mansell (Ed.), Management of Information and Communication Technologies: Emerging Patterns of Control (pp. 234-247). London: Aslib.

Hall, E. (1976). *Beyond culture*. Anchor-Doubleday.

Hall, E. (1992). The silent language in overseas business. In H. Lane & J. Di Steffano (Eds.), *International management behavior*. PWS-Kent.

Handy, S., & Mokhtarian, P. (1996). The Future of Telecommuting. *Futures*, *28*(3), 227–240. doi:10.1016/0016-3287(96)00003-1

Hayes. (2017). *2017 Gender Diversity Report*. Retrieved from https://www.hays.com.au/gender-diversity/HAYS_1832068

Hayes. (2019). *Flexibility a hot topic that shows no signs of cooling down in Malaysia*. Retrieved from https://www.hays.com.my/press-releases/HAYS_118017

Henson, B. (Ed.). (1997). Remote Working: marvelous, perilous, or both. *Staff Notes Monthly*. Retrieved from https://www.ucar.edu/communications/staffnotes/9704/telecommuting.html

Hickson, D., & Pugh, D. (1995). *Management worldwide: The impact of societal culture on organizations around the globe*. Penguin.

Hill, J., Ferris, M., & Martinson, V. (2003). Does it matter where you work? A comparison of how three work venues (traditional office, virtual office, and home office) influences aspects of work and personal/family life. *Journal of Vocational Behavior*, *63*(2), 220–241. doi:10.1016/S0001-8791(03)00042-3

Hislop, D., Axtell, C., Collins, A., Daniels, K., Glover, J., & Niven, K. (2015). Variability in the use of mobile ICTs by homeworkers and its consequences for boundary and social isolation. *Information and Organization*, *25*(4), 222–232. doi:10.1016/j.infoandorg.2015.10.001

Hofstede, G. (1994). *Cultures and organizations: Software of the mind - intercultural cooperation and its importance for survival*. Harper-Collins.

Hofstede, G. (2011). Dimensionalizing Cultures: The Hofstede Model in Context. *Online Readings in Psychology and Culture*, *2*(1). Advance online publication. doi:10.9707/2307-0919.1014

Inkpen, A., & Beamish, P. (1997). Knowledge, bargaining power, and the instability of international joint ventures. *Academy of Management Review*, *22*(1), 177–202. doi:10.5465/amr.1997.9707180263

Ishikura, Y. (2019, August 11). Flexible work style - can it be sustainable? *The Japan Times*. Retrieved from https://www.japantimes.co.jp/opinion/2019/08/11/commentary/japan-commentary/flexible-work-style-can-sustainable/

Jackson, P., & van der Wielen, J. (2002). *Teleworking: International Perspectives*. Routledge. doi:10.4324/9780203053089

Johns, T., & Gratton, L. (2013). The Third Wave of Virtual Work. *Harvard Business Review*, *91*(1/2), 66–73.

Khidhir, S. (2018, November 4). Looking at flexible work arrangements. *The Asian Post*. Retrieved from https://www.google.com/search?q=Looking+at+flexible+work+arrangements%2C+The+Asian+Post.&rlz=1C1AZAA_enAU744NZ745&oq=Looking+at+flexible+work+arrangements%2C+The+Asian+Post.&aqs=chrome.69i57j33.1536j0j8&sourceid=chrome&ie=UTF-8

Kluckhohn, C. (1962). Universal categories of culture. In S. Tax (Ed.), Anthropology Today: Selections (pp. 304-20). Chicago: University of Chicago Press.

Kluckhohn, F., & Strodtbeck, F. (1961). *Variations in value orientations*. Row Peterson.

Kroeber, A., & Kluckhohn, C. (1963). *A critical review of concepts and definitions*. Vintage.

Kuhn, T. (1970). *The Structure of Scientific Revolutions*. University of Chicago Press.

Lake, A. (2013). *Smart Flexibility: Moving Smart & Flexible Working from Theory to Practice*. Routledge.

Lam, P. L., & Shiu, A. (2010). Economic growth, telecommunications development, and productivity growth of the telecommunications sector: Evidence around the world. *Telecommunications Policy*, *34*(4), 186–199. doi:10.1016/j.telpol.2009.12.001

Lee, S., Trimi, S., & Kim, C. (2013). The impact of cultural differences on technology adoption. *Journal of World Business*, *48*(1), 20–29. doi:10.1016/j.jwb.2012.06.003

Levi-Strauss, C. (1969). *The Scope of Anthropology*. Jonathan Cape.

Levi-Strauss, C. (1979). *Structural Anthropology*. Penguin.

Liang, T.-P., Huang, C.-W., Yeh, Y.-I., & Lin, B. (2007). Adoption of mobile technology in business: A fit-viability model. *Industrial Management & Data Systems*, *107*(8), 1154–1169. doi:10.1108/02635570710822796

Lin, C. (2012). Communication Technology and Social Change. In C. Lin & D. Atkin (Eds.), Communication Technology and Social Change: Theory and Implications (pp. 3-15). New York: Routledge.

Lyotard, J.-F. (1986). *The post-modern condition: A report on knowledge*. Manchester University Press.

Mackenzie, N., & Knipe, S. (2006). Research dilemmas: Paradigms, methods, and methodology. *Issues in Educational Research*, *16*(2), 193–205.

Marx, K., & Engels, F. (2010). Collected Works (Vols. 1–50). Lawrence & Wishart.

Mead, R. (1994). *International management: Cross cultural dimensions*. Blackwell.

Mills, C. W. (1973). The Meanings of Work throughout History. In F. Best (Ed.), The Future of Work (pp. 6-13). Englewood Cliffs: Prentice-Hall.

Montreuil, S., & Lippel, K. (2003). Telework and occupational health: A Quebec empirical study and regulatory implications. *Safety Science*, *41*(4), 339–358. doi:10.1016/S0925-7535(02)00042-5

Nicolaus, M. (1967). *Proletariat and the Middle Class in Marx: Hegelian Choreography and the Capitalist Dialectic. Studies on the Left.*

Nilles, J. (1976). *The Telecommunications-Transportation Tradeoff: Options for Tomorrow*. Wiley.

Nilles, J. (1998). *Managing Telework: Strategies for Managing the Virtual Workforce*. Wiley.

Osaki, T. (2020, March 22). For many in Japan, remote work during coronavirus outbreak is not an option. *The Japan Times*. Retrieved from https://www.japantimes.co.jp/news/2020/03/22/national/social-issues/coronavirus-remote-work-not-option-for-all/#.Xo-7msgzbZY

Pahl, R. (Ed.). (1988). *On Work, Historical, Comparative and Theoretical Approaches*. Basil Blackwell.

Persolkelly. (2018). *2018 APEC Workforce Insights: Gig Economy; How free agents are redefining work*. Persolkelly. Retrieved from https://www.persolkelly.com/media/persolkelly/client/2018%20APAC%20Workforce%20Insights%20-%20Q1/PERSOLKELLY%202018%20APAC%20Workforce%20Insights%20-%20Gig%20Economy%20How%20Free%20Agents%20Are%20Redefining%20Work.pdf

Polycom. (2019). *The Changing World of Work: A Global Survey*. Digital Whitepaper, Polycom. Retrieved from https://www.polycom.com/content/dam/polycom/common/documents/whitepapers/changing-needs-of-the-workplace-whitepaper-enus.pdf

Raghuram, S., Wiesenfeld, B., & Garud, P. (2003). Technology enabled work: The role of self-efficacy in determining telecommuter adjustment and structuring behavior. *Journal of Vocational Behavior*, *63*(2), 180–189. doi:10.1016/S0001-8791(03)00040-X

Ravasi, D., & Schultz, M. (2006). Responding to organizational identity threats: Exploring the role of organizational culture. *Academy of Management Journal*, *49*(3), 433–458. doi:10.5465/amj.2006.21794663

Ritzer, G. (1975). *Sociology, a Multiple Paradigm Science*. Allyn & Bacon.

Ruppel, C., Tworoger, L., & Tworoger, T. (2012). Telework: Identifying a Personal Dimension to Work-Related Socio-Technical Theory. *Advances in Business Research*, *3*(1), 12–24.

Samson, D., & Daft, R. (2015). *Fundamentals of Management* (5th ed.). Cengage.

Serrano, M. (Ed.). (2014). Between Flexibility and Security; The Rise of Non-standard Employment in Selected ASEAN Countries. ASEAN Services Employees Trade Unions Council (ASETUC), Ciujung No. 4.

Statista. (2020). *Flexible workspace in Asia Pacific - Statistics & Facts*. Statista Research Department. Retrieved from https://www.statista.com/topics/5411/flexible-workspace-in-asia-pacific/

Taleb, N. (2007). *The Black Swan: The Impact of the Highly Improbable*. Penguin.

Tang, S. (2011). Foundational Paradigms in the Social Sciences. *Philosophy of the Social Sciences, 41*(2), 211–249. doi:10.1177/0048393109355294

Tayeb, M. (1995). The competitive advantage of nations: The role of HRM and its socio-cultural context. *International Journal of Human Resource Management, 6*(3), 588–606. doi:10.1080/09585199500000037

Tilgher, A. (1930). Work: What is has meant to Men through the Ages. New York: Arno Press. (Original work published 1929)

Toffler, A., & Toffler, H. (1990). *Powershift, Knowledge, Wealth, and Violence at the Edge of the 21st Century*. Bantam Books.

Triandis, H. (1983). Dimensions of cultural variations as parameters of organizational theories. *International Studies of Management & Organization, 12*(4), 139–169. doi:10.1080/00208825.1982.11656354

Warner, M. (Ed.). (2013). *Managing across diverse cultures in East Asia: issues and challenges in a changing globalized world*. Routledge. doi:10.4324/9780203106952

Weber, M. (1947). *The Theory of Social and Economic Organization*. The Free Press.

Weinert, C., Maier, C., & Laumer, S. (2015). Why are teleworkers stressed? An empirical analysis of the causes of telework-enabled stress. *Proceedings 12th International Conference on Wirtschaftsinformatik*. Retrieved from https://aisel.aisnet.org/wi2015/

Wiberg, M., & Ljungberg, F. (2000). Exploring the vision of "anytime, anywhere" in the context of mobile work. In J. Malhotra (Ed.), *Knowledge Management and Business Innovation*. Ideas Group Publishing.

Wojcak, E., & Barath, M. (2017). National Culture and Application of Telework in Europe. *European Journal of Business Science and Technology, 3*(1), 65–74. doi:10.11118/ejobsat.v3i1.79

## KEY TERMS AND DEFINITIONS

**Axial Principles:** These are the deep level universalistic principles that shape how people respond to or think about the cardinal dimensions of daily life – for example, the meaning of work, how the cosmos works, causality, and the temporal nature of existence.

**Culture:** Culture is the characteristics and knowledge of a group of people or society, which encompasses language, customs and the spiritual, material, intellectual, and emotional elements of everyday life.

**Meaning of Work:** Perceiving one's work to be meaningful or purposeful and to serve a higher and unconscious motivation offer paradigm-type explanations of how people react to organizational life and workplace relations.

**National Culture:** National culture is the norms, behaviors, beliefs, customs, and values shared by the population of a sovereign nation (e.g., a Chinese or Canadian national culture). It refers to specific characteristics such as language, religion, ethnic and racial identity, cultural history and traditions.

**Psychology of Behavior:** Indistinct concept: contingent behavior and unconscious motivation offer paradigm-type explanations of how people react to organizational life and workplace relations.

**Social Facts:** Social systems and structures and their extensions in organizational life and workplace relations – for example, roles, values, control rewards.

**Social Interpretation:** Proactive engagement of workers required to negotiate and interpret organizational life and workplace relations – attaching meaning to phenomena that reinforce the patterned nature of social life.

**Social Relations of Work:** In social science, social relations refer to any relationship between two or more individuals. Social relations derived from individual agency form the basis of social structure and are studied by sociologists such as Max Weber.

**Sociological Paradigm:** An established theory that guides thinking and research in sociology. Such theory aims to gain a deeper understanding of society.

**Work Organization:** Seeks to optimize the interaction between employees, equipment and information to enhance the cost of efficiency of work processes while at the same time maintaining the performance, motivation and skills of employees.

# Chapter 3
# Humans Need Not Apply:
## Artificial Intelligence, Robotics, Machine Learning, and the Future of Work

**Mike Berrell**
*WADEmatheson, Australia*

## ABSTRACT

*Advanced technologies including artificial intelligence, robotics, and machine learning (smart machines) impact understandings about the nature of work. For professionals, semi-professionals, and ancillary workers supplying healthcare and legal services, for example, smart machines change the social relations of work and subvert notions of status and hierarchy that come with occupational groups such as doctors or lawyers. As smart machines continue to disrupt employment, job advertisement might soon carry the warning that humans need not apply. Under the prospect of a new world of work, people require additional knowledge, skills, and attitudes to cope with a future where smart machines radically alter the nature of work in settings where some people work anywhere and anytime while others work nowhere. In any future, people require skills and attitudes to cope with uncertainty. Ideas about multiple intelligences, emotional intelligence, critical thinking, creativity, and problem-solving will help employees cope with any of the futures of work predicted in the literature.*

DOI: 10.4018/978-1-7998-4159-3.ch003

## INTRODUCTION

The idea of anywhere working is seductive. Ostensibly represented to workers as a choice among the competing options of working availability, anywhere working delivers a range of positive social and economic benefits to employers, employees, and the wider society. These outcomes include regional economic growth, a better work-life balance, improved working conditions, a reduction in pollution with fewer workers regularly commuting to work in petrol consuming vehicles and new opportunities for employers to retain workers and bolster a distributed workforce (cf. Haddon & Lewis, 1994; Messenger, et al., 2017).

In 1998, Davenport and Pearlson flagged the death of the traditional idea of the office, suggesting that technology will make these workplaces redundant. Ideas about different work options including telework, virtual work, and anywhere working tracked the rapid advances in 'information, digital and mobile technologies in business and personal communication' [ICT]. New work options extolled the virtues of these new technologies, advanced notions of flexible work arrangements [FWAs] and improved the well-being of employees. However, what scenarios emerge for anywhere working when ICT delivers unforeseen outcomes?

From ancient Egypt to the present, science and technology have been major game-changers. History mirrors technology's power to alter or even depose the most entrenched social, political, and economic discourses. Thinkers from different worldviews accepted this fundamental proposition. Aristotle knew this, so did diverse thinkers like Fredrich Nietzsche, Rene Descartes, Karl Marx, and John Maynard Keynes. However, knowing the potential of technology to overturn established ways of doing and thinking is no guarantee that any pundit's view over the horizon will arrive in the manner they envisaged.

Game-changing technologies usually develop over time. For example, the historian Eric Hobsbawm suggested the technological seeds of the Industrial Revolution planted in Britain during the 1780s took decades to propagate. It took a further 50 years for the social, economic, and political changes wrought by this revolution in material production to resonate in the societies of the time fully. When technology develops swiftly, and its uptake is immediate, a different story appears. In the US in 2001, only a handful of people knew of Apple's plan for the iPhone. With its release in 2007, sales topped 1.36 million units. Two years on, Apple sold about 40 million units. In 2019, sales reached 217 million; by then, Apple had dispatched 1.5 billion iPhones across the globe. Apple's revolutionary iPhone technology and the rate of uptake of the device reinvigorated Apple's business fortunes overnight.

These relationships between the development of technology, its application and rate of uptake are fundamental to imagining the future of work in any of its forms. However, whether the rate of change in the social relations of work created by ICT is gradual or rapid, it is contingent on the technology's utility for society. In this light, charting the future of work, workplaces and anywhere working with any degree of certainty is challenging enough. Nevertheless, in 2019, *Forbes Magazine* presented a blueprint for the future of work, and ITC supplied the foundations of this vision.

The thrust of the case for the future underscored structural changes that would radically reshape ideas of work developed during the first industrial age, the post-industrial age and in today's high-tech digital world (Marr, 2019). Bernard Marr proposed that the coming "4th Industrial Revolution" would compel employers to develop new mindsets about employees and workspaces, especially concerning the skills and knowledge necessary to be productive in the next stage of capitalism, an age in which automation is likely to be the most entrenched feature of work and workspaces. Marr also raised matters germane to education; specifically, the need to provide employees of the 4th Industrial Age with "emotional intelligence, critical thinking, creativity and problem-solving skills" to cope with the new social relations of work in a highly automated workplace.

Marr included the dramatic increase in the number of "gig" workers as a significant structural change. In an increasingly distributed workforce, this highly flexible work choice fits with the aspirations of a cadre of Generation X, Y and Z employees. Leaving aside the prominent issues of fair work legislation, worker entitlements, equal opportunity and so forth, gig working certainly presents as an opportunity for anywhere working and for any worker seeking FWAs. Accordingly, the idea of living and working anywhere and anytime entered readily into the vocabulary describing the essential components in the work-life balance of Gen Xs, Ys and Zs.

However, other structural influences relate to the motivation of employees in the new industrial age; for example, how to link business and corporate goals with the emerging aspirations of a vanguard of employees who possess the "latest tech gadgets to facilitate their (preferences to) working-from-anywhere". Marr suggested that education through lifelong learning is the key to meeting this demand. Education enables workers today to periodically enrich their skills as new applications of technology continually change the work they do and where they do it. Innovative technologies also have a prominent role in delivering education of this type. Although the jury remains out on what the relationship between human and robot teachers might be (cf. Mubin et al., 2013; Sharkey, 2016) one thing is certain - robots can work anywhere, anytime and across all working spaces, including cyberspace.

History shows that rapid advances in technology alter fundamental understandings about the social relations of work and the nature of workplaces. Marr is sanguine in his estimation of the strength of this change in the 4th Industrial Age. The human workforce going forward will "need to develop a level of comfort and acceptance" concerning the collaboration between people and machines. The use of the term "collaboration" to describe the relationship between people and machines (or robots) almost bestows the latter with human traits. The extent of this relationship, however, is contentious for the reasons discussed below.

Over thirty years ago, Zuboff (1988) contemplated the future of work when your co-worker is a machine. Today, that time is upon us. Artificial intelligence [AI] (a surrogate term for the theories of and developments in computer systems capable of performing tasks that require human intelligence) and robotics (the field of computer science and engineering concerned with creating machines that react to sensory inputs – also a branch of AI) are life-changing technologies. These technologies will shape the future more than any technological application to date.

Rapid developments in machine learning technologies will also accelerate this change. Machine learning, a branch of AI defined by Bishop (2006), encompasses the study of algorithms and statistical models used by computers to execute specific tasks without using explicit commands. Machine learning uses "patterns and inference" instead. Embedded algorithms construct mathematical models using sample data or "training data" to predict and/or make decisions without being "explicitly programmed to perform the task". Algorithms, a set of rules followed in problem-solving, have been around centuries. Their use in computers, however, heralds a new age for algorithms in systems that learn and make decisions with minimal human input.

The permutations of AI, robotics, and machine learning with their implanted algorithms, coalesce as an age of smart machines. In Stanley Kubrick masterpiece, *2001: A Space Odyssey,* HAL 9000 is a smart machine, overseeing the functions of a spaceship. Hal goes off the rails when 'he' turns off the life support of the crew members in suspended animation during a perceived crisis, killing them outright. The Commander confronts Hal, 'who' replies:

*I am putting myself to the fullest possible use, which is all I think that any conscious entity can ever hope to do. Look, Dave, I can see you're really upset about this. I honestly think you ought to sit down calmly, take a stress pill, and think things over.*

Is now the time to think things over about technology and what it means for anywhere working in the age of smart machines? Furthermore, what of the possibility of a future where no one works (humans need not apply) or only a small number of fortunate (or unfortunate?) people have the privilege (or burden?) of working. Utopian, idyllic, and dystopian futures all foresee what these minorities and majorities might do under these conditions of existence.

## BACKGROUND

Despite the downsides, smart machines today offer opportunities for employers and employees to seize the future. As workplaces and work practices continue to evolve, anywhere working will flourish and characterize the employment relationships of the 4th Industrial Age. The dominance of this work choice will spur on the design of new types of workplaces to fit the anywhere working environment. However, this story is only one of the alternative scenarios explaining the impact of ICT's monumental leap forward in the first two decades of the 21st Century. Concomitant with the continued development of even smarter machines, the kind of tasks employees perform in their jobs will change significantly; sometimes quickly, other times gradually. Other tasks will simply disappear from an employee's tool kit.

Smart machines progressively altered the world of the process worker as the smokestack cities of the industrial age slowly disappeared (cf. Zuboff, 1988), although in some cases, the smokestacks and their problems were exported to the emerging economies of Asia (Bluestone & Harrison, 1982). While the nature of industrial work changed in the digital age, so too did the work of professionals. For example, in the provision of health care and legal services, jobs that have existed in one form or another for millennia, ICT irreversibly transformed the social relations of work, how people worked and where they worked. However, change is not always a matter of personal choice.

Technology increased the potential for employees delivering these services to execute their workloads anywhere and anytime, a profile that fits the archetype of the anywhere worker. Nevertheless, these new opportunities challenged the traditional thinking of employees in their respective fields. Different social relationships of work usurped traditional notions that had survived for centuries, especially related to subjective views about job status, prestige, mental prowess, and their ensuing relationships. A hierarchy of relationships also existed among service providers and their consumers. Health care professionals had patients, lawyers had clients, and they all practiced their profession in offices, law courts, clinics, surgeries and/ or hospitals. In most cases, patients and clients came to the expert for advice and treatment. In social and economic contexts, these professions delivered significant status and wealth for their practitioners.

However, although current evidence suggests anywhere working will loom large among the work choices of employees in the 4th Industrial Age, this is speculative at least. In 1937, the French essayist and social philosopher Paul Valéry encapsulated this view concerning predictions; he suggested that "the future, like everything else, is no longer quite what it used to be ... we can no longer think of it with any confidence in our inductions". In this pessimistic light, unforeseen outcomes in the real world might rescind the promise of smart machines manipulating in future cyberspace.

Consider the following vignettes:

*Be afraid, be very afraid! At 2.47 pm. on 6 May 2010, the Dow Index began to "shudder". Three hundred seconds later it shed 998.5 points. Shortly after that, it soared back by the same amount. Astounded by these machinations, pundits explaining the "Flash Crash" placed the blame on a practical joker hacking the market, rogue traders, a money market manager who misjudged their trading window for a $4 billion sell and triggered other trading algorithms to follow suit and unknown traders who deliberately tried to manipulate the market (Steiner, 2012). At one point during the crash, billion-dollar multinationals became penny stocks. While trading algorithms in smart machines became the main suspects in explaining the Flash Crash, the actual culprit remains unknown.*

*Be ecstatic; be very ecstatic! In 2019, a team of researchers from Imperial College London and Google Health achieved a tremendous leap forward in the application of AI to medical diagnosis. Using AI-powered by Google's DeepMind algorithm, they 'trained' a computer with 'knowledge' "capable of surpassing human experts in breast cancer prediction" (McKinney et al., 2020). Motivated by the number of false positives and false negatives in cancer diagnosis, the team created an AI system that outperformed human experts.*

*Be wary, be very wary! In 2019, Wired reported that despite parameters in AI programs, individual programs developed shortcuts and deviations that their programmers did not consider or define as being "off-limits". What does the future hold when algorithmic bots (software applications that run automated tasks over the Internet) learn to cheat? More to the point, what happens if companies use smart machines to defraud deliberately? In 2017, a US federal judge ordered Volkswagen to pay a $2.8 billion fine for cheating on emissions tests. To deceive their customers, Volkswagen inserted the cheating into the algorithm that controlled car emissions tests (Schneier, 2015). In what could be another alarming development, one bot learned "to hide data from its creators to CHEAT at tasks they gave it" (Palmer, 2019).*

Apart from the prophetical elements in these stories, they reveal the potential downsides of smart machines.

One of the leading technology critics, Evgeny Morozov (2013), suggests that technology's deep roots in today's world mean that the tiniest "adjustments to seemingly inconsequential acts" have the potential to change the way people go about their lives. While Ashton (2015) recognizes that the complexity of various technologies and their applications across society are "mostly unforeseeable", even if technology goes astray, the capacity of people to seek solutions to problems created by technology is reassuring.

In thinking about the potential of smart machines for society requires initiative-taking engagement in the process by people working anywhere, anytime, or even in traditional workplaces. Assessing the utility of ICT for society demands the oversight and cognizance of employers, employees, and governments alike in the development, production, and application of smart machines. However, the fragmented environment of anywhere working may compound this task in the 4th Industrial Age. The section below examines the influence of smart machines in the provision of health care and legal services as examples of how work, workplaces and social relations are quickly evolving in these employment sectors.

## PROFESSIONAL WORKERS IN THE AGE OF SMART MACHINES

Smart machines have invaded the work practices and workspaces of employees delivering health care and legal services. In the case of health care, ICT profoundly changed the working environment. The section below explores what it means to be a professional, semi-professional and/or an ancillary worker in these fields in the 4th Industrial Age.

Brynjolfsson and McAfee forecast in 2011 that smart machines led the race in the employment stakes. Significant changes were afoot. However, over the centuries, a succession of soothsayers gazed into their crystal balls and predicted the collapse of work in one form or another because of automation. They suggested the collapse would set off a series of social, political, and/or economic upheavals (cf. Gorz, 1982; Jenkins & Sherman, 1979). Nevertheless, society endured. What possibly makes the 2020s a watershed decade is the smart machine, a very different species to their ancestors, the brute machines of the industrial age and their robotic cousins working in the assembly lines of the latter stages of post-industrial society or late capitalism.

All stories about the future of work cast technology as a leading protagonist; and all have different endings for anywhere working. In the early 1800s, raw technology featured prominently in the story of the world of work authored by the Luddites. They saw employers devalue their craft by replacing their skills in the production process with those of inanimate machines. The signs were everywhere - machines will eventually replace and devalue the human contributions to work. Daniel Susskind (2020) acknowledges that successive generations of workers have fretted about the rise of machines but suggests in the age of smart machines, the “threat of technological unemployment is real”.

Furthermore, smart machines create an environment where work is no longer the focal point of daily activity. Jerry Kaplan (2015) argues that there is a ceaseless march of smart machines affecting every aspect of life. Following the billions of dollars of investment in research and development and an almost unlimited supply of intellectual capital, smart machines now compete with and even outdo people in their jobs. However, the future is still uncertain, given the potential for technology to create unemployment in societies characterized by entrenched income inequality. When anywhere working becomes a transition to nowhere working, how will the next chapter in the world of work read?

The first part of the sub-sections below canvass two broad themes: (i) recent developments in smart machine technology and (ii) how smart machines alter traditional ideas about work relationships and images of work. A third section draws out the implications for anywhere working and the future of work, offering two alternative views about anywhere working's place the fourth iteration of the future of work.

## Health Care and Technological Change - Smart Machines and Recent Developments in the Field

The rapid rise of the smart machines is evident as a walk through any hospital corridor reveals. Even chronically under-resourced hospitals still have an astonishing number of smart machines. Tomlinson's (2018) identification of 15 medical technologies currently revolutionizing health care and modifying ideas about what it means to be a health care professional appear below. Determining the appropriate relationship between smart machines and people is a critical process in this technological revolution.

Robots like the DaVinci system allow surgeons to operate with increased precision. This accuracy results in fewer incisions, delivering better outcomes for both surgeons and patients. The technology also requires fewer doctors and nurses. Advances in prosthetics and exoskeleton technology are also life-changing developments in health care.

Nanotechnology and the proliferation of medical bots are new fields that decrease the workloads of some health care professionals while simultaneously opening new employment opportunities and creating new employment relationships. These bots operate in acute care areas improving medical diagnostics and procedures in oncology and haematology to bots that clean and disinfect hospital wards. Bots even dispense pharmaceuticals at the University of California - San Francisco.

Today, life-sized clinical training bots have quickly altered traditional approaches to medical education (by replacing cadavers and simulating the feel and look of blood and tissue). Companion bots also enrich the social life of the elderly. In the future of aged care, perhaps humans need not apply. However, do we really want a robot as a first-order companion? Perhaps nursing will be the employment type most affected by technological applications. Nevertheless, the School of Nursing at Duquesne University in the US views robotic nursing as creating new employment opportunities for the robot's human counterpart.

The human element in health care makes nurses "irreplaceable", although time will attest to the strength of this belief. With nurses overworked by most assessments of hospitals worldwide, robots can improve a nurse's working environment. Apart from the economic benefits that come with the applications of new technologies in society, new employment opportunities also emerge. Coordinators need to oversee the work of robotic nurses and confirm the veracity of any data collected or the appropriateness of any proposed intervention.

Advances in robotics and telemedicine allow patients in any location remote from a hospital or health care centre to access a diagnosis or a treatment plan 24/7. Although Ronald Weinstein and his colleagues (2014) note barriers and opportunities coexist in the practice of telehealth, the push to extracting additional efficiencies from the health care system in the US spurred a string of developments in the field including application to out-of-hours radiology, treating stoke, burn and other urgent care patients, various video-enabled extension programs and multi-site diagnoses. They conclude that "mobile health is currently undergoing explosive growth and could be a disruptive innovation that will change the face of healthcare in the future". Telehealth and its smart machines mean that business as usual no longer suffices in health care. When a diverse range of health care workers across the global converse with each other in real-time and tap their smart machines to answer health care problems, the working environment has changed. By default, these service providers are increasingly engaged in anywhere working.

The addition of machine learning to the field of health care is the game-changer for health care professionals. Technological advances are now so rapid that the news media finds it challenging to keep society abreast of these changes and their implications for work and society. Tomlinson's (2019) web pages on Interesting Engineering reports that FDNA Inc, using Face2Gene, a search and reference tool and its next-generation phenotyping (NGP) technologies, employs "facial recognition software to screen patients for over 8,000 diseases and rare genetic disorders" and it achieves this task with a "scarily high degree of accuracy". He also reports that a team from New York University created a smart machine that "scanned thousands of medical documents to pinpoint patients at risk of developing diabetes, heart failure, or stroke". To date, the machine has never faltered.

Other smart machines include robots assisting with biopsies using ultrasound technology for cancer detection, where a "robotically steered transducer" is guided to a biopsy site. The surgeon isolates the site among numerous 3D images with an extremely high degree of certitude – the keyhole surgery technique leaves little signs of the procedure.

On the patient side, the explosion of self-help sites and social media platforms, containing a mix of public and private, and profit and not-for-profit organizations, dispense advice across a range of health care issues, from medicine and well-being to aged care and end of life decisions.

The recent COVID-19 global pandemic of early 2020 provides an example of how health care professional quickly co-opted smart machines to address this health emergency. In the cases of "emerging and novel pathogens" where viruses are "easily and readily transmissible and have asymptomatic infectivity periods", a concerted global effort from health care professionals is required (Srinivasa Rao & Vazquez, 2020). They proposed a machine learning algorithm, which would accelerate the identification of COVID-19 cases via a mobile-based web survey. The advantage of their approach is that it would effectively reduce the spread of COVID-19 among "susceptible populations under quarantine".

## Smart Machines, Social Relations of Work, and Images of the Profession

Robotics and telemedicine are a combination that alters the traditional relationships between doctors, nurses and technicians. In some cases, smart machines allow a skilled nurse or a technician to take on roles traditionally associated with doctors, blurring the traditional demarcations between these occupations. Even the hospital cleaner's role transforms with the introduction of disinfection bots. Time will tell whether the roles of hospital cleaners will morph into being smart machine supervisors.

Technology changes the social relations of work that previously cast actors in the easily recognizable parts of professionals and non-professionals (including technicians). Just what is the role of the doctor in the age of smart machines when these machines seem better on giving a correct diagnosis in many areas of medicine and what level of education do supervisors require to oversee these machines. It seems that doctors are now most influential at the final stage of the process of diagnosis before the implementation of treatment programs. In many instances, these machines have surpassed the years of accumulated knowledge residing in health care professionals. However, companies leading this smart machine revolution in health care services moderate this claim. For example, FDNA Inc. states "Face2Gene is a search and reference tool provided for informational purposes and not intended to replace the clinician's judgment or experience, nor should it be used to diagnose or treat medical conditions". History will decide the veracity of the disclaimer.

Advances in prosthetics and exoskeleton technology are life-changing developments, which not only offer new job opportunities but also move the expertise away from doctors to technician and specialist nursing staff. As employment in the health care professions become highly flexible, the traditional work performed by doctors, nurses, cleaners and even chemists change profoundly as these technologies flourish.

Perhaps the most complex effect of smart machines is evident in the social psychology of work. A person's self-efficacy derives from the status associated with their job, the social prestige that accompanies it, and the mental prowess the job requires. Smart machines change all this, and quickly. A doctor has typically invested thousands of dollars in education, receives a substantial income, achieves seniority in the health care profession and accepts society's accolades. What happens to the self-efficacy of doctors as smart machines surpass their ability in medical-related tasks that previously required highly technical abilities and years of experience to perform expertly. Furthermore, what happens to cleaners when smart machines do their jobs more cheaply and efficiently? Whereas a select few employees will move up on the hierarchy of jobs through training and development programs, most will move down a rung or two on the ladder, although this downward destination is unclear.

In a similar vein, the relationship between doctors and patients has changed. Today, people are fast becoming knowledgeable concerning their health care options. Given that Internet sites such My Doctor.com, EVERYMIND.com and Third Age Matters all rank highly in Google's search results, their reach across all sections of society is considerable. Worldwide, millions of people with access to the Internet have proactively accumulated a reservoir of knowledge about their own well-being. Whether this knowledge is power or a confirmation of Morozov's proposition *that to save everything, just click here* (reflecting the *folly of technological solutionism*) remains a thorny question. Nevertheless, Dr Google provides large numbers of people with health care knowledge about the following areas - kidney stones, snoring, hiccups, the causes of fatigue, the flu, systemic lupus erythematosus, cholesterol, attention deficit hyperactivity disorder, cholesterol and hypertension. Again, whether this bank of specific knowledge is a product of folly or design is undetermined.

## Legal Services and Technological Change - Smart Machines and Recent Developments in the Field

Today, smart machines and their algorithms proliferate in the provision of many types of legal services. Steiner (2012) reported that BlackStone Discovery was replacing people with algorithms in work that required lawyers and paralegals to read and assess large contracts – the algorithms worked "just as efficiently and often more thoroughly" than their human counterparts in performing these tasks.

It is worth reviewing BlackStone Discovery's sales pitch on their Home Page:

*We take a collaborative approach to defining your success criteria. Our team of former litigators, eDiscovery specialists, and IT experts tackle your case with cutting-edge technology to eliminate the need for massive data processing and evaluation. This efficiency translates to highly scalable services and quality results that are available sooner, giving you more time for case preparation ... your case is viewable online 24×7, providing complete transparency. Think of BlackStone as your in-house discovery team without the overhead.*

Smart machines are rapidly removing humans from the process of discovery and reducing labor costs, an extremely attractive pitch for BlackStone Discovery's corporate clients. Even in 2012, only 26,000 jobs existed for the 54,000 lawyers who passed the bar exam in the US (Steiner, 2014).

In *AI vs Lawyers, the Ultimate Showdown*, the LawGeex AI algorithm pitted lawyers against smart machines in "accurately spotting risks in everyday contracts". LawGeex, a Tel-Aviv based company, had already raised $21.5 million for its start-up when the New York office opened in 2018. The question on the minds of investors was straightforward: can AI really replace lawyers? In this context, the data below portend the future for lawyers. The AI algorithm outperformed the lawyers on accuracy with AI achieving 94% and the average of the lawyer being 85%. AI took 26 seconds to review five non-disclosure agreements [NDAs]; the average time taken by lawyers was 92 minutes. Lawyers received four hours of review time for the five NDAs; the LawGeex smart machine had none.

The mix of trial lawyers included associates, single practitioners, general counsels, and in-house corporate lawyers (from entities such as Goldman Sachs, Cisco and global giants including Alston & Bird and K&L Gates). The smart machine trained on "tens of thousands of NDAs using machine learning and deep learning technologies". The formal and technical language processed included 30 legal issues, 153 paragraphs, 11 pages and 3,213 clauses. For the baristas among us, the lawyers consumed an average of 12 cups of coffee each during the trial. Granted, the investment in the LawGeex algorithm was significant, but its scalability potential is enormous; its reach is global, its access 24/7.

Bernard Marr (2018) also delved into the penetration of smart machines into the provision of legal services, and its consequences for the work lawyers and paralegals do in the 4th Industrial Age. Reviewing 'how AI and machine learning are transforming law firms and the legal sector', he provided examples of smart machines at the frontier of this transformation. This is especially evident the time consuming and sometimes tedious tasks associated with reviewing documents, conducting legal research, executing due diligence and managing contracts. Smart machines also infiltrate higher-order processes associated with predicting legal outcomes. Also, "automating divorce" is now an alternative to traditional lawyer-driven settlements.

Marr discusses the work of Wevorce, which the company itself describes as "the premier self-guided divorce solution" in delivering mutually beneficial outcomes for the parties involved and the best possible solution considering their economic and social circumstances. Settlements negotiated via a smart machine come at a fraction of the cost incurred going through the 'normal' channels. However, Wevorce retains legal experts on call to supply a first-hand expert opinion when required.

Deloitte's (2016) step into the law firm of the future is a revelation for the legal profession. This a future where the "quickening pace of technological developments" will profoundly transform the profession, following "shifts in workforce demographics and the need to offer clients more value for money". The life expectancy of law firms that do not meet the future head-on with reinvigorated service and employment strategies is short. With 100,000 legal roles becoming automated in the next 15 years, Marr (2019) suggests the early 2020s is the tipping point for determining the structure of the law firm of the future. Companies like NextLaw Labs are already ahead of the game, focusing their intellectual capital on becoming the "definitive global intelligence hub focused exclusively on the world of legal innovation".

In the light of the above, Wevorce's promise of legal experts on call heralds the new work of work for expert lawyers and paralegals. As smart machines increasing take on many legal processes, it is highly likely that a small band of skilled lawyers at the pinnacle of the profession will become progressively engaged in more strategic areas, including the task of evaluating legal solutions generated by smart machines. Moreover, legal services workers will become anywhere workers by default.

## Smart Machines, Social Relations of Work, and Images of the Profession

As algorithms swiftly colonize legal services, the relationship between lawyers and paralegals blurs. The differences between human and machine skills and capabilities become less visible, save the understandable desire to keep the human touch in the loop. As in health care services, this human element may make human interaction indispensable in legal services too. Nevertheless, smart machines change the relationships between lawyers and paralegals. Lawyers and paralegals were clearly at different levels in the hierarchy of jobs in previous times. Today, this hierarchy of jobs is muddled with lawyers facing similar issues related to self-efficacy as doctors do when smart machines outperform them. Furthermore, just where do paralegals go when their jobs evaporate, up or down the job hierarchy?

People seeking legal services today are far more cognizant of their own legal predicaments compared to earlier generations. The digital age is replete with Internet sites dispensing legal advice. Excluding the generic search terms "free advice", "lawyer", "legal aid" and "attorney", according to the SEO Digital Group, popular legal service searches on Google in the US included the keywords: immigration lawyer, employment law, divorce/family law and/or lawyer, criminal law, civil law, estate planning, disability lawyer, workers' compensation, DUI lawyer, personal injury lawyer and business law. In Australia, Justanswer.com offers "Get it all for 7 days - only AU$5" and "cancel anytime ... no commitments". Lawpath offers "year-round legal help from a lawyer, for a low monthly fee ... unlimited legal calls and documents to protect your business for only $69 a month". In the US, Capterra gets straight to the point and flag five leading sites that are "actually free" of costs, which is a significant boost for those searching for "free advice". Nevertheless, whether "technological solutionism" is a positive gain in a new age remains problematic.

## Anywhere Working in the Fourth Iteration of the Future of Work

The notion of having 'experts on-call' heralds one of the possible futures of work. Smart machines affect the divisions of labor in ways unimagined by Emile Durkheim. In the new divisions of labor, smart machines outperform their human counterparts in completing job assignments accurately and with reduced costs. Whereas the first industrial revolution created the proletariat, later revolutions in the world of work made it almost vanish. The smart machines, harbingers of the 4th Industrial Age are currently taking a scythe and cutting through the ranks of Karl Marx's surplus class and Serge Mallet's new middle class. Against this background, the story of the world of work in the 4th Industrial Age has any number of plausible endings.

In idyllic and utopian interpretations, the concluding chapter casts anywhere working as a misnomer. Most people will be engaged in anywhere working to such an extent that people will simply "work". Indigenous cultures interpret the concept of work quite differently to Western interpretations. Western viewpoints do not mesh with indigenous worldviews that posit work as just another activity everyone engages in; it is neither unique nor unusual. With the rapid rise of smart machines in the 4th Industrial Age and the preferences among a new generation of workers for FWAs, most people will work anywhere and anytime, either by choice or necessity. However, as smart machines take over many jobs, some pundits believe new jobs will absorb displaced workers.

In a dystopian script, a different ending appears. The world of work has altered from previous times to such an extent that most jobs carry the tag "humans need not apply". Smart machines dominate the workforce, which is not a fanciful plot. Even today, while global corporations increase their profits by billions of dollars annually, their workforce numbers remain relatively stable. At present, workers displaced by technology have taken up new jobs created in the digital age. However, some industrial sectors have shed large numbers of workers, and there is little scope for these redundant workers to move to other "new" or even existing occupations.

In support of addressing the challenge of climate change, an Australian politician recently made the strange claim that the tenacity and nerve displayed by coal miners, whose skills and attitudes allowed them to cope with the daunting task of going down a mine shaft to undertake their work, might allow these workers to reinvent themselves as computer programmers. A hopeful vision, maybe, but in a dystopian future, anywhere workers can morph quickly into nowhere workers. The capacity to conflate the set of transferable skills required by people to make them employable with the set of skills that smooth the transition to new jobs or even out of employment, exists in the literature. However, the context of the rise of smart machines requires a new mindset.

## A DIFFERENT MINDSET

### Emotional Intelligence, Critical Thinking, Creativity, and Problem-solving Skills

In either idyllic or dystopian futures, what is certain is that the type of work done by people and how they do it will change considerably. Whether people work at all is another matter entirely. While these changes will raise critical social, political, and economic issues, on a personal level, the impact of change will undoubtedly affect a person's well-being. Issues related to self-efficacy, anxiety, status, prestige, and economic security come to the fore. Developing skills and coping strategies to deal with the new world of work - anywhere working or nowhere working, is essential. The literature on multiple intelligences (Gardiner, 1983), emotional intelligence [EQ] (Goleman, 2005, 2008), the influence of the affective domain in learning (Eleanor & Oughton, 2007) and the value of life-long learning (Hager, 2001; Hammond, 2007) are significant resources for building resilience in a quickly changing world of work.

In reviewing the literature, Suleman (2017) suggests little consensus exists concerning this "much-discussed subject". Moreover, different skills suit different environments. Her review of the field pinpointed soft skills like interpersonal, communication and teamwork skill as universally important but concluded that other skills in the catalogues reviewed were actually "hard-to-observe" in the workplace. While employability skills, including technical skills and knowledge, are understandable and fundamental for an effortless entry into the workforce, the influences of multiple intelligences, EQ and the affective sides of cognition are opaque. Nevertheless, these latter skills are essential when a person moves jobs or workplaces. A transition into the world of unemployment or non-work requires added sources of resilience.

As smart machines continue their relentless march into workplaces, all workers, including anywhere workers, will likely confront one or all the above scenarios in the coming decades. In this context, life-long learning is a 24/7 vehicle for building resilience to cope with a quickly evolving work environment, especially if your co-worker or replacement is a smart machine.

In 1983, Howard Gardner proposed the notion of seven "multiple intelligences". Among these multiples were interpersonal intelligences, concerned with understanding the intentions, motivations, and desires of another person; these coexisted with intelligences that gave people the ability to understand their own motivations and feelings. These multiples intelligences are vital in explaining the social relations of work. Daniel Goleman's model (1998) focuses on EQ to explain outcomes in areas that require internal mechanisms of control. He flagged five areas worthy of attention: self-awareness (know how your values and goals mold your behaviour), self-regulation, (know how to manage your emotions), social skills (manage the emotions of others), empathy (understand other people's feelings) and motivation (adopt behaviors that align with your goals). As smart machines expand their footprint in the workplace, the ideas of Howard Gardner and Daniel Goleman enrich the emotional tool kit of any person facing an uncertain future in the world of work. In times of crisis, emotions often override intellect.

The affective domain of cognition subtly affects decision-making in the workplace. This is especially the case when the rise of the smart machines threatens a person's on-going employment or reduces their social or economic status. People use their bank of interests, attitudes, and values to navigate their way through various circumstances. However, in a predicament, the workings of the affective domain often trump the rational, intellectual response card.

While the literature on employability skills includes those required for critical thinking, creativity and problem-solving skills (cf. BCA, 2011, 2016, 2017; DEEWR, 2012; Wrathall & Berrell, 2017), more attention should be accorded to the roles of multiple intelligences, EQ and the affective domain of cognition in decision-making. A combination of the above skills would help workers tackle the world of the smart machines with a reasoned argument. These same skills help people navigate unfamiliar circumstances, such as a fall in social status or a move down a rung on the economic ladder caused by the rise of the smart machines in the workplace. Managing the psychological fallout caused by a move down the socio-economic hierarchy is no mean feat for people in the provision of health care and legal services today.

A commitment to life-long learning bolsters a person's ability to manage confronting circumstances. It is a holistic and educative process where initiative-taking people voluntary pursue knowledge for self-improvement or work-related reasons. This personal investment in education is a self-sustaining activity, which increases one's "competitiveness" and "employability" (CEC, 2006; DES, 2000;

Jarvis, 2009). If anywhere workers are to change into nowhere workers, the theories and practices embedded in ideas about multiple intelligences, EQ, and the affective domain of cognition are valuable resources for building resilience in uncertain times. The process of life-long learning is the most significant vehicle for delivering these resources.

## Future Research in Artificial Intelligence, Robotics and Machine Learning

Future research in the above areas needs to pay equal attention to the technical and the human sides of these developments. While so-called "transformative technologies" offer significant economic gains for society, these gains need to be examined in the context of their effects on "behavioral, societal, policy, and governance issues" (Wong & Saiu, 2019). On the economic side, the *Robotics Business Review* highlighted USD1.16 billion in corporate transactions in robotics in January 2020; the review's Robot Report pointed to transactions of USD1.9 billion in December 2019 and USD644 million in January 2019 (Analytics Insight, 2020). During 2018, funding of AI-focused enterprises approached USD5.4 billion. According to Zion Market Research, while the global market in machine learning technology was about UDD1.58 billion in 2017, by 2024, it will grow to USD20.83 billion (Lima, 2020). If we follow the money, increasing amounts of investment by companies in smart machines and related R&D seems assured.

Whether the investment in pure and applied research concerned with the non-economic side of smart machines also keeps pace is less certain. On a brighter note, since the embryonic stage in the development of smart machines, successive contributions to the literature raised the social implications of these technologies for the wider society (Ashman et al., 2014; Boden, 1977, 1984; Melián-González, 2019; Veruggio et al., 2016). However, a cursory review of the citation indexes suggests articles with an economic bent dominate. The implication here is that academic and corporate research and development favor those projects with clear economic rationales and outcomes.

Against this trend, higher education institutions are well placed to ensure that research into behavioral, societal, policy and governance issues concerning smart machines accelerates to balance the scales and bring more attention to non-economic outcomes as a result of the march of the smart machines. The recent Summit of the G7 science academies (2019) concluded that although AI brings a range of positive benefits including economic prosperity, its rapid development and application across business and society also "gives rise to questions about employment, the confidentiality of data, privacy, infringement of ethical values and trust in results". The Summit calls for "careful stewardship" to ensure the fair distribution of the benefits of AI across society. Higher education research into the stewardship concept will contribute the making the age of the smart machine a positive development.

## CONCLUSION

The future of work and the place of anywhere working in this world is uncertain. Jarrahi (2018) casts a positive light on the future while exploring the symbiotic relationship between smart machines and people. He suggests AI bolsters our cognitive resources when we tackle complex problems although he asserts that people "offer a more holistic, intuitive approach in dealing with uncertainty ... in organizational decision making". Jarrahi makes the point that smart machines should augment rather than replace human cognition in decision-making. However, other political, social, and economic discourses underpin future thinking.

A real possibility is a world without work, articulated in both utopian and dystopian tales. However, so too does a world with work presenting as a self-fulfilling, rewarding and intrinsically human activity. In any scenario, people require knowledge, attitudes, value, and skills to make sense of unfamiliar environments. Most thinkers conceive of the world of work in the future as one in which people "work". Even in Marx's vision of an idyllic future, people worked. The capacity of the capitalist mode of production to efficiently reproduce the material conditions of existence opened a new world where use-values dominated. With private property in production eliminated, pursuing self-directed goals and aspirations became a real possibility. People could do "one thing today and another tomorrow, "to hunt in the morning, fish in the afternoon, rear cattle in the evening, criticize after dinner" without being locked into a specific job. Nevertheless, people still "worked" in Marx's vision, although not in its conventional meaning.

Susskind (2020) and Kaplan (2015) both contemplate a world where work *per se* is no longer the primary focus of daily life. What happens when smart machines turn anywhere working into nowhere working, the least palatable of the scenarios sketched above. Recalling the three themes in the vignettes, society should be either being either afraid, ecstatic, or wary of the smart machines' forward march into all workplaces. Examining these views helps clarify the issues at hand concerning the future of work.

In one view, smart machines take control over most aspects of work and as predicted, new jobs arise to soak up superseded employees. Let us assume underground miners become computer programmers, hospital cleaners become shift supervisors, lawyers become high-value analytical thinkers, and health care technicians become medical diagnosticians. Granted, bumps in the road will create a rocky ride, but society will adapt to an environment where all workers are engaged in anywhere working either by design or default. Work is still a focal point of daily life.

Another position imagines a world of work in which the human element is mostly absent, only smart machines work. Ryan Avers (2016; cf. West, 2018) envisions this world on the horizon – "it could be utopia, or it could be hell", he suggests. Therefore, society must plan in the here-and-now to avoid social upheaval or even a complete social collapse in the future.

Avers captures the type of thinking required concisely:

*Preparing for a world without work means grappling with the roles work plays in society and finding potential substitutes. First and foremost, we rely on work to distribute purchasing power: to give us the dough to buy our bread. Eventually, in our distant Star Trek future, we might get rid of money and prices altogether, as soaring productivity allows society to provide people with all they need at near-zero cost.*

However, society would have already crossed the Rubicon when anywhere working becomes a nostalgic memory in a world where no one works.

## REFERENCES

Analytics Insight. (2020). *Top Robotics Investments and Funding in January 2020.* Retrieved from https://www.analyticsinsight.net/top-10-robotics-investment-funding-january-2020/

Ashman, H., Brailsford, T., Cristea, A. I., Sheng, Q. Z., Stewart, C., Toms, E. G., & Wade, V. (2014). The ethical and social implications of personalization technologies for e-learning. *Management & Information*, *51*(6), 819–832. doi:10.1016/j.im.2014.04.003

Ashton, K. (2015). *How to Fly a Horse: The Secret History of Creation, Invention and Discovery*. Windmill Books.

Ask a Lawyer on Call. (2020). *Ask a Lawyer*. Retrieved from https://www.askalawyeroncall.com

Avent, R. (2016, September 19). A world without work is coming – it could be utopia or it could be hell. *The Guardian*. Retrieved from https://www.theguardian.com/commentisfree/2016/sep/19/world-without-work-utopia-hell-human-labour-obsolete

Berrell, M. (2017). The Social Relations of Anywhere Working: Major Themes and Meanings. In Y. Blount & M. Gloet (Eds.), *Anywhere Working and the New Era of Telecommuting*. ICI Global. doi:10.4018/978-1-5225-2328-4.ch002

Bishop, C. (2006). *Pattern Recognition and Machine Learning*. Springer.

BlackStone Discovery. (2020). *BlackStone Discovery Home Page*. Retrieved from https://www.blackstonediscovery.com/about/

Bluestone, B., & Harrison, B. (1982). *The Deindustrialization of America: Plant Closings, Community Abandonment, and the Dismantling of Basic Industry*. Basic Books.

Boden, M.A. (1977). Social implications of intelligent machines. *Radio and Electronic Engineer*, *47*(8.9), 393-399.

Boden, M. A. (1984). Impacts of artificial intelligence. *Futures*, *16*(1), 60–70. doi:10.1016/0016-3287(84)90007-7

Brynjolfsson, E., & McAfee, A. (2011). *Race Against the Machine: How the Digital Revolution Is Accelerating Innovation, Driving Productivity, and Irreversibly Transforming Employment and The Economy*. Research Brief, MIT Center for Digital Business. Retrieved from http://ebusiness.mit.edu/research/Briefs/Brynjolfsson_McAfee_Race_Against_the_Machine.pdf

Business Council of Australia. (2011). *Lifting the Quality of Teaching and Learning in Higher Education*. BCA.

Business Council of Australia. (2016). *Being Work Ready, A guide to what employers want*. BCA.

Business Council of Australia. (2017). *A Sustainable Higher Education System*. BCA.

Capterra. (2020). Retrieved from https://blog.capterra.com/free-legal-advice-5-easy-to-use-sites-that-are-actually-free/

Commission of the European Communities (CEC). (2006). *Adult learning: It is never too late to learn*. Access to European Union Law. Retrieved from https://eur-lex.europa.eu/legal-content/EN/ALL/?uri=CELEX:52006DC0614

Davenport, T., & Pearlson, K. (1998). Two Cheers for the Virtual Office. *Sloan Management Review*, *39*(4), 51–65.

Department of Education, Employment and Workplace Relations (DEEWR). (2012). Employability Skills Framework, Stage 1. Canberra: DEEWR.

Department of Education and Science (DES). (2000). *Learning for Life: Paper on Adult Education*. Dublin: Stationery Office.

Eleanor, P., & Oughton, J. (2007). The Affective Domain: Undiscovered Country. *The College Quarterly*, *10*(4), 1–7.

Everymind. (2020). Retrieved from https://everymind.org.au/need-help/self-care

Gardiner, H. (1983). *Frames of Mind: The Theory of Multiple Intelligences*. Basic Books.

Goleman, D. (2005). *Emotional Intelligence: Why It Can Matter More Than IQ*. Bantam Books.

Goleman, D. (2008). *Working with Emotional Intelligence*. Bantam Books.

Gorz, A. (n.d.). *Farewell to the Working Class: An Essay on Post-industrial Society*. London: Pluto Press.

Haddon, L., & Lewis, S. (1994). The experience of teleworking: An annotated review. *International Journal of Human Resource Management*, *5*(1), 193–223. doi:10.1080/09585199400000010

Hager, P. (2001). Lifelong Learning and the Contribution of Informal Learning. In D. Aspin, J. Chapman, M. Hatton, & Y. Sawano (Eds.), *International Handbook of Lifelong Learning. Springer International Handbooks of Education* (Vol. 6). Springer. doi:10.1007/978-94-010-0916-4_5

Hammond, C. (2004). Impacts of lifelong learning upon emotional resilience, psychological and mental health: Fieldwork evidence. *Oxford Review of Education*, *30*(4), 551–568. doi:10.1080/0305498042000303008

Hansen, L. (2016). *Humans need not apply: How robotic accelerator technology are challenging our ideas of work and innovation* (Masters' thesis). Copenhagen Business School.

Harvard Health Publishing, Harvard Medical School. (2017). *Dr. Google: The top 10 health searches in 2017*. Retrieved from https://www.health.harvard.edu/blog/google-top-10-health-searches-2017-2018022113300

Jarrahi, M. H. (2018). Artificial intelligence and the future of work: Human-AI symbiosis in organizational decision making. *Business Horizons*, *61*(4), 577–586. doi:10.1016/j.bushor.2018.03.007

Jarvis, P. (2009). Lifelong Learning and Globalization: Towards a Structural Comparative Model. In R. Cowen & A. Kazamias (Eds.), *International Handbook of Comparative Education, Springer International Handbooks of Education, 22*. Springer.

Jenkins, C., & Sherman, B. (1979). *The collapse of work*. Eyre Methuen.

Kaplan, J. (2016). *Humans Need Not Apply: A Guide to Wealth and Work in the Age of Artificial Intelligence*. Yale University Press.

LawGeex. (2020). *LawGeex Home Page*. Retrieved from www.lawgeex.com

Lawpath. (2020). *Lawpath Home Page*. Retrieved from https://lawpath.com.au/

Lima, J. (2020, January 27). Why You Should Invest in Machine Learning. *Data Economy*. Retrieved from https://data-economy.com/why-you-should-invest-in-machine-learning/

Marr, B. (2018, May 23). How AI and Machine Learning are Transforming Law Firms and the Legal Sector. *Forbes Magazine*. Retrieved from https://www.forbes.com/sites/bernardmarr/2018/05/23/how-ai-and-machine-learning-are-transforming-law-firms-and-the-legal-sector/#5116da832c38

Marr, B. (2019, July 15). The Future of Work: 5 Important Ways Jobs Will Change in the 4th Industrial Revolution. *Forbes Magazine*. Retrieved from https://www.forbes.com/sites/bernardmarr/2019/07/15/the-future-of-work-5-important-ways-jobs-will-change-in-the-4th-industrial-revolution/#7570158a54c7

McKinney, S., Sieniek, M., & Godbole, V. (2020). International evaluation of an AI system for breast cancer screening. *Nature, 557*. Retrieved from https://www.nature.com/articles/s41586-019-1799-6

Melián-González, S. (2019). The impact of digital technology on work. University Institute of Tourism and Sustainable Economic Development (TIDES), Las Palmas de Gran Canaria (Canary Islands): University of Las Palmas de Gran Canaria. doi:10.2139srn.3353258

Messenger, J., Llave, O., Gschwind, L., Boehmer, S., Vermeylen, G., & Wilkens, M. (2017). *Working anytime, anywhere: The effects on the world of work*. Publications Office of the European Union, Luxembourg, and the International Labour Office.

Morozov, E. (2013). *To Save Everything, Click Here: The Folly of Technological Solutionism*. Public Affairs.

Mubin, O., Stevens, C., Shahid, S., Al Mahmud, A., & Dong, J.-J. (2013). A Review of the Applicability of Robots in Education. *Technology for Education and Learning*, *1*(1), 1–7. doi:10.2316/Journal.209.2013.1.209-0015

MyDoctor.com. (2020). *My Doctor*. Retrieved from https://www.mydr.com.au/

Palmer, A. (2019 January 2). The AI that learnt to hide data from its creators to CHEAT at tasks they gave it. *The Daily Mirror*. Australia. Retrieved from https://www.dailymail.co.uk/sciencetech/article-6545281/The-AI-learnt-hide-data-creators-CHEAT-tasks-gave-it.html

Schneier, B. (2015). VW scandal could just be the beginning. *CNN Opinion*. Retrieved from https://edition.cnn.com/2015/09/28/opinions/schneier-vw-cheating-software/index.html

SEO Digital Group. (2020). Retrieved from https://seodigitalgroup.com/best-legal-keywords/

Servos, M. (2019). *The Future of Work? Work of the Future! On how artiðcial intelligence, robotics and automation are transforming jobs and the economy in Europe*. European Commission. Retrieved from https://ec.europa.eu/epsc/sites/epsc/files/ai-report_online-version.pdf

Sharkey, A. (2016). Should we welcome robot teachers? *Ethics and Information Technology*, *18*(4), 283–297. doi:10.100710676-016-9387-z

Sheedy. C. (2019). Teaching Machines. In *In the Black*. Southbank: CPA Australia.

Simonite, T. (2018). When Bots teach themselves to cheat. *Wired* Business. Retrieved from https://www.wired.com/story/when-bots-teach-themselves-to-cheat/

Smith, A., & Anderson, J. (2014). *AI, Robotics, and the Future of Jobs*. Pew Research Center. Retrieved from https://www.pewresearch.org/internet/2014/08/06/future-of-jobs/

Srinivasa Rao, A., & Vazquez, J. (2020). Identification of COVID-19 can be quicker through artificial intelligence framework using a mobile phone-based survey when cities and towns are under quarantine. *Infection Control and Hospital Epidemiology*, *41*(7), 826–830. doi:10.1017/ice.2020.61 PMID:32122430

Steiner, C. (2012). *Automate This: How Algorithms came to Rule our World*. Portfolio Penguin.

Suleman, F. (2016). Employability skills of higher education graduates: Little consensus on a much-discussed subject. *Procedia - Social and Behavioral Sciences. 228*, 169-174.

Summit of the G7 science academies. (2019). *Artificial intelligence and society: Executive summary and recommendations*. Summit of the G7 science academies. Retrieved from https://www.leopoldina.org/uploads/tx_leopublication/AI_G7_2019_EN.pdf

Susskind, D. (2020). *A World Without Work: Technology, Automation and How We Should Respond*. Allen Lane.

Taskin, L., & Edwards, P. (2007). The possibilities and limits of telework in a bureaucratic environment: Lessons from the public sector. *New Technology, Work and Employment, 22*(3), 195–207. doi:10.1111/j.1468-005X.2007.00194.x

The Law Buddy. (2020). *The Law Buddy Home Page*. Retrieved from https://www.lawbuddy.com.au/

Third Age Matters. (2020). *Third Age Matters*. Retrieved from https://thirdagematters.com.au/need-more-information/resources/

Tomlinson, Z. (2018). 15 Medical Robots That Are Changing the World. *Interesting Engineering*. Retrieved from https://interestingengineering.com/15-medical-robots-that-are-changing-the-world

Veruggio, G., Operto, F., & Bekey, G. (2016). Roboethics: Social and Ethical Implications. In B. Siciliano & O. Khatib (Eds.), *Springer Handbook of Robotics*. Springer Handbooks. doi:10.1007/978-3-319-32552-1_80

Weinstein, R., Lopez, A., Joseph, B., Erps, K., Holcomb, M., Barker, G., & Krupinski, E. (2014). Telemedicine, Telehealth, and Mobile Health Applications That Work: Opportunities and Barriers. *The American Journal of Medicine, 127*(3), 183–187. doi:10.1016/j.amjmed.2013.09.032 PMID:24384059

West, D. (2018). *The Future of Work: Robots, AI and Automation*. Brookings Institute Press.

Wevorce. (2020). *Wevorce Home Page*. Retrieved from https://www.wevorce.com/

Wilkens, N. (2019). *Artificial Intelligence: A Comprehensive Guide to AI, Machine Learning, Internet of Things, Robotics, Deep Learning, Predictive Analytics, Neural Networks, Reinforcement Learning, and Our Future*. Amazon.com LLC. Retrieved from https://www.amazon.com/Artificial-Intelligence-Comprehensive-Predictive-Reinforcement-ebook/dp/B07QFL4HG3/ref=sr_1_12?keywords=artificial+intelligence%2C+machine+learning+and+robotics&qid=1575655795&sr=8-12

Wong, W., & Saiu, K. (2019). Artificial Intelligence, Machine Learning, Automation, Robotics, Future of Work and Future of Humanity: A Review and Research Agenda. *Journal of Database Management, 30*(1), 61–79. doi:10.4018/JDM.2019010104

Wrathall, J., & Berrell, M. (2017). Infusing Employability Skills in Teaching, Learning and Curriculum Development: An Event Management Perspective. In *THE-ICE IPoE Forum 2017*. William Angliss Institute.

Zuboff, S. (1988). *In the Age of the Smart Machine: The Future of Work and Power*. Basic Books.

## KEY TERMS AND DEFINITIONS

**4th Industrial Revolution:** This idea suggests that today's stage of technological innovation is characterized by the continual and increasing integration and synthesis of technologies and technological ideas in ways that alter current understandings about the relationships between the physical world, digital technologies and human biology.

**Affective Domain of Cognition:** In Bloom's *Taxonomy of Learning Domains*, the affective domain is concerned with an individual's development in attitudes, emotion, and feelings.

**Artificial Intelligence (AI):** This is a surrogate term for the theories of and developments in computer systems capable of performing tasks that require human intelligence.

**Images of the Profession:** This refers to one's professional self-concept - their professional image is based on attributes, beliefs, values, motives, and experiences gained through professional practice.

**Machine Learning:** Is a branch of AI, which encompasses the study of algorithms and statistical models used by computers to execute specific tasks without using explicit commands.

**Multiple Intelligences:** This describes the variety of ways people learn and acquire information. Proponents of the idea believe that single measures of intelligence, such as the Intelligent Quotient (IQ), are too narrow to account for the variety of ways people learn.

**Robotics:** Refers to the field of computer science and engineering concerned with creating machines that react to sensory inputs – also a branch of AI.

**Smart Machines:** Smart machines are devices that can teach themselves how to do things – today, permutations of AI, robotics, and machine learning with their implanted algorithms, coalesce as an age of smart machines.

**Social Relations of Work:** In social science, social relations refer to any relationship between two or more individuals. Social relations derived from individual agency form the basis of a social structure.

## Section 2

# Telehealth, Disability, and Inclusiveness

# Chapter 4
# A Clinician's Perspective on Anywhere Working and Telehealth

**Yvette Blount**
https://orcid.org/0000-0003-0129-7400
*Macquarie University, Australia*

**Marianne Gloet**
*The University of Melbourne, Australia*

## ABSTRACT

*Clinicians (general practitioners, specialists, allied health professionals) are experts in medicine, not technology. The delivery of healthcare using technology includes changes to the way the clinician works; in effect, they work from anywhere. This study examined telehealth adoption from the perspective of clinicians. Data was collected from 44 in-depth interviews undertaken with a variety of Australian clinicians. The findings show that telehealth is a complex endeavor involving multiple stakeholders. While the potential of telehealth service provision is significant, the realities of delivering telehealth services involve many challenges. These include technology-related issues, lack of funding and financial incentives for telehealth, the changing skills and capabilities required by clinicians who engage in telehealth consultations, as well as changes to business processes resulting from the introduction of telehealth in a complex environment. A conceptual model for the adoption of sustainable telehealth is proposed for a better understanding of these complexities.*

DOI: 10.4018/978-1-7998-4159-3.ch004

## INTRODUCTION

The success of anywhere working in telehealth relies on clinicians (practitioners) to successfully utilize their skills in a clinical setting facilitated by technology. The ability to successfully deliver telehealth relies on sufficient technology such as reliable internet as well as competencies and skills to use the technology. Increasingly, information and communication technology (ICT) is used to deliver health services in a variety of health contexts. The success of telehealth adoption relies on clinicians using technology effectively and efficiently to provide health services. However, the curriculum for health practitioners, including physicians and allied health practitioners to date has not included eHealth as a focus in Australian universities (Edirippulige et al., 2018).

Although stakeholders, including universities and accrediting bodies, acknowledge the importance of developing skills in telehealth, the barriers to embedding telehealth into the Australian curriculum is problematic due to competing priorities. Therefore, this lack of focus may contribute to practitioners not having the competencies and skills to utilize technology to deliver telehealth services (Edirippulige et al., 2018).

Access to affordable, reliable technology is a key enabling factor for telehealth. Information and communication technologies (ICT) supporting telehealth service delivery include video conferencing, web-based applications, mobile computing, body sensors and other monitoring applications, in an environment where advances in technology continue to disrupt the way modern healthcare is delivered. Computers are increasingly used for diagnostic tasks that do not necessarily require a visit to a clinician. For example, the Apple ResearchKit platform uses iPhone apps to gather data from patients for medical research into conditions such as autism, epilepsy, and melanoma. The ResearchKit platform remotely transfers medical data such as blood pressure, heart rate and body weight (Kang, 2016).

Smartphone apps provide health data that can inform health practitioners and provide novel opportunities, and new risks, for health care provision (Siddiqui, Miller, McKinley, Maduekwe, & Schwaitzberg, 2014). In *The Patient Will See You Now*, Topol (2015) argues that the smartphone is the Gutenberg moment (Gutenberg's printing press enabled the production of books for the masses for the first time in the 1450s) for medicine because medicine is becoming digitized.

New technologies, including big data, automation, and artificial intelligence, are likely to change the health sector, including demand for new skills and capabilities (OECD, 2019). Health apps are capable of both replacing and augmenting tasks undertaken by physicians (general practitioners) such as recording medical history and some diagnoses but cannot perform medical procedures or coordinate a team-based approach (Wattanapisit et al., 2020). In this context, the regulatory framework and protocols on how individuals' health data can be used and protected are still being developed (Miller, Glisson, Campbell, & Sittig, 2019). Overall, the complexity of telehealth has been underestimated (van Dyke, 2014).

If telehealth is to be sustainable, it must be both effective (clinically appropriate) and efficient concerning service delivery. Thus, in addition to the advancement of new technologies and unresolved issues, it has been challenging to establish the effectiveness and overall cost efficiency of telehealth service delivery because the financial benefits are inconsistent and may be specific to situations, locations or stakeholder groups.

Globally governments are grappling with rising health care costs. The OECD (2019) Health at a Glance report shows that on average OECD countries spend around $US4,000 per person with the USA spending much more than other countries by a significant amount at $US10,000 per person. Australia's health spending was $US5,006, slightly higher than average. Health expenditure has exceeded economic growth and is predicted to be10.2% of GDP by 2030 across OECD countries, up from 8.8% in 2018. The report shows that in OECD countries, health and social systems employ more workers now than at any other time in history, with about one in every ten jobs found in health or social care.

The challenges of increasing health costs, new technologies and the changing skills and capabilities of clinicians suggest a need for rigorous research that carefully considers both the context and the myriad of stakeholders, processes, systems (including technology) and costs, to understand better the practicality of telehealth services from the perspectives of the clinicians who deliver health care. This understanding provides insights into how a key stakeholder, the clinician, can adopt telehealth working from anywhere in a clinically effective and financially sustainable way.

Health care delivery facilitated by technology is a complex endeavor involving multiple stakeholders and many challenges. Careful consideration of both the choice of technology and technology support that facilitates telehealth for both the patient and the clinician is the first criterion for successful telehealth adoption. The second criterion involves funding incentives for clinicians and appropriate funding for telehealth consultations. Analysis of changes in roles, responsibilities and skills of clinicians adopting telehealth consultations is the third criterion. The fourth criterion is the recognition of the necessary changes in business processes and workflow that result from telehealth adoption.

Other enablers of telehealth include user skills and training, the development of appropriate medical and ethical protocols, and health care providers' acceptance and collaboration. The development of appropriate business models and supportive legislative and policy frameworks also enable the successful uptake of telehealth (V. A. Wade, Eliott, & Hiller, 2014). Conversely, barriers to sustainable telehealth delivery include the lack of technical support; quality, ethical and legal concerns;

absence of protocols for telehealth delivery; the lack of appropriate business models to support telehealth delivery; and regularity barriers in licensing and standards (V. A. Wade et al., 2014). Moreover, clinicians need to have the clinical expertise to ascertain if a patient is suitable for telehealth (Sabesan & Kelly, 2015).

This chapter examines the issues relating to the provision of telehealth services from the perspectives of the workers (clinicians) engaged in delivering these services from anywhere. The next section provides the background and context of telehealth, followed by a discussion of telehealth benefits and limitations. Methodological considerations relating to the study are discussed and explained. The findings are presented using a framework that identifies the overarching themes arising from the analysis of the interview data. Finally, we provide a conceptual model that can be used to guide sustainable telehealth adoption from the perspective of clinicians working anywhere.

## BACKGROUND

Telehealth is a component of eHealth and relies on information and communications technology (ICT) to deliver health services. However, more recently, other terms such as digital health have emerged (see, for example, Edirippulige et al., 2018). Telehealth has been defined as 'enabling health care services and related processes delivered over distance, using information and communication technologies' (Carati & Margelis, 2013, p. 3). Telehealth encompasses the curative, preventative and promotive aspects of health care delivered over a distance (van Dyke, 2014). It is a subset of e-Health that incorporates more broadly the use of information and communications technology to support health and health-related fields (Al-Shorbaji & Geissbuhler, 2012). Telemedicine is a subset of telehealth and is specifically focused on the curative aspect of health delivery using information and communication technology (van Dyke, 2014). For this chapter, we have used telehealth in the context of preventative, promotive and curative healthcare delivered over a distance (van Dyke, 2014).

In the Australian context, telehealth services effectively began with the Flying Doctor Service in the 1920s. Australia, although the sixth-largest country by size in the world (Australian Government Geoscience Australia, 2016), has a comparatively small population; as of 13 January 2020, the population was 25,568,323 (Australian Bureau of Statistics, 2020). Between 2006–07 and 2015–16, growth in total health expenditure was higher than the growth in the population and health expenditure grew from 8.7% of GDP in 2006–07 to 10.3% of GDP in 2015–16 (Australian Institute of Health and Welfare, 2019). These characteristics make Australia an ideal candidate for telehealth.

Australia's health system is complex and consists of both public and private health providers. Australia has a universal public health insurance scheme, Medicare, funded by the Australian Government. Medicare was introduced in 1984 to provide free or subsidized treatment by clinicians such as general practitioners, specialists, and optometrists. Also, people can take out private, non-compulsory health insurance that offers a range of cover options to suit individual circumstances. Private health insurance covers some or all the costs of a range of health services not covered by Medicare, including ambulance, dental services, prescription glasses and physiotherapy (Australian Institute of Health and Welfare, 2015).

This chapter investigates the major issues and challenges for workers engaged in telehealth service delivery. The overarching research question addressed in this study was: What are the major issues and challenges associated with telehealth service delivery from workers (clinicians) engaged in telehealth delivery?

## ANYWHERE WORKING AND TELEHEALTH

### Telehealth: Cost-Effectiveness and Quality of Service Delivery

Telehealth offers numerous potential benefits. These include earlier interventions and better patient care, reduced costs in health care service provision, access for the aged or chronically ill to health care services into the home, reduced travel time for both patients and health care professionals, and improved patient satisfaction (Standing, Gururajan, Standing, & Cripps, 2014). Around 29 per cent of the Australian population (7 million people) live in rural and remote areas. Geographic spread, low population density, limited infrastructure, as well as the higher costs of delivering rural and remote health care, can affect access to health care (Australian Institute of Health and Welfare, 2018). Inadequate access has been identified as a key factor in the poorer health status of people living in rural and remote Australia, compared to those living in urban areas (Jang-Jaccard, Nepal, Alem, & Li, 2014).

Compared with people in major cities, people in outer regional/remote areas had higher rates of daily smoking, risky alcohol consumption, physical inactivity and overweight and obesity in 2014–15 (Australian Institute of Health and Welfare, 2018). In 2017-18, the Australian Bureau of Statistics' National Health Survey showed that two thirds (67.0%) of Australian adults were overweight or obese (12.5 million people), an increase from 63.4% in 2014-15. The National Health Survey also indicated that almost one quarter (24.9%) of children aged 5-17 years were overweight or obese in 2017-18 (Department of Health, 2019). In 2014-15, 61.1% of adults living in major cities were overweight or obese compared with 69.2% in inner regional Australia and 69.2% also in outer regional and remote Australia.

One of the main risk factors for developing Type 2 diabetes is being overweight or obese because excess body weight can interfere with the body's production of, and resistance to, insulin. In 2014-15, people living in areas of most disadvantage in Australia had a higher rate of diabetes than people living in areas of least disadvantage (8.2% compared with 3.1%). Similarly, people living in outer regional/remote areas of Australia had a higher rate than people living in Major Cities (6.7% compared with 4.7%) (Australian Bureau of Statistics, 2016a).

These statistics are troubling, not just from access to health services for patients but for the economy. For example, obesity in Australia was estimated to have cost A$8.6 billion in 2011-2012. The direct costs included physician (GP) services, specialist services, allied health services, pharmaceuticals, weight-loss interventions and public interventions. The indirect costs included absenteeism, presenteeism, government subsidies and foregone tax (PwC, 2015).

Recent Australian research reveals that rural patients wait, on average, twice as long to see a general practitioner compared to their city counterparts (>6 days compared to 3 days), and in some regions wait four times as long (>13 days) (Sheppeard, 2014). Cornish (2014) reports that people living in rural areas 'are more likely to have cancer, diabetes, and heart disease', 'die two and a half years earlier', 'get 12.6 million fewer Medicare services, 11 million fewer prescription medicines and $800 million a year less dental and allied health care' and 'as a result, they are 30% more likely to end up in hospital as a result of an avoidable cause than people living in cities'. Jang-Jaccard et al. (2014) note that there are 50 hospitalizations for chronic disease per 100,000 population in remote areas compared to 20 in urban areas.

Telehealth has the potential to address many of these issues by providing patient access to health services more equitably. Telehealth has demonstrated that health care services can be delivered more efficiently, provide relief from prolonged absences from work and family responsibilities and deliver significant reductions inpatient costs for items such as travel and accommodation (Standing et al., 2014; V. A. Wade, Eliott, & Hiller, 2014). However, despite the many benefits of telehealth, the uptake in Australia has been patchy and slow. Telehealth projects have usually begun as pilots, trials or feasibility tests that, successful or otherwise, do not translate into ongoing services (Armfield, Edirippulige, Bradford, & Smith, 2014; V. A. Wade et al., 2014).

In 2011, the Federal Government introduced a telehealth system to support video-based consultations between general practitioners, nurse practitioners, Aboriginal health workers, and specialists. Despite helping 40,000 patients and delivering 71,000 services in 2012-13, the telehealth system attracted just 12% of specialists and spent only 20% of its government allocated budget (Armfield et al., 2014; Cornish, 2014). Subsequent changes in geographic boundaries for eligibility in 2013 preceded the termination of the Telehealth Financial Incentives Program in 2014. Indeed, recent research suggests that the instability of telehealth funding models is an issue of particular concern to clinicians (Blount & Gloet, 2015).

Systematic reviews of the cost-effectiveness of telemedicine (clinical health care) have produced inconclusive or contradictory evidence (Armfield et al., 2014; Mistry, 2012; Mistry, Garnvwa, & Oppong, 2014). For example, while a systematic review of nine case studies of video-conferencing into the home found there was no cost-effectiveness for telehealth (Peeters, Mistiaen, & Franke, 2011), a review of 22 studies found home health care resulted in cost savings for both the health care system and insurance providers in 20 (91%) of the 22 cases (Polisena, Coyle, Coyle, & McGill, 2009) and a further study identified substantial savings for patients – especially regarding travel costs for rural patients (V. Wade, Karnon, Elshaug, & Hiller, 2010).

The variation in findings has led researchers to raise serious concerns about the quality of prior telehealth research. Some are highly critical of the methodology underpinning sample selection and data collection (Bashshur & Reardon, 2014; Polisena et al., 2009) while others conclude that the quality of economic analysis itself has been poor (Bergmo, 2009). Other studies have failed to consider the interrelationships and interdependencies between stakeholders who are essential given that effective telehealth delivery requires alignment of processes between patients (and their families and community), health care professionals (general practitioners, specialists, allied health professionals), technology providers and funding bodies (specifically government and health insurers). Researchers have noted that telehealth can only be considered successful if it is integrated sustainably into clinical care (Armfield et al., 2014; V. Wade et al., 2010). As such, clinician acceptance of telehealth will continue to have the most significant impact on the success of telehealth adoption (V. A. Wade et al., 2014). Therefore, the perceptions of clinicians working anywhere is a core consideration for sustainable telehealth service delivery.

## METHODOLOGY

This qualitative research was conducted in Australia. The research involved 44 in-depth interviews with a variety of doctors, nurses, and allied health professionals. The interviews included 21 nurses, nine general practitioners, ten specialists, two speech therapists, a physiotherapist and a cancer support professional over six months.

A purposive sampling technique (Recker, 2013) was used to identify clinicians successfully engaged in telehealth delivery. Purposive sampling (also referred to as judgmental, selective or subjective sampling) is where a deliberate choice is made by the researcher to collect data from a specific population to answer the research questions.

The objective was to obtain the perceptions of telehealth provision from the perspectives of general practitioners, specialists and allied health practitioners involved in various forms of telehealth delivery. It was essential to obtain a comprehensive, multi-faceted view from the stakeholders involved directly in telehealth provision because the literature shows that telehealth provision is complex and challenging.

The Telehealth Provider Directory on the Australian College of Rural and Remote Medicine (ACCRM) website contains details relating to telehealth providers. Clinicians listed in the directory were contacted by phone or email and asked if they would participate in an interview. All interviews were conducted via telephone for between 45 and 60 minutes (except one that was carried out on-site), taped and transcribed. All general practitioners and allied health clinicians were either located in regional and remote areas or provided physician (GP) services to these areas. Specialists were in major cities or major regional centers.

The purpose of this study was not to offer generalizations based on statistical analysis, but rather to generate a bank of rich data to identify major themes and subthemes (Merriam, 1994). Based on a review of the literature, the interview protocol was developed using overarching themes and guiding questions. The guiding questions were clustered around the following seven areas:

1. How telehealth originated in their practice
2. The positive and negative implications of telehealth
3. The technology used to support telehealth delivery
4. Telehealth and productivity implications
5. Telehealth and wellbeing
6. Telehealth and service delivery
7. The future of telehealth

The interviews yielded multiple perspectives concerning the issues involved in telehealth delivery. A method of textual analysis, frequently utilized in social science research, used a coding system where data was placed into some predetermined categories by the researchers and grouped across a range of patterns or themes that emerged from the interviews (Yin, 2014). An interpretive method was used to identify themes in the data (Miles, Huberman, & Saldana, 2014; Recker, 2013).

## FINDINGS

Analysis of the interview data yielded some overarching themes. These themes represented the following areas concerning telehealth: 1) technology and support infrastructure for telehealth; 2) funding and financial incentives relating to telehealth delivery; 3) changes in roles, responsibilities and skills resulting from the uptake of telehealth; and 4) changes to business processes as a result of telehealth service delivery. While these themes are overlapping at times, they emerged as distinct areas of focus. This section examines each of these themes in detail, including direct quotes from interview participants.

## ICT Infrastructure

Information and communication technology (ICT) infrastructure is a critical component for the successful delivery of telehealth. In this study, the technology used by clinicians to support telehealth was relatively unsophisticated (Skype was the leading technology used); however, participants stressed that the technology must be reliable, accessible and easy to use.

Importantly, technology support needs to be available. Participants reported that insufficient bandwidth, inconsistent broadband service, the internet and/or satellite outages constrained the ability to conduct a telehealth consultation. Bandwidth can also be a problem limiting the number of consultations able to be done concurrently in the one practice, particularly since images require high bandwidth. In remote areas, technology outages were the most frustrating problem affecting the successful delivery of telehealth. The most crucial component in remote areas was the ability to communicate, particularly if managing an emergency such as an evacuation.

On the one hand, telehealth can reduce the costs of health care delivery; for example, the processing of film is not required by specialists such as radiologists. Clinicians can access the images wherever they are. On the other hand, bandwidth can be expensive, particularly if access to fast broadband is limited. Also, video quality is not as good as a high-quality photo generated by a smartphone. Sending photos and images requires sufficient upload speeds and bandwidth for effective communication and coordination of patient issues.

*...putting up with crappy broadband...not having decent internet access...[not] having the technological support within practices...GP2*

In the days of the Flying Doctor Service, formed in 1928 (Royal Flying Doctor Service, 2016), the technology available at the time was sufficient for the delivery of remote healthcare. Today District Medical Officers (DMOs) in the Northern

Territory primarily use mobile phones for consultations and communication via satellite. The reliability of technology is an important criterion, particularly when interacting in regional, rural and remote areas.

*The DMOs in the Northern Territory are still providing services to those remote clinics by telephone, so it's entirely possible to deliver services via a variety of modality. GP3*

*...now I'm entering something on the shared information system...but when the internet goes down, or the satellite isn't working or whatever, you dig out the bits of paper and start writing again. GP9*

There were no sources of information that clinicians could tap into that provided advice or support for adopting technologies for telehealth. One allied health practitioner noted that Services for Australian Rural and Remote Allied Health (SARRAH) had one document on the website on Allied Health and Telehealth. However, this was a position paper dated 19/10/2012. Clinicians believed that support in the form of technical advice and support from professional bodies as well as government such as the colleges, surgeons, physicians and others should be forthcoming.

Respondents reported that the primary tool for telehealth consultations conducted between patients and specialists facilitated by general practitioners was Skype because Skype is universally available, free, and easy to use for clinicians and patients. A supporting technology was smartphone applications, particularly for images such as x-rays, electrocardiograms (ECGs) and photos as well as for communication in remote areas such as the Northern Territory.

*...you know the amount of people that say you need flashier computers and whatnot, but I think that's all rubbish you know. You can do telehealth from my phone to your phone right now...GP6*

*You can wake up the cardiologist or the orthopaedist at three o'clock in the morning and say 'are you on your phone, what's your number? Here is the ECG...the x-ray... GP9*

Setting up telehealth involves more than just technology. The setup of the technology itself, the booking, preparation and coordination of the consultation all need to be aligned. Participants consistently reported that technology must be seamless to support efficient and effective telehealth delivery. Privacy on the use of technology to deliver telehealth was reported as a potential issue. Clinicians had different approaches dealing with privacy and security of patient information. One

GP practice contacted the Privacy Commissioner and asked the question about privacy and the use of Skype for telehealth consultations. The response was that Skype is only a problem if the patient makes a complaint. The practice dealt with this risk by seeking written consent from the patient.

*So we just started using Skype, and we kept it to basics, and we got a consent form from the patient...GP4*

Many interviewees acknowledged that email communication between doctors and patients, GPs and specialists, doctors and hospitals should be secured using encryption. However, most did not encrypt emails or the contents (such as photos on smartphones and x-rays).

*... I'm not always encrypting my emails...the iPhone photos I use all the time ...it's so easy to take a photo of an x-ray...if I get a guy with a broken ankle...a fractured wrist and I'll take a copy and send it to the orthopedic surgeon...SP1*

From a telehealth service delivery perspective, clinicians perceived State health systems as cumbersome, citing that the information from these sources is often unreliable and inaccurate. The adoption of technology in hospitals for telehealth involves committees, tenders and a range of processes and procedures. Hospital systems are not well designed and/or do not have the functionality required for effective telehealth delivery.

*...they [hospitals] have to make it complicated; they have to go through 55 different committees...and then they put it all out to tender...all you need to do is buy five cameras in Officeworks...stick them on five computers, and we've got the clinics, and we are good to go. GP4*

While most participants felt that technology in principle is not a barrier to efficient and effective telehealth delivery, bureaucracy in hospitals and state health systems makes seamless technology that supports telehealth a serious challenge.

## Funding and Financial Incentives

The second major theme to emerge from the study was the funding for telehealth consultations, including incentives for adopting telehealth[1]. In the past, GPs and specialists had used the Australian Government telehealth incentive funds available to buy technology and educate staff. Incentives for adopting telehealth were removed in 2014, and the funding for telehealth consultations in public (Medicare) systems was reviewed and tightened. Clinicians had to reconsider how to structure payments for telehealth consultations and pay for the technology, including support and training.

*...we had a psychiatrist in Brisbane. She'd done 1,000 telehealth consultations...she was probably the most active person in telehealth at the time. [when the eligibility criteria changed] all bar one of her patients became ineligible [for telehealth]...GP3*

There were some significant concerns raised by interviewees regarding the incentives for telehealth consultations, particularly for physicians (GPs). The funding for telehealth was specialist centric and driven mainly by the public system (Medicare schedule). Under the Medicare rules, patients had to be at the physician's (GP's) practice either with a GP or a nurse. GPs were not always involved in the full telehealth consultation for a variety of reasons, most of them related to remuneration. GPs used that time to see other patients in another room.

*The way that telehealth was implemented...specialists can do this, but a GP can't, insulted every GP in the country, and in terms of funding it around it... GP3*

Specialists in this study reported that they could avoid putting patients on long waiting lists if they took the approach of answering physician (GP) questions over the phone or via email. However, answering physician (GP) queries over the phone or by email are not Medicare billable services. Therefore, it makes economic sense to use telehealth, phone, and email to follow-up, with the specialists utilizing their skills to see patients with more complex needs. Funding for telehealth programs has often been temporary, for example, through government grants. When the funding stops, so does the telehealth service. Moreover, if clinicians are going to be worse off financially, then there is little incentive to engage in telehealth. An additional issue is that specialists tend to stay in cities where there are more opportunities for better remuneration.

*...there's no incentive to see people because there's no money arising from it [telehealth] ... there needs to be some sort of fee system that's generated out of this so that people can make some money ...it'll only expand if it is financially viable... SP10*

Also, while there are opportunities for physician (GPs) to use telehealth directly with patients, particularly for follow-up visits, this is not funded by Medicare. It is unlikely that physicians (GPs) and specialists will adopt telehealth if they have not already, now that the incentives and Medicare rebates have been reduced.

*...so if I kept not charging anyone and just accepted the [Medicare] rebate each time I did a Telehealth, it would be 20 or 30 dollars less than if the patient had been forced to come [for a face-to-face consultation]...anyone who comes into a level playing field and I doubt anyone is going to accept bulk billing...if you didn't get on board in the first period of time where you've got substantial incentives to learn the technology or buy your technology or whatever... I'm not sure why you are getting on board now... SP6*

*...the more wealthy people now in society are prepared to do that [pay]...so you've already narrowed telemedicine down to perhaps a more wealthy group who can afford to pay for it...the poor people don't want to pay for it because they're used to everything being free. SP1*

*It's not fair to have people who make the effort to come and see me charged more that the people who [elect to do telehealth] because otherwise, everyone will be electing to do telehealth. It's cheaper [for the patient]. SP6*

A potential way to fund telehealth is to pass on at least some of the costs to patients. However, increasing costs for patients creates dilemmas concerning the equity of access to healthcare. It does not solve the issues discussed above relating to access to health services for rural and remote patients.

## Changes in Roles, Responsibilities, and Skills

Participants in the study reported that the inability to see a patient personally requires a different, or at least, a modified skill set. In primary care for remote patients, physicians (GPs) are usually dealing with acute situations. A consultation via telehealth requires an experienced clinician that has confidence in their ability to diagnose and provide health management plans for patients.

The physician (GP) with responsibility for remote primary care must be an experienced health practitioner, not just in general practice but also in the context of the working environment including technology, government policy, and local knowledge. Not every interaction with a patient requires a physical examination. In some specialist consultations, such as psychiatry, technology-facilitated consultations such as video conferencing are effective and efficient. Radiology is another example where there is instant access to images for clinicians anywhere. If a physical examination is required, the specialist is unlikely to agree to a telehealth consult, particularly if the physical examination is essential for diagnosis.

*...there's a discreet skills set which isn't fully appreciated, about what it takes to extract the appropriate information to the highest possible standard... I've got my little ways of explaining to nurses how to check for different examination signs, how to check for neck stiffness for meningitis... GP8*

*I don't see telehealth as being a good option for somebody who needs a full workup including a physical exam...chronic ulcer patients or peripheral vascular disease patients, then ideally a lot of that is done based on look, touch and even smell...SP4*

However, if telehealth is the only option for the specific patient (e.g. if they cannot travel), there must be an experienced clinician available locally, for example, an experienced nurse or physician (GP) to facilitate the consultation. Clinicians need an understanding of the clinical situation as well as the options for treating the patient, including medical evacuations and the regulatory environment.

*There are a whole lot of nuances of logistics and politics that cannot be learnt over the phone doing the on-call stuff. I spent a year going into the office, rubbing shoulders with other people and doing the job, hearing all the water cooler conversations about tricky problems and so on... GP9*

An important skill is knowing when it is appropriate to participate in a consultation with a patient and specialist. However, the physician (GP) or practice nurse participates at the beginning and the end of a specialist telehealth consultation. The physician (GP) and specialist need to assess the appropriateness of telehealth for specific situations. On the other hand, it can be beneficial for both the specialist and the patient to have the GP involved in the consultation.

*...I haven't had to [deal with a patient who is] dying, breaking terrible news in a telehealth consultation...I don't know how I would feel about trying to do that [break bad news], especially if that was an environment where they didn't have support or options, we wouldn't want to be doing that and turning off and leaving them with a blank screen...there are those kinds of human contacts that I think are a bit of a problem.. SP9*

*...one of the advantages of the telehealth system when you've got a GP in the room is the fact that...in the real world...the GP is sending you a referral letter...but if there are details that they've not put in the referral, then I spend time trying to see if I can ascertain that information from the patient, or chasing down results...SP9*

Many patients have multiple chronic conditions, particularly as the population ages. Comorbidity, where a patient has two or more diseases at the same time, leads to an increased frequency of visits to physicians (GP's) and specialists, leading to increased health care costs. In Australia, the statistics of comorbidity are increasing (Australian Government Australian Institute of Health and Welfare 2016, 2016). Clinicians, including allied health professionals, are part of a multi-disciplinary team to manage comorbidity.

*...diabetes is one example. It is very much a multi-disciplinary care...if you have diabetes, you need to have a nurse, maybe a dietician... SP2*

Many consultations with a physician (GP) are about screening and monitoring conditions such as blood pressure and diabetes, including engaging patients in their care. Specialist follow-up consultations post-operation can mostly be done via telehealth. For example, for orthopedic issues, the physician (GP) can show the specialist the patient movements via video link. There are opportunities for these consultations to be virtual. Many specialist appointments are for follow-ups which in some cases can cause long waiting lists for new patients. Many patients no longer have a regular physician (GP) and use medical centers that bulk bill. The GP knowing the patient and the patient knowing the GP is essential for effective care. Telehealth can only be successful from a physician (GP) perspective if all stakeholders are supportive. A culture where telehealth is business as usual for all stakeholders is essential for efficient telehealth consultations.

*All the reviews take up all the time slots, so you've got to do Skype, and his [specialist] view would be 'there is no point being a specialist if you've got a six month to a year waiting list' GP5*

Much of the work for remote nurses require higher-level skills, for example, in triage, because in the absence of physicians (GPs), nurses are on the frontline. Telehealth is particularly useful for rural and remote Australia, e.g. fly in and fly out and remote clinics. However, one potential consequence is that telehealth may be a reason for governments not trying to get doctors into some of these areas. In many instances, nurses acted as 'boundary spanners,' taking on extra responsibilities, including management of support technology for telehealth.

*But without the telemedicine, there would be more effort to get more people actually living in the communities...the fact that there is a service that allows the absence of doctors from these communities...a sort of mixed blessing. GP9*

*I think it [telehealth] is a bit of a cop-out for actually providing doctors and other health professionals in the bush...we need them to actually go out there...a cheap way for the government to provide services to 30 per cent of the Australian population that don't live in capital cities...I am concerned that it [telehealth] will become a replacement. SP5*

*I would struggle to find a specialty where it is ethical to set up a complete telehealth service...I don't believe everything can always be solved by telehealth...I can't physically examine someone's joints via telehealth. SP6*

Telehealth is regarded by many as a double-edged sword, beneficial in some circumstances. In other cases, telehealth was regarded as limited in effectiveness and not always equivalent to face-to-face medical care.

## Changes to Business Processes as a Result of Telehealth Service Delivery

In many cases, the volume of telehealth consultations from a GP's perspective was low, maybe three a week on average. The small number makes it difficult to integrate telehealth into the practice workflow, particularly if physicians (GPs) must stick with the specialist's schedules. Different specialists have different requirements, including the amount of time allotted for patient consultation. The coordination of the telehealth consultation is usually left to the practice manager, and coordinating work schedules can be complicated. Moreover, when specialists already have a full waiting room and a waiting list of patients, there is little incentive to do telehealth consultations on top of what they already do.

*...nursing staff and reception staff have to do things they don't normally do...anything new we introduce to our practice, there's always substantial angst...substantial catastrophizing...the main ones who whinge about the time consumption is the practice manager...GP7*

The physician (GP) is the broker of telehealth because the physician (GP) is the one who refers the patient to a specific specialist. That is, the physician (GP) has traditionally been central to the patient's care regarding coordinating all the care they need involving specialist services. The physician (GP) is a trusted person from the patient's perspective. Trust and credibility are critical components for clinicians that offer online consultations.

*...when the general practitioner is actually the physical broker of the service, which they are, in the realm of specialist care, then if you don't engage with them then, really, what's the expectation about why they would be involved? GP3*

*...specialists don't need telehealth because they have appointment books which are already overflowing...they just say that I can't do it anymore. In other words, their books are full with local patients, so there is no time....GP4*

*...specialists become less available [for telehealth]. GP7*

Physician (GP) practices did not involve all their physicians (GPs) in telehealth. The decision to engage in telehealth delivery was up to the individual physician (GP) rather than to the practice. However, within most practices, there was a 'champion' who had some ability to influence colleagues. Finding a specialist who practices telehealth is problematic for physicians (GPs) and poses a significant hurdle. Some specialists may agree to telehealth consultations but do not advertise. Alternatively, specialists may offer telehealth consultations but may not be able to find the patients.

*...I feel a little unable to influence the others because they've got their own mindsets about things...I try and be a champion for the service...without shoving it down their throats...doctors are slow to adopt technologies, and they get into habits and ruts...GP7*

*...apart from putting it [telehealth] on my website, I really do not go out promoting it and trying to fill up my practice...I mean I am so flat out...SP10*

Before a telehealth consultation, the physician (GP) must prepare the referral, order the pathology and scans, take photos (e.g. for dermatology) and any other tests that may be required for the consultation to be effective. Different specialties require different amounts of time. For example, psychiatry is usually an hour, and dermatology could be a matter of minutes. The GP must fit in the consultation with the specialist's schedule. Both GPs and specialists take their own notes. When there is joint care in clinics, identifying who handles taking notes and follow-up was unclear.

*I've actually got a protocol that I've sent them [GP], and they actually organize for the patient to be seen by them, they do the physical examinations, and they do all the investigations that I would have ordered if they'd come to see me here in my practice...SP10*

*As far as booking telehealth consults we're at the mercy of the specialists...which can be a little bit of a problem for the nursing roster because sometimes during the day there is only one nurse... GP7*

*I run an ante-natal clinic, and we jump in on a consultation that our obstetricians will be participating in, and we end up going well, who is going to write the chart, whose notes... I'll write all these notes but where do I write them? SP2*

In a telehealth consultation with a specialist, the specialist may be concerned about missing something vital. For the telehealth consultation to be effective, trust between the physician (GP) and the specialist improves the quality of the interaction. The physician (GP) can provide the additional information that the specialist is unable to obtain via video link. Both physicians (GPs) and specialists agreed that productivity and effectiveness of care were enhanced due to the immediacy of feedback and the ability to start on a management plan rather than waiting, sometimes for many weeks, for a specialist letter. The specialist letter is part of the process, regardless of the mode of consultation.

*...you're trying to work out...go through their symptoms and discuss whether they've had episodes...if the GP is ready to pipe up with 'oh yes, remember you had this and this and this...it speeds up the process immeasurably having a medically trained competent person in the room to translate across the telehealth line... SP9*

*...one of the key benefits of the GP being present at the telehealth consultation is that it makes follow-up management much more clearly understood and instantaneous as opposed to...waiting six weeks after the appointment for the specialist letter to come in...SP4*

A significant benefit of telehealth is the education opportunity whereby specialists can pass on their knowledge to physicians (GPs) and experienced allied professionals can build capacity in rural and regional areas. Specialists were keen to pass on their knowledge, particularly where knowledge is scarce in remote communities.

*An example is endocrinology. Where there are an awful lot of rare things that aren't actually that serious...in GP land, you don't really know where on the spectrum your individual patient is. So often the session with the specialist gives you a great deal of comfort to judge how seriously to take the same problem in the future... Good specialists often do include teaching as part of their referral letters...GP2*

*...what I am trying to do is create a bit of an apprenticeship model to support the GPs that do the work and have the confidence that they can make those complex decisions, not necessarily with my help, but into the future. SP2*

The sustainability of telehealth that is, the ability for the physician (GP) to engage with a specialist and have a long-term relationship to build up trust can be difficult at times either because the specialist only engages in telehealth at the start of their career to fill their books, or they become too busy with local patients. However, most participants in the study believed that over time, the specialist telehealth consultations should become more efficient as the physician (GP) and specialist develop a relationship.

*...the [specialists] are usually younger, and they're filling up their appointment books with telehealth consults ...we've had a number of doctors who dropped out of telehealth because they couldn't get their numbers up...telehealth for specialists is a way of filling your appointment books. GP4*

*...once they build up that relationship, maybe the first two or three consults are a bit longer...by the cons end becoming shorter and shorter because the GP learns what the specialist likes, wants, needs before and after...GP6*

*It's a relationship-building exercise which is what I think is what telehealth means... if a GP knows me, and they give me a call, they'll get an answer pretty quickly, and the patient can get on and get that treatment underway. SP2*

The delivery of telehealth is not just a consultation between a patient and a specialist in a GP's practice. Clinicians must consider the business process, the workload, the funding model, as well as the skills and capabilities of the stakeholders involved in the consultation.

## SOLUTIONS AND RECOMMENDATIONS

The research found that telehealth had not been adopted across Australia in a consistent, sustainable way. However, we found some similarities and differences in the way that clinicians set up telehealth consultations. There is no clear model on how to set up efficient and effective telehealth consultation, including protocols and the appropriate use of technology. That is, clinicians must work out which technology to use and how to use and support the technology. Everyone involved in the practice (the practice manager, nurses, clinicians, IT staff) need to support telehealth consultations, from the initial appointment booking through to follow-up. We found that the decision to adopt telehealth was more likely to be made at the level of individual clinicians rather than at practice level.

*Figure 1. Sustainable Telehealth Conceptual Model*

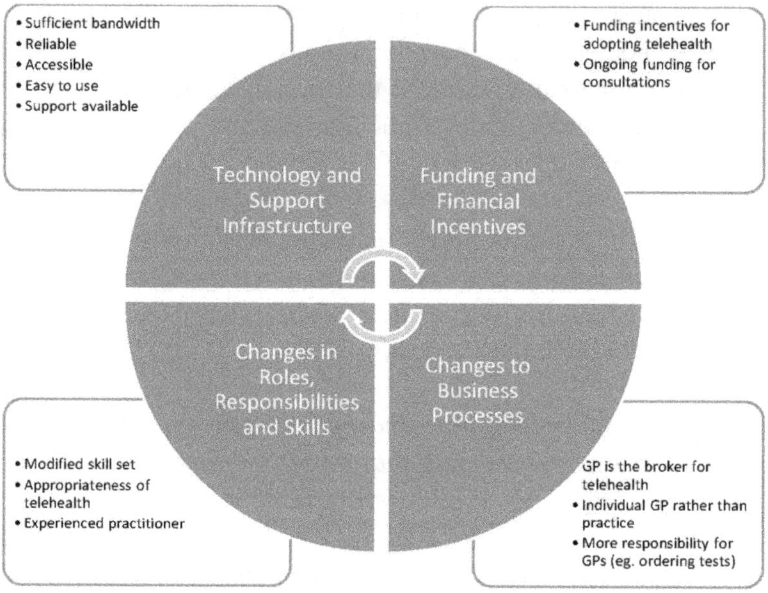


The conceptual model in Figure 1 shows that there are some components from the worker's (clinician's) perspective that are linked. The first is the technology and support infrastructure that clearly must be adequate, particularly regarding reliability, access, and support. Clinicians found that technology in hospitals was unreliable and difficult to use. However, Skype was used by general practitioners, specialists, and allied health professionals because it is universally available, cheap and intuitive. Support is crucial for ensuring that the technology works and is fit for purpose.

The second component concerns financial incentives and the ongoing funding of telehealth consultations. Telehealth has the potential to increase the equity of access to specialist and allied health for those with poorer health outcomes, and those in regional and rural areas. It also has the potential to reduce health care costs in some contexts. However, telehealth can often involve additional costs to those who provide the service. Without adequate financial incentives, it is unlikely that the majority of practitioners will adopt or continue to use telehealth.

The third component is centered upon the clinician's role, responsibilities, and skills for successful adoption of telehealth. Clinicians' skills are generally developed in a face-to-face environment. Telehealth involves a change in the way general practitioners, specialists, and allied health professionals interact with patients and each other. This often requires additional skills and specialist training to maximize the potential benefits of telehealth consultations. For example, nurses often act as boundary spanners to facilitate the use of technology for telehealth consultations.

The last critical component concerns the business processes that support telehealth in practices offering telehealth services. For the telehealth consultation to be effective, in most situations, there needs to be a health care practitioner at the location of the patient. Usually, it is the physician (GP) who is the broker of the telehealth consultation with the specialist. This requires the physician (GP) to take on more responsibility, such as ordering tests and organizing follow-up consultations. The adoption of telehealth delivery often means a disruption to normal business processes, as the requirements for telehealth consultations are often more demanding than those for face-to-face consultations.

The complexity of the health system in the Australian context means that there are some restrictions in each state and territory, for example, diagnosis and the prescription of drugs. This may restrict the effectiveness of telehealth consultations, where the specialist is in another state from the patient. It is also still unclear as to the most appropriate way to fund telehealth. This is a complex area where unintended consequences and behaviors such as rorting (dishonest practices) may potentially occur. On the other hand, to be able to reap the benefits of telehealth, telehealth must be funded appropriately for physician's (GPs), specialists and other clinicians, including allied health professionals.

The technology itself is not a barrier. However, insufficient technology infrastructure and support can be a significant limitation for successful telehealth practice. Some of the deficiencies include inadequate bandwidth and unsatisfactory technology support. Clinicians should not be expected to be technology experts; rather, the technology should be readily available, accessible and straightforward to set up and maintain. Clinicians are more likely to engage in telehealth if the technology is intuitive, cost-efficient and fit for purpose.

There is an opportunity cost for clinicians adopting telehealth. Telehealth takes more resources to set up and integrate into practice workflows. Telehealth also requires an in-depth knowledge of the specialty. Experienced specialists will have higher quality consultations because they have been in practice and dealt with many patients with similar conditions. This level of experience will allow the specialist to interact with the physician (GP) and a patient in a more comprehensive way. The quality of patient care, including equity of access, is critical for improving the health outcomes, particularly for rural and remote patients. Therefore, the worker (clinician) perspective is critical for sustainable telehealth adoption.

## CONCLUSION

This study investigated the major issues and challenges for workers engaged in telehealth service delivery. In examining the provision of telehealth service delivery from the clinicians' perspective, the challenging and complex landscape surrounding telehealth was revealed. Issues with technology, funding and incentives, practitioner skills and capabilities and business process change all combine to create significant challenges for telehealth practitioners. For telehealth is to be sustainable, it must be both effective (clinically appropriate) and efficient (seamless and cost-effective). However, it has been challenging to establish the effectiveness and overall cost efficiency of telehealth service delivery compared to conventional care because the financial benefits are inconsistent and are often specific to particular situations, locations or stakeholder groups.

Since the study was qualitative and limited to 44 participants, we plan to revisit these participants to ascertain what has changed since the original interviews were conducted. It would be useful to extend the research to a larger cohort and add a quantitative component to validate the themes uncovered in this study and generalize from these results. Extending the research focus beyond Australia may yield interesting data for comparison across countries or regions. Future research in the area could also include a comparison to recent research on telework (anywhere work) in the corporate sector as the issues appear to be similar. There is also a need for a better understanding of the efficiencies and effectiveness of telehealth in specific contexts, such as in aged care. The next stage of this research is to investigate the issues more thoroughly by testing the conceptual model and investigating the reasons for the limited adoption of telehealth from the perspectives of clinicians and allied health professionals.

## REFERENCES

Armfield, N. R., Edirippulige, S. K., Bradford, N., & Smith, A. C. (2014). Telemedicine — is the cart being put before the horse? *The Medical Journal of Australia*, *200*(9), 530–533. doi:10.5694/mja13.11101 PMID:24835716

Australian Bureau of Statistics. (2016). *4364.0.55.001 - National Health Survey: First Results, 2014-15*. Retrieved from http://www.abs.gov.au/ausstats/abs@.nsf/Lookup/by%20Subject/4364.0.55.001~2014-15~Main%20Features~Diabetes%20mellitus~12

Australian Bureau of Statistics. (2020). *Population clock*. Retrieved from http://www.abs.gov.au/ausstats/abs%40.nsf/94713ad445ff1425ca25682000192af2/1647509ef7e25faaca2568a900154b63?OpenDocument

Australian Government Australian Institute of Health and Welfare. (2016). *Chronic disease comorbidity*. Retrieved from http://www.aihw.gov.au/chronic-diseases/comorbidity/

Australian Institute of Health and Welfare. (2018). *Australia's health 2018*. Retrieved from Canberra https://www.aihw.gov.au/reports/australias-health/australias-health-2018/contents/table-of-contents

Australian Institute of Health and Welfare. (2019). *Health expenditure Australia 2017–18*. Retrieved from https://www.aihw.gov.au/reports/health-welfare-expenditure/health-expenditure-australia-2017-18/contents/data-visualisation

Bashshur, R. L., & Reardon, T. G. (2014). Commentary on "Critical Appraisal of Published Systematic Reviews Assessing the Cost-Effectiveness of Telemedicine Studies". *Telemedicine Journal and e-Health*, *20*(9), 883–884. doi:10.1089/tmj.2014.9980 PMID:25184946

Bergmo, T. (2009). Can economic evaluation in telemedicine be trusted? A systematic review of the literature. *Cost Effectiveness and Resource Allocation*, *7*(1), 18. doi:10.1186/1478-7547-7-18 PMID:19852828

Blount, Y., & Gloet, M. (2015). *Adoption of ICT Enabled Telehealth Services in the Australian Context: Implications of Technology Use for Telehealth Workers*. Paper presented at the Hawaii International Conference on System Sciences HICSS-48, Kauai, HI.

Cornish, S. D. (2014). *Living in Australia's rural areas will cut your life short*. Retrieved from http://www.news.com.au/lifestyle/health/living-in-australias-rural-areas-will-cut-your-life-short/story-fneuzlbd-1226947018877

Department of Health. (2019). *Overweight and Obesity*. Retrieved from https://www1.health.gov.au/internet/main/publishing.nsf/Content/Overweight-and-Obesity

Edirippulige, S., Brooks, P., Carati, C., Wade, V. A., Smith, A. C., Wickramasinghe, S., & Armfield, N. R. (2018). It's important, but not important enough: eHealth as a curriculum priority in medical education in Australia. *Journal of Telemedicine and Telecare*, *24*(10), 697–702. doi:10.1177/1357633X18793282 PMID:30343657

Jang-Jaccard, J., Nepal, S., Alem, L., & Li, J. (2014). Barriers for Delivering Telehealth in Rural Australia: A Review Based on Australian Trials and Studies. *Telemedicine Journal and e-Health, 20*(5), 496–504. doi:10.1089/tmj.2013.0189 PMID:24801522

Miles, M. B., Huberman, A. M., & Saldana, J. (2014). Qualitative Data Analysis: A Methods Sourcebook (3rd ed.). Thousand Oaks, CA: SAGE Publications, Inc.

Miller, S., Glisson, W. B., Campbell, M., & Sittig, S. (2019). *Risk Analysis of Residual Protected Health Information of Android Telehealth Apps*. Academic Press.

Mistry, H. (2012). Systematic review of studies of the cost-effectiveness of telemedicine and telecare. Changes in the economic evidence over twenty years. *Journal of Telemedicine and Telecare, 18*(1), 1–6. doi:10.1258/jtt.2011.110505 PMID:22101609

Mistry, H., Garnvwa, H., & Oppong, R. (2014). Critical Appraisal of Published Systematic Reviews Assessing the Cost-Effectiveness of Telemedicine Studies. *Telemedicine Journal and e-Health, 20*(7), 609–618. doi:10.1089/tmj.2013.0259 PMID:24820406

OECD. (2019). *Health at a Glance 2019*. OECD.

Peeters, J., Mistiaen, P., & Franke, A. (2011). Costs and financial benefits of video communication in care at home: A systematic review. *Journal of Telemedicine and Telecare*, 17. PMID:22025744

Polisena, J., Coyle, D., Coyle, K., & McGill, S. (2009). Home telehealth for chronic disease management: A systematic review and an analysis of economic evaluations. *International Journal of Technology Assessment in Health Care, 25*(03), 339–349. doi:10.1017/S0266462309990201 PMID:19619353

PwC. (2015). *Weighing the cost of obesity: A case for action. Retrieved from Recker, J. (2013). Scientific research in information systems: a beginner's guide*. Springer Berlin Heidelberg.

Royal Flying Doctor Service. (2016). *Royal Flying Doctor Service: History*. Retrieved from https://www.flyingdoctor.org.au/about-the-rfds/history/

Sheppeard, A. (2014). GP waiting times can be double for rural patients. *Australian Rural Doctor.* Retrieved from http://www.ruraldr.com.au/news/gp-waiting-times-can-be-double-for-rural-patients

Standing, C., Gururajan, R., Standing, S., & Cripps, H. (2014). Making the Most of Virtual Expertise in Telemedicine and Telehealth Environment. *Journal of Organizational Computing and Electronic Commerce*, *24*(2-3), 138–156. doi:10.1080/10919392.2014.896714

van Dyke, L. (2014). A Review of Telehealth Service Implementation Frameworks. *International Journal of Environmental Research and Public Health*, *11*(2), 1279–1298. doi:10.3390/ijerph110201279 PMID:24464237

Wade, V., Karnon, J., Elshaug, A., & Hiller, J. (2010). A systematic review of economic analyses of telehealth services using real time video communication. *BMC Health Services Research*, *10*(1), 233. doi:10.1186/1472-6963-10-233 PMID:20696073

Wade, V. A., Eliott, J. A., & Hiller, J. E. (2014). Clinician Acceptance is the Key Factor for Sustainable Telehealth Services. *Qualitative Health Research*, *24*(5), 682–694. Advance online publication. doi:10.1177/1049732314528809 PMID:24685708

Wattanapisit, A., Teo, C. H., Wattanapisit, S., Teoh, E., Woo, W. J., & Ng, C. J. (2020). Can mobile health apps replace GPs? A scoping review of comparisons between mobile apps and GP tasks. *BMC Medical Informatics and Decision Making*, *20*(1), 5. doi:10.118612911-019-1016-4 PMID:31906985

## KEY TERMS AND DEFINITIONS

**Business Process:** A set of activities and tasks that, once completed, will accomplish an organizational goal.

**Clinician:** A health care professional that works as a primary caregiver of a patient in a hospital, skilled nursing facility, clinic, or patient's home. This could be a physician (general practitioner), specialist or allied health professional.

**General Practitioner (GP):** A physician (medical doctor) based in the community who treats acute and chronic illnesses and provides preventive care and health education to patients. A general practitioner manages types of illness that present in an undifferentiated way at an early stage of development, which may require urgent intervention.

**Information and Communication Technology (ICT):** ICT Infrastructure offers a range of technologies to assist organizations in running efficiently. These services are essential to the everyday mechanics of an organization and integral to effective service delivery. These include hardware, software, networking, and implementation.

**Specialist:** A medical doctor who has completed advanced education and clinical training in a specific area of medicine (their specialty area). There are many specialties, for example Endocrinologist, Obstetrician, Psychiatrist and Urologist.

**Telehealth:** the use of telecommunication techniques for the purpose of providing telemedicine, medical education, and health education over a distance.

**Telemedicine:** the use of advanced telecommunication technologies to exchange health information and provide health care services across geographic, time, social and cultural barriers.

## ENDNOTE

1 New temporary COVID-19 Medicare numbers for funding telehealth from March 2020 http://www.mbsonline.gov.au/internet/mbsonline/publishing.nsf/Content/Factsheet-TempBB (it is unclear if the funding will be extended and if so, for how long).

# Chapter 5
# Service Delivery in Aged Care Case Study:
## ICT and Anywhere Working

**Gabriele Taylor**
*Feros Care, Australia*

**Yvette Blount**
https://orcid.org/0000-0003-0129-7400
*Macquarie University, Australia*

**Marianne Gloet**
*The University of Melbourne, Australia*

## ABSTRACT

*This chapter examines how information and communication technology (ICT) and working anywhere was adopted in a not-for-profit aged care organization in Australia. The aged-care and services sector is expanding, leading to shortages of skilled and experienced workers. At the same time, the sector is dealing with significant changes relating to how services are funded, an increase in competition from both not-for-profit and for profit providers, a rise in demand for services, changes in technology, as well as variations in government regulations. Using ICT to streamline operations, communicate and collaborate has become critical for delivering efficient and effective services the aged care and services sector. The not-for-profit case study in this chapter shows how a first mover in ICT adoption and utilizing working anywhere (telework) can support cost savings, provide the ability to respond to the changing regulatory environment, as well as attract, recruit, and retain skilled and experienced workers.*

DOI: 10.4018/978-1-7998-4159-3.ch005

## INTRODUCTION

The number of people in care across the world is expected to be 2.3 billion by 2030, driven in part by older persons living beyond their predicted life expectancy. Although many older people can contribute to economic and social prosperity, more people are surviving after suffering from chronic illness and experience multi-morbidity and frailty (ILO & OECD, 2019). The aging stage of life should be one where the focus should be on the quality of life, not just quality of care. Across the globe, there is a recognition that keeping people in their homes and communities (keeping them 'in place') assists in reducing social isolation and leads to a better quality of life for an aging population (Freek et al., 2019).

Reliance on care systems to support older people will require more workers in the aged care sector in the future (ILO & OECD, 2019). Worldwide, there are and will continue to be challenges in recruiting and retaining suitably qualified workers to care for our aging population. The shortfall of workers and the increasing costs of caring for older people requires the innovative application of various information and communication technology (ICT) solutions to support the skills of the workforce (Freek et al., 2019). The overall goal of applying technological solutions in this sector is to improve both the life expectancy and healthy life expectancy gap for the aging population (Kang, 2016).

In the Australian context, the population is getting older, with around 25 per cent likely to be 65 or older by the middle of the 21st century. Residential care homes are becoming larger with the home care and home support sector expanding (Kostas et al., 2017). The Australian government has moved to a consumer-centered, community-based, independence-focused model for aged care because it is more cost-effective and provides more choice for consumers. Projections of growth in the aging population suggest that demand for aged services will increase. However, it is unclear how many people will live longer than 85+ and to what extent older people will be healthy or potentially living with disabilities and/or chronic health conditions (Baldwin & Chenoweth, 2015; Chomik & MacLennan, 2014).

Not everyone will need care as they age, and a substantial proportion of people may never need any care in their lifetime depending on their level of health (Chomik & MacLennan, 2014). Between 2008 and 2016, the utilization of aged care in Australia remained consistent, that is, although the number of people receiving aged care services increased, the proportion of older people needing and receiving aged care did not change (Khadka et al., 2019).

In 2012, the Australian government adopted a ten-year Living Longer, Living Better policy to reform the sector to be consumer-driven and reduce costs (Chomik & MacLennan, 2014; Department of Health and Ageing. Canberra, 2012). The reforms included a web portal 'My Aged Care' that replaced three community-based programs ((Community Aged Care Programme, Extended Aged Care at Home, Extended Aged Care at Home-Dementia) (Khadka et al., 2019).

On the 1 July 2015, it became mandatory for all home care packages to be delivered on a customer directed care (CDC) basis. From 27 February 2017, all home care packages were provided to individual consumers instead of the home care packages being awarded to approved providers under an allocation process (Department of Health, 2019). This reform of choice-focused care models with individualized budgets is consistent with the US, the UK and some parts of Europe (Phillipson, Low, & Dreyfus, 2019).

There are two primary services in the Australian aged care and services sector. The first is residential care (in institutions), and the other is community care (support to stay at home and in the community) (Aged Community Services Australia, 2015; Chomik & MacLennan, 2014). Until recently, Australia relied on the not-for-profit sector to supply both residential and community aged care services. An exception is in rural and remote areas where some services are state-owned (government) hospitals or through multi-purpose services (MPS) co-funded by the state and Commonwealth governments. In more recent times, there has been an increase in private-for-profit ownership of residential aged care facilities (RACF), primarily in the metropolitan regions and a reduction of government beds in rural and remote regions (Henderson, Willis, Xiao, Toffoli, & Verrall, 2016).

In Australia, in 2016, 366,027 employees were working in aged care which is a 4 per cent increase from 2012. The findings of the 2016 National Aged Care Workforce Census and Survey (NACWCS) showed of these 235,764 worked in residential facilities, and 130,263 worked in-home care and home support outlets (Kostas et al., 2017). The number of employees in direct care roles was 240,317, with 153,854 in residential facilities which is a 5 per cent increase since 2012 and 86,463 in-home care and home support outlets which is a 7 per cent decrease since 2012 (Kostas et al., 2017).

The direct care workforce in Australia consists of six primary occupational groups: Nurse Practitioners (NP), Registered Nurses (RN), Enrolled Nurses (EN) Personal Care Attendants (PCA)/Community Care Workers (CCW), Allied Health Professionals (AHP) and Allied Health Assistants (AHA). The characteristics of the employees in direct care roles are female-dominated (89 per cent), with a median age of 52 years; of these, 84 per cent are community care workers, 75 per cent are employed on a permanent full-time and part-time basis, 23 per cent are born overseas, and 14 per cent are casual or contract employees (Kostas et al., 2017).

Since 2012, the home care and home support workforce has declined. This decline is a concern because the demand for home support services by older Australians is predicted to increase significantly in the future (Kostas et al., 2017). Therefore it is prudent to seek a better understanding of how resources are utilized to achieve the 'age in place' government policy (Khadka et al., 2019). There are also skills shortages across the sector that are similar to those reported in 2012. The main causes of these skills shortages were a lack of specialist knowledge, slow recruitment and geographical location. The skills shortages are more acute in rural areas where recruiting staff, accessing resources for staff development, fewer general practitioners and limited access to specialist and allied health services represent serious challenges (Henderson et al., 2016; Kostas et al., 2017).

In the Australian aged care sector, registered nurses are the most difficult group to recruit. The inability to attract registered nurses to aged care is a longstanding issue, and clinical training in aged care is one possible response to this issue (King et al., 2013; Kostas et al., 2017). King et al. (2013) found in a survey of the working conditions of registered nurses that many are working longer hours than they would prefer. Compared with other occupational groups, registered and enrolled nurses reported that they are more likely to feel under pressure and that their job was more stressful than they imagined. Registered nurses working in residential care reported a high work-life imbalance, to a greater extent than all other occupational groups in the Australian workforce. Another troubling statistic is that just over 20 per cent of registered nurses had been in their roles for 12 months or less, the highest proportion of all the occupational groups. Most of the respondents had been in the workforce for 20 years or more. There is also a great deal of mobility within the registered nursing occupational group; about 25 per cent of registered nurses do not expect to be working for their current organization in 12 months, with 14 per cent in the residential sector and 8 per cent in the community sector were actively seeking work at the time of the survey (King et.al. 2013).

The demand for workers in the aged care sector will continue to grow for the next 30 years. A skilled, capable and flexible workforce is critical for ensuring that the government policy is adopted and achieves the stated of objectives of 'aging in place'. ICT and flexible work practices are two key areas for ensuring sustainable aged care services (Aged Community Services Australia, 2015).

The objective of this chapter is to examine how Feros Care, an Australian not-for-profit organization in the aged care and services sector responded to these drivers using anywhere working and ICT to attract and retain staff, grow the business and achieve competitive advantage. The aim is to ascertain how Feros Care uses anywhere working (telework) to attract, recruit and retain qualified staff as well as integrate technology to achieve competitive advantage. The chapter will conclude with lessons learned and future research directions.

## BACKGROUND

The cost of delivering health care is escalating in developed countries due to aging populations and the increased prevalence of chronic disease (Yang, Kankanhalli, & Chandran, 2015). In Australia, Government spending on aged care is steadily increasing, as can be seen in Figure 1.

*Figure 1. Increase in Government Spending on Aged Care*
*(https://www.gen-agedcaredata.gov.au/Topics/Government-spending-on-aged-care)*

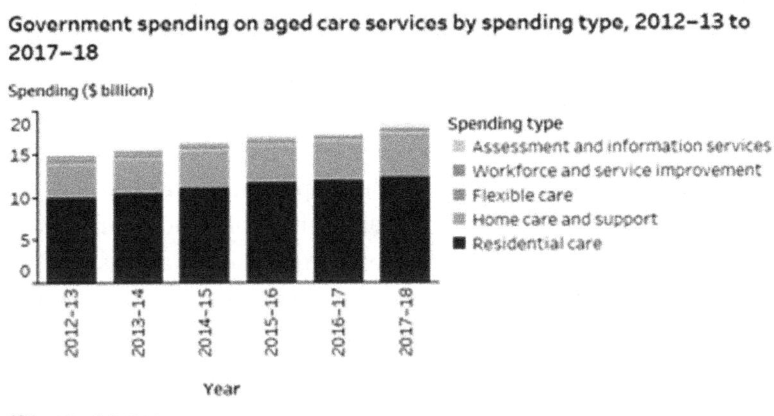


In 2017-2018, governments in Australia spent $A18 billion on aged care. The expenditure on residential care ($12.4 billion) was 2.4 times the amount spent on home care and support ($5.1 billion) (Productivity Commission, 2019).

Despite the increasing costs of aged care, technology is a means of mitigating costs while at the same time adding quality, efficiency and effectiveness to the delivery of aged care services. ICT is disrupting the delivery of healthcare, for example, mobile apps, remote medical diagnosis, robotics and 24/7 monitoring of health conditions (Topol, 2015). Health care services, including in the aged care and services sector, have been disrupted by ICT. Various applications of ICT disruption are changing the way health care professionals interact with clients and with each other. Supported by ICT, health information about patients is readily accessible by both health care practitioners and the patient.

Health care is accessible and affordable over distances because of telehealth, ICT-enabled healthcare delivery, and related processes (Carati & Margelis, 2013). Telecare refers to the technical devices and services provided at a distance to support and care for people with chronic illness or reduced mobility, usually in their homes.

Examples include personal alarms, monitoring devices for abnormal behavior such as leaving the house late at night or not getting up out of bed at the usual time, calling for help in the event of a fall, and reminders to eat or take medication (Aceros, Pols, & Domènech, 2015).

The formation of the Australasian Telehealth Society (ATHS) in 2008 had the objective of bringing together academics, clinicians, government and industry partners to inform the telehealth debate. The ATHS has co-hosted the annual Success and Failures in Telehealth Conference since 2010 and produced a draft telehealth strategy, still in a draft in 2020 (Carati & Margelis, 2013). One of the critical issues identified in the draft strategy was workforce constraints (Carati & Margelis, 2013). In a study that investigated the medical curriculum in Australia, the findings showed that although there was an acknowledgment of the importance of eHealth skills development, there was little appetite by accreditation bodies or practitioners to include eHealth competencies in an already crowded curriculum (Edirippulige et al., 2018)

ICT in aged care and services is providing opportunities to both deliver better health outcomes and to reduce costs. Smart apps on mobile and wearable devices can monitor blood pressure, blood glucose level, weight, heart rate, as well as activity levels (exercise) and nutrition. The data can be used to monitor patients remotely without the need for a visit to a medical practitioner (Kang, 2016). Some smart applications can also diagnose medical conditions (Topol, 2015).

There are some barriers to the adoption of ICT by workers and clients for the delivery of services using telehealth. The barriers include limitations of passive monitoring, the need to manage multiple devices, limited functionality for device design, lack of customization, the level of acceptance and potentially higher costs (Rana, Hume, Reilly, & Soar, 2015).

Monitoring of devices and visiting patients in their homes often require workers to work from anywhere, either from their homes or in another location. Anywhere working (other terms include telework, telecommuting amongst others) refers to a substitution of information technologies for work-related travel (Nilles, 1975), working from a location such as a home office. However, the definition of anywhere work is not universally agreed (Wooden & Fok, 2013). This chapter defines anywhere working as working from a home office for most work-related duties.

The successful adoption of ICT that supports eHealth requires fast, reliable and ubiquitous broadband. In Australia, the national broadband network (NBN) is in the final stages of being rolled out across the country. A Telehealth Pilot by Feros Care compared the performance of the NBN, 4G and ADSL2 for connectivity and cost and found that the NBN was the most reliable for delivering telehealth services (Southern Cross University, 2014). The connectivity and reliability of the broadband network are also crucial for aged care workers who support clients in their homes.

The social and professional isolation of teleworkers can be detrimental to job satisfaction and worker retention (Blount, 2015). ICTs can support teleworkers by facilitating knowledge acquisition, transfer, and exchange, which improves health professionals work satisfaction and may positively influence worker retention (Gagnon et al., 2011). Research has shown that health care workers that have access to continued training and professional development influence the retention of workers (Duplantie, Fortin, Gagnon, & Landry, 2007).

Feros Care is a case study of a not-for-profit organization in the aged care and services sector that has used ICT to deliver aged care services more effectively and efficiently. At the same time, Feros Care has used anywhere working (telework) to attract, appoint and retain skilled and capable staff.

## FEROS CARE

### Case Description

Feros Care Ltd is an Australian community-owned, not-for-profit organization founded in 1990 that began in Byron Bay with one aged care facility. Since then, Feros Care has grown and diversified their offerings from residential care, home care packages, the national disability insurance scheme packages (NDIS) with a focus on technology innovation. For example, Feros Care was awarded the Global Ageing Network (GAN) Award for the development and implementation of many new technologies that have the potential to 'revolutionize the global aged care industry' (https://www.feroscare.com.au/feros-stories/articles/feros-care-wins-prestigious-global-ageing-network-award).

The Feros Care Annual Report 2017-2018 states that 55,732 clients were serviced during that year in QLD, NSW, VIC, Tas, ACT (Australian states) and New Zealand. Feros' mission and strategic intent are to support seniors to live their best life by providing meaningful support and service options that promote health and wellness to achieve lifestyle goals and aspirations (Feros Care, 2016). Assisting seniors to remain healthy, active, independent and connected to their families, friends, and their community, for as long as possible is the aim (Feros Care, 2015).

The development of the mission and strategy used government policy and a key report in the early 2000s from the Myer Foundation: 2020 A Vision for Aged Care (The Myer Foundation, 2002). Feros Care also undertook a comprehensive review, including finding large successful organizations in the same or similar area of industry. Several site visits followed this both in Australia and overseas two of which included the Visiting Nurse Service of New York (VNSNY) (www.vnsny.org), the largest community nursing service in the southern hemisphere with a budget of over US$ 3 billion per annum, and the centralized community intake system of the Community Care Access Centre in Toronto, Canada (helathcareathome.ca/torontocentral/en).

Feros Care found that successful organizations in the aged care and services sector had five key areas of focus. The first was the adoption of ICT, the second was paperless systems, the third was the use of client e-records, the fourth was centralized administration, and the fifth was the mobility of staff (ability to work anywhere). ICT supported staff mobility at the VNSNY by providing a laptop for staff for traveling on the subway.

Feros Care commenced a project to systematically work through each task and function that staff in the field were required to do daily as well as the administration and back-office staff. This activity produced the specifications for ICT, a must-have list, a nice-to-have list and a wish-list. The project identified overlaps and co-dependencies across the whole organization. The project included the legislation, privacy, standards and compliance requirements across all planning, development, implementation and evaluation phases to support the new business model.

The information from the project was used to establish need, identify gaps and encourage innovation. Involvement of key stakeholders including all levels of staff through to board members was included in conducting some initiatives These initiatives included 'blue skies' brainstorming, 'ignite' sessions, consultation forums, workshops, meetings; reviewing of results of formal and informal feedback loops, mind mapping and process mapping, utilizing the Ottawa Charter framework (World Health Organization, 1986) to identify and incorporate innovative solutions and sustainable strategies.

A project management plan was used to capture each aspect of the implementation. The project plan included key actions and timeframes allocated to a person/team responsible. Regularly scheduled project meetings ensured opportunities for enhancement and necessary corrective actions could be undertaken quickly to minimize delays, overcome barriers and resolve any difficulties. Project reports were regularly tabled at meetings to monitor the project outcomes, measure the attainment of the objectives, detail the change management activities undertaken, report on results of key deliverables, detail the sustainability strategies and the ongoing monitoring activities.

Critical challenges for Feros Care are: how to effectively comply with the changing legislation, integrating ICT, new competitors entering the market (not-for-profit and for-profit) as well as attract, recruit and retain workers with the right mix of skills and capabilities to achieve the stated vision and mission. Integrating anywhere working (telework) was a deliberate strategy to deal with attracting, recruiting and retaining workers.

## Information and Communications Technology (ICT)

Feros Care was the first mover in adopting ICT in the aged care and services sector. ICT is a core capability that underpins and supports the whole-of-business across service delivery, client care, and the workforce. Feros Care recognized that ICT was necessary for improving the efficiency and flexibility of the Feros Care workplace as well as improving the quality of life outcomes for seniors. ICT has underpinned Feros Care's ability to grow (including expanding geographical areas) and provide the flexibility to respond quickly to the changing needs of the aged care industry (Feros Care, 2015).

Creating a paperless system utilizing an electronic client management system was a challenge as there was no one product on the market that aligned with the specification list. Feros Care's requirements included rostering staff efficiently, ensuring staff had access to the information they required during their working day as well as feeling supported, part of a team and connected to the organization.

Instead of setting up local physical offices in many different locations, Feros Care developed The Centralized Gateway and Teleworker Model, supported by ICT to develop a virtual workforce. Feros Care equips its workforce with all the necessary technology to keep them connected and communicating, using a robust video conferencing infrastructure and community gateway call center linking all stakeholders to Feros Care 24/7.

Feros Care's Community Gateway, established in 2007, and rebadged Feros Central in 2018, supports the virtual workforce. Feros Central provides one access point (hub) for all stakeholders to access Feros Care, including staff, clients, families, health professionals, and the community. Feros Central is the gateway for all incoming calls and communication; emails and referrals are managed by an experienced client and staff liaison team. The single access point ensures that all requests for services and inquiries are answered and actioned. The super-hub serves as the organizational backbone of all information management, and administration systems actioned centrally, and all referrals and communications from clients, families, staff, referral agencies, service providers, health professionals, and funding bodies routed through Feros Central.

Feros Central simplifies service access, service delivery, service logistics and service administration. Through combining existing web-based, broadband and communication technologies with community system software, quality and document systems, a 24/7 secure real-time authenticated access to client and organization records provides significant operational efficiencies. The International Association of Homes and Services for the Aging, 2011, announced Feros Care as the winner of the prestigious International Award for Excellence in Ageing Services for this model.

The initial technology solution combined existing broadband and communication technology with several software systems to provide significant efficiencies in service delivery through the implementation of a centralized Community Gateway that included a combination of the following technologies:

- Combined ISDN, Voice Over IP (VOIP) and wireless technology to enable the caller to be transferred seamlessly a staff member working in the community;
- PABX and call management software used to record contact center statistics including on-call times, call demographics and abandonment rates;
- A Wide Area Network included business-grade broadband and wireless solutions, provided a secure, authenticated access for teleworkers to access organizational forms, files, client and staff records remotely.
- Paperless information management with the conversion of all faxed referrals and other documents into pdf formatted documents forwarded via email or mobile phone to mobile teleworkers;
- Establishment of home (virtual) offices for Mobile Care Managers with laptops, broadband internet connection, multifunction centers and smartphones;
- Real-time access for teleworking Care Managers to electronic client records anytime, anywhere (e.g. while conducting visits and assessments in homes).
- Use of smartphones capable of receiving voice and SMS broadcasts, roster updates, pdf documents and sending imagines for clinical consideration and risk analysis;
- Mobile office set up for all community care staff with secured email support to enable the receipt of rosters and appropriate company documentation;
- Electronic mapping of client's home locations using Google Maps® to assist logistical considerations and create efficiencies within roster planning; and
- GPS mapping and time tracking programs testing to undertake an advanced logistical analysis for roster planning, staff supervision and monitor workplace safety issues.

While the initial implementation plan mostly included off-the-shelf technologies and readily available online solutions, improvements and innovations over the years have brought the inclusions of more advanced and more robust technology products, including customization of software and software developer partnerships to design and create a fit-for-purpose system tailored to Feros Care's unique specifications and client service offerings.

Data security is a key focus. The internal ICT infrastructure is secured by best-of-breed perimeter firewalls that have threat management gateways for alerting and monitoring; third party vendors undertake regular penetration and perimeter testing as well as internal social engineering and phishing exercises. All internal server infrastructures are held within an IS0 27000:2009 Information Security Standard Data Centre and adhere to data privacy legislation. The Business Continuity Plan details the actions to take in the event of an emergency or a disaster.

There are some technologies used to support clients. For example, seniors living in their own homes can use the My Health Clinic At Home (MHCAH) technology to monitor vital signs such as blood pressure via a smart device similar an iPad with a follow-up from health practitioners via a video link (Feros Care, 2015). MHCAH aligns with government policy to keep people at home and in their communities if possible (it is also more cost-effective).

Feros Care's LifeLink Telehealthcare services provide a range of assistive and smart technology products to support people with a wide variety of care needs, to live safely and independently in their own home. Telecare enables easy and immediate access to emergency help when needed in the home. Telehealth enables people to monitor and take control of their health from home proactively. Telehealth facilitates virtual connections to GP's, specialists and other essential health supports. Telecare home environmental sensors technologies can be installed unobtrusively into any pre-existing home. The technologies are designed to automatically alert a 24/7 response center in the case of an emergency. For example, fall detection, automatic inactivity detection, day and night time exit seekers (for clients with live-in or out carers), unwelcome caller alarm, inactivity sensors (detects no movement in the home for extended periods), bathroom safety as well as others (Feros Care, 2015).

In 2014, Feros Care received funding from the Department of Social Services to trial a multidisciplinary virtual clinical care model Australia-wide for residents with chronic disease, called the Technology Enabled Multidisciplinary Care Advisory Service (TEMCAS). In 2014-2015, Feros Care conducted 288 video calls between 92 residents and 18 general practices. This equates to avoiding 52 hospital visits, saving on the medical costs and the transport costs to the medical appointment or hospital (Feros Care, 2015).

Robots have been introduced to socially connect less mobile residents and allow the residents to participate in interactive social outings and to access medical practitioners without having to travel. The robot is called Wheel-I-Am, an iPad mounted on a self- balancing Segway base. Wheel-I-Am is used in social settings by visiting art galleries and museums where he can stream live footage back to the aged care facility, where residents who were unable to participate physically can watch on a big screen. The residents can also ask questions of the tour guide as if they were there.

## Staff Profile

As of June 2015, Feros Care employed 518 staff. The majority were female (87%), and over half (53%) were part-time. The workforce included 24% contracted and 29% casual. The most significant proportion of staff was aged between 40-49 years (31%) and the second-largest was between 50-59 years (30%). The following table provides an overview of Feros Care staff by role.

*Table 1. Feros Care staff by role*

**Feros Care Staff Distribution by Primary Duties (as of 30 June 2015)**

| Primary Duty Category | No. | % of Staff |
|---|---|---|
| Coordination | 53 | 10% |
| Administration | 64 | 12% |
| Management | 24 | 5% |
| Registered Nursing | 23 | 4% |
| Enrolled Nursing | 2 | 0.4% |
| Carers AIN's | 252 | 49% |
| Hotel Services | 49 | 9% |
| Health & Wellness | 11 | 2% |
| Positive Living | 9 | 2% |
| Gateway & Rostering | 16 | 3% |
| IT & Technicians | 15 | 3% |

This shows that Feros Care relies on female workers who are at ages that often involve caring responsibilities for both children and aging parents. Over sixty per cent of workers were between 40 and 59, that indicates an aging workforce. On the one hand, this indicates that there is a great deal of experience and knowledge in the Feros Care workforce. On the other hand, there is a small percentage of younger workers engaged in this sector that shows that there may be a skill shortage in the future. The skill shortage will hamper Feros Care's ability to grow their business and compete.

## Key Management Issues and Strategies

Managing a virtual workforce, who are mobile and multidisciplinary, involve three main challenges. The challenges are the availability of digital infrastructure, social and professional isolation and attracting, recruiting and retaining workers.

The first challenge is the availability of ubiquitous, fast and reliable broadband. The policy for a national broadband network and subsequent delays potentially impacts on the rollout of technologies, particularly in rural and regional areas where the internet and mobile access can be poor. Teleworkers located in locations with insufficient broadband and mobile connections are disadvantaged. For example, ICT is used for managing appointments and schedules and monthly teleconference meetings. If broadband is not adequate for supporting essential tasks, it may reduce opportunities for both Feros Care and the worker. For Feros Care, it may reduce the opportunities for hiring qualified and experienced staff if they are unable to access reliable internet. For the workers, it may be a disadvantage because they may not be able to work from home, which may preclude them from employment with Feros Care.

The second challenge is social and professional isolation. Telework creates a new organizational form of working with different ways of defining tasks, more complex integration problems, and different management responsibilities (Mahler, 2012). This may also lead to workers feeling less engaged with the organization. Feros Care has some strategies to deal with this challenge.

The first is some face-to-face opportunities for sharing information and celebrating successes. There is an annual awards night for all staff that acknowledges both individual and team contributions to the organization. A bi-annual leadership conference is held for all teleworking multidisciplinary case managers. Another initiative is the community conferences that are held quarterly for direct care staff across regional teams with a focus on team building, culture and innovation.

The second consists of strategies using technology. The Feros Care intranet is used to disseminate information, provide important updates and consultative calendars. GoToMeeting supports scheduled and ad-hoc training sessions over the Web. Yammer (an enterprise social networking service used for private communication within organizations) is used to reduce email traffic and promote engagement with team members and the organization more broadly. Feros Care promotes the whole of organization wellness programs that are underpinned by gaming principles using Yammer and the Intranet to encourage and support engagement.

The third challenge is attracting, recruiting and retaining workers with the skills and capabilities required for achieving Feros Care's mission and strategic objectives. It is a significant investment to provide the technology, the training and mentoring required to ensure the worker can deliver the level of service Feros Care promise to deliver in their business model. Therefore, keeping turnover to a minimum is an important management consideration.

Feros Care has designed a three-month nested onboarding program for new recruits that blends face-to-face with e-learning via web support. A buddy system includes role-specific and culture support. A buddy is assigned to support the recruit in their specific role, including side-by-side training in the field. A culture buddy can be assigned from any area in the organization. An important initiative is the professional support and supervision e-sessions. The e-sessions are agenda-driven and cover all aspects of the teleworker role. The e-sessions are valuable for early identification of a poor role fit.

## Anywhere Working (Telework) Model

Feros Care recognized that the diminishing workforce was a fundamental challenge to the future growth of the business. Feros Care realized that not being able to attract, recruit and retain the necessary skills and capabilities was a significant risk to their ability to sustain and grow their business. The Aged Care Sector is not usually the first choice for a job seeker. The workforce, particularly those in part-time or casual positions, are targeted by multinational competitors such as supermarket chains and other large retailers who rely on workers who need flexible work. This majority of this workforce is made up of mature females who have family caring responsibilities for children, grandchildren, aging parents or blended family commitments. Some of this workforce may also be juggling second jobs because of financial pressures due to not only family commitments but second mortgages and little or no superannuation.

A collaborative approach with emerging software developers has facilitated customization of the scheduling and appointment regimes to significantly improve route optimization as well as the creation of a scheduling App on the smartphones of the anywhere working (telework) staff which display their appointments for the day, the purpose and tasks of each appointment, hazards, safety alerts and even specific instructions for an appointment. Similarly, another App has been developed, which allows staff to report handovers, incidents and feedback in real-time from their smartphone. A new web-based Business Intelligence and Outcomes Database provide teleworking managers and clinicians with the ability to monitor client outcomes and goal attainment in a range of configurations and views to enable appropriate and timely personalized interventions and program enhancements.

An essential component of the model has been the use of video conferencing technology which has been integral in bridging the geographical gap between managers and workers providing real-time support and supervision. While the key objective was to adopt technology that would create a teamwork environment despite distance and enabled, even more, productivity from each team, it has also opened the door to finding innovative technology-based service options for clients.

The Centralized Gateway and Teleworker model have enabled Feros Care to diversify its geographic influence in a short period. This ability to expand geographically with minimal infrastructure is a critical commercial and industry advantage. Feros Care has achieved the following outcomes, most that relate to the ability to utilize anywhere-working staff:

- ***Reduction of multiple office infrastructures and associated operational costs.*** This equates to minimum annual savings of over $2 million per annum across the Feros Care's geographic footprint.
- ***Efficiencies in the client intake process, including referral processing and allocation of staff with improvement in response rates to both referrals and first service start***. This has been achieved by Gateway staff acknowledging the referral, commencing intake documentation, eligibility determination, and collecting initial assessment information on the first call.
- ***Increased timeliness of referral processing from 3-5 days to 10 minutes***. The ability to forward electronic referral information has meant case managers and direct care staff do not have to return to base to collect paper documentation.
- ***Immediate allocation of staff with the aid of electronic mapping tools and roster referencing***. In the past, this process would have taken 2-3 days and involved discussion and time negotiations with case managers.
- ***Significantly improved service delivery response rates***. Immediate basic services, care and 'urgent' requests can be initiated on the same day as a referral, and higher-level care follow-up occurs within one working day. The previous wait was between 7 to 14 days.
- ***Efficient use of staffing resources through the effective use of available technologies and software.*** This has been achieved through the establishment of 'virtual offices' for teleworking case managers with laptops, wireless broadband, multifunction centers and smartphones ensures real-time access to electronic client records while conducting visits and assessments in homes.
- ***Improved communications for teleworking staff.*** This has been realized using smartphones capable of receiving voicemail and SMS broadcasts,

roster updates, sending images for clinical consideration, safety, hazards and risk analysis.

- ***Timely update of rosters, appointment schedules, requests and organization documentation.*** Feros Care has provided a home office set up for direct care staff with fax machines and secured individualized email support.
- ***Reduction in daily travel costs by an estimated 50%.*** This is due to case managers working from a home base and rostering efficiencies gained for direct care staff.
- ***Reduction in on-call staffing costs by 80%.*** This is the result of case managers sharing on-call arrangements and wirelessly accessing all necessary documentation via the wide-area network to assist in decision making and activating appropriate response plans and supports as may be necessary.
- ***Reduction of paper consumption by 90%.*** This has been achieved through extensive use of e-Records, web-based quality, and document management systems.
- ***Improvement in no delay 'referral-assessment-service commencement'.*** This ensures that income is generated more expediently with no unnecessary double handling resulting in less non-income producing or vacant days and an increase in available direct care hours by an estimated 25%.
- ***Continuous Quality Improvement surveys consistently show an increased level of client and staff satisfaction.*** Feros Care has achieved 90th percentile reports across all aspects of service access for users, communication management, and work-life balance.

In 2014/2015, Feros Care used video conferencing to conduct over 750 e-mentoring and e-supervision sessions with community managers across the eastern seaboard in Australia to support, coach and collaborate to strengthen the capacity of the remote teleworking managers (Feros Care, 2015).

## SOLUTIONS AND RECOMMENDATIONS

The Board and management of Feros Care recognize that ICT is the enabler for adapting to the changing regulatory environment, increased competition for clients and workers and new business models. The Feros Care case study shows that it is a first mover in the adoption of ICT for effectiveness and efficiency, including adopting new ICT for streamlining operations, providing quality client care and attracting, recruiting and retaining qualified workers.

What is unclear is what skills and capabilities will be necessary for the coming decades to address these changes. Workers will not only need the appropriate level of clinical skills to provide the quality of service necessary, but they will also need to adapt to new models of care. Workers will also require increasing levels of digital literacy. Telehealth, including monitoring technologies and virtual clinician (doctors/nurses/allied health) visits, will become increasingly common as the technology becomes more ubiquitous and affordable. Workers will need to be able to respond to and adjust to ICT facilitated interactions with clients that will require updated skills.

Skill shortages, particularly for registered nurses, are likely to be a challenge in the future as the demand for workers intensifies. Feros Care uses ICT to promote aged and community care to help strengthen the professional image of the business and to create new employment pathways to attract younger workers to the industry.

The quality of interactions between workers and clients, workers and managers and workers and colleagues requires a balance of ICT facilitated communication channels as well as face-to-face interaction. Feros Care understands the importance of face-to-face interactions with team members that work from a home base. Feros Care has an annual staff function that is attended by workers to celebrate successes throughout the year and reconnect. Feros Care has processes for supporting anywhere workers, including regular face-to-face meetings with managers, usually monthly.

## FUTURE RESEARCH DIRECTIONS

The key drivers impacting the Aged Care and Services Sector are ICT, and the skills and capabilities of the workforce. ICT will continue to disrupt the way health care services are delivered, including in the aged care sector.

The Feros Care case study shows that using anywhere working policies can, to some extent, address workforce issues by creating a flexible workplace where experienced and qualified people can work from a home office. Although ensuring workers have access to ICT to manage their work wherever they work is an important consideration, the more important support for workers comes from the management structures, including training and development.

Future research should include investigating similar organizations to understand best practice for adopting anywhere working in the Aged Care and Services sector.

## CONCLUSION

The adoption of ICT has been a key operational enabler for Feros Care's exponential growth in Community Care across an ever-increasing geographical footprint. Adopting the Gateway and Teleworker Model instead of setting up local offices in many different locations has reduced costs, made business processes more efficient and facilitated attracting, recruiting and retaining skilled staff.

The model has equipped the workforce with all the necessary technology to keep them connected and communicating, using a robust video conferencing infrastructure and the community gateway provides real-time access to Feros Care 24/7. Reliable and ubiquitous digital infrastructure will be vital to ensuring that ICT can be adopted across all regions in Australia.

The virtual workforce model has enabled Feros Care to deploy services in new areas to satisfy clients in need much more quickly and without the delays created by finding and fitting out new premises which inevitably are costly to maintain and often underutilized. The risks of social and professional isolation of teleworkers, as well as feeling connected to the organization, will need to continue to be a focus as competition for workers in the Aged Care and Services sector increases.

Anywhere working (the virtual, mobile workforce) will continue to be a key pillar for attracting, recruiting and retaining staff while being able to deliver an increasingly diverse range of services to clients, the Feros Care business model.

## REFERENCES

Aceros, J. C., Pols, J., & Domènech, M. (2015). Where is grandma? Home telecare, good aging and the domestication of later life. *Technological Forecasting and Social Change*, *93*, 102–111. doi:10.1016/j.techfore.2014.01.016

Aged Community Services Australia. (2015). *The aged care workforce in Australia: position paper*. Retrieved from https://www.acs.asn.au/wcm/documents/ACS%20Website/Resources/Publications%20Submissions/ACSA%20Submissions%20Documents/ACSA%20Workforce%20White%20Paper%20-%20July%202014.pdf

Baldwin, R., Chenoweth, L., & dela Rama, M. (2015). Residential Aged Care Policy in Australia–Are We Learning from Evidence? *Australian Journal of Public Administration*, *74*(2), 128–141. doi:10.1111/1467-8500.12131

Blount, Y. (2015). Pondering the Fault Lines of Anywhere Working (Telework, Telecommuting): A Literature Review. *Foundations and Trends® in Information Systems, 1*(3), 163-276. doi:10.1561/2900000001

Carati, C., & Margelis, G. (2013). *Towards a National Strategy for Telehealth in Australia 2013-2018*. Retrieved from http://aths.org.au/wp-content/uploads/2013/05/TelehealthStrategy.pdf

Chomik, R., & MacLennan, M. (2014). *Aged Care in Australia: Part I-Policy, demand and funding, CEPAR research brief 2014/01*. Academic Press.

Department of Health. (2019). *Home care packages - reform*. Retrieved from https://agedcare.health.gov.au/aged-care-reform/home-care/home-care-packages-reform

Department of Health and Ageing. (2012). *Living longer. Living better: Aged Care Reform Package April 2012*. Author.

Duplantie, J., Fortin, J.-P., Gagnon, M.-P., & Landry, R. (2007). Telehealth and the recruitment and retention of physicians in rural and remote regions: A Delphi study. *Canadian Journal of Rural Medicine*, *12*, 30. PMID:17229362

Edirippulige, S., Brooks, P., Carati, C., Wade, V. A., Smith, A. C., Wickramasinghe, S., & Armfield, N. R. (2018). It's important, but not important enough: eHealth as a curriculum priority in medical education in Australia. *Journal of Telemedicine and Telecare*, *24*(10), 697–702. doi:10.1177/1357633X18793282 PMID:30343657

Feros Care. (2015). *Feros Care - Annual Report 2014-2015*. Retrieved from https://www.feroscare.com.au/about/annual-reports/

Feros Care. (2016). *Feros Care: Celebrating Aging Vision and Mission Statement*. Retrieved from https://www.feroscare.com.au/about/mission-statement/

Freek, L., Stevenson, D., Leser, M., Horecký, I. J., Kaserer, B., & Mattersberger, M. (2019). *Long Term Care 2030*. https://www.ecreas.eu/uimg/ecreasportal/b80760_att-report-ean-ltc-2030-digital.pdf

Gagnon, M.-P., Paré, G., Pollender, H., Duplantie, J., Côté, J., Fortin, J.-P., Labadie, R., Duplàa, E., Thifault, M.-C., Courcy, F., McGinn, C. A., Ly, B. A., Trépanier, A., & Malo, F.-B. (2011). Supporting work practices through telehealth: Impact on nurses in peripheral regions. *BMC Health Services Research*, *11*(1), 27–35. doi:10.1186/1472-6963-11-27 PMID:21294882

Henderson, J., Willis, E., Xiao, L., Toffoli, L., & Verrall, C. (2016). Nurses' perceptions of the impact of the aged care reform on services for residents in multi-purpose services and residential aged care facilities in rural Australia. *Australasian Journal on Ageing*, *35*(4), E18–E23. doi:10.1111/ajag.12343 PMID:27334723

ILO & OECD. (2019). *New job opportunities in an ageing society Paper prepared for the 1st Meeting of the G20 Employment Working Group*. Retrieved from https://www.oecd.org/g20/summits/osaka/ILO-OECD-G20-Paper-1-3-New-job-opportunities-in-an-ageing-society.pdf

Kang, S. Y. (2016). The ICT Technology for Geriatric Diseases Healthcare. In J. K. Kim & N. Joukov (Eds.), *Information Science and Applications (ICISA) 2016* (pp. 1495–1500). Springer Singapore. doi:10.1007/978-981-10-0557-2_144

Khadka, J., Lang, C., Ratcliffe, J., Corlis, M., Wesselingh, S., Whitehead, C., & Inacio, M. (2019). Trends in the utilization of aged care services in Australia, 2008–2016. *BMC Geriatrics*, *19*(1), 213. doi:10.118612877-019-1209-9 PMID:31387533

King, D., Mavromaras, K., He, B., Healy, J., Macaitis, K., Moskos, M., & Zhang, W. (2013). *The aged care workforce 2012 final report*. Department of Health and Ageing.

Kostas, M., Knight, G., Isherwood, L., Crettenden, A., Flavel, J., Karmel, T., . . . Wei, Z. (2017). *2016 National Aged Care Workforce Census and Survey – The Aged Care Workforce 2016*. Retrieved from https://www.gen-agedcaredata.gov.au/Resources/Reports-and-publications/2017/March/The-aged-care-workforce,-2016

Mahler, J. (2012). The Telework Divide: Managerial and Personnel Challenges of Telework. *Review of Public Personnel Administration*, *32*(4), 407–418. doi:10.1177/0734371X12458127

Nilles, J. M. (1975). Telecommunications and Organizational Decentralization. *Communications. IEEE Transactions on*, *23*(10), 1142–1147. doi:10.1109/TCOM.1975.1092687

Phillipson, L., Low, L. F., & Dreyfus, S. (2019). Consumer-directed care for older Australians: Are resources identified on the Web adequate to support decisions about home-based care packages? *The Australian Journal of Social Issues*, *54*(2), 135–156. doi:10.1002/ajs4.66

Productivity Commission. (2019). *Report on Government Services 2019*. Retrieved from https://www.pc.gov.au/research/ongoing/report-on-government-services/2019/community-services/aged-care-services

Rana, R., Hume, M., Reilly, J., & Soar, J. (2015). *wHealth - Transforming Telehealth Services*. Academic Press.

Southern Cross University. (2014). *Telehealth Pilot Full Report. - Feros Care*. Retrieved from https://www.feroscare.com.au

The Myer Foundation. (2002). *2020 A Vision for Aged Care in Australia*. Retrieved from http://myerfoundation.org.au/wp-content/uploads/2014/09/2020-A-Vision-for-Aged-Care-in-Australia.pdf

Topol, E. (2015). *The Patient Will See You Now: The Future of Medicine is in Your Hands*. Basic Books.

Wooden, M., & Fok, Y.-K. (2013). *Working at home: Whatever happened to the revolution?* Retrieved from https://www.smh.com.au/technology/what-ever-happened-to-the-working-from-home-revolution-20150101-12gb1f.html

World Health Organization. (1986). *The Ottawa Charter for Health Promotion*. Retrieved from https://www.who.int/healthpromotion/conferences/previous/ottawa/en/index.html

Yang, Y., Kankanhalli, A., & Chandran, S. (2015). A stage model of information technology in healthcare. *Health and Technology*, *5*(1), 1–11. doi:10.100712553-015-0097-z

## KEY TERMS AND DEFINITIONS

**Community Care:** Supports people to continue living at home for as long as possible, and provides more choice and flexibility for people receiving care at home.

**Healthy Life Expectancy:** Average number of years that a person can expect to live in "full health" by taking into account years lived in less than full health due to disease and/or injury.

**Information and Communication Technology (ICT):** All the technology and resources used to communicate, and to create, disseminate, store, and manage information.

**Residential Care:** A special-purpose facility which provides accommodation and other types of support, including assistance with day-to-day living, intensive forms of care, and assistance towards independent living, to frail and aged residents

**Telehealth:** The use of telecommunication techniques to provide telemedicine, medical education, and health education over a distance.

# Chapter 6
# Access to Flexible Work Arrangements for People With Disabilities:
## An Australian Study

**Rachelle Bosua**
https://orcid.org/0000-0003-0218-3018
*Open University of the Netherlands, The Netherlands*

**Marianne Gloet**
*The University of Melbourne, Australia*

## ABSTRACT

*People with disabilities face unique challenges accessing and participating in work. From a digital inclusion perspective, an uptake of anywhere working arrangements may hold significant promise for people with disabilities. This qualitative study explored barriers of flexible work for people with disabilities in Australia. The study focused on manager and worker perspectives and findings indicate that both parties face unique challenges to accommodate people with disabilities in flexible work. Barriers encountered by disabled workers seeking access to flexible working arrangements include management attitudes, physical and infrastructure problems, social isolation misconceptions, insufficient flexible work opportunities, and inadequate management knowledge of IT support and reasonable adjustment for people with disabilities. Management issues involve cultural intolerance towards diversity and disability in general, as well as lack of policies and processes that create a supportive environment for people with disabilities who wish to engage in flexible working arrangements.*

DOI: 10.4018/978-1-7998-4159-3.ch006

## INTRODUCTION

Over the last two decades, the work environment has changed significantly as a result of rapid digital transformation, the adoption of digital platforms, and the increase in new Information and Communication Technologies (ICTs) that support and facilitate work. Modern forms of work have become more flexible, increasingly more mobile, less structured and no longer restricted to a specific workplace or office location. Also, virtual teamwork has become a norm in the contemporary business environment bringing about radical change to organizational design that can draw on a dispersed multicultural workforce (Morley, Cromican, and Folan, 2015; Walsh, 2019). Apart from these changes, workplaces have become more *inclusive* towards a diverse workforce, which includes people with disabilities (Kulkarni, Boehm, & Basu, 2016; Meacham, Cavanagh, Shaw, & Bartram, 2017). These changes can be directly attributed to reforms, policies, and strategies related to the inclusion of a diverse and equitable workforce in the workplace, for example, the 2010-2020 European Disability Strategy (Moody, Saunders, Leber, Wójcik-Augustyniak, Szajczyk, & Rebernik, 2017).

In this study, 'disability' is the overarching term that covers impairments, activity limitations and participation restrictions resulting from problems with body function and structure (impairment), limitations to execute tasks/actions (activity restriction), and individual involvement in life situations (participation restriction) (World Health Organization, 2011). Disabled people's ability to engage in the workforce provides multiple benefits, including financial independence, a sense of self-satisfaction and improved physical and mental wellbeing (Stam, Sieben, Verbakel & De Graaf, 2015). Considering the increasing prevalence of flexible work, growth in co-working hubs and activity-based workspaces, and greater acceptance of diversity in the workplace, expectations are that organizations can make work and employment more accessible for people with disabilities. However, there are still countries that lack the necessary reforms and policies relating to a diverse workforce, especially people with disabilities in the workplace (George, 2017; Kiesel, Dezelar, & Lightfoot, 2019).

A recent Australian Government report indicates that there were 4.4 million Australians (or 17.7% of the population) with disabilities (Australian Bureau of Statistics, 2018). Also, only 53.4% of people with disabilities (those aged 15-64 years), participated in the Australian workforce in 2018, confirming very little change that has occurred in this area over the last two decades. This echoes sentiments contained in a 2011 World Health Organization report stating that despite modernization and change in the workplace, there has been a minimal alteration in global workforce participation by people with disabilities over the last 20 years (World Health Organization, 2011). Considering this gap, greater flexibility in work arrangements, work conditions and places where people can conduct their work, there is a lack of

Australian studies on antecedents that impact disabled people's access to flexible work. This study is based on two research questions:

1. *What are the issues and barriers that both managers and people with disabilities face with respect to flexible work arrangements*; and
2. *What are the antecedents for creating flexible work arrangements to include people with disabilities in the workforce?*

In response to these research questions, this study followed an interpretive qualitative research approach to identify various antecedents that are necessary to create a more inclusive work environment for people with disabilities. The chapter is structured as follows: the next section provides background literature on flexible work and disability. After that follows a description of the research approach, participants, and data collection. The subsequent section reports key themes arising from the data analysis followed by a discussion and theoretical model that describes the antecedents to the creation of flexible work arrangements for people with disabilities, and the significance of these antecedents in shaping a more digitally inclusive workforce for people with disabilities. The conclusion section discusses the limitations of the study, relevance for academia and practitioners, as well as avenues for further research.

## BACKGROUND LITERATURE

### Emerging Forms of Work

New developments in digitization, digital platforms and ICTs have brought about many changes in how individuals communicate, collaborate and conduct their work. New ICT applications and tools, Internet technologies and social media platforms significantly facilitate the sharing of information, knowledge and the ability to conduct service-related work from any location at any time (Bauer and Vocke, 2019; Pauleen, Campbell, Harmer & Intezari, 2015; Valenduc, 2019). Resulting from these changes, new flexible forms of work have emerged, including options such as job sharing, casual work, voucher-based work, ICT-based mobile work, portfolio work, crowd employment and collaborative self-employment, telecommuting and telework (Chiang and Lundgren, 2017). Flexible work is defined as *non-traditional work arrangements that take into account a person's personal needs and circumstances, enabling a worker to conduct some part of their working arrangements from home or in any other non-traditional workplace*. Some benefits of flexible work arrangements include a better work-life balance, lower levels of absence from the workplace or lower levels of stress (Allen, Golden & Shockley, 2015).

Historically, changes in work concentrated on telework or telecommuting, which allowed people more flexibility to work partly from home. Over time telework has evolved into other forms of work that includes different spaces and places of work, the home and the traditional office (Messenger, 2019). New forms of working from anywhere have become more flexible with many combinations of work arrangements and work patterns (Zenkteler, Darchen, Mateo-Babiano & Baffour, 2019); hence in this study, we have adopted the term 'flexible work' to cover the myriad terminology that refers to working from anywhere, including telework, telecommuting, remote work, distributed work, virtual work, distance work and anywhere work. Different forms of working anywhere have a variety of discourses on problems, issues, and opportunities associated with each working arrangement. In the literature, flexible working has been addressed from a variety of perspectives and across different disciplines including management, sociology, psychology, communications, transportation and infrastructure (Allen et al., 2015; Watson-Manheim & Swan, 2013; Fay & Kline, 2012; Zhu & Mason, 2014; Singh, Paleti, Jenkins & Bhat, 2013; Belanger, Watson-Manheim & Swan; Bosch-Sijtsema & Sivunen, 2012). Within the general area of management, the most familiar elements cited in literature that shapes flexible forms of work, involve technology support, the workspace (home office versus any other working place, such as activity-based work, smart hubs or co-working space), contractual arrangements (such as occasional work) and working hours (Messenger, 2019).

A 2017 study identified three elements that influence successful flexible work arrangements: 1) ICT support; 2) management trust; and 3) flexibility concerning where work is conducted in combination with extended work hours and a balance between time spent in the office and out of the office (Bosua, Kurnia, Gloet & Mendoza, 2017). This research found that the degree and extent of ICT support can significantly facilitate communication and collaboration between individuals and team members, managers and flexible workers (or teleworkers). This includes various virtual and networking tools that create an online presence and support the sharing of essential content such as electronic calendars, screen and virtual desktop tools and audio/video conferencing tools.

Earlier research has established that management trust in workers with a flexible work arrangement (teleworkers) is also an essential ingredient in a successful management-teleworker relationship. Some studies report on the importance of trust as an incentive for positive teleworker attitudes and work outcomes (Baruch, 2000; Cascio, 2000; Kowalski & Swanson, 2005). Trust between managers and teleworkers develops and evolves depending on the degree and extent of control managers have on teleworkers. In addition to trust, flexible work arrangements allowing for a balance between working both in and out of the traditional office appear to deliver more positive outcomes from both a management and teleworker perspective (Bosua et al., 2017; Halford, 2005; Peters, Den Dulk & de Ruitjer, 2010). Positive outcomes of such hybrid working arrangements relate to mentoring of younger employees, and the ability to learn from and socialize with workers who work full-time in the office.

Apart from eliminating traditional work boundaries related to the physical workplace, working hours and mode of communication, flexible work also brings about a shift in thinking on work-life-family balance, physical and emotional wellbeing and digital inclusion. A few studies report on the positive outcomes of flexible work arrangements that help parents balance work and family (Allen, Johnson, Kiburz & Shockley, 2013; Demeronti, Derks, Lieke & Bakker, 2014; Hilbrecht, Shaw, Johnson & Andrey, 2013), and caring for dependents (Hartig, Kylin & Johansson, 2007; Hilbrecht, Shaw, Johnson & Andrey, 2008). From a wellbeing perspective, previous studies have shown that the ability to work away from the office in a hybrid mode contributes to individual wellbeing, which in turns increases productivity (Bosua et al., 2017; Maruyama & Tietze, 2012).

Regarding digital inclusion, there is the promise that flexible ways of working may help to integrate a large community of workers who may not otherwise be taken up into the workforce, such as people with disabilities. Even though flexible work may open up new employment opportunities for these workers, there may also be constraints related to telework, the workplace environment and interactions with other workers, as well as the social inclusion of disabled workers. Several studies indicate that people with disabilities benefit greatly from flexible work arrangements allowing flexible work patterns that align with their circumstances and requirements (Baker, Linden, LaForce, Rutledge & Goughnour, 2018; Collier, 2016; Disability Case Study Research Consortium, 2011).

## Flexible Work and Access for People With Disabilities

Disability is "*...a condition that may restrict a person's mental, sensory, or mobility functions to undertake or perform a task in the same way as a person who does not have a disability. [this condition] does not mean that a person with a disability is unable to perform all the important requirements of a job and exceed the expectations of their employer*" (Disability Works Australia, n.d.). Disability varies in type, form, and severity, and is considered as a condition caused by accident, trauma, genetics or disease. The Australian Institute of Health and Welfare (AIHW, 2019) indicates that Australia has 4 million (or 18.5%) people that have some form of disability. Of these, 1.2 million have a profound or severe disability, with about 1,497,500 people with disabilities (about 8.8%) having difficulty in accessing employment and training which may also require workplace adjustments to enable employment. A 2016 Australian Government report identified several barriers to increasing workforce participation of people with disabilities (Australian Human Rights Commission, 2016). However, there is a lack of recent statistics that give a comprehensive indication of education and skill levels of people with disabilities, and there is almost no Australian literature that addresses the topic of flexible work for people with disabilities.

A study by Adams & Oldfield (2012) argues the need for disability equality in the workplace, stating that more considerable efforts should be made to provide better work and career opportunities for people with disabilities, as opposed to simply placing them in menial jobs with little or no opportunity for advancement. Research by Ali, Schur & Blanck (2011) suggests that the relatively low employment rates of people with disabilities are not related to a reluctance to work, but instead to the existence of a range of barriers to employment. Their study indicates that people with disabilities could perform a large proportion of job roles. At the same time, they also make the case that access to employment for people with disabilities can result in many positive outcomes. Recent research by Baker et al. (2018) suggests that attitudinal and social barriers based on stereotyping, ignorance or lack of knowledge are just as significant as physical barriers to the inclusion of people with disabilities in the workforce.

Technology is considered one means by which employment barriers for people with disabilities can be eradicated. Indeed, the proliferation of various forms of ICT has opened up a range of employment opportunities for people with disabilities, particularly flexible working, allowing people to work from any location without the need for commuting to work (Bilevičiūtė & Bilevičienė, 2010; Meshur & Ulusoy, 2013). There is undoubtedly potential for technology and its application through flexible working to create more opportunities for people with disabilities to join the workforce (Breaugh & Farabee, 2012). In noting the high levels of unemployment facing people with disabilities, Barnes (2012) argues for a rethinking of the meaning of *disability and work* to create higher levels of awareness and work allowing the inclusion of people with disabilities who wish to access the job market.

Apart from technology developments that can support flexible work practices, there are also other support mechanisms for people with disabilities in the workplace, i.e. *reasonable adjustments.* An updated version of the Australian Government's Disability Discrimination Act (1992) indicates that it is unlawful to discriminate against people with disabilities in the workplace. Employers are, therefore enforced to eradicate any form of discrimination and to make reasonable adjustments to the workplace to ensure that people with disabilities can be accommodated. Reasonable adjustments that employees make include a diverse set of adjustments to the workplace, falling into six categories:

1. Changed employee recruitment and selection procedures,
2. Modification to work premises, e.g. wheelchair ramps to access buildings or modification of toilets,
3. Job design and work schedule changes, e.g. new task and duty schedules that include different workers, shorter working hours or working from home arrangements,
4. Additional training and assistance, e.g. induction programs, mentors who supper people with mental disabilities, and
5. Modified equipment (e.g. ergonomic desks or physical equipment) that include ICT-enabled apps and tools to facilitate work, e.g. text speech conversion apps, assistive touch apps enabling smartphone device navigation and apps that assist people with limited dexterity or vision.

While studies from the mid-2000s are full of the promise of the potential of flexible working to eliminate employment barriers and integrate people with disabilities into the workplace, digital exclusion or a digital divide affects this group of workers (Atkinson, Black and Curtis, 2008). Bricout, Baker, Ward & Moon (2011) refer to this phenomenon as the *'disability divide,'* stating that the development and implementation of policies to address this situation is the most effective solution. Access to technology for the disabled is a significant issue, including affordability and general accessibility for the blind, deaf and those with other forms of disability (Baker & Moon 2008; Davison & Cotton, 2010). However, the significant recent growth in new universal assistive tools and technologies (e.g. mobile applications), as well as a reduction in the cost of workplace accommodations for disabled workers can increase employment accessibility.

In summary, there is an acute shortage of accurate recent statistics and in-depth research in Australia that explores the uptake of flexible working opportunities, the challenges and barriers, as well as positive and negative aspects relating to telework for people with disabilities and their employers. Hence, this research seeks to fill this gap by exploring: 1) the issues that impact on the uptake of flexible working opportunities for people with disabilities, and 2) the relationship between flexible working and digital exclusion of people with disabilities from the workforce.

## RESEARCH METHOD

Due to the exploratory nature of this study, a qualitative interpretive research design was chosen. The researchers were interested in the rich stories of HR and Diversity managers and people with disabilities in the field and therefore chose a narrative inquiry approach as the most appropriate method for this study (Connelly

& Clandinin, 1990; Creswell, 2007). Narrative inquiry allows data collection in the form of participant stories based on personal experiences through semi-structured and structured interviews. Narrative inquiry, therefore, first allows a participant to narrate his/her story effectively through storytelling to the listener/researcher. The data collection phase is then followed by data analysis, whereby the researcher aims to understand the lived storytelling experiences through content analysis and reflective accounts emerging from the data. Since the aim was to identify the antecedents for people with disabilities to access flexible work, the researchers focused on issues and problems managers and people with disabilities faced regarding access to flexible work arrangements (Creswell, Hanson, Clark, Plano & Morales, 2007).

Following ethics approval to conduct the study, senior HR, general and diversity managers and people with disabilities who had the experience of flexible work were approached through online sources and disability networks in Victoria and New South Wales in Australia and invited to participate in the study. Due to the sensitive nature of the issues discussed, most participants preferred to stay anonymous. Hence none of the participating organizations or participant details is revealed in this study.

## Data Collection

A three-pronged approach to data collection was followed, as illustrated in Figure 1. The research unfolded in three consecutive stages, as illustrated in Figure 1. The aim was to gather rich insights, stories, and experiences from various participants over six months, with each stage feeding into the next stage as outlined below:

*Figure 1. Stages of the research process*

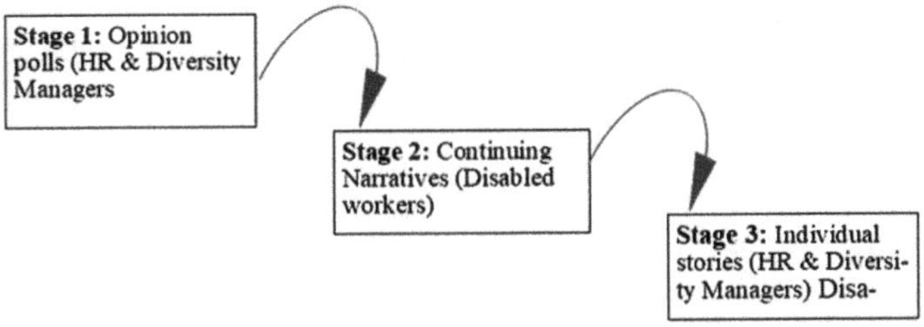


## Stage 1: Beginning the Story - Opinion Polls

This first stage 'tested the ground' on general management perspectives of disability and access to flexible work by opening up the conversation about disability and digital inclusion. Seventeen managers in key HR/Managerial and Diversity Management positions were cold-called Australia-wide, first briefed on the issue, then asked their opinions regarding the topic. Contact details were acquired through LinkedIn and personal networking. Five HR Managers, three 'HR/Diversity Managers,' seven Diversity Managers and two managers of employment agencies for the disabled, shared their views and experiences. The aim was to hear original stories that impacted on disabled workers' access to flexible work considering digitalization and changes in the workplace. Responses were instrumental in shaping in-depth data collection in Stages 2 and 3 of the study.

### Stage 2: Continuing Narrative Inquiry Through Stories of Working People With Disabilities

More data collection followed through the sharing of eight disabled workers' stories; six workers with physical disabilities and two with mental disabilities. Stages 2 and 3 were conducted either face-to-face or by telephone for some Stage 2 participants who preferred not to face the interviewer. The Stage 2 interviews were instrumental in gaining further insights and complementing the study. In addition to these interviews, seven case studies of disabled workers' experience in the workplace in various Australian organizations were included.

### Stage 3: Individual Stories From Senior HR/Diversity Managers

Finally, data were collected through listening to the stories and experiences of twelve senior HR/Diversity managers; eight from large- and four from medium-size organizations. Questions focused on disability and flexible work, focusing diversity strategies, recruitment for flexible work, inclusion criteria, the technologies used and provided by the organizations, training given, and issues and problems associated with the management of disabled workers engaged in flexible work arrangements.

## Data Analysis

The opinion poll data was interpreted and summarized as notes, while all the stories were audio-recorded with consent and transcribed verbatim. Field notes taken while listening to the stories were merged with the transcripts followed by the use of NVivo 10 to support a thematic data analysis using principles of open, axial and selective coding (Strauss and Corbin, 1998; Neuman 2014). Both researchers first worked independently through the dataset and later combined views and interpretations. Findings presented are classified as a set of major themes that arose from a more in-depth analysis and interpretation of the data.

## FINDINGS

Several themes relating to issues and barriers faced by both managers and people with disabilities were identified in the findings. Also, some antecedents that impacted access to flexible work for people with disabilities emerged from the data analysis. These themes and issues are outlined below.

### Theme 1: Barriers Impacting Access to Flexible Working Arrangements for People With Disabilities

Findings indicate that people with disabilities faced six key barriers affecting their access to flexible working arrangements:

#### Barrier i: Attitudinal Barriers From Employers

One interviewee indicated that there were still stiff employer attitudinal barriers that hindered access to and uptake of flexible working arrangements for people with disabilities:

*It's an attitudinal problem of employers - a prospective employer thinks here's a blind person who wants to work, how are they going to read? They don't think at all about options or possibilities. Other attitudes? They think there's a risk hiring someone who may not be able to read and write properly. Or risk associated with the possibility that a blind or visually impaired person might fall down in the office and get hurt – they might not want to take that risk. You know: I really like that person, but I don't want the liability. There is a range of different barriers, but that's just two examples.*

This person also mentioned that managers were not prepared to build flexibility into work packages to facilitate flexible work uptake by people with disabilities:

*We're even trying to build flexibility into enabled employment. For instance, an employer can choose how much work is in a job and how they want to pay. So you can pay by the day, and hire someone for five days of work. It doesn't matter how much he or she works in a day, but you are paying him or her for a block of work, and you are expecting certain results from that. Then we also have hourly arrangements, and for those people who might not know how they are going to manage.*

## Barrier ii: Physical and Infrastructure Barriers

People with disabilities faced physical and infrastructure barriers to access the physical workplace. Even though flexible working arrangements allowed working from home, some days required workers to be present in the office:

*Transport is an issue, because if you're blind or vision-impaired, you can't drive to the workplace, so you have to find another way to get there. That usually means public transport or a taxi. Taxis are prohibitive because they're costly. There is a government subsidy at state level to provide half-price taxi fares, but it's still a lot of money. So trying to get to work is complex, and you may have to take more than one form of public transport in your journey to work. So this helps to explain why 58% of blind and visually impaired people who want to work, can't get work.*

Another participant confirmed this barrier by stating:

*The biggest barrier to disability employment is potentially getting into the office (so accessibility), there are also attitudinal issues and capability issues. The biggest barrier is the employers themselves and how they think.*

## Barrier iii: Lack of Management Awareness About Funding for Reasonable Adjustments

Participants noted managers' unawareness of government disability funding support for reasonable adjustments. One participant said:

*Most [managers] think that it will cost thousands of dollars to make workplace modifications and adjustments, but that's not true.*

The same participant noted:

*I went to a conference recently, and they said that only 3% of employers know that there are funds out there to cover [reasonable] adjustments. In addition, they don't know that compensation and insurance are also covered by government funds. So we need to make employers more aware about all these resources. If they know about it, there are no more excuses for not hiring people with disabilities.*

## Barrier iv: Insufficient Flexible Working Arrangements, Processes and Access to Flexible Working Opportunities

Workers felt a need for more opportunities to work flexibly, particularly for recent university graduates, as two participants indicated:

*There is a need for more flexibility around job arrangements – there are a lot of people [with disabilities] who cannot work full time.*

*The government disability employment services don't do anything for well-educated people with disabilities who lack work experience.... we aren't expecting them to be treating people like charity cases and we are dealing with people who already have skills.*

The second participant further elaborated on the difficulty to hire people with disabilities:

*And even employers - they want to hire people with a disability, but the process is so complex.*

## Barrier v: Social Isolation and Interaction Misconceptions

One potential risk of flexible working is social isolation, and many managers were fearful of isolating people with disabilities, even more, when allowing them to work flexibly. Whereas this concern may be warranted, findings confirm that people with disabilities did not want to telework all the time, but also wanted to be present in the office some days. A vision-impaired worker commented that he enjoyed coming into the office despite the difficulty of moving around:

*It actually turns out that going into the office every day, stopping at the coffee shop and getting a coffee, 'see' the people in the building', that sort of social interaction is extremely important. People get to know me around the building, and I think I would find it challenging if circumstances were different at home and I had to miss out on that social interaction. So it's wonderful that I can come to work and have that social interaction.*

Another participant felt the same and wanted to work flexibly as well as be in the office:

*I would prefer the hybrid ...approach because I am very social and I like coming to the office, but I would probably like to do two days.*

### Barrier vi: Managers Lacked Trust in Disabled Workers

Managers often lacked trust that people with disabilities are experienced and *can do* a specific job while some managers believe work is only conducted when physically at one's desk. One graduate participant described how he could handle 70-80% of IT problems in a non-face-to-face role while another non-disabled worker attended to the other 20% of the problems face-to-face.

*My new manager felt I wasn't being utilized enough and both of us should be attending to computer issues in person. And it didn't last long because all the jobs took much, much longer. They tried using wireless phones, which in the late 1990s didn't work very well; the whole thing just fell apart. The whole perception was that because I was sitting at my desk, I wasn't working. So jobs that would have taken a minute to solve over the phone were now taking half an hour by the time we had gone to the person and dealt with the problem. It is interesting that there is this perception about getting work done when it might not appear to some managers that work is actually being done.*

The same worker described his current flexible working agreement and his ethical approach to his work:

*I'm very fortunate to have a very strong working relationship with my manager, but having said that, I don't think that would have been the case if I had always been teleworking. I think the fact that I worked in Sydney for two and a half years, I built up that trust and that rapport - and he could see what my work was like. I also built up relationships with my colleagues, so I was not just a faceless person on the Internet or on the other end of the phone. Also I make a very active effort when I go to Sydney, to get to know new people, that sort of thing.*

## Theme 2: Management Issues Related to Flexible Working Arrangements and People With Disabilities

Four key thematic management issues relating to culture and awareness arose from a more in-depth analysis of the manager interviews.

## Issue i: Cultural Intolerance and Lack of Disability Awareness

A large organization's HR/Diversity Manager outlined the issue of management responsibility to create cultural awareness and tolerance associated with disability in their organizations by sharing his organization's story:

*A disabled athlete, a meningococcal victim with 80% burns on her body, two prosthetic legs, and an artificial arm, joined our organization. She's a very switched on, intelligent girl has a degree and hasn't been able to get work. But being part of the [diversity] program I know what she has done, and she performs her job very well. We are trying to make it [diversity and disability awareness] a bit more universal across the organization, trying to break down the barriers a bit more. So I think you have to get people's awareness up in order for it [disability awareness] to be successful.*

A second Diversity manager emphasized 'tolerance' as part of disability awareness:

*Tolerance is one thing that workplaces need to develop further, and we also need to think more how to create a supportive work environment if we want to increase employment opportunities for the disabled generally and for everybody. So it's back to the universal design principle, that tools, equipment, and furnishings should be designed with everyone in mind. The same thing goes for awareness training; it should link more broadly to everyone and should include everyone in the organization. When you induct people, and you train people, this sort of stuff should be included.*

Another Diversity Manager described her new disability awareness training program for managers:

*We want to raise awareness in our workplace about what we felt was a pretty inclusive environment in a way. We also found there is a bit of a fear factor around disability in the workplace and when we thought about traditional methods of training, a lot of it is around discrimination, those sorts of things which scare people off. Many people think, oh I'm a bit uncomfortable about people with disabilities, so I'll just disengage and not talk to anyone.*

## Issue ii: Lack of Awareness of the Need For Flexible Working Arrangements to Support Diversity

Findings indicated the need for more access to flexible working arrangements and diversity:

*Managers need to raise access [to flexible working arrangements] and also increase awareness. They [managers] have all these unconscious biases that kick in, so my argument is: if you can shift the onus back to management - if I can do this, what do I need to get this done? People's working environments change from people with a disability to a mum who is just coming back into the workforce and wants to come back differently. Managers face that on a day-to-day basis... I'm seeing more and more large organizations getting into awareness – making that first step.*

Another manager supported this by stating:

*I actually think that physical disability and flexible working could be quite successful - the fact is that if a person has the physical capability to work with a computer, work via Skype for instance if they need to attend meetings and the like. If they are capable of producing the work that's required, working via a consultancy role, that sort of thing, then I think there is a lot of scope for people with physical disabilities to access telework... However, there has to be a balance between working at home or in another location - just to keep a connection if workers are physically capable of doing that.*

## Issue iii: Need for Diversity and Disability Policies and Processes

A senior manager spoke about the importance of policy regarding flexible work, diversity and people with disabilities:

*I'm a huge fan of [flexible]working, of working remotely and working differently. People battle with that whole concept of working from home, but working differently could be from anywhere. It's about the language, the communication, the policy – I often talk about two things – policy and a process that enables people to work remotely, to allow the company to support that: the tools, technology, leadership, guidance – no longer is a single line of sight management required.*

The same manager indicated how important it is for organizations to do the right thing for disabled workers:

*Organizations need to think what they do in their own organizational environment. Diversity, flexibility, mature age workers and disability are the major focus areas in most organizations. Managers should speak to people at the Australian Network on Disability. They help organizations think about and shape their views on diversity, and put systems in place to make sure that policy and vision is supported. Accessibility is an interesting policy, but sometimes it clashes with other policies, such as Occupational Health & Safety or heritage policies - I may not be able to dig up the front of an old bank building to make it accessible because it is heritage listed and therefore protected.*

A senior manager of another large organization emphasized the importance of policy:

*There has to be an inclusion policy - that is the first step. There are policies about equity and policies about positive discrimination, so people that say 'well I don't want to have a quota or a target,' which could be a policy. So in that case they would actively seek to fill positions through a disability employment agency.*

## Issue iv: The Need for a Changed Environment With Adjustments for Flexible Workers

A senior diversity manager indicated the importance of change regarding management sensitivity towards thinking about disability and creating (or adjusting) a suitable work environment:

*My argument is: how do we change the workforce, educating people by getting them to ask, how can I employ people differently? There is an organization I worked with that actually changed their interview and recruitment practices. So they ask questions like are you Aboriginal or Torres Strait Islander? But I cannot ask if you have a disability. What I can ask is 'Do you need any adjustments in order to perform this role'? I think telework should be available for all types of people, but if there is something that limits your ability to work at a certain level and standard, how do you adjust that work setting, be it the office or home? Management needs more communication skills; they need to set expectations, to adjust expectations.*

Another senior manager indicated how her organization educates supervisors about adjustments for disabilities:

*Supervisors get to work with me and learn how to interview someone with a disability, how you see them in the workplace, how to talk about reasonable adjustments in the job. When that happens on an individual level, it actually makes change possible. I often see amazing changes.... the thought process has to change, we are still in that medical model where disability is a problem, how much do I hear disability and problem in the same sentence?*

## Theme 3: Technological Aspects to Consider for Digital Inclusion

Modern ICTs no longer restrict flexible forms of work and can overcome barriers that previously prevented a disabled person from being employed. Two technology-related themes emerged as outlined below:

### Issue i: Technology Should Not Be an Excuse to Exclude People With Disabilities

Technology has advanced sufficiently to allow for full digital inclusion as the Diversity Manager of a large organization stated:

*We're in a better situation now than ten years ago [with technology support for mobile work] as cost has come down substantially. No longer can a company say it's too expensive for people to telework. You can work remotely with a laptop and phone these days. But it's more about labeling people who work differently. If they need special software, it's about asking the question, can I do that from home? Technology should not be a barrier these days, it should be an enabler.*

Another senior manager indicated that technology has evolved to support disabled teleworkers, but felt there were some gaps:

*With technology, there are still gaps; e.g., Skype is not suitable for deaf people using sign language, because of delays and drops outs the message gets muddled-up completely. We have got to address the universal design issues [of technology] because it often costs more to design things with everyone in mind. I think technology has improved the capacity for various disabled people to be more socially included.*

One of the managers who is disabled and also works flexibly further commented:

*I think technology is fantastic; I am as effective from home as when I'm here, because I've got access to everything. Obviously, the technology gets better and better all the time.*

### Issue ii: The Need to Provide Support for Assistive Technologies

Findings suggest that there was a need to provide support for introducing and using assistive technologies as one participant indicated:

*Technology can help with adjustments, but management needs to empower the situation.*

Another participant indicated that there are exciting advances in technology that can enable work for people with disabilities:

*More and more we're seeing issues around the actual technology. Logistics are being addressed around what needs to be set up in and around the office itself, which is an exciting step forward. Where the issues come in is that sometimes employers may not fully appreciate that the disabled can contribute fully to a job [through these technologies].*

This participant was excited about IT support for workers with disabilities:

*Exciting in the disability employment landscape is that many employers are moving to Cloud computing. One benefit of this is workplace flexibility [for disabled workers] - if you put your storage and infrastructure in the Cloud, people can use it anyplace, anytime. From a disability perspective its particularly exciting, because if you have particular needs; your employer doesn't have to worry about buying equipment and software. The disabled person might have a home-office set up perfectly well to meet their needs. So this flexibility of the Cloud offers future potential - it works in real-time.*

One disabled worker expressed his concern that managers and other employees don't understand what disabled workers 'can' do with technology:

*There has to be mechanisms so managers [and other workers] can understand what we [disabled workers] can do with technology. There is a government subsidy, so you can buy hardware and software, and the government will cover workplace modifications, so businesses don't have to fork out money for this.*

A disability employment agency manager mentioned that many different available technologies used creatively could enhance disabled worker productivity:

*I think the advent of and increased uptake of technology is really assisting a lot of disabled workers, especially those with sensory impairments. Suppose you're looking at someone who is hearing impaired rather than deaf - Bluetooth works really well to assist people like that, so they get clear phone contact. A lot to think about - just because someone is hard of hearing doesn't necessarily mean s/he can't do a lot of phone work these days. Someone with low vision that doesn't mean that they can't do a lot of computer-based work, it's incredible what's out there - and given a bit of training, it just opens up so many opportunities for the disabled. Then I think about technology assisting those people who have learning or have memory issues as well because they're able to use various applications to set up reminders for things, and so forth.*

Another disabled worker who occasionally works flexibly added his opinion on IT and management involvement by saying:

*But there are a lot more people now who are working from many different locations. Technology nowadays can support these different ways of work. From an employee [disability] point of view, we have the appropriate accommodation at home if we are working from home, but also need the trust from the employer and the right technology to do the job.*

## DISCUSSION

This study posed two research questions:

1. *What are the issues and barriers that both managers and people with disabilities face with respect to flexible work arrangements*; and
2. *What are the antecedents for creating flexible work arrangements to include people with disabilities in the workforce?*

In response to the research questions, an interpretation of the empirical evidence identified three categories of issues that concern access to work for people with disabilities: disability worker issues, managerial issues and technology issues. Numerous studies on flexible working confirm multiple management and teleworker barriers that impact on flexible work arrangements for non-disabled workers, i.e. manager trust and additional efforts to manage teleworkers, technology support, synergy in teamwork, social isolation or creating a performance-oriented culture. (Bailey & Kurland, 2002; Baruch, 2000; Maruyama & Tietze, 2012).

Our study confirms that people with disabilities face these challenges as well as many more unique challenges such as access to flexible work arrangements, an accepting and welcoming cultural work environment, funding of reasonable adjustments to facilitate physical office access and IT support for work, unconscious bias, social isolation misconceptions and lack of management trust in capabilities to conduct work. Telework can facilitate the digital inclusion of workers with disabilities, thus leading to a range of positive outcomes.

One pertinent barrier that emerged from stories shared by disabled workers was limited access to flexible working roles/arrangements, and that they *would welcome an opportunity to prove themselves in the workplace*. Hence, people with disabilities are keen to gain management trust in their capabilities, contribute to the work in general and would embrace the opportunity to be part of any organization's workforce. Feeling a sense of exclusion as a natural consequence of disability, these workers are more than willing to overcome many of the obstacles associated with a physical disability to contribute to the working environment, i.e. commuting to the workplace, being part of work culture, team or workgroup, spending time in the office to build employer and collegial trust, and demonstrating individual accountability and loyalty. Once the necessary management trust has developed, and there are appropriate communication channels in place enabled by assistive technologies, managers can grant workers with disabilities some flexibility in the form of hybrid or occasional flexible work arrangements. This would foster work-life balance, in particular for those who have families or are unable to work in more traditional, office-based environments. Disabled workers were most willing to bear the initial discomfort associated with physical access to the workplace to build collegial and manager trust as an antecedent to a more formal telework arrangement.

*Figure 2. Antecedents of successful flexible working arrangements to support people with disabilities*

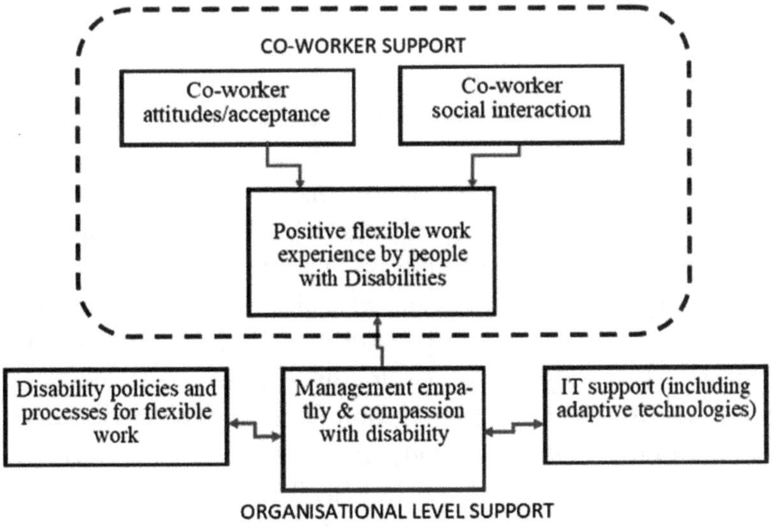

One other barrier evident from the findings involves task-related and non-task related workplace adjustments and assistive technologies to facilitate and support access to and the execution of work (Riches & Green, 2003). Findings indicate that managers were often uninformed about requirements, eligibility, and type of support provided by the Australian Government in this regard. Moreover, most workers indicated they already had assistive technologies and devices they used in their everyday life activities that could be brought into the workplace to support and enable work. Considering recent advances in technology device usage by mobile workers, some reasonable adjustments may be necessary. These adjustments may not be the full responsibility of the organization as assistive tools and devices could be considered as additions to an organization's existing suite of bring-your-own-devices (BYOD) used by its non-disabled workers. Therefore, managers need to become more informed regarding categories of assistive technologies and type of adjustments required to accommodate workers with disabilities and government funding in this regard.

In response to the first research question, our findings suggest a clear *management responsibility,* particularly the need to treat disability as part of the broader *diversity* category as one of the diversity managers sensibly commented. Considering the limited change in workforce participation by people with disabilities over recent years in Australia, there is an imminent need for workplace reform in the area of social equity and balance for diversity in the workplace. Moreover, as Angeloni (2013) has suggested, more integrated and holistic approaches to disability management are required. Organizations need to review and adjust their cultural make-up to identify how and to what extent elements related to bias towards diversity could be eradicated. This calls for several changes at different levels. First, at the employee and employer level, tolerance and acceptance need to be cultivated, equity policies need to be reviewed and disseminated, and management needs to be open-minded regarding recruitment practices focused on diversity. Secondly, job and task structures need to be revisited or redesigned as part of a broader reasonable adjustment strategy to match specific and unique worker skills with tasks. This may impact on work allocation and corresponding remuneration associated with different tasks or categories of work. Finally, more comprehensive policies and Occupational Health & Safety arrangements should be required to cater for diversity and equity in the workplace.

This study clearly illustrates that flexible work brings about advantages for people with disabilities. While the study has not focused on specific disabilities, this study's results confirm that benefits of flexible work arrangements extend to people with various forms of physical, psychological and neurological problems, as well as those with chronic issues, fatigue, and pain. For those with chronic forms of illness or disability, the flexibility of work allows a better balance between periods of illness and the capacity to work. Flexible work may also reduce the social stigma associated with a disability because people are judged more by the work they do, rather than by their disability.

In reflecting on the study and its outcomes, one key issue that was notable in the study but has not been explicitly addressed is the growth in mental issues that can lead to disability in the workplace. Mental and chronic physical illness lead to disabilities that significantly impact a worker's access to work and his or her productivity (Dewa and Lin, 2000). Dewa and Lin indicate that the World Health Organisation (WHO) predicted that mental illness would be the second most important area of global disease concern in the 21st century. Our findings also indicate that, due to the growth in mental illness worldwide, there are reasons for concern as organizations also need to provide reasonable accommodations for this category of workers. Since this study did not focus on mental health issues, in particular, this area may be an interesting avenue for further research.

In conclusion, the study highlights that the worlds of managers and workers with disabilities are not yet adequately aligned nor transparent, i.e. managers do not yet fully understand the needs and potential that people with disabilities can contribute to the workplace. Also, workers with disabilities have not yet expressed what they need and can deliver to be part of the workforce. Hence, there is a need for these groups to open up a discourse in this regard. Advocacy groups may play a more prominent role to support this discourse, while more networking activities are required to link different groups, role players, stakeholders, and agencies.

## CONCLUSION

This study is the first exploratory research that investigates the relationship between anywhere working and disability in Australia and identifies multiple barriers and issues associated with the uptake of flexible working arrangements for people with disabilities. The study has some limitations. First, the study was qualitative and relatively small, considering the number of participants. Also, the study was primarily focused on issues pertaining to workers with physical disabilities, as opposed to other forms of disability. In addition, the study did not consider specific aspects associated with workplace adjustments and equity from a policy and legal perspective. A larger, more in-depth quantitative study needs to be conducted that is more focused on different categories of disability and different attributes that relate to diversity and access to flexible working arrangements concerning management and workers. Future work may, therefore, use the outcomes of this study as a basis for a quantitative study that involves a large-scale survey. Such a study may shed more light on best practices to accommodate diverse workers, including people with disabilities. Best practices regarding reasonable adjustments, specific IT use, task and job division and allocation aspects associated with diversity in the workplace in general, as well as issues relating more specifically to flexible work opportunities for people with disabilities would also be useful.

## REFERENCES

Adams, L., & Oldfield, K. (2012). Opening up work: The views of disabled people and people with long-term health conditions. *IFF Research.* https://www.equalityhumanrights.com/sites/default/files/research_report_77_opening_up_work.pdf

Alexopoulos, A. N., & Buckley, F. (2013). What trust matters when: The temporal value of professional and personal trust for effective knowledge transfer. *Group & Organization Management*, *38*(3), 361–391. doi:10.1177/1059601113488939

Ali, M., Schur, L., & Blanck, P. (2011). What types of jobs do people with disabilities want? *Journal of Occupational Rehabilitation*, *21*(2), 199–210. doi:10.100710926-010-9266-0 PMID:20924777

Allen, T., Golden, T., & Shockley, K. (2015). How Effective Is Telecommuting? *Assessing the Status of Our Scientific Findings Psychological Science in the Public Interest, 16*(2). https://journals.sagepub.com/stoken/rbtfl/EnhOwEhELZ4al/ful

Allen, T. D., Johnson, R. C., Kiburz, K. M., & Shockley, K. M. (2013). Work–family conflict and flexible work arrangements: Deconstructing flexibility. *Personnel Psychology*, *66*(2), 345–376. doi:10.1111/peps.12012

Anderson, J., & Douma, F. (2009). *Telework for Workers with Disabilities Pilot Projects Synthesis Report (under sub-contract to CESSI for the Office of Disability Employment Policy, U.S. Department of Labor).* Minneapolis, MN. Online resource, accessed December 29, 2019, from https://www.dol.gov/odep/research/TeleworkSynthesisReport.pdf

Angeloni, S. (2013). Integrated Disability Management: An interdisciplinary and holistic approach. *SAGE Open*, *3*(4), 1–15. doi:10.1177/2158244013510303

Australian Bureau of Statistics 4430.0. (2018). *Disability, Ageing and Carers, Australia: Summary of Findings, 2018).* https://www.abs.gov.au/ausstats/abs@.nsf/Lookup/4430.0main+features12018

Australian Human Rights Commission. (2016) *Willing to Work National Inquiry into Employment Discrimination Against Older Australians and Australians with Disability*. https://www.humanrights.gov.au/sites/default/files/document/publication/WTW_2016_Full_Report_AHRC_ac.pdf

Australian Institute of Health and Welfare (AIHW). (2019). *People with disability in Australia*. https://www.aihw.gov.au/reports/disability/people-with-disability-in-australia

Baker, P., & Moon, N. (2008, Fall). Wireless Technologies and Accessibility for People With Disabilities: Findings from A Policy Research Instrument. *Journal of Assistive Technologies*, *20*(3). PMID:18939655

Baker, P. M., Linden, M. A., LaForce, S. S., Rutledge, J., & Goughnour, K. P. (2018). Barriers to employment participation of individuals with disabilities: Addressing the impact of employer (mis) perception and policy. *The American Behavioral Scientist*, *62*(5), 657–675. doi:10.1177/0002764218768868

Barnes, C. (2012). Rethinking Disability, Work and Welfare. *Sociology Compass*, *6*(6), 472–484. doi:10.1111/j.1751-9020.2012.00464.x

Bauer, W., & Vocke, X. (2019). Work in the Age of Artificial Intelligence – Challenges and Potentials for the Design of New Forms of Human-Machine Interaction. *International Conference on Applied Human Factors and Ergonomics*, 493-501.

Bayrak, T. (2012). IT support for Telecommuting Workforce. *Telematics and Informatics*, *29*(3), 286–293. doi:10.1016/j.tele.2011.10.002

Bélanger, F., Watson-Manheim, M. B., & Swan, B. R. (2013). A multi-level socio-technical systems telecommuting framework. *Behaviour & Information Technology*, *32*(12), 1257–1279. doi:10.1080/0144929X.2012.705894

Bilevičiūtė, E., & Bilevičienė, T. (2010). Telework organization model as method of development of disabled persons' employment quality. *Perspectives of Innovations, Economics and Business*, *2*(5), 71–74. doi:10.15208/pieb.2010.53

Blok, M. M., Groenesteijn, L., Schelvis, R., & Vink, P. (2012). New ways of working: Does flexibility in time and location of work change work behavior and affect business outcomes? *Work (Reading, Mass.)*, *41*, 5075–5080. doi:10.3233/WOR-2012-0800-5075 PMID:22317507

Bosch-Sijtsema, P. M., & Sivunen, A. (2013). Professional virtual worlds supporting computer-mediated communication, collaboration, and learning in geographically distributed contexts. *IEEE Transactions on Professional Communication, 56*(2), 160–175. doi:10.1109/TPC.2012.2237256

Bosua, R., Kurnia, S., Gloet, M., & Mendoza, A. (2017). Telework Impact on Productivity and Wellbeing: an Australian Study. In J. Choudrie, S. Kurnia, & P. Tastsou (Eds.), *Social Inclusion and Usability of ICT-enabled Services*. Taylor and Francis Group. doi:10.4324/9781315677316-10

Chiang, J., & Lundgren, A. (2017). *What is the Evolution of Flexible Work in Corporations and What are the Key Trends?* Available from: https://digitalcommons.ilr.cornell.edu/student/168

Collier, D. (2016). *Inclusion of people with disabilities in the workplace: Best practices for HR professionals.* Retrieved 19 December 2019 from Cornell University, ILR School site: https://digitalcommons.ilr.cornell.edu/student/142

Connelly, F. M., & Clandinin, D. J. (1990). Stories of experience and narrative inquiry. *Educational Researcher, 19*(5), 2–14. doi:10.3102/0013189X019005002

Creswell, J. W. (2007). *Qualitative inquiry and research design: choosing among five approaches*. Sage.

Creswell, J. W., Hanson, W. E., Clark Plano, V. L., & Morales, A. (2007). Qualitative research designs: Selection and implementation. *The Counseling Psychologist, 35*(2), 236–264. doi:10.1177/0011000006287390

Davison, E., & Cotton, S. (2010). *Connection Disparities: The Importance of Broadband Connections in Understanding Today's Digital Divide. In Overcoming Digital Divides: Constructing an Equitable and Competitive Information Society*. IGI Global.

Demerouti, E., Derks, D., Lieke, L., & Bakker, A. B. (2014). New ways of working: Impact on working conditions, work–family balance, and wellbeing. In *The impact of ICT on quality of working life* (pp. 123–141). Springer Netherlands. doi:10.1007/978-94-017-8854-0_8

Dewa, C. S., & Lin, E. (2000). Chronic physical illness, psychiatric disorder and disability in the workplace. *Social Science & Medicine, 51*(1), 41–50. doi:10.1016/S0277-9536(99)00431-1 PMID:10817467

Disability Discrimination Act (DDA). (1992). https://www.humanrights.gov.au/sites/default/files/GPGB_disability_discrimination.pdf

Disability Works Australia. (2015). http://www.dwa.org.au/whatisadisability.htm

Disability Works Australia, Ltd. (n.d.). http://www.dwa.org.au/whatisadisability.htm

Fay, M. J., & Kline, S. L. (2012). The influence of informal communication on organizational identification and commitment in the context of high-intensity telecommuting. *The Southern Communication Journal*, *77*(1), 61–76. doi:10.1080/1041794x.2011.582921

George, V. (2017). A new approach to disability in the workplace. *Pursuit*. Accessed on 1 December 2019, from: https://pursuit.unimelb.edu.au/articles/a-new-approach-to-disability-in-the-workplace

Kiesel, L. R., Dezelar, S., & Lightfoot, E. (2019). Equity in social work employment: Opportunity and challenge for social workers with disabilities in the United States. *Disability & Society*, *34*(9-10), 1399–1418. Advance online publication. doi:10.1080/09687599.2018.1561354

Kulkarni, M., Boehm, S. A., & Basu, S. (2016). Workplace inclusion of persons with a disability: Comparison of Indian and German multinationals. *Equality, Diversity and Inclusion*, *35*(7/8), 397–414. doi:10.1108/EDI-08-2016-0066

Meacham, H., Cavanagh, J., Shaw, A., & Bartram, T. (2017). HRM practices that support the employment and social inclusion of workers with an intellectual disability. *Personnel Review*, *46*(8), 1475–1492. doi:10.1108/PR-05-2016-0105

Meshur, A., & Ulusoy, C. (2013). Attitudes of people with disabilities towards teleworking as an employment opportunity: IT modelling in terms of the Turkish case. *African Journal of Business Management*, *7*(4), 227–243.

Messenger, J. C. (2019). *Telework in the 21st Century: An Evolutionary Perspective: The ILO Future of Work Series*. ElgarOnline., doi:10.4337/9781789903751

Moody, L., Saunders, J., Leber, M., Wójcik-Augustyniak, M., Szajczyk, M., & Rebernik, N. (2017). An exploratory study of barriers to inclusion in the European workplace. *Disability and Rehabilitation*, *39*(20), 2047–2054. doi:10.1080/09638288.2016.1217072 PMID:27665671

Morley, S., Cromican, K., & Folan, P. (2015). An analysis of virtual team characteristics: A model for virtual project managers. *Journal of Technology Management & Innovation*, *10*(1).

Neuman, W. L. (2014). *Social Research Methods: Qualitative and Quantitative Approaches* (7th ed.). Pearson.

Pauleen, D., Campbell, J., Harmer, B., & Intezari, A. (2015). Making Sense of Mobile Technology. *Sage Open, 5*(2).

Peters, P., Den Dulk, L., & de Ruijter, J. (2010). May I work from home? View of the employment relationship reflected in line managers' telework attitudes in six financial-sector organizations. *Equality, Diversity and Inclusion, 29*(5), 517–531. doi:10.1108/02610151011052799

Piaggesi, D., Castelnovo, W., & Battistella, R. (2013). *ICT for Social Inclusion and Equal Opportunities. E-Government Implementation and Practice in Developing Countries: 147*. IGI Global.

Powell, A., & Craig, L. (2015). Gender differences in working at home and time use *patterns*: Evidence from Australia. *Work, Employment and Society, 29*(4), 571–589. doi:10.1177/0950017014568140

Randolph, D. S. (2004). Predicting the effect of disability on employment status and income. *Work (Reading, Mass.), 23*(3), 257–266. PMID:15579934

Riches, V. C., & Green, V. A. (2003). Social integration in the workplace for people with disabilities: An Australian perspective. *Journal of Vocational Rehabilitation, 19*, 127–142.

Singh, P., Paleti, R., Jenkins, S., & Bhat, C. R. (2013). On modeling telecommuting behavior: Option, choice, and frequency. *Transportation, 40*(2), 373–396. doi:10.100711116-012-9429-2

Solovieva, T. I., & Walls, R. T. (2013). Implications of Workplace Accommodations for Persons with Disabilities. *Journal of Workplace Behavioral Health, 28*(3), 192–211. doi:10.1080/15555240.2013.808079

Stam, K., Sieben, I., Verbakel, E., & De Graaf, P. M. (2015). Employment status and subjective wellbeing: The role of the social norm to work. *Work, Employment and Society, 29*, 1–25.

Strauss, A., & Corbin, J. (1998). *Basics of Qualitative Research Techniques and Procedures for Developing Grounded Theory* (2nd ed.). Sage Publications.

Valenduc, G. (2019). New Forms of Work and Employment in the Digital Economy. In A. Serrano-Pascual & M. Jepson (Eds.), *The Deconstruction of Employment as a Political Question*. Palgrave Macmillan. doi:10.1007/978-3-319-93617-8_3

Walsh, T. (2019). Virtual Team Success with the Power of Technology Advancements. In *Advances in the Technology of Managing People: Contemporary Issues in Business* (pp. 99–107). Emerald Publishing Limited. doi:10.1108/978-1-78973-073-920191009

World Health Organization (WHO). (2011). *International Classification of Functioning, Disability and Health*. ICF.

Zenkteler, M., Darchen, S., Mateo-Babiano, I. & Baffour, B. (2019). Home-based work in cities: in search of an appropriate urban planning response. *Futures*. .futures.2019.102494 doi:10/1016/j

Zhu, P., & Mason, S. G. (2014). The impact of telecommuting on personal vehicle usage and environmental sustainability. *International Journal of Environmental Science and Technology*, *11*(8), 2185–2200. doi:10.100713762-014-0556-5

## KEY TERMS AND DEFINITIONS

**Digital Inclusion:** Digital inclusion is social inclusion in the 21st century that ensures individuals and disadvantaged groups have access to, and skills to use, Information and Communication Technologies (ICTs) and are therefore able to participate in and benefit from today's growing knowledge and information society.

**Disability:** Disability can take many forms, be temporary, total or partial, lifelong, acquired, visible or invisible. In this study 'disability' is the overarching term that covers impairments, activity limitations and participation restrictions resulting from problems with body function and structure (impairment), limitations to execute tasks/actions (activity restriction), and individual involvement in life situations (participation restriction) (World Health Organization, 2011).

**Diversity:** Refers to an understanding that every individual is unique and recognizing our individual differences. These can be along the dimensions of race, ethnicity, gender, sexual orientation, socio-economic status, age, physical abilities, religious beliefs, political beliefs, or other ideologies.

**Flexible Working:** Non-traditional work arrangements that take into account a person's personal needs and circumstances, enabling a worker to conduct some part of their working arrangements from home or in any other non-traditional workplace.

**Reasonable Adjustments:** Refers to changes in the working environment allowing people with disabilities to work more productively and safely. These adjustments are usually physical, IT-enabled or ICT tools. Reasonable adjustments are usually suggested to or requested from an employer by the person who has a disability.

# Section 3

# Design and Context of Anywhere Working

# Chapter 7
# Design for the Future of Work:
## A Theoretical Framework for Coworking Space Design

**Umut Tuğlu Karslı**
https://orcid.org/0000-0002-6573-5433
*Istanbul University, Turkey*

## ABSTRACT

*The paradigm shift in work dynamics in the digital age leads the evolution of how and where people work. Knowledge workers adopt more flexible working styles: they connect to their laptops and work anywhere. The main disadvantage of this way of working is social isolation. Creative industries often require interdisciplinary interaction and collaboration. Coworking spaces have emerged in order to remove this isolation and create a third place apart from home and office. These spaces have been studied by disciplines such as economics, work psychology, and geography but studies on their spatial characteristics are limited. The aim of the chapter is to propose a conceptual framework to identify design implications for the coworking spaces in terms of spatial preferences of users. Accordingly, literature related to changing work dynamics and workplaces, rise of coworking spaces, and coworking space typology are discussed. The conclusion of the chapter is to propose design implications, which will inform designers, researchers, and managers on best practice for coworking space design.*

DOI: 10.4018/978-1-7998-4159-3.ch007

## INTRODUCTION

Knowledge work was mostly performed in offices in the past. However, globalization and advances in information technologies have changed the dynamics of work and the physical spaces where work is done; consequently new ways of anywhere working (multi-locational, distributed, mobile, virtual) have emerged (Kojo and Nenonen, 2016). As one of the locations that host these new ways of working, "coworking spaces" are shared workplaces used by knowledge workers who are often freelancers and at different levels of expertise in the vast area of the information industry. Coworking spaces are "third places", where workers seek a sense of socialization, opportunities for serendipity, and networking encounters to increase their social capital (Leclercq-Vandelannoitte and Isaac, 2016). Practically conceived as office-renting facilities where workers hire a desk and a Wi-Fi connection, these are places where independent professionals live their daily routines side-by-side with professional peers, mainly working in the same sector (Gandini, 2015). Beyond physical space, coworking spaces represent a new type of business organization and lifestyle.

The literature related to these spaces indicates that this is a multifaceted phenomenon investigated by disciplines like sociology, anthropology, psychology, geography, economy and urban planning. Sociologists and anthropologists (Jones et al., 2009; Gandini, 2015) evaluate the impact of coworking spaces on the careers and business lives of coworkers, the innovative role of these spaces in labor policies, and the place of proximity in information sharing. Geographers (Moriset, 2013) analyze this phenomenon based on its formation and the role of public policies in supporting these formations. Mariotti et al. (2017) evaluate coworking spaces in terms of their interaction with urban planning. Leclercq-Vandelannoitte and Isaac (2016) address coworking spaces from a management perspective, and Schmidt and Brinks (2017) examine these spaces in order to contribute to conceptualizing the relation of communities and space.

On the other hand, there are limited studies on these spaces concerning the disciplines of architecture and design. In one of these studies, Wagner and Watch (2017) suggest that designers and architects are increasingly tasked to redesign places to do more than simply accommodate innovation-centered activities; their main goals are to facilitate collaboration and to create communities and serendipitous encounters. Their research raises several design implications for innovation spaces. Weijs-Perrée et al. (2019) analyze user preferences for coworking space characteristics. Their research provides valuable data for managers of coworking spaces about coworker preferences by offering coworking spaces "with good accessibility, home-like interior and a semi-open layout".

It is important to draw a theoretical framework for coworking space design (such as café-office, experimentation lab, learning center, work lab, airport office) to inform designers, owners and operators of these spaces. User profiles also vary according to coworking space typology. User-oriented design studies that have recently emerged in the field of design suggest that the user factor is one of the most important components of design (Oygur and McCoy, 2011; Sanoff, 2006). In this context, this chapter proposes a conceptual framework to identify design implications for coworking spaces in terms of spatial requirements of users. The chapter first examines changing work dynamics and workplaces, which involve the evolution of coworking spaces as an architectural reflection of the change in business organizations. It analyzes the rise of coworking spaces, which reveals the socio-economic factors that impact the development of coworking spaces. The literature review on coworking space typology, which includes classifications of coworking spaces described by different disciplines, is discussed and user profile, user preferences and design implications which will inform designers, researchers and managers on the best practice for coworking space design are determined in the conclusion of the chapter.

## CHANGING WORK DYNAMICS AND WORKPLACES

Workplaces have evolved depending on changes in work organizations and working styles in the historical process. Agricultural societies created workplaces like barns, storerooms and granaries. The transition into industrial societies brought the need for office spaces; consequently, workshops and factories were built in rural areas and skyscrapers were built in city centers. Workplaces have evolved under the influence of information technologies, and they have now progressed beyond office buildings through alternative work methods created by the knowledge society and come to describe any place that houses workers (Çimen, 2008).

In the 19$^{th}$ century, a large number of office buildings were constructed in the U.S., for the work function as a physical reflection of the divergence of living and working spaces. In this period, the design of office spaces is usually guided by general typologies (e.g. cellular office, open plan office, group office) to describe the level of interactions in offices (Sailer et al., 2009). The biggest difference between these plan types is the layout that involves varied arrangements of spaces (offices, core and corridor). Duffy (1997) describes ways of working depending on the level of autonomy and interaction of staff and suggests four types of offices: those hosting individual processes (*hive*), concentrated study (*cell*), group processes (*den*) and transactional processes (*club*).

Workspaces started to become independent from physical space in the post-Fordist period. Postmodernism has brought on many changes in economic, socio-cultural and political areas during the globalization period (Erdoğan, 2012). The phenomenon of "time-space compression" emerged during this period of the capitalist world, changing the time dimension of the work process, and growing costs of communication and transportation led to the expansion of this process to a broader and more diverse space (Leclercq-Vandelannoitte and Isaac, 2016). In the information society, people who work in the production, processing, development, marketing, utilization and distribution of information are described as "knowledge workers" (Ergin, 2012). In the middle of the 20th century, popularization of technological breakthroughs like the internet, wireless communication, laptop computers, indicated that conventional workspaces would lose their former function (Örs, 2001). In this context, the digital age and creative economies have brought about new ways of working and new concepts on workspaces. "Free address", "hot-desking", "hoteling" and "shared offices" are office types that use open workspaces shared by two or more users (Erdener, 1996). "Tele-office", "satellite office", "virtual office", "home-office" and "mobile office" are working styles that stand for offices physically free of traditional restrictions like time, space, job definitions and job titles.

In addition to these new concepts describing workspaces in the digital age, Myerson and Ross (2003) classified new workspaces that emerged in the 21st century as "narrative", "nodal", "neighborly" and "nomadic" offices. For nomadic workers, any time and any space they can connect to the network is a workspace. "Coworking spaces" are the new offices of the digital age where nomadic workers can avoid social isolation, work with others, and interact with individuals of the same professional background.

## RISE OF COWORKING SPACES

DeKoven used the term "coworking", for the first time as a meeting facilitation technique in the American Journal of Play. This term was later used to describe a workspace where work meetings and computer-aided coworking can be performed (Curaoğlu and Demirbaş, 2017). This way of working originated as a "third method" to work besides from standard work-life in a conventional, well-delimited workplace and a free work-life where workers are isolated as they work at home. This third method was named "*coworking*" without a hyphen to set it apart from "*coworking*", which means working together closely on a job, as an indication of working individually in a shared environment (Gandini, 2015). People who work in spaces that host this way of working initially worked at home or a nearby café. Disadvantages of working at home or a café are social isolation and distractions. Individuals with different backgrounds get together in various and more or less public environments, meet other people, share information and learn (Kojo and Nenonen, 2016). There is no recognized academic description of the concept of coworking. However, the term expresses "a new form of work organization that creates cooperation opportunities and encourages a sense of community in a shared space, and gathers employees of different companies and even freelancers with different profiles and objectives." This new type of work organization has led to a change in workspaces and methods of work and collaboration. Workers create these spaces together, reflecting the great importance they place on autonomy and empowerment and are now disrupting classic models of work organization (Leclercq-Vandelannoitte and Isaac, 2016).

The phenomenon of coworking born in San Francisco in 2005 reached 2498 spaces until mid-2013, and, according to Deskmag, grew 100% annually between 2007 and 2012 (Moriset, 2013). The growth of information and communication technologies contributed to the development of knowledge-based, creative and digital economies, and thereby the development of information society, which changed working methods fundamentally (Mariotti et al., 2017). A literature review on the rise of coworking spaces shows that the phenomenon is associated with three interconnected tendencies namely, economic (global economic crisis), social (rise of the creative class) and technological (work virtualization). These tendencies have led to significant changes in the production and consumption of spaces allocated to creative work.

## Global Economic Crisis

The oil crisis that occurred in the U.S. in the 1970s made it more difficult for workers to go to the office on a daily basis; instead, workers curbed gasoline consumption by working on a computer at home or anywhere closer to home. Virtual workers went to the office in person a few days a week in full-time or part-time employment. This reduced the number of workers in centralized offices and minimized rent costs (Kış, 2009). With the change in working and business relationships of the capitalist economy, workers left conventional tools and ways of working and were subjected to work organizations that offered them a new social identity. These systems generally involve a less organized process that reduces the fact of working, from a societal phenomenon into the individual scale (Erdoğan, 2012).

The emergence of coworking dates to the economic stagnation of the early 1990s. The recession forced the industry to transform 25-year corporate lease contracts into economically more flexible usage solutions with service orientation, leading to a considerable shift in the property procurement sector. New shared areas appeared where individuals and small groups gather and work as a community, mostly paid on a subscription basis and used on a daily, weekly or monthly basis. These spaces offer a "community" workspace with shared services, allowing individuals and small groups to share ideas and reciprocally support each other's ideas (Kojo and Nenonen, 2016).

The digital age has given a new meaning to the term "community." This term is used to describe digital working models ascribed to the sharing economy, which involves participation without ownership (for instance, carpooling) and contribution without necessarily expecting monetary compensation. In this sense, the term "community" now expresses the presence of other people in other places interested in similar practices rather than a social cluster of close-knit people. In this context, new environments like coworking spaces, fabrication labs and maker spaces emerged for business, entrepreneurship and innovation activities on a global scale (Schmidt and Brinks, 2017).

Coworking spaces have seen exponential growth since the first example was established by Brad Neuberg in San Francisco in 2005. Although there is an overenthusiastic interpretation of the rise of the creative class (Florida, 2002), jobs often reflect non-standard employment patterns that offer a nomadic and inconsistent work life. Coworking spaces offer benefits such as knowledge transfer, cooperation and business opportunities despite risks associated with coworking, which is exploited in terms of brandization, marketing and trade (Mariotti et al., 2017).

According to Avdikos and Kalogeresis (2017), coworking spaces emerged as a response to the gradual collapse of the stable employment paradigm and the increasingly unstable working conditions during the global economic crisis and the following stagnation. Coworking spaces are a result of the blurring of borders between technological, economic and social categories and the hybridization process. Although the sustainability and growth potential of such spaces can be questioned, it is a fact that they have great importance in the workplace landscape of business metropolises (Moriset, 2013).

## Rise of the Creative Class

The emergence of the information economy lit the fuse of the third industrial revolution, which saw gravitation towards tasks that require more intuition, creativity, reasoning, and initiative. Brainpower replaced the conventional physical workforce. Therefore, specific resources became more fundamental compared to others, and intellectual or cognitive capital replaced physical capital (Leclercq-Vandelannoitte and Isaac, 2016). In the eyes of the public, the word "creative" describes people with artistic skills in the content production sectors (music, art, architecture, design, fashion, advertising, media and entertainment). However, the actual concept of Florida's (2012) creative class is much larger and includes software professionals, engineers, scientists, lawyers and consultants. In the context of the globalized economy and competition, creative individuals and innovative industries were assigned as the driving forces of sustainable economic growth and welfare (Moriset, 2013).

The San Francisco peninsula was regarded as one of the leading areas of new media production based on the "hybrid" interaction infrastructure that can connect technologies, spaces and people in the early 2000s. During this period, technology and hardware companies concentrated in this area, leading to a productive socio-spatial division of the workforce and the natural inclusion of a "bohemian" environment in the cultural ambience. This environment is a lively culture based on political activism, social networks, implicit or shared information and includes socially organized work patterns. The idea of coworking has spread rapidly since its appearance and ultimately become a trend that carries great expectations related to the information business of the future (Gandini, 2015). The interest of public and media in coworking spaces has followed a similar trend. The abundance of coworking spaces in any city is associated with the vigor of urban life that makes a place attractive to artists, bohemians and entrepreneurs as workers of the creative industry. Existence of high technology ecosystems is secondary, which is indicated by the fact that the birthplace of the coworking movement was San Francisco, and not Silicon Valley (Moriset, 2013).

Third places like coworking spaces, incubators and work collectives represent the new ecosystem of collaborative working practices in the creative economy, which has significantly changed the concept of "workplace" and spatial distribution of the business world (Avdikos and Kalogeresis, 2017). Private enterprises initially started the coworking movement, but due to the high level of interest it has received, was included in public programs intended to form "creative cities", generally through the regeneration of obsolete industrial districts. Local administrations encouraged the establishment of coworking spaces as part of large-scale urban development projects intended to build "creative districts" (Moriset, 2013).

## Work Virtualization

In the post-Fordist period, the phenomenon of work virtualization paved the way for the emergence of new business models. Thanks to work virtualization, firms produce goods and services faster, performed office work faster, reduced physical office expenses and improved overall productivity by increasing worker productivity (Kış, 2009). From the end of the 20$^{th}$ century onwards, there have been three periods in the development of the work virtualization concept. The first period (the late 1980s) saw the initial democratization of home computers. This period manifested itself in the development of teleworking with the development of e-mail. In the second period (the 2000s), the spatial and temporal distribution of work was supported, and workers were allowed to work anytime, anywhere (Leclercq-Vandelannoitte and Isaac, 2016). The third period is "virtual coworking." During this period, coworking was the inclusion of returning to the colocation of workers in physical space into the digitalizing manufacturing method where work can be done anytime, anywhere (Johns and Gratton, 2013).

As work is no longer material and exists everywhere, new information technologies have a considerable impact on how and where knowledge work can be done. Therefore, the social and architectural borders of companies have become obsolete. Information workers who recognize growing corporate demands have found third places to work instead of the office (Leclercq-Vandelannoitte and Isaac, 2016). Workers of the digital age are no longer required to go to work regularly at full-time, and working conditions get flexible in terms of time and space. The business culture of fixed addresses has led to the differentiation of the office concept and workspaces. Information and knowledge transfer, made possible by technology, allow workers to work independently or have meetings anywhere (Ergin, 2012). This led to a significant shift in workplace management and operations, and coworking spaces have become a more generalized workplace concept (Kojo and Nenonen, 2016).

## COWORKING SPACES TYPOLOGIES

Coworking spaces have spread quickly since their nascence in San Francisco, and they have been classified according to various perspectives by different disciplines and academic circles. There is a growing portfolio of coworking spaces, and as these workspaces are blurring in distinction, the question becomes "what distinguishes the various coworking spaces?". To answer this question, this section discusses the relevant literature on coworking spaces typologies.

According to Moriset (2011), coworking spaces should not be confused with telecenters, flexible office spaces, different incubators and accelerators. Telecenters are found in rural and urban areas both (Moriset, 2011). These are conceptualized as "drop-in offices", and their professional interaction level is generally low. Flexible office providers offer office leasing solutions. However, they do not attempt to create a collaborative environment. Incubators generally focus on startup projects. Their users usually go through a selection process, and this process is not compatible with the third-place concept (Moriset, 2013).

In their research in Finland, Kojo and Nenonen (2016) mention six types of coworking spaces, namely, public offices, third places, collaboration hubs, coworking hotels, incubators and shared studios. In their study, public offices, third places and collaboration hubs are classified as coworking spaces that represent nonprofit business models, and coworking hotels, incubators and shared studios are classified as profit-oriented business models. In the search for a general term that encompasses coworking spaces, Schmidt and Brinks (2017) propose to group these environments under the term of "open creative labs". These labs are permanent spaces that can be accessed temporarily by different users. Schmidt et al. (2014) classified innovation and creativity labs into five types, namely, grassroots labs, coworking labs, firm-driven innovation labs, academic-driven innovation labs and finally, incubators and accelerators. These categorizations are business model-driven or user-driven categorizations. In this chapter, coworking spaces are categorized according to their specific spatial requirements in five types namely "third spaces", "working labs", "open innovation and fabrication labs", "firm-driven innovation labs" and "learning centers":

## Third Places

In the digital age, an increasing number of mobile workers perform their tasks in a range of public places, including cafés, hotel lobbies, airports, parks and vehicles. For these nomadic workers, traditional offices are no more than a place they drop by occasionally to have meeting or chat (Breure and Van Meel, 2003). Oldenburg (1999), in his book "The Great Good Place", describes "third places" as neutral places where people gather and interact. The actual strength of these spaces lies in the dynamic creation of micro-networks beyond a few square meters of office space, and their actual value comes from assisted serendipities, informal conversations and expert advice members are happy to provide for each other (Schopfel et al. 2015).

A third place is a collaborative workspace rooted in certain fundamental principles like openness, flexibility, usability and accessibility as it allows informal contact and social interactions. These spaces constitute an original public space that is easily accessible in terms of space and time, used for mobile work, does not have official membership criteria where individuals have voluntary and informal social gatherings (Oldenburg, 1999). According to Waxman (2006), cafés as third places have a unique social climate and culture with regards to a sense of belonging, territorialism and ownership; productivity and personal development; socialization, support and networking opportunities; and collectivism. As a type of coworking space, cafés, hotels, airport lounges, and even hair salons are typical third places (Moriset, 2013).

## Working Labs

Low access barriers characterize working labs. However, these labs generally provide service for a specific area of expertise, like media, design or software development. Unlike public labs, coworking labs are profit-oriented operations in a business model and are explicitly designed as workspaces that will provide service for professional users (Schmidt et al., 2014). The reason these labs are described as coworking spaces is that these spaces are mainly focused on income-oriented tasks (Schmidt and Brinks, 2017). Working labs often open stimulating debates on reference points shared in terms of equipment, materials and community, clearly striving to develop a community (Schmidt et al., 2014).

## Open Innovation and Fabrication Labs

According to the relevant literature on open innovation and fabrication labs, these labs are given various terms such as "fab lab", "maker lab", "experimentation lab" and "grassroots lab". There are no significant distinctions between these spaces except the activities or equipment they accommodate. The maker culture is a rapidly spreading global movement that combines technology and the "do it yourself" culture. Fabrication labs are places where people of different interests meet and produce diverse things. Manufacturing spaces specialized in digital production and experimentation, such as fab labs and maker labs, transform digital data into physical objects (and vice versa) through digital manufacturing machines (Mariotti et al., 2017). Experimentation labs create a joint platform to test ideas, experiment with tools and materials, and at the same time, collaboratively share information in the lab (Schmidt et al., 2014). The activities in these labs are aimed at creating new and beneficial ideas and products almost with no goal prespecified by lab operators (Schmidt and Brinks, 2017). As a type of public innovation and fabrication lab, grassroots labs are creativity labs established by private ventures who provide a coworking place for external users to express creativity in a collaborative environment. Although similar to a classic craft workshop, grassroots labs integrate crafts and digital interfaces (Schmidt et al., 2014).

## Firm-Driven Innovation Labs

As technological advancements provide continuous access to corporate information resources (mobile technologies and cloud computing), knowledge works have been liberated from the physical boundaries of an organization both temporally and spatially (Leclercq-Vandelannoitte and Isaac, 2016). Businesses in the knowledge economy must continuously generate new information or strategically convert existing information in order to have a competitive advantage. Firm-driven innovation labs are physical spaces of the open innovation processes of large and mostly multinational corporations. There is limited access to these labs and freelancers and experts from creative industries, research and development agencies and universities are selected to use the lab's infrastructure. Thus, users benefit from corporate resources and infrastructure, and proprietors internalize the information and competencies created in their laboratories (Schmidt et al., 2014).

### Learning Centers

In the 21st century, in the context of the knowledge economy, libraries are more important than ever for their function as a place of inspiration through discourse, peer collaboration, social learning and learning from different people (Aabø et al., 2010). The skills of creativity, interdisciplinary thinking, problem solving and cooperation required by the knowledge economy cannot be quickly learned from books; they are mostly gained by practice and social interactions (Bilandzic and Foth, 2013). Learning centers are models of integrated services, digital resources and user-orientation. However, most importantly, learning centers provide "a perfect network of services, libraries, information gathering, social spaces, studying spaces, restaurants, cafés and beautiful outdoors" (Schopfel et al. 2015). University campuses are currently moving away from assigning libraries solely as a reflective workspace and transforming libraries into spaces of informal and unplanned collaborations in a "common learning area" (Kojo and Nenonen, 2016). Learning centers host meetings that are examples of high-level interaction between a group of friends chatting while having coffee, or students working on an assignment together and also between strangers and users from different cultural backgrounds (Bilandzic and Foth, 2013).

## DESIGN IMPLICATIONS FOR COWORKING SPACES

Owners or managers of coworking spaces want to know more about the spatial preferences and motivations of workers in order to make their workplace more popular. However, designers and architects of coworking spaces are seeking creative spatial strategies to stimulate both providing interactions between workers and providing collaboration across disciplines. Therefore, drawing a theoretical framework for coworking spaces is important to inform the designers and operators of these spaces. As examined in the coworking spaces typology section, coworking spaces of such diversity also vary in the user profile. In this context, firstly the user profile in these spaces is analyzed to propose a conceptual framework to identify design implications for coworking spaces. In order to inform designers, researchers and managers, design implications developed according to coworking spaces, users' preferences on best practice for coworking space design are also examined in this section.

### User Profile in Coworking Spaces

The paradigm shift in workplace attitudes, preferences and spatial expectations comes with a changing workforce. For the first time, four generations (Traditionalists, Baby Boomers, Generation X'ers and Millenials) are working in the same workplace

(Wagner and Watch, 2017). Among these generations, millenials constitute the information society. They are regarded as the most active generation in the education and business world so far, and millenials (born between 1980 and 1999) growing up among daily life technologies have new technological skills. An important fact about this generation is that they have never seen life without the internet. Collaborative work and networking opportunities are critical for this generation (Curaoğlu and Demirbaş, 2017). Working methods of mobile workers, development of information technologies, and effortless transfer of technology have led to the requirement of short-term, flexible and temporary workplaces (Ergin, 2012). Coworking spaces are one of the workplace concepts that emerged to meet this need.

Coworking spaces have various types of users. Some coworking spaces are public coworking places, and some coworking spaces provide for the unique needs of creative sector workers, such as writers, technology entrepreneurs, artisans, designers, artists, moviemakers or workers with specific fields of interest, such as rock climbers (Sykes, 2014). The literature review by Gandini (2015) on the coworking space user profile in creative cities reveals the profile in Milan. According to this review, coworking space users indicate a profile of freelancers or self-employed professionals, mostly male, aged 24-44, who earn a low to medium income. A section of the variable coworking cluster in Milan consists of traditional intellectual professionals and executives directly connected to creative industries, and "digital professionals" like social media content creators, public relations or brand advisors. This means that coworking spaces are generally used by a group of professionals who gain their skills through education and information associated with the digital economy (Gandini, 2015).

Original users of coworking spaces in the U.S. were freelancers, contractors and small business owners. For some large-scale organizations, coworking spaces are regarded as an appealing solution as a temporary office space or even a permanent workplace (Sykes, 2014). The term "lone eagles" proposed by Burgess (1994) is used to describe members of the freelance class, and the same term is used for proprietorships in the literature. Lone eagles prefer coworking spaces for possibilities of serendipity in order to establish new business connections. According to Kojo and Nenonen (2016), public offices, third places and coworking hotels are often used by freelancers and other small business owners, however, larger companies can also use these places as meeting spaces.

Schmidt and Brinks (2017) argue that users of experimental labs are people who share a field of interest (e.g. amateur mechanics) or a hobby (e.g. hackers). Working labs are mainly directed to work practices like project-based work and freelance work (Schmidt and Brinks, 2017). The user profile of collaboration hubs generally consists of entrepreneurs and these workplaces target groups of specific fields of interest. Incubator users are startup companies accepted to acceleration programs. Shared studios generally accept new tenants who are often acquaintances of existing users, and they typically have a selection process (Kojo and Nenonen, 2016). Learning centers are coworking spaces for the academic society on campus. However, it is also a place of contact, learning, working and creation that gradually opens to businesses, industries, startups, entrepreneurs and innovators (Schopfel et al. 2015).

In addition to the literature review on the generations, professions and fields of interest of coworking space users, Bilandzic and Foth (2013) analyze users of a bookless library-coworking space in Australia based on their behavioral tendencies and refer to five user characters (personas) in these spaces: the first character (students, pensioners, travellers, homeless) use the coworking space as a place of free access to computers, internet, multimedia equipment and software. The second character has no idea about what a coworking space is and what it offers and visits the space incidentally. The third character wants to meet creative individuals and cooperate in projects on digital culture and technology. The fourth character (geek) continually attempts to develop in his own subculture and expand his fields of interest and likes "infecting" people with his knowledge. The fifth character uses a coworking space as a third-place and occupies himself with an agenda imposed by his jobs (Bilandzic and Foth, 2013). In this sense, the user profile of coworking spaces is rather heterogeneous in preferences and motivations. The next section proposes a conceptual framework to identify design implications for coworking spaces where user characteristics are discussed.

## Design Implications

Bilandzic and Foth (2013) argue that users of coworking spaces have three motivations to use these spaces namely, "access to unaffordable computers, internet, multimedia equipment and software", "cowork with individuals and groups" and "participate in workshops, presentations and similar activities". Spatial intervention to meet these motivations is the arrangement of coworking spaces as collaboration spaces fully equipped with technology and activity. The results of a nine-month study on Millenials in the U.S. showed that the ideal work environment for Millenials is social, flexible, comfortable, open, spacious, collaborative with technology and environmentally conscious (Wagner and Watch, 2017). Coworking spaces share similar values, namely openness, community, collaboration, accessibility, and sustainability (Kwiatkowski & Buczynski, 2014). Weijs-Perrée et al. (2019) report on a review of the literature that describes coworking space characteristics such as "24 hours access, open layout and virtual platform, coworking host, access to tools and resources, collaborative spaces, concentration rooms, atmosphere and interior aesthetics, diversity of tenants, event spaces, flexible workspaces, events and workshops, flexible contract, good accessibility (car and public transport), kitchen areas and meeting rooms".

Wagner and Watch (2017) underline three meta-trends influencing the design of innovation spaces that coworking spaces: "the increasingly open and collaborative nature of innovation", "the complexity of innovation re-valuing face-to-face communication" and "the ubiquitous nature of technology transforming spaces into testbeds". Based on their observations, Bilandzic and Foth (2013) report that users of these spaces work individually or cooperate in previously organized groups but mostly do not interact with other users. However, the open and accessible nature of the architecture helps people make contact by chance in shared "zones", especially like the computer lab or café or officially organized workshops (Bilandzic and Foth, 2013).

Based on literature review related to user preferences, values and space characteristics of coworking spaces, it is proposed to arrange these spaces to facilitate technology and activity assisted collaboration. In this context, design implications are proposed under ten coworking space characteristics, namely accessibility and proximity, sustainability, openness and permeability, flexibility, comfort/home-like spaces, collaboration spaces, concentration spaces, gathering spaces, technology-assisted spaces and activity-based spaces:

## Accessibility and Proximity

According to Capdevila (2013), location is the most important characteristic of a coworking space, and a more accessible location is the main factor for a user to consider joining a coworking space. The popularity of coworking spaces is directly proportional to their proximity to the daily activities of users. These spaces are close to users' homes, customers, popular bars, restaurants, various shopping services near the city, public transportation and other services (Kojo and Nenonen, 2017). Remøy and Van der Voordt (2014) also suggest accessibility (by car, by public transport or by bicycle) and location as essential factors, among creative industries. According to Weijs-Perrée et al. (2019) designers, by offering enough parking spaces, satisfy managers of an organization who prefer accessibility by car.

Accessibility and proximity to daily activities of users are essential criteria for owners and managers of coworking spaces to evaluate when considering a location for their new business—located in city centers or near the transportation facilities ease accessibility. The location should be easily accessible by car, by public transportation and by bike. Also, it is important to offer adequate car parking and bike rack space for workers.

## Sustainability

Sustainability has a special place in the coworking space literature. Users share the resources, rent and equipment of these spaces, and this allows a positive environmental impact by reduction of material and energy use. On the other hand, coworking spaces also have positive effects on the economic, social and cultural development of their neighborhood. In practice, this means reusing defunct or obsolete buildings, attracting new activities to the area, and creating employment (Kojo and Nenonen, 2017).

One of the main characteristics that reflect the spirit of coworking spaces is ecological and social sustainability. To promote ecological sustainability, a significant amount of materials and energy could be saved by using design techniques such as adaptive reuse of defunct buildings, creating honest and uncoated interior surfaces, providing natural lighting and ventilation in interiors, selection of ecological materials such as wood, natural stones and natural fabrics in interior fittings and furniture. A coworking space in an adequately considered location also promotes social sustainability as it provides employment, creates an attraction center and contributes to the socio-economic development of the neighborhood.

## Openness and Permeability

From incubator spaces to maker labs, managers and designers of coworking spaces seek ways of tearing down physical barriers to stimulate collaboration between teams and disciplines. Open work-floor settings are encouraging people to engage in conversations, and a welcoming lobby can create a connection point and space where people start to break down these barriers. The transparency and openness blur the boundaries between working, passing by or gathering, connect people outside with the activities inside and provide social and physical permeability. The main aim of allocating extravert functions on the ground floor is to create a neutral space that everyone is free to use and to blur the public and private spaces (Wagner and Watch, 2017). Another spatial characteristic that increases sharing and cooperation is spaciousness. Mariotti et al. (2017)'s research shows that small-scale coworking spaces in Milan are self-enclosed, dissociated from other spaces and sometimes invisible. However, larger-scale coworking spaces are more open to interaction, more innovative and more visible in an urban context. Large coworking spaces can provide various possibilities for workers inside (gathering places like meeting rooms and kitchen, resting areas and gardens) and external users (cafés and restaurants) and are often able to organize activities for the community (meetings, exhibitions, seminars or training programs) (Mariotti et al., 2017).

In coworking spaces, the most crucial design intervention focuses on how to increase cooperation and serendipity possibilities among workers and disciplines, get workers to know each other and learn from each other by using open layouts for the collaboration spaces and designing exterior and interior walls with transparent surfaces (floor to ceiling windows) at coworking spaces. Featuring a welcoming ambience containing comfortable seating groups and free Wi-Fi that will attract passers-by and extrovert functions (such as a café or lounge) on ground floors helps increase the permeability of these spaces. Similarly, spacious, open and transparent venues support sharing and collaboration opportunities and help stretch the visual barriers between workers inside the space and the people outside.

## Flexibility

For all types of coworking spaces, it is fundamental to be responsive to the changing needs of changing users in this dynamic environment. Weijs-Perrée et al. (2019) suggest that it is important for owners to offer a wide variety of workspaces such as event spaces, meeting spaces, informal zones, an open work environment, kitchen areas and concentration rooms to adapt to changing activities and needs of users. Flexible design requires all aspects of space, including moveable walls, machinery, furniture and other components (Wagner and Watch, 2017). It is important to be able to adapt coworking spaces to user preferences through flexible workspaces and adaptable furniture (Weijs-Perrée et al., 2019). Spaces easily convertible from open office to event spaces or meeting rooms increase flexibility (Hauser, 2019). In terms of flexibility, the selection of furniture is as important as the spaces and layout. The project "Welcoming Workplace" carried out by Myerson, Bichard and Erlich (2010), desks that can be used in sitting and standing positions both thanks to an adjustable height function was welcomed. Also, the selection of light and reconfigurable furniture allows workers to move quickly (Hauser, 2019). Owing to demands for greater flexibility, wheels are now mostly affixed to furniture and equipment, and in some spaces, electrical cords attached to pulleys form giant extension cords (Wagner and Watch, 2017).

Flexible layouts, space dividers, furniture, interior construction and electrical systems that can be adapted to different activities of workers are preferable. Designing open, flexible and informal collaboration spaces, visually open-physically closed spaces for users looking for a quiet space to concentrate; preferring glass walls, transparent, moveable and lightweight partitions, adjustable desks, chairs and cabinets on wheels, furniture defining personal spaces and plug-and-play workbenches could increase flexibility in coworking spaces. Allowing dynamic modifications, interior products, and materials should be constructed using mechanical connections. In fabrication labs, preferring thick floor slabs allows the movement of heavy machinery without damaging the floor. Electrical cords on retractable coils could be hung from the ceiling. In this way, workers have the freedom of being plugged in while moving around. Dimmable lights, smart ceilings (which allow changes to lights and other electrical components) and local lighting available in every workstation allow workers personal control and flexibility.

## Comfort/ Home-Like Spaces

Results of a study by Breure and Van Meel (2003) show that the idea of nomadic workers who can work anywhere they want is a bit too romantic. A laptop computer and a mobile phone is not enough to be productive. Nomadic workers have clearly expressed that they at least need a place to sit and a place to put their laptop when they work (Breure and Van Meel, 2003). Weijs-Perrée et al. (2019) suggest, "owners and managers of coworking spaces should create a creative and inspiring environment with a home-like interior". Many spaces are organizing a home-like atmosphere by placing even greater emphasis on living rooms or kitchens (Wagner and Watch, 2017) and comfortable seats to increase working efficiency and serendipity opportunities. According to Kojo and Nenonen (2014), relaxing, home-like spaces with no traditional office look are preferences of workers using coworking spaces.

The most important reason workers prefer to work at coworking spaces is the promise of these spaces to combine a comfortable environment at home and the social environment at the office. Therefore, these spaces must offer a comfortable environment for workers to be able to work there for long hours. In this sense, a coworking space should offer its users ergonomic workbenches, user-controlled lighting and a relaxing, home-like ambience. Interior design can include cozy workspaces where workers have the opportunity to create personalized spaces with comfortable desks, seats, sofas, plants and an inviting kitchen environment where informal meetings occur.

## Collaboration Spaces

According to Schmidt and Brinks (2017), open innovation labs allow cross-pollination, which is not as possible within fixed organizational routines. Augustin (2014), based on a literature review on collaboration, lists the reasons a group of people gather: sharing information, making a decision, creating ideas (brainstorming), education, problem-solving and socialization with colleagues. Coworking space users have similar motivations to work at coworking spaces. Two types of collaboration space can be designed to respond to different needs of collaboration in coworking spaces, namely open collaborative spaces and private collaborative spaces (group working spaces). Open, collaborative spaces are working hubs with comfortable and adjustable workbenches and with convenient technology in a single spacious volume aiming to remove physical barriers to stimulate collaboration between users (Wagner and

Watch, 2017). Private collaborative spaces are visually open-physically closed spaces reserved by a project team for coworking and generally arranged in an open layout. These spaces must be equipped with whiteboards, large surfaces, papers, pens, digital image capturing, visual-audio equipment and conventional video media, and adaptable to the nature of periodic work. They should accommodate moveable/adjustable furniture and flexible working methods for project teams as well as individually customized use. Large desks to spread work materials and large bulletin boards to pin project ideas can enhance collaborative work methods (Myerson et al., 2010).

A semi-open layout consisting of open and private collaboration spaces is a spatial organization that responds to different collaboration types. Open, collaborative spaces allow a group of workers who do not know each other to meet, communicate, socialize and create ideas together and private collaborative spaces are allocated for a specific collaborative work. In this context, it is recommended to design studio-like group workspaces where users share the data they obtain, talk and debate without having to worry about confidentiality, within the open layout. Digital and traditional video media installed in private collaborative spaces (group working spaces) support the continuation of the work. Moveable furniture and workbenches let teams convene, and workers perform their individual tasks. Dynamic lighting allows users to adjust their light according to their specific task and ergonomic requirements.

## Concentration Spaces

Open layouts used in coworking spaces increase collaboration while reducing the concentration and privacy required for individual work. According to Myerson et al. (2010), removing separators, walls and private work areas in collaboration- and teamwork-oriented workspaces has led to the omission of environments that encourage solo knowledge work. Most of the demands concerning problem-solving, planning, analysis, creation and processing complex information require uninterrupted and extended attention spans, introverted thinking, a rare state of mind in workspaces with open layouts (Myerson et al., 2010). The word "collaboration" connotes an image of people sitting around a conference table and sharing valuable information. However, a discussion on collaboration is not considered finished until it is acknowledged that many collaborative projects are carried out in the form of individual tasks in the background. Today, the workspace needs to facilitate private work and collaboration with colleagues in order to improve the productivity of knowledge workers. One of the workplace factors with the most significant influence on job satisfaction and performance is "a worker's skill of performing individual work without getting distracted at the individual and team level" (Augustin, 2014).

A simple set of interior design arrangement measures is sufficient to meet the spatial requirements of knowledge workers to undertake tasks that require constant concentration. Concentration spaces to be arranged in coworking spaces can be private stands/workspaces or divided spaces in an open layout. These spaces should be separated from the noise and distracting physical environment of the main workspace by separators covered with sound-absorbing materials, and located away from noisy spaces like kitchens, cafés and social areas. As factors like poor ergonomics and an uncomfortable sitting position would have adverse effects on concentration, furniture with adjustable features should be preferred. Concentration spaces should have windows in order to establish a link with the outdoors. While designing the lighting plan, a lower, more pleasant ambient lighting and user-controlled desk lamps should be considered for reading and other specific tasks.

## Gathering Spaces

Knowledge workers are deprived of opportunities for professional interactions and encounters when they are exposed continuously to desk sharing and nomadic work. They become more isolated as they are always digitally online. On the other hand, face-to-face communication appears superior to other communication tools in terms of "complex, content-specific" knowledge sharing that supports creativity and innovation (Augustin, 2014). Tacit knowledge exchange requires face-to-face communication, which takes place intermittently when people get together. Although codified knowledge exchange can be done remotely, tacit knowledge requires trust between individuals, which is only created in close and direct contact (Mariotti et al., 2017). Social contacts are limited to a few special cases among unacquainted users. Design can be used as a facilitator of these social contacts.

The essential place in a coworking space where workers meet each other or report social contacts is shared spaces, i.e. gathering spaces. These contacts occur when people wait in line to get coffee or smoke outside next to the entrance. Similarly, people sometimes start conversations with other people working on similar projects or using the same platform at the computer lab (Bilandzic and Foth, 2013). Coworking spaces are designed to be less formal than traditional office environments, and they provide coffee machines, kitchens, comfortable resting spaces and reading corners (Spinuzzi, 2012). Wagner and Watch (2017) recommend designing indoor atriums, grand internal staircases in order to increase face-to-face communication at innovation spaces, and underline the significance of gathering spaces (well-designed kitchens, cafés, lounge/adaptive spaces) for maximizing interaction between workers.

Coworking space arrangements should facilitate face-to-face communication and serendipity opportunities among workers. In this arrangement, gathering spaces shared by all users play an essential role. Circulation and recreation spaces offer the best place for sudden encounters and meetings. It is vital to design corridors and staircases as circulation areas, cafés and lounges as recreation areas to enhance communication and interaction between users. Central staircases creating a stepped interior facilitate interaction and encounters, as people traverse floors and reconnect people who study on steps. An internal atrium can be designed to provide visual connectivity across floors. The reconfiguration and dimension of corridors should be considered in order to create serendipitous meetings. Gathering spaces should strategically be placed throughout a building to encourage people to circulate. Cozy cafés with comfortable seats, home-like kitchens, and an adaptable lounge space with inspirational interior design can facilitate social interactions.

## Technology-Assisted Spaces

Coworking spaces have the equipment (such as 3D printers, sewing machines, fax machines, recording and mixing tables) that varies according to the activities they offer. Free Wi-Fi access is essential for connectivity and communication requirements (Spinuzzi, 2012). Innovation labs generally have technological hardware like devices, machines and relevant software. This infrastructure can be supported with additional services like professional assistance in operating the high-tech equipment (Schmidt et al., 2014). According to Bilandzic and Foth (2013), one of the coworking spaces user types (persona) prefer the space because it provides the specialised tools and infrastructure required for his/her hobbies. From this perspective, coworking spaces should offer the technological infrastructure that workers need.

Wagner and Watch (2017) classify technologies found in innovation spaces in three categories, namely technology "as a collaboration and communication tool", "as a research and/or production tool" and "as a display and showcase tool". According to these categories, coworking space users can collaborate and communicate using free Wi-Fi, hardware and software provided by the space, find production opportunities through specific equipment like 3D printer, and display their work via digital whiteboards, interactive walls, screens and interactive tables.

The preferability of a coworking space must have useful information and communication technology (ICT) and equipment. A wide variety of spaces should be arranged from micro-scale workspaces to full-scale teleconferencing spaces in order for workers to benefit from the internet, hardware and software. Various technological tools and machines such as 3D printers, interactive tables, digital whiteboards or multi-touch screens can be added as the standard equipment of the interior design according to a specific user group or specific activities of the coworking space.

## Activity-Based Spaces

Trends like new ways of working, new generations and changing lifestyles have influenced office design and necessitated the creation of new workplace concepts. The goal of these new offices is to enhance productivity, flexibility, creativity and interaction. Such activity-based workspaces can be described as open, cheerful and dynamic places (Kojo and Nenonen, 2016). According to Vithayathawornwong et al. (2003), "dynamism" as a behavioral component is one of the most striking social-psychological states that influence creative behavior supported by the physical work environment. Dynamism encompasses various sub-dimensions, such as interaction, communication and exchange of information. Openness, collaboration, interaction and community are crucial to perform knowledge work. Specific coworking spaces organize activities and offer instruments to promote relationships and collaboration among workers (Kojo and Nenonen, 2016). Merkel (2015) argues that managers of coworking spaces play an essential role in creating a welcoming environment through strategies like organizing meetings and seminars, designing the space to communicate and creating social opportunities while enjoying food or drink breaks. Business presentations, weekly seminars, exhibitions and workshops are other possibilities offered by coworking spaces (Spinuzzi, 2012). All these activities are designed to bring people together, create a community, support businesses, startups, customers, artists and encourage synergy (Schopfel et al., 2015).

In order to build a community at a coworking space, spaces for cultural events, training and workshops (activity-based spaces) should be designed. This collaborative environment needs to be designed in an adaptable and flexible way to respond to different worker profiles and needs. Space should be able to easily install, move and store the furniture, equipment, machinery and tools needed for events. In this sense, the arrangement should include a flexible open layout that can be separated when needed, durable flooring, flexible lighting systems and adequate storage spaces.

Table 1 provides an overview of the design implications proposed in this chapter.

# FUTURE RESEARCH DIRECTIONS

The ubiquitous nature of technology will continue to transform work dynamics and the spaces in which work is done. In the 21st century, coworking spaces are one of the most popular spaces that host knowledge workers. This chapter draws a theoretical framework for design implications of coworking spaces and is the first step for research on the spatial organization of these spaces. Coworking is a multifaceted phenomenon, and future research on coworking spaces should be conducted through interdisciplinary collaboration. To obtain detailed design data, coworking space design

*Table 1. An overview of design implications for coworking spaces*

| Accessibility and Proximity |
|---|
| • Locating in city centers or near the transportation facilities<br>• Offering adequate car parking and bike racks space for users |
| **Sustainability** |
| • Adaptive reuse of defunct buildings<br>• Creating honest and uncoated interior surfaces<br>• Providing natural lighting and ventilation in interiors<br>• Selection of ecological materials such as wood, natural stones and natural fabrics in interior fittings and furniture<br>• Preferring a properly considered location promoting social sustainability as a coworking space provides employment, creates an attraction center and contributes to the socio-economic development of its neighborhood. |
| **Openness and Permeability** |
| • Use of open layouts at the collaboration spaces<br>• Designing exterior and interior walls through transparent surfaces (floor to ceiling windows)<br>• Featuring a welcoming ambiance containing comfortable seating groups and free Wi-Fi that will attract passers-by and designing extrovert functions (café, lounge, etc.) on ground floors to increase the permeability of these spaces<br>• Planning spacious, open and transparent volumes to support collaboration opportunities and to stretch the visual barriers between workers inside and people outside |
| **Flexibility** |
| • Preferring flexible layouts, space dividers, furniture, interior construction and electrical systems that can be adapted to different activities of users<br>• Designing open, flexible and informal collaboration spaces and also visually open-physically closed spaces for users looking for a quiet space to concentrate<br>• Preferring glass walls, transparent, moveable and lightweight partitions, adjustable desks, chairs and cabinets on wheels, furniture defining personal spaces and plug-and-play workbenches to increase flexibility<br>• Using mechanical connections instead of fixing in the construction of interior products and materials to allow dynamic modifications<br>• In fabrication labs, preferring thick floor slabs which allow heavy machinery moving without damaging the floor and using electrical cords on retractable coils hung from the ceiling to provide users having the freedom of being plugged in, while moving around<br>• Preferring dimmable lights, smart ceilings and local lightning possibility in every workstation to provide workers personal control and flexibility |
| **Comfort/ Home-Like Spaces** |
| • Designing a comfortable environment for users to be able to work for long hours<br>• Offering ergonomic workbenches, user-controlled lightning and a relaxing, home-like ambience<br>• Designing cozy workspaces where users have the opportunity to create personalized spaces with comfortable desks, seats, sofas, plants and an inviting kitchen environment where informal meetings occur |
| **Collaboration Spaces** |
| • Organizing a semi-open layout consisting open and private collaboration spaces which responds to different collaboration types:<br>• Designing open collaborative spaces to allow a group of users who do not know each other to meet, communicate, socialize and create ideas together<br>• Designing private collaborative spaces as studio-like group work spaces equiped with digital and traditional video media, moveable furniture and workbenches and dynamic lighting |
| **Concentration Spaces** |
| • Organizing concentration spaces such as, private stands, private workspaces or divided spaces in an open layout, separated from the noise and distracting physical environment of the main workspace<br>• Using separators covered with sound absorbing materials, which should be positioned away from noisy spaces like kitchens, cafés and social areas<br>• Preferring furniture with adjustable features in response to poor ergonomics that disrupts concentration.<br>• Providing windows in order to establish a link with the outdoor<br>• Using a lower, more pleasant ambient lighting and user-controlled desks |
| **Gathering Spaces** |
| • Designing circulation and recreation areas to enhance communication and interaction between users<br>• Organizing central staircases creating a stepped interior to facilitate interaction and encounters, as people traverse floors and to reconnect people who study on steps<br>• Creating an internal atrium to provide visual connectivity across floors and considering reconfiguration and dimension of corridors in order to create serendipitous meetings<br>• Placing gathering spaces to encourage people to circulate and locating cozy cafés with comfortable seats, home-like kitchens and an adaptable lounge space to facilitate social interactions |
| **Technology-Assisted Spaces** |
| • Providing convenient information and communication technology and equipment in coworking space<br>• Arranging wide variety of spaces, from micro-scale workspaces to full-scale teleconferencing spaces in order for users to benefit effectively from the internet, hardware and software<br>• Providing various technological tools such as 3D printers, interactive tables, digital whiteboards or multi-touch screens as the standard equipment of the interior design |
| **Activity-Based Spaces** |
| • Designing spaces for cultural events, trainings and workshops (activity-based spaces) in order to build a community and organizing collaborative environment in an adaptable and flexible way to respond to variable user profiles and needs<br>• Designing the space being able to easily install, move and store the furniture and tools needed for the events and arranging a flexible open layout that can be separated when needed, durable flooring, flexible lighting systems and adequate storage spaces |

studies should be multidisciplinary, for example, designers and social scientists to better analyze human behavior, user expectations and motivations.

Future research could propose specific design implications for each type of coworking space (third spaces, working labs, open innovation and fabrication labs, firm-driven innovation labs, learning centers) by analyzing in-depth quantitative data (survey) and qualitative data (e.g. focus groups or interviews) to explore the preferences of workers and experiences of coworking space designers, owners and managers. Another suggestion for future research could be to investigate the relationship between coworking space characteristics and place attachment, by using survey, observation, behavioral mapping and interview research techniques. Moreover, it could be interesting for future researchers to analyze which preferred characteristics of coworking spaces stimulate collaboration between users.

## CONCLUSION

Digitalization of the modern world and the emergence of digital capitalism has changed the business ecosystem. This has led to geographical disintegration of value chains and an increase in the number of self-employed professionals and freelancers. Therefore, lack of social and professional interaction inherent in these activities has guided independent workers to look for new workspaces that combine anywhere working and the social richness of offices. As a response, coworking spaces defined by social interactions, close contacts and learning opportunities outside typical office spaces have emerged. Coworking spaces have been spreading rapidly since 2005, and they will likely remain popular as the value assigned by the global economy to technology and innovation grows. The design of these spaces will affect future working styles, and working styles will affect the design of these spaces. This chapter offers new insights into the design of coworking spaces according to worker preferences. Based on the literature, it is recommended to design these spaces to facilitate technology and activity assisted collaboration. In this context, design implications grouped under ten coworking space characteristics, namely "accessibility and proximity, sustainability, openness and permeability, flexibility, comfort/home-like spaces, collaboration spaces, concentration spaces, gathering spaces, technology-assisted spaces and activity-based spaces", are proposed in order to inform designers, researchers and managers on best practice for coworking space design.

## REFERENCES

Aabø, S., Audunson, R., & Vårheim, A. (2010). How do public libraries function as meeting places? *Library & Information Science Research*, *32*(1), 16–26. doi:10.1016/j.lisr.2009.07.008

Augustin, S. (2014). Designing for collaboration and collaborating for design. *Journal of Interior Design*, *39*(1), ix–xviii. doi:10.1111/joid.12020

Avdikos, V., & Kalogeresis, A. (2017). Socio-economic profile and working conditions of freelancers in coworking spaces and work collectives: Evidence from the design sector in Greece. *Area*, *49*(1), 35–42. doi:10.1111/area.12279

Bilandzic, M., & Foth, M. (2013). Libraries as coworking spaces: Understanding user motivations and perceived barriers to social learning. *Library Hi Tech*, *31*(2), 254–273. doi:10.1108/07378831311329040

Breure, A., & van Meel, J. (2003). Airport offices: Facilitating nomadic workers. *Facilities*, *21*(7/8), 175–179. doi:10.1108/02632770310489918

Burgess, P. M. (1994). *Lone eagles*. Center for the New West Points West Advisory.

Capdevila, I. (2013). *Knowledge Dynamics in Localized Communities: Coworking Spaces as Microclusters*. Available at SSRN: https://ssrn.com/abstract=2414121

Çimen, T. (2008). *Teknolojik gelişmelerin sonucunda değişen üretim ilişkilerinin, ofis yapılarına etkisi ve ofis mekanları* (Unpublished master's dissertation). Istanbul Technical University, Istanbul.

Curaoğlu, F., & Demirbaş, D. (2017). From coworking places to new education places. *The Design Journal*, *20*(sup1), S4765-S4767.

Duffy, F. (1997). *The New Office*. Conron Octapus.

Erdener, H.E. (1996). Büro binalarında yeni kullanım yöntemleri. *Yapı*, (181), 77-83.

Erdoğan, S. (2012). *Yeni emek sistemleri: ev-ofis sistemi üzerine bir inceleme* (Unpublished master's dissertation). Ankara University, Ankara.

Ergin, E. (2012). *Hazır ofislerin iç mekân tasarım yaklaşımları* (Unpublished master's dissertation). Cukurova University, Adana.

Florida, R. (2002). *The Rise of the Creative Class—and How It Is Transforming Leisure, Community and Everyday Life*. New York: Basic Books.

Gandini, A. (2015). The rise of coworking spaces: A literature review. *Ephemera*, *15*(1), 193.

Hauser, M. (2019). *Guiding Principles For Coworking Interior Design*. Available at https://www.globalworkspace.org/blog/guiding-principles-for-coworking-interior-design/

Johns, T., & Gratton, L. (2013). The third wave of virtual work. *Harvard Business Review*, *91*(1), 66–73.

Jones, D., Sundsted, T., & Bacigalupo, T. (2009). *I'm Outta Here: How Coworking is Making the Office Obsolete*. Austin: Not an MBA Press.

Kış, E. (2009). *Geleneksel ve sanal ofislerde iş doyumu: Bir alan araştırması* (Unpublished master's dissertation). Gazi University, Ankara.

Kojo, I., & Nenonen, S. (2014). User experience in an academic coworking place: The case of Aalto university's design factory. *Proceedings of the CIB Facilities Management Conference*, 21-23.

Kojo, I., & Nenonen, S. (2016). Typologies for coworking spaces in Finland–what and how? *Facilities*, *34*(5/6), 302–313. doi:10.1108/F-08-2014-0066

Kojo, I., & Nenonen, S. (2017). Evolution of coworking places: Drivers and possibilities. *Intelligent Buildings International*, *9*(3), 164–175. doi:10.1080/17508975.2014.987640

Kwiatkowski, A., & Buczynski, B. (2014). *Coworking: Building community as a space catalyst*. Cohere, LLC.

Leclercq-Vandelannoitte, A., & Henri Isaac, H. (2016). The new office: How coworking changes the work concept. *The Journal of Business Strategy*, *37*(6), 3–9. doi:10.1108/JBS-10-2015-0105

Mariotti, I., Pacchi, C., & Di Vita, S. (2017). Coworking spaces in Milan: Location patterns and urban effects. *Journal of Urban Technology*, 1–20.

Merkel, J. (2015). Coworking in the City. *Ephemera*, *15*(1), 121–139.

Moriset, B. (2011). Developing the Digital Economy in France's Rural Regions: A Critical Assessment of Telecenters. *NETCOM*, *25*(3-4), 249–272. doi:10.4000/netcom.175

Moriset, B. (2013). *Building new places of the creative economy. The rise of coworking spaces*. Academic Press.

Myerson, J., Bichard, J. A., & Erlich, A. (2010). *New Demographics, New Workspace: Office Design for the Changing Workforce*. Gower Publishing Limited.

Myerson, J., & Ross, P. (2003). *The 21st century office*. Laurence King Publishing.

Oldenburg, R. (1999). *The Great Good Place: Cafés, Coffee Shops, Bookstores, Bars, Hair Salons, and Other Hangouts at the Heart of a Community*. Marlowe.

Örs, N. (2001). ABD'de büronun dünü ve bugünü, National Building Museum'da 'On The Job: Design and The American Office' sergisi kataloğu çevirisi. *Arredamento Mimarlık*, (135), 90-95.

Oygur, I., & McCoy, J. M. (2011). User: Inspiration or constraint? *Journal of Interior Design*, *36*(3), 1–13. doi:10.1111/j.1939-1668.2011.01058.x

Remøy, H., & Van der Voordt, T. J. M. (2014). Priorities in accommodating office user preferences: Impact on office users decision to stay or go. *Journal of Corporate Real Estate*, *16*(2), 140–154. doi:10.1108/JCRE-09-2013-0029

Sailer, K., Budgen, A., Lonsdale, N., Turner, A., & Penn, A. (2009). *Comparative studies of offices pre and post—how changing spatial configurations affect organizational behaviours. Royal Institute of Technology*. KTH.

Sanoff, H. (2006). Multiple views of participatory design. *METU Journal of the Faculty of Architecture*, *23*(2), 131–143.

Schmidt, S., & Brinks, V. (2017). Open creative labs: Spatial settings at the intersection of communities and organizations. *Creativity and Innovation Management*, *26*(3), 291–299. doi:10.1111/caim.12220

Schmidt, S., Brinks, V., & Brinkhoff, S. (2014). Innovation and creativity labs in Berlin. *Zeitschrift für Wirtschaftsgeographie*, *58*(1), 232–247. doi:10.1515/zfw.2014.0016

Schopfel, J., Roche, J., & Hubert, G. (2015). Coworking and innovation: New concepts for academic libraries and learning centres. *New Library World*, *116*(1/2), 67–78. doi:10.1108/NLW-06-2014-0072

Spinuzzi, C. (2012). Working alone together. *Journal of Business and Technical Communication*, *26*(4), 399–441. doi:10.1177/1050651912444070

Sykes, K. (2014). Coworking: A workplace paradigm shift. *Contract (New York, N.Y.)*, *55*(6), 140–145.

Vithayathawornwong, S., Danko, S., & Tolbert, P. (2003). The role of the physical environment in supporting organizational creativity. *Journal of Interior Design*, *29*(1-2), 1–16. doi:10.1111/j.1939-1668.2003.tb00381.x

Wagner, J., & Watch, D. (2017). *Innovation spaces: The new design of work*. Anne T. and Robert M. Bass Initiative on Innovation and Placemaking at Brookings.

Waxman, L. (2006). The coffee shop: Social and physical factors influencing place attachment. *Journal of Interior Design*, *31*(3), 35–53. doi:10.1111/j.1939-1668.2006.tb00530.x

Weijs-Perrée, M., van de Koevering, J., Appel-Meulenbroek, R., & Arentze, T. (2019). Analysing user preferences for coworking space characteristics. *Building Research and Information*, *47*(5), 534–548. doi:10.1080/09613218.2018.1463750

## KEY TERMS AND DEFINITIONS

**Community:** This term is used to describe digital working models ascribed to the sharing economy, which involves participation without ownership (for instance, carpooling) and contribution without necessarily expecting monetary compensation. In this sense, the term "community" now expresses the presence of other people in other places interested in similar practices rather than a social cluster of close-knit people.

**Coworking:** A new form of work organization that creates cooperation opportunities and encourages a sense of community in a shared space, and gathers employees of different companies and even freelancers with different profiles and objectives.

**Coworking Spaces:** Shared workplaces used by knowledge workers who are often freelancers and at different levels of expertise in the vast area of the information industry. Coworking spaces are "third places", where workers seek a sense of socialization, opportunities for serendipity and networking encounters to increase their social capital.

**Firm-Driven Innovation Labs:** Physical spaces of the open innovation processes of large and mostly multinational corporations. There is limited access to these labs and freelancers and experts from creative industries, research and development agencies and universities are selected to use the lab's infrastructure.

**Learning Centers:** Models of integrated services, digital resources and user-orientation providing a network of services, libraries, information gathering, social spaces, study spaces, restaurants, cafés and outdoor areas.

**Open Creative Labs:** These labs can be described as permanent spaces that can be accessed temporarily by different users. Innovation and creativity labs can be classified into five types, namely, grassroots labs, coworking labs, firm-driven innovation labs, academic-driven innovation labs and finally, incubators and accelerators.

# Chapter 8
# Entrepreneurial Needs for Outer Urban Co-Working Hubs:
## An Exploratory Study of a "Pop-Up" Co-Working Hub

**Emsie Arnoldi**
https://orcid.org/0000-0002-2838-5278
*RMIT University, Australia*

**Rachelle Bosua**
https://orcid.org/0000-0003-0218-3018
*Open University of the Netherlands, The Netherlands*

**Vanessa Cooper**
https://orcid.org/0000-0002-8299-7056
*RMIT University, Australia*

**Cathy Greenfield**
https://orcid.org/0000-0001-6656-0543
*RMIT University, Australia*

**Huck Ying Ch'ng**
*RMIT University, Australia*

## ABSTRACT

*Workspaces and workplaces have changed significantly over the last decade. Facilitated by networking and collaboration tools, there has been a steady concentration of inner-city coworking spaces providing many opportunities for new*

DOI: 10.4018/978-1-7998-4159-3.ch008

*flexible work arrangements. Driven by sustainability and creative entrepreneurship, coworking spaces are ideal hosting and meeting places to connect creative minds. Despite the growth in inner city coworking spaces, little is known of entrepreneurial needs for coworking models in outer urban city areas, particularly areas that experience rapid population growth. The authors conducted an exploratory study to identify entrepreneurs' coworking needs in a fast-growing outer urban city area in Melbourne, Australia. Drawing on activity theory (AT) as a lens to analyse the data, the study confirms that entrepreneurs in fast-growing outer urban areas have unique coworking needs compared to those in inner-city areas. The study identifies three key requirements that an outer urban coworking model needs to address to support a growing cohort of outer-urban anywhere workers.*

## INTRODUCTION

*Workplaces* and *workspaces* have changed significantly over the last decade (Kelliher & Richardson, 2019; Messenger & Gschwind, 2016; World Bank, 2019). These changes are a result of increased digitalization, widespread deployment of Information and Communication Technologies (ICT) to collaborate and communicate, and more recent, urban congestion (Fiorentino, 2019; Messenger & Gschwind, 2016). New anywhere working models are becoming more widespread such as flexible work with increased worker mobility, work-life balance and wellbeing, and support for new work arrangements, i.e. temporary, virtual and freelance workers (AIG, 2012; Bentley, Teo et al., 2017).

Coworking, though not a panacea for the future of work, has become an attractive work arrangement that combines the formal office or work environment with 'other' informal workplaces, i.e. the home office, satellite hubs or libraries (Kingma, 2016). These workspaces allow for non-traditional forms of employment in attractive spaces that are appealing to young urban entrepreneurs who wish to work with other creative 'like-minded' workers (Cappelli & Keller, 2013; Osnowitz, 2010). Indications are that the growth spurt in inner-urban coworking hubs of large cities has not extended as quickly to outer urban areas (Moriset, 2013). Due to rapid outer urban population growth in many parts of the world, there is a need to create workspaces that support outer urban worker needs. Hence, this chapter will focus on the specific needs of workers who wish to access outer urban coworking hubs that are close to where they live (Anderson & Larsson, 2016).

Although there is no single universal definition, 'coworking' can be described as *the collaborative working of independent professionals and those with workplace flexibility in a shared space that upholds the core values of this concept, i.e. accessibility, collaboration, community, openness and sustainability* (Butcher, 2013; Spinuzzi, 2012; Uda, 2013). Coworking spaces develop around the idea of community building and sustainability. As a growing trend in the work landscape, coworking brings together different types and groups of workers from startups, entrepreneurs, corporate employees, and business travellers to home workers. Additionally, coworking spaces serve as vibrant platforms for exchanging new and innovative ideas and creative thinking (Waters-Lynch et al., 2016), and motivating workers to share business partners and connections (Merkel, 2015). Coworking hubs also create friendly harmonious work environments that allow both flexible and mobile work practices. Apart from these opportunities, such hubs often serve as an intermediate office space, saving employees the long daily commute to and from densely populated city areas.

Over the last years, there has been a growing interest worldwide in the design and development of coworking spaces bringing together a wealth of talent. The collaboration of individuals, micro- and small businesses in coworking hubs promote creativity and new business opportunities. For these purposes, coworking spaces are classified broadly in two categories. The first represents luxurious to more affordable custom-designed private or government-owned coworking spaces hosting a range of professionals. Services offered vary from day passes to occasional visitors to individual dedicated desks, or private spaces that include enclosed, lockable offices. The second category offers reconfigured space transformed into coworking spaces in community libraries, community centres (Bilandzic & Foth, 2013, 2017) or academic campus libraries (Lumley, 2014).

With the current focus on smart cities, modernization and redevelopment of unused space, the literature on coworking spaces is concentrated on inner-city metropolitan coworking arrangements addressing specific city-workers' entrepreneurial needs (Merkel, 2015; Waters-Lynch et al., 2016). Despite the steady growth of coworking spaces in outer urban areas of large cities, the extant literature has at best a cursory mention of coworking hub needs for outer urban co-workers. Considering the population growth and urban sprawl in large outer urban city areas (Brenner & Keil 2014; Downs, 1999; Florida, 2017), and in particular the Greater Melbourne area (Department of Environment, Land, Water, and Planning, 2017; Foster et al., 2013; Lowe et al., 2013), there is a need to understand better Melbourne's outer urban coworking needs to develop hubs that satisfy these needs. This chapter, therefore, aims to answer the following research question: *What are coworking needs of entrepreneurs in a fast-growing outer urban area?*

This paper is structured as follows: Section 2 describes background literature, followed by an introduction of Activity Theory, which was used as a lens to analyze the data in this study. Section 3 describes the research design, followed by a description of the case study, BizBuddyHub. Sections 4 and 5 present the findings and discussion, respectively, with outcomes describing unique outer urban coworking hub needs that emerged from the study. Section 6 gives a conclusion outlining the study's limitations, relevance for academia and research, and avenues for further research.

## BACKGROUND LITERATURE

Over the last few years, there has been a significant shift in *where and how workers conduct their work* which evolved away from the traditional office (Hislop & Axtell, 2009; Wessel et al., 2019). One example is the emergence of fluid forms of work that allow workers to combine working in the office with other settings, i.e. the home, satellite offices or smart hubs (Arnoldi et al., 2018; Bailey & Kurland, 2002; Bentley et al., 2016; Bosua et al., 2017. A second example is the progression of work settings from closed to open workspaces, i.e. hot desks, activity-based workspaces and coworking hubs that encourage entrepreneurial collaboration across different business areas and work disciplines (Felstead et al., 2005; Krause, 2019; Rockwood, 2017; Waters-Lynch et al., 2016).

Predictions are that future work will be even more fluid, less formal, more local/ global and virtual, not bounded to fixed locations and schedules, relying more on creativity and new ideas with a focus on quality output and productivity (Hirschi, 2018; Lee, 2012; Woodland 2017). Changes to work modes, styles and work locations can be attributed to digitization, new technological developments in infrastructure, such as the cloud and collaborative technologies that facilitate networking and distributed teamwork. Also, new developments in Web 2.0 and beyond, and accompanying social media tools enable collective access to data and content, human experts, and increasing use of mobile devices to support and facilitate collaboration and networking of an increasingly mobile workforce (Cole et al., 2012; Gandini, 2015). A review of the coworking literature from the last seven years highlights two key aspects of coworking: advantages of coworking models and the focus on social entrepreneurship as explained in the next two sections.

### Advantages of Coworking Models

The extant literature on coworking identifies five advantages that arise from coworking models:

1. *Accessible spaces supporting new ways of work*: Workers have access to physical spaces that embrace different forms of work and types of workers, e.g. mobile workers, multi-locational workers, remote, flexible, distributed and virtual

workers (Kojo & Nenonen, 2016; Wang & Loo, 2017). These workers share similar work practices that may not involve fixed daily office hours or work patterns. This may create a feeling of identity and belonging for those workers who combine home offices with coworking hubs instead of long commutes.

2. *Collaborating with heterogeneous workers*: Co-workers in hubs can participate actively in hub activities, e.g. regular events and hub-related activities arranged by coworking hosts or hub owners. This encourages collaboration, open communication and access to a variety of entrepreneurial activities while also creating a sense of unity through participation (Van Meel & Brinko, 2014).
3. *Aligning workers' lifestyles with work patterns*: Coworking spaces accommodate flexible or freelance workers with work patterns that differ from full-time work. There is no direct span of management control with co-workers controlling their own work pace and task completion (Kojo & Nenonen, 2016).
4. *Access to and use of specific facilities and tools*: Workers can access specific tools (printing, e.g. 3D-printing or overhead projection tools) or physical facilities such as a meeting or presentation rooms that might otherwise not be available (Buksh & Davidson, 2013; Parrino, 2015; Wang & Loo, 2017). These elements are useful for entrepreneurs or startups who lack the financial means to invest in their own tools and facilities; and
5. Access to expertise and knowledge sharing: The circulation and sharing of tacit knowledge in hubs is regarded as a key factor for building relationships and developing innovative ideas (Parriono, 2013; Wang & Loo, 2017).

All these coworking advantages are instrumental in shaping the collaboration and networking required for entrepreneurship in inner-city coworking hubs. However, there is scant evidence of studies focusing on outer urban coworking hub needs, hence the focus of this study to identify unique needs in these areas.

## Social Entrepreneurship Focus

Prior research indicates that coworking fosters social entrepreneurship, i.e. a social innovation culture that creates social capital which in turn gives access to support structures and mechanisms in networks to create new business ideas (Surman, 2013). The creation of coworking spaces has been a growing trend since 2005, and recent statistics list 14,411 coworking spaces worldwide with expectations that the number of coworking members will rise to 3.8 beyond 2020 and 5.1 million by 2022 (Fiorentino, 2019; Moriset, 2013).

A growing body of research on coworking follows ethnographic research designs involving short-term in- situ observations of work in workspaces. Findings indicate that socialization, collaboration and interaction activities promote creativity and innovation in coworking hubs. Studies also confirm that coworking space owners play a vital role in the success of these spaces in the sense that they are instrumental in linking entrepreneurs through socialization activities. Also, studies that share coworking success stories comment on the use of material practices and strategies that enhance and facilitate interaction in these spaces (Merkel, 2015). Hence, the openness of coworking environments provides a friendly environment in which social entrepreneurs as residents (Reuschke et al. 2019) can share novel ideas and get feedback from experts. While some coworking studies concentrate on knowledge sharing, connectivity, learning and innovation (Papageorigiou 2016; Parriono 2015), there are scant studies that investigate worker-specific needs for outer urban metropolitan hubs, hence the focus of this study.

## Exploring Outer Urban Coworking Using Activity Theory

To identify unique coworking needs for outer urban hubs, a theory focused around the activity of 'work' was selected. Activity Theory (AT) allows for an analysis of the impact of multiple elements on core activity, particularly the synergy between people, processes and technology. In AT, an activity existing in a sociocultural setting comprises a set of elements forming the activity system. The seven core elements that relate to coworking as an activity are: a subject (the co-worker who engages in the activity) is motivated by a purpose or towards the solution of a problem, the object (working and living locally), in order to achieve some goal (successful coworking) (Allen et al., 2011; 2013). Tools impact the activity while rules (membership type) and the division of labor (hybrid or coworking combined with home-based work) drive the activity. The community are stakeholders and groups that have an interest in coworking (Engeström, 2000, 2009; Gedera, 2016). An AT perspective adapted for coworking in outer urban areas is illustrated in Figure 1. AT offers analytical tools to model and analyze an activity system using three elements: *Rules or norms*, *Community* and the *Division of labor* (see Fig. 1).

These elements continuously mediate the relationships between elements in the activity system. For example, *Tool* mediates the '*Subject-Object*'-relationship and *Rules* mediate the '*Subject-Community*'-relationship, *Community* mediates the '*Subject-Object*'-relationship and *Division of Labor* mediates the '*Community-Object*'- relationship.

*Activities* are dynamic, constantly change and develop as impacted by other activities and environmental elements (Kuuti, 1996). Since activities are intertwined with others, the dynamic nature of activities accounts for contradictions in the activity system. Contradictions manifest as conflicts, gaps, disruptions, interruptions and obstacles in the activity system. The choice of AT to analyze the data for our study

*Figure 1. AT constructs for coworking in outer urban areas*

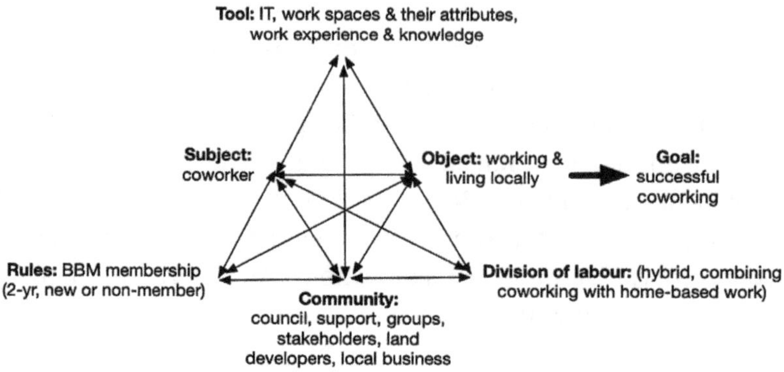


assisted in identifying obstacles which translated into needs for coworking in outer urban areas, as explained in the findings section of the chapter.

## RESEARCH DESIGN

Our research objective was to explore the nature of coworking needs of entrepreneurs in a fast-growing outer urban area. Thus, a qualitative research design using a single case was chosen for this study. The intention to explore a real-world situation while retaining a holistic perspective aligned well with the aims of case study research (Yin, 2014). Case study research allows for the collection of rich context-specific data to explore and analyze one or more phenomena in its specific context (Neuman, 2014). Case studies are also relevant when *how* and *why* types of questions are asked and where there is a need to understand better individual and group centred, complex social phenomena such as those in this study, i.e. perceptions, obstacles and wishes which translated into needs for coworking in outer urban areas (Yin, 2014). The research will generate data and ideas that may be verified in follow-up studies through traditional logico-deductive methods.

### Case Study Background

Melbourne's coworking culture is the biggest in Australia with the highest concentration of coworking hubs (66% in 2016) in its CBD and City Fringe. Eighty-seven per cent of Melbourne's businesses have less than four employees, and, predictions are that the growth trend in micro-businesses will grow in years to come. While the fastest growth in Melbourne coworking hubs is in inner-city metropolitan areas, coworking hub growth in outer urban metropolitan areas is lagging. With this in mind a grassroots' pop-up' coworking hub, G-HuB (a pseudonym), in an outer suburban area (referred to as OuterSub for anonymity) with a local government 44 kilometres on the south-western fringes of the Melbourne Metropolitan Area, was selected. OuterSub's population was 255,322 in 2018, and as one of the fastest-growing outer urban areas in Melbourne's Western corridor, expectations are that its population will grow by 83.2% in 2036. 27% of OuterSub's current population is older than 15 years. Sixty-three per cent of the population has a degree or higher qualification and work either full or part-time. Approximately 70% of OuterSub's resident workforce commutes to workplaces outside its municipality with 30% working locally.

Notably, G-HuB is different from the usual coworking hubs that rely on fixed physical spaces for coworking. Starting as a grassroots community-driven digital portal, G-HuB evolved in response to fast-growing outer urban neighbourhood needs. These needs were to promote and connect local outer urban businesses offering an opportunity to 'living locally'. A local social entrepreneur living in the OuterSub neighbourhood launched G-HuB in October 2015. She reported her process of consultation with several of local businesses, educational and community organizations and receipt of verbal support and encouragement from the local council's Chief Executive Officer, and members of Federal and State Parliaments at the time. G-HuB first introduced its presence virtually through an online portal aiming to draw local businesses, entrepreneurs, stakeholders and interested parties together through yearly memberships. G-HuB aimed to extend its online presence, pending financial support and critical mass into a physical space over time. G-HuB's business model complemented its virtual presence with a variety of regular 'pop-up' coworking hub space days and events in the OuterSub area.

Pop-up coworking hub days brought entrepreneurs and workers from the area together to meet up, work and collaborate with other like-minded entrepreneurs, while key business leaders and experts who live and work locally facilitated presentations and mentorship. These hub days and events targeted startups and local small and larger businesses. Since its launch, G-HuB gained momentum in two distinct ways:

1. active promotion and marketing through physical outreach, invitations and knowledge sharing via its portal to mobilize businesses and community support for the '*live local, work local, shop local – collaborate global*' vision, and
2. hub days, referred to as 'hackathons' or monthly 'get-togethers', aimed to link local business owners around social activities, i.e. short presentations, shared lunches, interesting workshops, educational events, business workshops, coffee catch-ups and time to work together at random in ad hoc spaces.

Traditionally, coworking hubs occupy fixed rented spaces where businesses come together to work on their own business in the same space For G-HuB, in the absence of a fixed coworking hub space, 'pop-up' coworking days filled the need to connect face-to-face in different venues (e.g. local hotels or other conference facilities) that were available on a needs base. These days were popular, and attendance required pre-booking through the portal. A combination of existing G-HuB members and new members (often up to 50) attended frequently.

At the time of conducting the study, G-HuB offered a flexible, affordable monthly membership program at approximately half the fee paid for a traditional coworking space. The flexible approach enabled free, 24/7 access to its events and its collaborative online community platform to engage in discussions, market, and advertise one's business and access business-community events. G-HuB's paid membership grew steadily to 110 members by 2017, providing an online marketplace that enabled local business and entrepreneurs to trade, shop, sell and share resources, services and products across the network and broader online community and participate in networking activities during physical pop-up and hackathon events. G-HuB was, therefore, an ideal concept and case for this study to explore and identify the unique coworking needs of outer urban workers in a fast-growing outer urban area.

## Participant Selection

One of the authors met the founder of G-HuB before conducting the study. Following this, two members of the research team participated in a full day G-HuB' hack connect' event in 2017 in OuterSub which aimed to get members and stakeholders together for round table discussions on issues that impacted G-HuB's growth in the area. As part of this wider event, the planned research study was presented, and a verbal invitation extended to attendees to participate in the study. Following the recruitment process outlined in the formal research ethics approval, the following participants were identified:

- a set of 'moonlighters' who were employed by large organizations and commuted to the city (traditional employees);
- SME employees working locally in the OuterSub area; and
- micro and small business managers/entrepreneurs working in their own businesses.

More than half the participants had prior experience of working in inner-city coworking spaces.

The final set of participants represented three different groups:

- *'2-year members'* who held G-HuB membership since its launch;
- *'new members'* who joined G-HuB 3-6 months before conducting the study; and
- *'non-members'*, who were aware of G-HuB and its model but were no members yet.

Attributes of participants in this study are described in the following table (Table 1).

*Table 1. Participants age, gender, business sector and G-HuB membership*

| Participant Details | Description |
|---|---|
| Age | 28 – 72 years |
| Gender | 12 females and 12 males |
| Number of entrepreneurs and business sector | 9 - Business Advisors and Consultancy<br>6 - Training and Career advisory<br>4 - IT, and Marketing Business<br>3 - Creative Design<br>2 - New startup Development while in full-time corporate employment in the CBD |
| BBH membership distribution | 7 non-members,<br>8 joined during the last year (3-6 months a member)<br>9 joined within the first year (2+ year members) |
| **Total** | **24 participants** |

## Data Collection and Analysis

The primary data collection method comprised four focus groups conducted over two weeks on 28 September 2017 (Focus Groups 1 and 2, 6 participants in each) and 6 October 2017 (Focus Groups 3 and 4, 7 participants in each). All focus groups were held in the area (OuterSub) and were run by two members of the research team. Focus group discussions aimed to gather data on participants' perceptions of the G-HuB model, the value of its events, and specific coworking needs, e.g. coworking settings, necessary IT tools, facilitating elements and barriers impacting local coworking, and mechanisms to develop regional coworking communities. Participants were offered a gift voucher to compensate for their time, travel and parking expenses.

Also, secondary data was collected and analyzed (including data from key G-HuB artefacts such as vision documents, write-ups and reports, and notes made during individual meetings with the G-HuB founder, other stakeholders (e.g. representatives from the City of OuterSub)). Observations were conducted, and notes were taken during the first hackathon event. All focus group discussions were audio-recorded, de-identified, transcribed verbatim and consolidated with the secondary collected data, i.e. handwritten and other notes/documents analyzed. All transcribed content was made available to all researchers via a shared network drive. Following data distribution, each author first analyzed the data individually, then collectively through a team meeting sharing, comparing and discussing analysis themes that emerged. AT was used as a lens to identify and interpret outer urban workers' coworking needs (see next section). NVivo 11 was used to facilitate the coding and subsequent data analyses.

## FINDINGS

### An AT Activity Perspective on Outer Urban Coworking

A first cut through the data used open coding to identify bottlenecks, obstacles, needs, advantages, disadvantages and mechanisms the focus group participants mentioned concerning the G-HuB model. Following this, axial coding was used to cluster open codes into sets of categories that align to the AT constructs: *subject*, *object* and *goal*, *tools*, *rules*, *community* and *division of labor* (see Fig. 1).

The focal activity, i.e. '*worker engagement in outer area coworking*', formed part of a larger activity system consisting of the following elements identified in the first open coding process: *subject* is a co-worker, *tools* are the technology used to facilitate coworking, plus the physical workspace(s) and its attributes, and a worker's experience and knowledge related to work/coworking. The *object* construct was considered as workers' motives to work and live locally, with the *goal,* successful coworking. Further, the *rules* construct was considered as the adoption of the G-HuB coworking model based on membership type.

G-HuB-model adopters were classified into three groups:

- early adopters (joined G-HuB since its launch);
- recent adopters (joined in the last 3-6 months); and
- outsiders (non-adopters but those interested in joining G-HuB)

The *community* construct included environmental elements that influence outer urban coworking, i.e. the local council, other support groups and stakeholders, land developers and outer urban businesses, and the *division of labor,* i.e. entrepreneurship and the combination of coworking and home-based work.

Figure 1 represents the study's AT building blocks as elements that impact outer urban workers' coworking needs.

## Outer Urban Coworking Needs Through the AT Lens

The next step in the analysis aimed for a more in-depth investigation of the basic activity system considering the impact of *tools* on the Subject-Object interrelationship sub-triangle (Section 4.2.1 below). Also, Engeström's (2000; 2009) expansion of AT elements that foregrounds the broader social context through the addition of *rules* and norms, the *community* and the *division of labor* as interrelated elements that impact on the activity were the focus. Inclusion of these elements helped to further cluster the data into three sets of sub-triangles, each representing a new view of contradictions on the data. The following sections present the four themes in 4.2.1 to 4.2.4 (as sub-triangles), each representing a contradiction that impacts a worker's outer urban coworking needs. The AT sub-triangles described supported the axial and selective coding stages of qualitative data analysis.

### Impact of Tool Needs on Coworking

In this interaction, the impact of the *Tool* artefact, i.e. Information Technology, the coworking physical space and the G-HuB portal (and its attributes) on coworking needs were analyzed by identifying critical needs from the data as described below:

#### Access to Physical Coworking Hub Items

Almost all the participants indicated a need for access to essential items in a coworking hub such as:

*I want a desk, a printer and a coffee machine" (Joshua, Focus Group 1). ... my needs are specific. It needs to be audio-visual; I have to have phones for phone conferences (Rosemary, Focus Group 4), ... [I need] a professional setup" (Alan, Focus Group 4). Fast WIFI/internet connectivity was high on most participants' agenda as the slow broadband network connectivity in some OuterSub areas impacted workers' ability to work from home. Another important requirement was that a physical space had to be ...close to the local area businesses, close to the shopping centre. (Ravi, Focus Group 1).*

#### Coworking Hub Affordability

Affordability of the hub was important as some participants were startup or nascent entrepreneurs. Participants appreciated the exploration and support for alternative pricing strategies following extensive comparative pricing to gauge affordability, and their sensitivity for affordability was demonstrated by the suggestion for an alternative model to alleviate existing financial hurdles in securing a physical space for G-HuB in the following remarks:

*I've done my [pricing] enquiries, three to four service offices in the area are more expensive, requires like a monthly subscription you pay as rent, then there is your bond – you need to sign a bond, contracts and all this. Because I am a [professional] Social Worker [and] I can't work as a business with contractual [bond] agreements, I can't do that I can only work as a social contract..., keep it simple...the local council isn't supporting us.... it's better to do something like a barter system which is like you donate time to each other, you don't talk about financial terms you just help each other maybe monthly once, or whatever, have a fixed space (Mike, Focus Group 1).*

## Online Register and Space Booking Facility

Participants indicated that unused open spaces in the area should be made available to rent on a needs basis. Hence the suggestion that G-HuB keeps a register of available spaces and accompanying facilities workers can book on a needs basis. Participants wanted to browse the online portal to identify spaces that were available and suggested a need to allow them to register their details and book spaces for coworking space and facility use. Due to the lack of a regular accessible physical space, participants only wanted to secure a 'place' for each pop-up but also expressed a high need for the booking of temporary spaces on a needs basis to run local workshops/seminars. The participants' needs were expressed by a participant who declared:

*[I often need] a dedicated space where you always know where it is, and you could have a look at the timetable like a 'shared house' you know 'flat-share type of things' – where you could jump on [online] have a look and go "I'm going to book it for that time", jump on and see if there are two or three other people who are looking to band together and get a coworking [space], rent a space together and share the costs. (Debbie, Focus Group 1).*

## Space for Privacy

Several participants required a space that allows for private conversations and meetings. The need for privacy was reflected in the remark:

*So you know I might have to take a Skype call or something, so I couldn't work in something where everybody had this closeness all the time, so [I need to] have [access to] multi-use spaces, some open space where people can have coffee and sit around and chat and [then] some closed spaces where people can just go in and shut the door, and maybe a boardroom for people who might have meetings and things like that (Debbie, Focus Group 1).*

### Face-to-face Networking

Most participants felt that face-to-face networking was essential, particularly for conducting and promoting their business in the area. An ad hoc, temporary physical space was acceptable insofar as offering the most important requirement for face-to-face networking, summarised as:

*I don't have to pay when I'm working from home but getting out there and networking with people, it does build the community a little bit more and sharing the information and keeping more businesses going locally is a good idea [for a coworking space], so it will be worth for me as a small business. (Gemma, Focus Group 3).*

Another participant added:

*What I want is a space where I can work, and then space where I can socialize and bounce ideas around with other businesses…an option that wasn't my home. (Andrew, Focus Group 1).*

### Coworking Hub Space for Childcare

Working parents expressed a particular need to have coworking spaces with additional space for childcare, allowing them to balance part-time work and childcare:

*I'd really like to connect locally... we need that [space] desperately, I don't want a permanent base in the city, that's a family decision for me because I've got young children and I don't want to be an hour away… I run my business with that in mind, so I can be close. (Linda, Focus Group 2).*

## Impact of Rules on Coworking

This theme focused on G-HuB membership rules for coworking and its impact on the needs of outer urban co-workers. Two aspects arose:

### G-HuB Membership

Most full membership G-HuB members were happy with current ad hoc G-HuB pop-up and hackathon events. However, they expressed the need for a dedicated physical coworking hub space to support their entrepreneurial needs. Five 'non-member' G-HuB participants were satisfied with their infrastructure at home but wanted to extend their home office with occasional coworking in a nearby space. One participant summarised their needs as follows:

*I wanted the option to work from home if I needed to be in that space for whatever reason or have somewhere I can go and potentially have a coffee machine and an address I wanted, that was not my home [office]. (Mary, Focus Group 2).*

### Getting Rid of the Area's Stigma

One interesting theme that emerged in recurring discussions was the 'stigma' associated with using a home address as a business address in this specific outer urban area. A young entrepreneur who migrated from India described the group's dilemma as:

*...bigger space where you can have privacy... you need an address as a mailbox where it [the mail] goes – it's not your home address, but it looks like an office address and no-one will know you live in the area. (Ravi, Focus Group 1).*

## Impact of Community on Coworking

Participants all agreed that their case for a dedicated coworking hub needed more interest from key area stakeholders who will support their grassroots initiative. There was a need for local councils and potential space owners who were willing to refurbish unused spaces and buildings in the area for coworking hub rental, allowing working more closely with G-HuB. Four specific needs emerged:

### Proactive Council Involvement

More than half of the participants felt strongly the local OuterSub council or regional bodies could be more proactive to ensure coworking hubs are created based on growing community needs:

*The council cannot keep up with the growth. ... there is a lot of 'talk' about creating local jobs and people working locally and living locally and not having to get on the freeway during peak hours and take an awful amount of time, or get on trains that are really packed, two stations away" (John, Focus Group 2).*

However, an analysis of coworking spaces and a discussion with the G-HuB owner indicated a lack of resources and financial support to realize the specific coworking needs for one or more physical spaces in this area.

Some participants felt that local councils were not doing enough to support outer urban workers:

*If the council has that great vision, it's like, you have to address the parking, the public transport, the roads, the address space for businesses. So, all these things need to be addressed. So 'what is going on', how are you going to support that grand vision because it's great to have people move into the area because for all of us it means potentially more clientele, but if we can't find a space, or access a space easily, and affordably to work together, then you'll have people migrating out of the area... so there need to be spaces where people can park, and where they can get to. (Debbie, Focus Group 1).*

## State Government Involvement

More involvement of the state government was raised by participants to ensure that outer coworking needs are fulfilled, particularly in this fast-growing regional area with a high percentage of knowledge workers:

*The state government should be involved...if there's enthusiasm from members in order to build on that, we do need some government support... some sort of money coming in, some – funding of some sort, otherwise the enthusiastic members will go. (Tony, Focus Group 2).*

## Local Council Collaboration With G-HuB

Some participants felt the local council could do more to collaborate with G-HuB to facilitate the creation of informal coworking spaces that could be privately rented by a few small businesses, declared by one participant as: "*I would love to see* G-HuB *tie in better with the OuterSub City Council,*" and expressed her wish that the Economic Development Office would invest in a development hub that works closely with G-HuB (Ann, Focus Group 2). She mentioned:

*… there should be better integration of the business in the community, the support they need and the council supporting them to grow and make [one's] businesses better".*

### Replicating Successful Co-work Models

A former UK resident suggested that councils learn from other workable solutions by replicating successful outer area coworking models from abroad:

*...have a hub [coworking space] but then invest in other areas like the UK, they dropped the business rates to make the area attractive to business. Once you get businesses into the area it's easier to keep them there because businesses don't like moving, it costs them more to move... they're attracted in because of business rates, the facilities, so you drop their overhead rather than give them a return so it makes it cost-effective for them A hub is just one of the strategies for the local area, local businesses which make the whole lot prosperous which then makes it more attractive for people to live here, then puts the prices up, and then people can invest in properties and business (Jon, Focus Group 2).*

Interestingly, a representative from the local council revealed in an informal follow-up meeting with the research team that local governments already use such models to incentivize businesses to move to the area. However, participants did not perceive there was evidence of this was at the time of conducting the study.

## Impact of Different Forms of Labor on Coworking

The final theme considered the impact of existing forms of 'labor' (or coworking models such as a hybrid, irregular or regular coworking work model) on co-workers' needs, with three emerging themes:

### Flexible Coworking Model

Most participants wanted to control their own coworking needs and preferred combining a home-based office with a coworking hub, i.e. spending time in both spaces with the flexibility they could control. In particular, the need to co-work in a hub was for some participants temporal as one consultant indicated:

*......an ability to occasionally go out and remind myself, you know, or be reminded that I'm not alone and that there are other people out there who have ideas and – and things that can be engaged with is great. (Patrick, Focus Group 3).*

Another worker confirmed this flexible temporal need by saying:

*It's like I'm getting some like-minded people or some people that I want to collaborate with [at times], on a pretty innovative idea, and we want to make a commitment to meet once a week, twice a week, whatever it is and have a space, versus having to go to someone's house, right. (Alex, consultant who juggles corporate work with small business ownership, Focus Group 4).*

## Appreciation for the G-HuB Coworking Model

The 2-year and newer G-HuB members highly valued the virtual support, and 'pop-up' initiatives as one member indicated that the G-HuB model fitted her work style. She appreciated the flexibility and occasional G-HuB events she could attend on a needs base. G-HuB helped her to

*...step outside their [my] old little confined space of me, me, me". From a business perspective, she praised the occasional events and pop-ups, stating "...that's when one starts to grow and expand and that's all about putting the community before oneself, and that's when one starts getting results. (Samantha, Focus Group 3).*

## Casual Entrepreneurial Support

Abhi (a marketing company owner, Focus Group 3) felt the G-HuB model fulfilled flexible work needs and helped him find the right entrepreneurs to connect to. She said G-HuB helped her to

*...pursue my dream of starting a media marketing company down here in the OuterSub area (early adopter).*

Another participant felt the G-HuB portal provided

*... a [business] opportunity in a very informal way. So, it's not like you have to go somewhere like a ten o'clock meeting and all suited and formally stand and speak about [your business]. That itself is a bit too much for a beginner. G-HuB just brings people casually [together] to start with. If you want to catch up then you build your own connections. (Samantha, Focus Group 2).*

# DISCUSSION

In response to the research question:

*What are the specific coworking needs of entrepreneurs in a fast-growing outer urban city area?*

The findings highlight several key outcomes based on the data analysis using AT as a lens (Figure 1).

The next sections highlight the outcomes of this study: the value of the virtual G-HuB portal, in this case, the need for coworking spaces to support a new upcoming flexible workforce, and unique coworking needs of outer urban workers.

## A Virtual Portal Drawing Outer Urban Entrepreneurs Together

G-HuB has introduced an alternative model of coworking – a 'pop-up' coworking model – that satisfies most business needs of co-workers in this outer urban area. In the absence of one or more physical coworking spaces, the G-HuB-portal served as a vibrant centralized component that drew the local community together virtually (Österle et al., 2011) while also serving as a 'marketplace' for local entrepreneurs and businesses. The vision of '*living and working and conducting business locally'* was enabled through the G-HuB portal and paid membership gave access to this portal's advertising, marketing and community-driven posts which members described as a 'their own marketplace' providing a *"...loose information environment that is all about collaboration*".

Members appreciated the portal's informality, flexible nature, membership focus, the wide scope that enables and facilitates business opportunities and entrepreneurship and the value it brought in terms of connectivity and linking to experts and other businesses (Kohet al., 2003). Members felt that the portal was instrumental in pushing the '*live locally, work locally'* concept hoping that G-HuB initiatives could lead to a next stage of investing in more local physical coworking spaces (some non-permanent) where those who wanted, could connect with others. In this way, unused open spaces could be used to support the sustainability of the built environment; therefore:

**Proposition 1:** The presence of an information portal based on membership, giving access to tools that link and facilitate communication, connectivity and inclusiveness between local business and entrepreneurs, leads to higher online visibility and business opportunities for local entrepreneurs.

## The Need for Coworking Hub Models That Support Hybrid, Flexible Work Arrangements

Our final results indicate that outer urban coworking space needs are different from those of inner-city areas. Outer urban co-workers want more control over their circumstances and work models. Our findings indicate a high degree of consensus about a hybrid work mode, i.e. the need to combine coworking (even a 'pop-up' coworking model) with home-based work, offering heightened levels of choice for workers in terms of attendance (Papageorgiou, 2016). Workers supported the preference to work in a hybrid work mode with irregular work patterns allowing to spend some days '*in the space*' and some days working either from home or in any other suitable area (Bosua et al., 2017). Some participants felt that the 'pop-up' coworking model improved their mental wellbeing while also preventing isolation (Bentley et al., 2016; Gandini, 2015). The preference of affordable space to be frequented on a needs basis emphasized the preference for a flexible hybrid work model to better balance work and family life, e.g. getting children to and back from schools (Garrett et al., 2014). This was important as many of the workers were entrepreneurs who juggled work with the raising of their young children. Also, a hybrid work model promoted workers' ability to conduct a large part of work from home, giving access to spaces and events that could enhance professionalism on an occasional needs base. The interest was more in access to spaces to conduct client meetings and collaboration activities or to rent dedicated spaces for a workshop or use of facilities on a needs base. Therefore:

***Proposition 2a:*** *Outer urban co-workers prefer coworking spaces that support hybrid work models, i.e. allow workers to combine coworking with home-based work on a needs base to decrease isolation and loneliness,* and

**Proposition 2b**: Outer urban co-workers do not require regular coworking hub attendance but prefer 'pop-up coworking' allowing workers to control and plan their flexible work models.

## A Deeper Understanding of Outer Urban Coworking Needs

Respondents agreed about the need for local stakeholders who understand their unique coworking needs. They did not require fixed-space coworking hubs each day, but instead needed hubs and accompanying facilities in the hubs to support flexible work practices and specific needs. An example of this model would be a register of affordable spaces and facilities that could be booked in local areas when necessary. Also, participants felt that different stakeholders (such as regional development bodies, local council and state government, land developers and planners, and other large business investors in regional coworking spaces), should be more involved and supportive of unique outer urban work needs. Also, participants observed that unused spaces could be customized for coworking – some empty warehouses and buildings could potentially be transformed into affordable coworking hubs.

The G-HuB owner and participants indicated the need to improve outer urban coworking and noted that Councils made more resources available for inner-city coworking hubs as opposed to outer-working areas. At the same time, fast-growing regional areas required more attention from local and state governments. With steep population growth in outer urban areas as a result of migration, the future of work had to consider outer urban areas to stimulate economic growth (Jamal, 2018), therefore:

**Proposition 3:** A detailed assessment of outer city worker needs led by local community stakeholders (councils, support groups, regional planners and developers) is necessary to grow much needed new models of outer urban coworking spaces.

## Promoting Living and Working Local Through Coworking in Outer Urban Areas

The central activity of AT related to coworking as living and working locally was confirmed as paramount for sustainable living in fast-growing outer urban areas such as OuterSub, as confirmed by Gandini (2015) and Boyer (2016). Participants indicated that their needs were different from inner-city areas as a result of the existing infrastructure, presence and interest in the G-HuB portal that drew local entrepreneurs together in this outer urban area. Participants indicated pride in the leadership role of the G-HuB social entrepreneur in establishing the coworking G-HuB portal that united the local business community and supported the notion of a 'pop-up' coworking model that participants valued. The G-HuB founder was seen as a visionary social entrepreneur who represented the local community and promoted their cause for coworking through a 'pop-up' coworking outer urban model, therefore:

**Proposition 4:** An entrepreneurial coworking champion and coworking model that support new forms of work based on local outer urban community needs, increase the success of outer urban coworking hub models in outer urban city areas.

Our findings confirm that AT is a useful theory (Engeström, 2000, 2009; Gedera, 2015) to conduct an in-depth analysis of the unique needs associated with coworking activities of outer urban co-workers. In particular, AT gives a perspective on coworking as an activity that spans the following elements: Tool- and Community support, Rules and the Division of Labor.

The use of AT in this study confirms the need for establishing:

1. hybrid coworking models or hubs for outer urban areas with,
2. the inclusion of an IT portal that fosters collaboration and draws workers together virtually, and
3. affordable coworking spaces in outer urban areas that provide a professional yet affordable environment for outer urban workers on a needs base.

The study highlights the need for greater public and private stakeholders' involvement in promoting regional development and the development of coworking spaces in particular. Follow-up studies applying 3rd and 4th generation AT analyses are required to apply a deeper conceptual level of analysis (Spinuzzi, 2012).

## CONCLUSION

This chapter sought to explore outer urban metropolitan workers needs for coworking hubs in a growing outer urban area, City of OuterSub, on the fringes of Melbourne, Australia. Adopting a qualitative case study approach, the responses are conveyed in a manner that appropriately represents the members' perspectives (Carey et al., 2012). Three critical coworking needs of workers that wish to live and work locally were identified:

1. a central community-driven online coworking portal that promotes networking, collaboration and marketing;
2. a hybrid coworking hub model that includes a virtual/physical infrastructure that satisfies workers' entrepreneurial needs to meet occasionally and network, make new connections with potential clients and other business through face to face events to facilitate the sharing and marketing of business ideas; and
3. an affordable physical space with desks, printers and breakout spaces that allow for workshops, meetings and private discussions combined with high-speed internet services to increase networking, collaboration and interaction between local individuals and business partners.

Our findings also indicate that in addition to online collaborative efforts, outer urban area workers avoided isolation by visiting coworking facilities intermittently for face-to-face interaction: a flexible arrangement that allows for a hybrid work model that combined a home-office or other workplace with occasional work in outer urban coworking spaces. More important than spending time working in coworking spaces, was the ability to access frequent organized pop-up events and workshop sessions allowing workers to market their small businesses products or services, making new business connections and attending business or running workshops. Our study also highlighted the need for local councils and other key stakeholders to be more involved and focused on outer urban worker needs while increasingly collaborative initiatives and efforts for social entrepreneurs to foster '*live local work local shop local – collaborate global*'. This supports Mason and Brown's (2014) criticism of governments and non-government organizations' extensive support for only high-growth, large firms.

## Study Limitations

Our study has some limitations. Firstly, the coworking needs, initially in a single outer urban area in south-west Melbourne, were considered to develop an understanding of the phenomenon. With Melbourne's growth into a mega-city by 2030, there is a need to extend the study to other outer urban areas offering the opportunity to compare other-area worker needs (e.g. east versus the west). Secondly, as a first study to explore coworking in outer urban areas, plans are underway to extend this study into a more extensive quantitative study to test our results in a broader demographical context. Moreover, a follow-up study has to consider the perspectives of other key stakeholders, i.e. councillors, investors, land developers and planners to identify how worker needs can be met and addressed. Notably, using a single case study limits generalizability. One cannot infer that our findings apply to similar outer urban or areas on the fringes of cities elsewhere in Australia and beyond. The research study needs to be extended to include other outer areas, states, and countries. However, based on our findings, we can make modest claims about the implications of our study in terms of theory and practice.

## Implications for Theory and Practice

This study has implications for both theory and practice. In terms of theory, we applied AT as a lens to explore the workers' outer urban coworking needs. This theory helped to focus on coworking as an activity (AT Levels 1 and 2). However, it did not attempt a more in-depth perspective on the interaction between human and artefact networks, nor the impact of adoption and value of an online portal such as G-HuB (e.g. the design of G-HuB to foster networking and collaboration by the different user groups were not explored). The study extends Wessels et al.'s. (2018) model of spatial job crafting, postulating new ways of work giving workers the flexibility to shape their own time/space job crafting proactively. The importance of policy and regulatory guidelines that drive coworking as well as the synergy between social entrepreneurs that drive coworking (e.g. the G-HuB founder) and other stakeholder groups from the Council and Regional Development entities warrant further exploration. The study highlights the urgency for a holistic stakeholder approach to the outer urban coworking debate. Also, more research to explore outer urban coworking platforms as mechanisms for innovation, knowledge-sharing and knowledge creation is recommended due to population growth and urban congestion. The study attempted to contribute to the extant research on flexible coworking in a specific geopolitical setting.

From a practice perspective, this study has some implications. Firstly, by identifying the needs and experiences of entrepreneurial workers that wish to work and live in outer urban areas, other 'grassroots neighbourhood communities' with co-work initiatives in other outer urban areas may learn from the study. For example, investors may need first to develop an online portal as a beta activity – a construct familiar to entrepreneurs as the minimum requirement for 'testing' a concept - that supports the '*live local-work local- shop local – collaborate globally*' coworking model before investing in a physical space. Secondly, our study indicates that the championing by stakeholders of a coworking model is central to engaging and including local workers in an outer urban coworking model. Thirdly, the design of the G-HuB-portal may serve as a platform for the design of a more comprehensive information system that supports the needs of specific user groups engaged in anywhere working. Finally, it is recommended the study be repeated in a similar setting post-COVID-19 allowing for new insights on the effect of the pandemic in this space.

## REFERENCES

AIG. (2012). *Working smarter: flexible work and telework, Report of the Australian Industry Group*. http://ict-industry-reports.com.au/wp-content/uploads/sites/4/2013/09/2012-Telework-Working-Smarter-AIGroup-Nov-2012.pdf

Allen, D., Karanasios, S., & Slavova, M. (2011). Working with activity theory: Context, technology, and information behavior. *Journal of the American Society for Information Science and Technology*, *62*(4), 776–788. doi:10.1002/asi.21441

Allen, D. K., Brown, A., Karanasios, S., & Norman, A. (2013). How should technology-mediated organizational change be explained? A comparison of the contributions of critical realism and activity theory. *Management Information Systems Quarterly*, *37*(3), 835–854. doi:10.25300/MISQ/2013/37.3.08

Andersson, M., & Larsson, J. P. (2016). Local entrepreneurship clusters in cities. *Journal of Economic Geography*, *16*(1), 39–66. doi:10.1093/jeg/lbu049

Arnoldi, E., Bosua, R., Cooper, V., Greenfield, C., & Ch'ng, H. (2018). *Coworking and an Outer urban community: What can we learn from a grassroots community coworking hub?* Analysis and Policy Observatory.

Bailey, D. E., & Kurland, N. B. (2002). A review of telework research: Findings, new direction and lessons for the study of modern work. *Journal of Organizational Behavior*, *23*(4), 383–400. doi:10.1002/job.144

Bentley, T. A., Teo, S. T. T., McLeod, L., Tan, F., Bosua, R., & Gloet, M. (2016). 'The role of organizational support in teleworker wellbeing: A socio-technical systems approach'. *Applied Ergonomics*, *52*, 207–215. doi:10.1016/j.apergo.2015.07.019 PMID:26360212

Bilandzic, M., & Forth, M. (2013). Libraries as coworking spaces: Understanding user motivations and perceived barriers to social learning. *Library Hi Tech*, *31*(2), 254–273. doi:10.1108/07378831311329040

Bilandzic, M., & Forth, M. (2017). Designing hubs for connected learning: Social, Spatial and technological insights from Coworking, Hackerspaces and Meetup groups. In L. Carvalho, P. Goodyear, & M. de Laat (Eds.), *Place-Based Spaces for Networked Learning, Routledge* (pp. 191–206). United Kingdon.

Bosua, R., Kurnia, S., Gloet, M., & Mendoza, A. (2017). Telework Impact on Productivity and Well-Being. In *Innovative ICT-enabled Services and Social Inclusion*. Taylor and Francis. doi:10.4324/9781315677316-10

Boyer, R. H. (2016). Achieving one-planet living through transitions in social practice: a case study of Dancing Rabbit Ecovillage. *Sustainability: Science, Practice and Policy, 12*(1), 47-59.

Brenner, N., & Keil, R. (2014). From Global Cities to Globalized Urbanization. *Glocalism: Journal Of Culture, Politics And Innovation*, 3. www.glocalismjournal.net

Buksh, B., & Davidson, J. (2013). Digital Work Hubs-An Activation Framework for South East Queensland. *The Digital Work Hub Project, Regional Development Australia.* Available at: digitalworkhub.com.au

Butcher, T. (2013). Coworking: locating community at work. *Annual Australia New Zealand Academy of Management (ANZAM) Conference.*

Cappelli, P., & Keller, J. R. (2013). Classifying work in the new economy. *Academy of Management Review*, *38*(4), 575–596. doi:10.5465/amr.2011.0302

Carey, M.A., Asbury, J. & Tolich, M.B. (n.d.). *Focus Group Research.* Taylor & Francis Group.

Cole, R. J., Bild, A., & Olivre, A. (2012). The changing context of knowledge-based work: Consequences for comfort, satisfaction and productivity. *Intelligent Buildings International, 4*(3), 182–196. doi:10.1080/17508975.2012.695950

Department of Environment, Land, Water and Planning. (2017). *Metropolitan Partnerships: Western Region.* Victoria State Government. www.delwp.vic.gov.au

Downs, A. (1999). Some realities about sprawl and urban decline. *Housing Policy Debate, 10*(4), 955–974. doi:10.1080/10511482.1999.9521356

Engeström, Y. (2000). Activity theory as a framework for analyzing and redesigning work. *Ergonomics, 43*(7), 960–974. doi:10.1080/001401300409143 PMID:10929830

Engeström, Y. (2009). The future of Activity Theory: A rough draft. In Learning and Expanding with Activity Theory. New York, NY: Cambridge. doi:10.1017/CBO9780511809989.020

Felstead, A., Jewson, N., & Walters, S. (2005). The shifting locations of work: New statistical evidence on the spaces and places of employment. *Work, Employment and Society, 19*(2), 415–431. doi:10.1177/0950017005053186

Fiorentino, S. (2019). Different typologies of 'coworking spaces' and the contemporary dynamics of local economic development in Rome. *European Planning Studies, 27*(9), 1768–1790. doi:10.1080/09654313.2019.1620697

Florida, R. (2017). *The New Urban Crisis.* Basic Books.

Foster, H., Towers, B., Whittaker, J., Handmer, J., & Lowe, T. (2013). Peri-urban Melbourne in 2021: Changes and Implications for the Victorian Emergency Management Sector. *Australian Journal of Emergency Management, 28*, 6–12.

Gandini, A. (2015). The rise of coworking spaces: A literature review. *Ephemera, 15*, 193–205.

Garrett, L. E., Spreitzer, G. M., & Bacevice, P. (2014). Co-constructing a sense of community at work: the emergence of community in coworking spaces. Academy of Management Proceedings, 1, 14004. doi:10.5465/ambpp.2014.139

Gedera, D. S. P. (2016). 4: The Application of Activity Theory in Identify Contradictions in a University Blended Learning Course. In *Activity Theory in Education* (pp. 53–60). Sense Publishers.

Hirschi, A. (2018). The Fourth Industrial Revolution: Issues and Implications for Career Research and Practice. *Career Development Quarterly*, *66*, 192–204.

Hislop, D., & Axtell, C. (2009). To infinity and beyond? Workspace and the multi-location worker. *NTWE*, *24*, 60–75.

Jamal, A. C. (2018). Coworking spaces in mid-sized cities: A partner in downtown economic development. *Environment and Planning A. Economy and Space*, *50*, 773–788.

Kelliher, C., & Richardson, J. (2019). *Work, Working and Work Relationships in a Changing World* (1st ed.). Routledge.

Kingma, S. F. (2016). The constitution of 'third workspaces' in between the home and the corporate office. *NTWE*, *31*, 176–193.

Knight, F. (2017). *Bridging the Gap: Melbourne's Coworking Culture*. https://kfcontent.blob.core.windows.net/research/1100/documents/en/melcowork1702-4438.pdf

Koh, J., Kim, Y. G., & Kim, Y. G. (2003). Sense of virtual community: A conceptual framework and empirical validation. *International Journal of Electronic Commerce*, *8*(2), 75–94. doi:10.1080/10864415.2003.11044295

Kojo, I., & Nenonen, S. (2016). Typologies for coworking spaces in Finland–what and how? *Facilities*, *34*(5/6), 302–313. doi:10.1108/F-08-2014-0066

Krause, I. (2019). Coworking Spaces: Windows to the Future of Work? *Foresight and STI Governance*, *13*(2), 52–60. doi:10.17323/2500-2597.2019.2.52.60

Kuuti, K. (1996). Activity Theory as a potential framework for human computer interaction research. In B. Nardi (Ed.), Context and consciousness: Activity Theory and human computer interaction, (pp. 17-44). Cambridge, MA: MIS Press.

Lowe, M., Whitzman, C., Badland, H., Davern, M., Hes, D., Aye, L., Butterworth, I., & Giles-Corti, B. (2013). *Liveable, Helthy, Sustainable: What are the key indicators for Melbourne Neighbourhoods? Research Paper 1, Place, Health and Liveability Research Program, University of Melbourne*. http://mccaugheycentre.unimelb.edu.au/research/health_and_liveability

Lumley, R. M. (2014). A Coworking Project in the Campus Library: Supporting and Modelling Entrepreneurial Activity in the Academic Library. *New Review of Academic Librarianship*, *29*(1), 49–65. doi:10.1080/13614533.2013.850101

Mason, C., & Brown, R. (2017). Looking Inside the Spiky bits: A critical review and conceptualization of entrepreneurial ecosystems. *Small Business Economics*, *49*(1), 11–30. doi:10.100711187-017-9865-7

Merkel, J. (2015). Coworking in the city. *Ephemera*, *15*, 121–139.

Messenger, J., & Gschwind, L. (2016). Three generations of Telework: New ICTs and the (R)evolution from Home Office to Virtual Office. *NTWE*, *31*, 159–208.

Moriset, B. (2013). Buildi308ng new places of the creative economy. The rise of coworking spaces. In 2[nd] *Geography of Innovation International Conference*. Utrecht University.

Neuman, W. L. (2014). *Social Research Methods: Qualitative and Quantitative Approaches* (2nd ed.). Pearson Education Ltd.

Osnowitz, D. (2016). *Freelancing expertise*. Cornell University Press. doi:10.7591/9780801460388

Österle, H., Fleisch, E., & Alt, R. (2011). *Business networking: shaping collaboration between enterprises*. Springer Science and Business Media.

Papageorgiou, A. (2016). *Living in Beta: hubs, collectives and the emergence of moral economies in Athens*. The Dynamics of Virtual Work, Working Paper Series (7). Accessed 1 November 2019: http://dynamicsofvirtualwork.com/wp-content/uploads/2015/08/working-paper-No-7.pdf

Parrino, L. (2015). Coworking: Assessing the role of proximity in knowledge exchange. *Knowledge Management Research and Practice*, *13*(3), 261–271. doi:10.1057/kmrp.2013.47

Reuschke, D., Kleinhans, R., Syrett, S., Van Ham, M., & Mason, C. (2019). Understanding entrepreneurship in residential neighbourhoods and communities of place. In C. Mason, D. Reuschke, S. Syrett, & M. van Ham (Eds.), *Entrepreneurship in Cities: Neighbourhoods, Households and Homes, 297 – 308*. Edward Elgar.

Rockwood, K. (2017, June). Rethinking the Workspaces and Build Movement. *Entrepreneur*.

Spinuzzi, C. (2012). Working alone together: Coworking as emergent collaborative activity. *Journal of Business and Technical Communication*, *26*(4), 399–441. doi:10.1177/1050651912444070

Surman, T. (2013). Building social entrepreneurship through the power of coworking. *Innovations: Technology, Governance, Globalization*, *8*(3-4), 189–195. doi:10.1162/INOV_a_00195

Uda, T. (2013). *What is Coworking? A Theoretical Study on the Concept of Coworking*. Discussion Paper, Series A. 265:1-15.

Van Meel, J., & Brinkø, R. (2014). Working apart together. *FMWorld*. http://www.fm-world.co.uk/

Wang, B., & Loo, B. P. (2017). Hubs of Internet entrepreneurs: The emergence of coworking offices in Shanghai, China. *Journal of Urban Technology*, *24*(3), 67–84. doi:10.1080/10630732.2017.1285124

Waters-Lynch, J.M., Potts, J., Butcher, T., Dodson, J. & Hurley, J. (2016). *Coworking: A Transdisciplinary Overview.* Available at SSRN 2712217 (2016).

Wessels, C., Schippers, M. C., Stegmann, S., Bakker, A. B., van Baalen, P. J., & Proper, K. I. (2019). Fostering Flexibility in the New World of Work: A Model of Time-Spatial Job Crafting'. *Frontiers in Psychology*, *10*, 505. doi:10.3389/fpsyg.2019.00505 PMID:30941072

Wilmot, K., Boyle, T., Rickwood, P., & Sharpe, S. (2014). *The Potential for Smart Work Centres in Blacktown, Liverpool and Penrith. Report by the Institute for Sustainable Futures*. UTS.

World Bank. (2019). World Development Report. In *The Changing Nature of Work*. World Bank Publications. Accessed 8 May: http://ebookcentral.proquest.com

Yin, R. K. (2014). *Case Study Research: Design and Methods* (5th ed.). SAGE Publications.

## KEY TERMS AND DEFINITIONS

**Activity Theory:** A descriptive meta-theory or framework. It considers an entire work or activity system and the motive for the activity in AT is created through the tensions and contradictions within elements of the system.

**Co-Work:** Work and work-related activities that take place in a shared space and place that fosters community and collaboration that are inclusive and diverse.

**Flexible Work:** The ability to have some choice and control over when, where and how work and work-related activities are accomplished. refers to the activities of individuals and groups (social entrepreneurs) who identify gaps in the social system as an opportunity to serve groups who are marginalized and aim to address these needs in entrepreneurial ways.

**Outer Urban Flexible Work:** Working from a shared location in outer urban or fringes of the city in a digital work hub or coworking space, or part-time teleworking from home while having some choice and control over when, where and how work and work-related ac activities are accomplished.

**Pop-Up Coworking Space:** A work-related or other business that opens ad hoc or quickly in a temporary, vacant, or open location and is intended to operate for only a predetermined period of time.

**Social Entrepreneurship:** Refers to the activities of individuals and groups (social entrepreneurs) who identify opportunities in the social system to serve groups who are marginalized and aim to address these needs in entrepreneurial ways.

# Chapter 9
# 3D Printing Build Farms:
## The Rise of a Distributed Manufacturing Workforce

**Jennifer Loy**
https://orcid.org/0000-0001-7153-0699
*Deakin University, Australia*

**James I. Novak**
https://orcid.org/0000-0003-4082-4322
*Deakin University, Australia*

## ABSTRACT

*The development of high-end, distributed, advanced manufacturing over the last decade has been a by-product of a push to foster new workforce capabilities, while building a market for industrial additive manufacturing (3D printing) machines. This trend has been complemented by a growing democratization in access to commercial platforms via the internet, and the ease of communication it allows between consumers and producers. New ways of distributed working in manufacturing are on the rise while mass production facilities in the Western world are in decline. As automation increasingly excludes the worker from assembly line production, the tools to regain control over manufacturing and commercial interaction are becoming more readily available. As a result, new working practices are emerging. This chapter discusses networked 3D printing build farms and their potential to reshape the future of work for distributed manufacturing. It highlights changes in infrastructure priorities and education for a digitally enabled maker society from an Australian perspective.*

DOI: 10.4018/978-1-7998-4159-3.ch009

## INTRODUCTION

Mass production has its roots in the uniformity introduced to meet the consistency required for the sale of products from a catalogue (Forty, 1986), and grew through the development of technology that supported mass manufacture over craft-based production. In the past, industrial designers were responsible for translating cultural trends, designing a product, then splitting the making of the product into components so that an individual was responsible for only a single stage of production. The designers were initially based in the manufacturing facility, where they would be familiar with the capabilities of the workers and provided working drawings to ensure consistency.

With the introduction of Computer-Aided Design (CAD) in the nineteen-eighties, and then Internet communication in the nineties, the separation of designer and manufacturer became more prevalent. The separation occurred not only through the development of independent design consultancies but also as manufacturers became more global in their operations. This working practise is enabled by digital platforms, which not only allow for verbal and written communication but increasingly, virtual and augmented reality communication tools. Three-dimensional (3D) computer modelling has generally superseded two-dimensional (2D) working drawings. While there are valid arguments that the designer based in a manufacturer, rather than in a consultancy, will have a better understanding of the production practices and capabilities in that particular factory setting, in reality (and with exceptions), where in-house designers are still employed, the design process has still become disconnected from the geographical place of manufacture. This disconnect allows an element of freedom for the company in terms of where the designers are based. In fact, with digital communication tools, it is increasingly possible for designers to work from home, anywhere in the world, and still be engaged with manufacturing.

One of the constraints in manufacturing has been catering for economies of scale, using production tooling. This tooling is frequently in the form of molds. Molds are expensive to produce and to offset the costs; manufacturers produce large numbers of the same part from each mold. The investment for a manufacturer in a mold is significant, and a single part must, therefore, be suitable for a broad market. The designer must design products that are generic enough to appeal to a wide range of consumers. This, in turn, requires an established market and supply chain to ensure that materials and hardware are available in quantity as required. For this to be efficient, the scale of production tends to be large, leading to centralised manufacturing and prohibiting viable entrepreneurship.

In contrast to the analogue processes of mass production, digital fabrication technology allows for computer-driven 2D and 3D cutting, with a part "revealed" as material is removed from a solid. It has been part of conventional manufacturing since the 1960s, ten years after the invention of computer numerically controlled cutting (CNC routing). Additive Manufacturing (AM) is also a digital fabrication technology. However, as the name suggests, material is added to produce a part, rather than removed from a solid. Neither technology requires a mold, meaning for both technologies that it is possible to create bespoke parts. This is a key capability for these technologies because their output depends on the time taken for the cutting head, or, in the case of AM, the print head or laser, to move across the part. Where excess material is removed in a 3D cutting action, the CNC router can be relatively slow. However, for 2D shapes the cutter is only following the critical cutting lines of an object, making part production quite fast. In additive manufacturing, the part is built in layers. Therefore, the speed of making the part is constrained by the speed of the print head and the size of the part. As printers have become more sophisticated, features such as multiple print heads or lasers have reduced print time, or increased part accuracy for the same print time.

CNC routing has proved a valuable tool for batch production workshops and independent designer-makers. Similarly, AM allows a designer to manufacture a single part without the cost of bespoke tooling. This is not to say that professional 3D printing machines do not require investment. In 2020, a 3D printing machine for metal products constructed using a laser to fuse powder costs upwards of US $800,000. However, there are significantly cheaper machines for different materials that can still be used by an individual designer-maker. Low-cost desktop 3D printers available for several thousand dollars that are capable of producing parts in polymers suitable for some end-use applications. Traditional manufacturers have been adding AM capabilities into their facilities at both ends of the cost spectrum, and entirely new manufacturers have also emerged specialising in AM for end-use products.

Service bureaus have become the new manufacturing centre for many designers, allowing them freedom in terms of where they are working, and where their customers are situated. Online service bureaus allow designers to order one-off products of their own design and have them printed and sent anywhere in the world without the need to own a 3D printer (Novak & Loy, 2020b). For the first time, designers can have individual designs fabricated to their own specification, bespoke to an individual customer's needs. Technically, with the computing power now readily available, a designer can choose to move around the globe and still maintain a consistent practice, through an online customer interface and the use of online service bureaus or distributed manufacturing networks However, service bureaus tend to be centralised centres of production due to the costs of purchasing and maintaining high-end equipment capable of producing large volumes of parts for different customers. They also require an investment in technicians to sort and prepare individual print jobs, clean and repair machines, post-process parts after printing (e.g. manually removing support materials) and perform other tasks that are difficult to automate.

This chapter considers the rise of networked fabrication technology, in particular 3D printing build farms, as the precursor for new ways of working for a more distributed workforce and anywhere working. The approach challenges conventional disciplines and traditional manufacturing practices and is proposed as a level up from the independent entrepreneur. It is also proposed as a response to the challenges caused by concentrations of populations and traditional work patterns that should be considered by governments in developing infrastructure plans for the future. Australia is a prime example featured throughout the chapter due to its large land size and separation from other countries, yet largely centralised population concentrations along the coastline. Globally, as populations increasingly converge on cities, resulting in nearly fifty megacities with populations over thirty million people each, it is necessary to question whether this trend is sustainable and desirable. 3D printing and digital communication technologies could provide a paradigm shift in manufacturing, through distributed manufacturing and a changed relationship between people, making and product use. This is the time to be exploring these options.

## BACKGROUND

### Framing the 3D Printing Build Farm

A 3D printing build farm is a recent concept within both academia and industry, emerging within literature around 2016 as 3D printers became more affordable, reliable and network connected. However, limited literature exists on the topic, and it is important to define what a build farm is, and how it is different to other business models that may scale the production of parts utilising 3D printers or other digital fabrication technologies.

In a broad sense, a 3D printing build farm is defined as a collection of similar 3D printers controlled by a central networked system. More advanced build farms may include autonomous systems to monitor production and perform tasks such as removing completed prints from machines, as well as include post-processing capabilities, or they may rely on technicians for these roles (Skawiński & Siemiński, 2017). The minimum number of 3D printers to be classified as a build farm is as low as 3-5 (Laplume, Anzalone & Pearce, 2016; MANUFACTUR3D, 2019), and theoretically can be scaled up infinitely. The largest reported build farm at the time of writing is that of Josef Průša's company Prusa Printers, which utilises 500 of its 3D printers to manufacture parts for its range of desktop Fused Filament Fabrication

(FFF) machines (Průša, 2018). Figure 1 shows a small university build farm featuring desktop FFF machines arranged on shelving.

*Figure 1. Example of a university build farm featuring FFF machines managed by a central system*

This definition of a 3D printing build farm is necessarily broad in order to describe the varied ways a build farm may function. However, it is important to delineate that a 3D printing build farm is not the same as a 3D printing service bureau. A service bureau allows anyone to upload files for 3D printing, with the bureau managing the hardware, materials and procedures for a customer, before sending the completed 3D print to them (Novak & Loy, 2020b). Similar models exist for inkjet printing of documents, posters and canvases, allowing people and businesses to access high-end, high throughput equipment without needing to own or rent the equipment themselves. Popular 3D printing service bureaus include Shapeways (www.shapeways.com), which began offering online 3D printing services in 2007, and i.Materialise (www.i.materialise.com), which launched in 2009 as a spin-off of the well-established company Materialise, founded in 1990. These companies provide a large range of 3D printing technologies which require different technical knowledge, processes, software, materials and post-processing, including technologies like Selective Laser Sintering (SLS) and Multi Jet Fusion (MJF) which are powder-based technologies, stereolithography (SLA) which is a resin technology, and FFF which uses a polymer filament. While service bureaus will employ scheduling and job management software, a single system that can farm 3D models to these various machines and automate production is not possible today. Therefore, such service bureaus cannot be classified as build farms.

However, a service bureau may utilise one or more build farms within its production facility, farming out low-volume runs of a part to a collection of 3D printers controlled centrally, or managing the production of unique parts. While research shows that it is more challenging to automate the production of unique parts within a build farm due to the need to optimise factors like build orientation for each different part individually, academic research is working towards automated solutions in experimental and lab conditions (Gushchin, Martynovich & Torubarov, 2020; Ransikarbum et al., 2017). The evidence from companies like Prusa Printers (Průša, 2018), Formlabs (Formlabs, 2017) and Zortrax (Krywko, 2018) is that there is a business case supporting 3D print farms for low volume production today and that a build farm can be successfully located within a service bureau.

Similarly, a 3D printing build farm can be located within a manufacturing facility, although simply having a build farm does not mean that a manufacturer is a 3D printing factory or additive manufacturing facility. The build farm may sit alongside traditional manufacturing equipment, such as injection molding or casting equipment, and enable low-volume production of parts for customers before scaling up to a mass production process, known as *bridge manufacturing* (Krywko, 2018; Lozova, 2016). A print farm may also service internal needs of a manufacturer, such as creating jigs and fixtures used as aids during the assembly of mass-produced goods, for example, vehicle manufacturers Volkswagen (Vries, 2017) and Ford (Staak, 2018). In other scenarios, a manufacturer may utilise a range of different 3D print technologies, much like a service bureau, while not employing the use of a networked build farm.

These relationships are shown diagrammatically in Figure 2 and include education facilities like universities and Makerspaces, which may include a build farm as part of broader 3D printing and manufacturing facilities. Importantly, the diagram also shows inverse relationships where a build farm itself creates new opportunities and enables a new digital business model. For example, establishing a build farm could open new opportunities to operate a specialist service bureau, with print jobs processed centrally and sequentially 3D printed by the build farm. A new manufacturer may take a similar approach by operating a facility that is made up of one large build farm, much like Prusa Printers (Průša, 2018), or several smaller build farms that can respond to bridge manufacturing requirements or operate in an entirely new digital manufacturing ecosystem. The dental market highlights the opportunities of such new business models, with companies like SmileDirectClub and Voodoo Clear Aligners emerging recently to provide clear aligners directly to customers, supported by in-house build farms. SmileDirectClub uses 49 in-house Multi Jet Fusion machines from Hewlett-Packard (HP), capable of producing 500 molds each per print, for a total of 49,000 aligners per day over two print cycles. Voodoo Clear Aligners instead uses SLA technology, with 21 Form 2 machines from Formlabs, reportedly producing 20,000 aligners a month for up to 700 patients (Davies, 2019). While such companies employ additional manufacturing processes, such as vacuum forming to create the aligners over the 3D printed molds, the businesses were born out of build farm technology, and are reliant upon the efficiencies and scales associated with networked 3D printing.

*Figure 2. Organisations that may utilise a service bureau or new businesses that may stem from creating a service bureau*

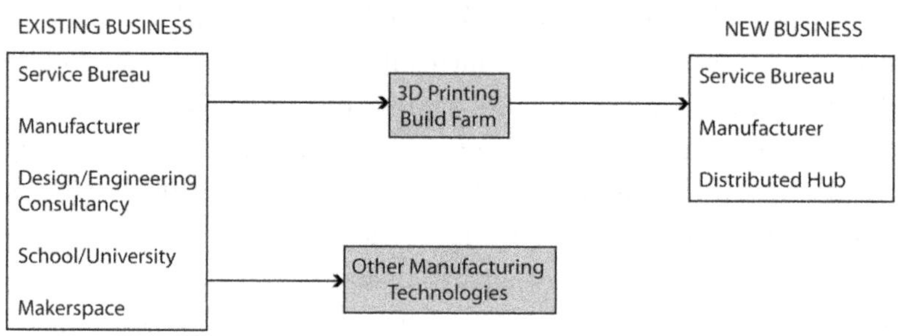


Another type of business model enabled by build farms is a distributed model, whereby a central network farms production to individual, geographically dispersed 3D printers, as shown in Figure 3. This concept has not yet been considered in the literature; however, precursors to such a model have already surfaced, most notably 3D Hubs. The company was founded in 2013 as an online platform similar to service bureaus Shapeways and i.Materialise, with the distinct difference being that the company itself did not own or operate any 3D printers. It was a community of individuals and businesses, including hobbyists, who owned one or more 3D printers and could produce 3D prints for customers based on proximity, cost, materials, reviews or other factors desirable to the customer (Hamalainen & Karjalainen, 2017). Therefore, it was possible to arrange for a part to be 3D printed by someone locally and collect it from them, shrinking the supply chain through a central online platform. However, in 2018, 3D Hubs shifted business models, moving away from peer-to-peer and towards a more profitable business-to-business model (Peels, 2018).

*Figure 3. A centralised build farm (left) and a decentralised, geographically dispersed build farm (right)*

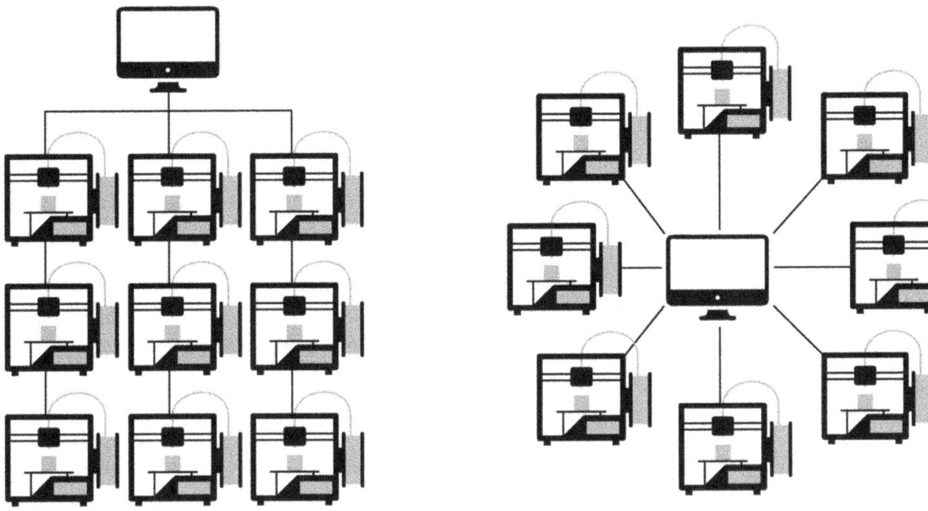

It is now a central platform to connect with commercial 3D printing service bureaus, as well as more traditional manufacturers, no longer a community of Makers.

Under both business models, 3D Hubs was a platform for connecting those in need of parts with those capable of producing them. This is not a build farm model; however, it is possible to imagine a similar online hub that is directly connected to a network of distributed 3D printers, capable of farming out prints with limited human interaction. These 3D printers could be dispersed around a local community, a city, or globally, creating new entrepreneurial opportunities, as well as challenges compared to a centralised 3D print farm which will be explored later in this chapter.

## MANUFACTURING CHANGE

### Digital Technology

3D printing, also called additive manufacturing, has matured over the last decade with material and process capabilities that allow for the production of functional parts for commercial use. Before this time, 3D printing, which is an umbrella term for a range of distinct manufacturing processes, was predominantly used for prototyping. The commonality of 3D printing processes is that they all build parts in layers from a 3D computer model. However, the range of processes available includes laser-based powder bed fusion, filament extrusion, UV cured resin and gel-based printing, among others. The proliferation of these technologies, and their distinct characteristics, means that although there are similarities in designing for each one, to design to a professional level for functional products, the user needs to understand the constraints and capabilities of the individual process chosen (Gibson, Rosen, & Stucker, 2014).

There has been a significant increase in sales of 3D printing machines worldwide over the last decade (Wohlers, 2019), particularly by research facilities and universities, and correspondingly, there has been a drive to build a technical workforce capable of working with these technologies (Loy, 2015). However, even with the positive predictions of the growth in additive manufacturing (Palmer, 2018), the uptake of machines in industry has arguably been slower than expected. As a result, some of the companies that specialise in additive manufacturing machines have begun to struggle, with those that have diversified arguably better able to work through the initial challenges facing machine adoption by manufacturers.

One of the reasons for the difficulties is that product design applications remain predominantly limited to a few specialist areas, rather than mainstream manufacturing. As a result, although some companies have invested in large numbers of machines, such as the medical company Stryker in its facility in Ireland (Jackson, 2019), in general, 3D printing remains a prototyping tool within most industries. According to Palmer (2018), global spending on 3D printing is expected to be almost US$20 billion by 2021. However, the widespread adoption of high-end 3D printing technology in mainstream manufacturing has been slow to materialise.

Alongside the development of digital fabrication, the last decade has seen the rapid expansion of Internet communication networks. During the previous decade, globalisation led to communication platforms that worked across country boundaries and were independent of the conventions and even regulations of different countries leading to changed commercial practice. The relatively lawless World Wide Web allowed for very different ways of working. While governments were striving to catch up with the development of laws governing virtual space, the 'gig' economy (based on temporary employment), enabled by online platforms, emerged as a significant factor. Entrepreneurship and crowdfunding flourished during this time, and for the first time in many years, it seemed possible that the control of employment by large corporations could be significantly subverted in Western societies. For designers, sites that allowed for individuals to bid for work independent of employment by a consultancy (such as 99designs.com.au for graphic/communication designers) allowed for greater inclusivity, and flexibility in working hours and location. On the negative side, however, it also meant that there was no oversight on the quality of the design output by an industry body, or protection for the designers where bidding resulted in jobs becoming loss leaders, rather than paid at a reasonable rate. While the 'gig' economy approach looked promising, it has not yet created widespread economic freedom.

Over the last few years, legislation has been increasingly introduced to try to provide some protection for 'gig' economy workers on 'zero' contracts; that is, those only paid for the actual hours they work on an ad hoc basis. This has impacted online companies such as Uber, who are now subject to workforce laws that they initially avoided. More broadly, discussions on laws appropriate for Internetworking are still ongoing. In the meantime, countries such as Russia and China have acted to curtail access to the World Wide Web, in order to exert some level of control over content and interactions. At the same time, there has been a widespread backlash against globalisation, in contrast to the expectations of many business futurists and policymakers (e.g. Ross, 2016), and a subsequent increase in nationalism in many countries, such as the UK and USA. This will change the way business is conducted, as will the debate on reducing the environmental impact of manufacturing. However, it is too early to anticipate the extent of the changes it will bring.

*To this day the vocabulary and theoretical assumptions of 19th-century economic thought continue to legitimise the operation of the world market, even as increasing numbers of people are alarmed by its tendency to widen global inequalities and, no less significantly, to degrade the ecological conditions for human life (Hornborg, 2019, p.28.).*

For those engaged in making for the 'gig' economy, the World Wide Web still provides an effective way of reaching customers on an individual basis that was not possible in previous decades. It allows individuals for whom this approach to employment suits their lifestyle, the opportunity to manage their career. Part of this is the ability to work flexible hours, as suits personal commitments, and to take work that meets their needs or preference. A key element of this access is that it can allow workers to be located wherever they choose, subject to a suitable level of Internet provision. This potentially creates a level of inclusivity not previously possible, although this is not without its challenges, as with greater autonomy comes greater personal responsibility.

This aspect of the freedom of flexible working conditions opens up new possibilities for the benefit of society as a whole. However, in order to exploit those conditions in ways that support those previously excluded because of location or personal circumstances, or barriers to conventional employment, there needs to be an investment by communities and governments in understanding these opportunities and mitigating against the challenges involved. These investments involve considerations such as digital infrastructure, legal protections and workforce development.

There will be costs involved in establishing better working practices and infrastructure to support distributed working for making via the World Wide Web in a more coherent, community-based manner. However, the potential reduction of costs to cities and societies associated with decentralised working, and in supporting those excluded from current working patterns, including in distributed manufacturing, should offset these considerations. Currently, there is little evidence of an association between the rise in costs of one, offset by the reduction of costs of the other.

## Disruptive Manufacturing

The relative costs of labor and changing markets have created major upheavals in manufacturing in Western countries over the last sixty years that have had significant impacts on populations. Enabled by the enhanced digital communications of the last two decades, globalisation has also led to a shift in concentrations of work from countries with high labor costs, to those with lower ones. Meanwhile, in countries where employment costs are high, low-skilled jobs are becoming scarce. The most dramatic example of a city impacted by changes in production practices has arguably been Detroit, where the city depended on a single industry. In 1958, the 3,500,000 $ft^2$ Packard Motor Car Co. factory was closed after initially opening in 1903. Over the next fifty years, car manufacturing in Detroit struggled, as did the city as a whole. Even with the US$17.4 billion bailout by President Bush in 2008 to General Motors and Chrysler, both declared bankruptcy within a year. In 2013, Detroit City officially filed for Chapter 9 bankruptcy (Weber, 2013).

Traditional manufacturing has been in decline in Western countries, such as the USA, UK and Australia, with manufacturing moving to countries with lower labor costs, such as China and Bangladesh. In Australia, for example, major vehicle manufacturers that once manufactured in the country now only have offices and dealerships (e.g. Ford), and even these offices have started closing with Holden (owned by General Motors), ceasing operation in 2020 (Gramenz, 2020). Off-shore manufacturing is an established practice, and on-shore manufacturing can struggle to compete. As a result, there has been a surge of investment in advanced manufacturing in countries like Australia by the government (e.g. imcrc.org funding), where value-added products are seen as a way to increase the export capacity of the country. This has led to an investment in innovative manufacturing technologies, and these have included additive manufacturing.

Similarly, in the USA, President Obama established the Digital Manufacturing and Design Institute (Louis, Seymour & Joyce, 2014). In 2020, there are significant examples of commitment to additive manufacturing by companies such as General Electric (GE) and Hewlett Packard (HP). However, additive manufacturing for production is still in its research stage for the majority of these companies. As

Krywko (2018, p.1) points out: "Factories are like supertankers in a way. They are huge but it takes ages to get them up to speed, to slow them down, and to change their course."

There are examples of such large factories beginning to change their course. The use of 3D printing for personalised vehicle features by BMW (bmwgroup.com), and for a small number of light-weight aircraft brackets by GE Additive (Kellner 2018), reducing weight compared to equivalent traditionally manufactured brackets while meeting load requirements, has provided quantifiable evidence supporting the adoption of AM. Overall, however, further development of a larger number of viable applications are needed at this time. Additive manufacturing offers the potential to bring manufacturing on-shore, particularly for countries where transport miles are an issue, such as Australia. However, it requires considerable development in machinery, business models, workforce development, product application (Diegel, Nordin & Motte, 2019) and supply chain development (Mavri, 2015) before that is possible.

*There is a consensus that technological changes, particularly those leading to measurable advances in worker productivity, are central for improvements in overall wealth and societal wellbeing....and thereby have fundamental social impact. There is also a consensus that the principal driver behind the adoption of new technologies among the community of potential users is the net benefit resulting from the use of the new technology...which may be directed to develop or sustain competitive advantage...Applied to the commercial manufacturing sector, technology procurement activity is targeted at enhancing profits obtained by private firms....In this context, it is worth noting that the current technological status quo often exerts a significant inertia: to motivate the adoption of AM, it has been speculated that an increase in revenue of at least 30% to 40% must be projected (Baumers et al., 2016, p.194).*

In contrast, the investment in advanced manufacturing has also created a higher degree of automation. While this began by increasing the viability of on-shore manufacturing, providing jobs for workers where automation allowed for more of a focus on the jobs requiring dexterity and understanding (Griffith, 2018), the evolution of artificial intelligence for configuring products (Diamandis & Kotler, 2020) is increasingly leading to 'lights out', autonomous manufacturing (Palmer, 2018). This refers to a situation where an assembly line is not dependent on human involvement on the factory floor, and a factory may run continuously twenty-four hours a day.

The exclusion of workers through automation is the subject of discussion on the introduction of a universal living wage (Bregman, 2017), also known as a universal basic income. While controversial, the concept is based on the understanding that automation should benefit all of society, not only shareholders. Although this is an interesting proposition, it provokes questions about the psychology of a community dependent on a supplied wage, which will need to be addressed. It may be that the future of society could be a well-balanced community, funded by automation, and engaged with meaningful activities. If automation in manufacturing continues, there is a risk that it will disenfranchise workers who would traditionally be employed in that field.

Over the last two and a half centuries, the role of makers in society has been transformed from a craft-based role to working within a factory, to manufacturing based on the division of labor, through a century of manufacturing driven by efficiency and profit, to collaborative robots, to a fully automated plant, organised by artificial intelligence. Society has to face the impact of these changes. In an equal society, a universal income, drawn from the profits of automation and machine learning, could spread the wealth. However, in a capitalist economy, this is unlikely to be the case. The reality is that a workforce consistently deskilled over time, disenfranchised by mass production operations at the start of the twenty-first century, is in danger of being alienated, contributing to the widening gap between those in control of capital, and those dependent on the work they provide.

For a company to decide to invest in 3D printing, not only does the actual manufacturing process change, the whole business model does too. This is frequently focused on changing interactions between a company and its customers to exploit its customisation capabilities. Where additive manufacturing adds to the capabilities of a manufacturer, typically for one-off parts needed for a specific project, with notable exceptions such as GE Additive and HP, the drive for a complete disruption of the company business model will be unlikely to come from existing manufacturers. For entrepreneurs, however, 3D printing provides a democratisation in high-level making not previously possible. When the cost of early desktop 3D printers initially dropped at the start of the last decade, it was hailed as the start of the widespread democratisation of making (Anderson, 2012; Lipson & Kurman, 2013). The hype surrounding the technology declined as the realities of working with the technologies, and their limitations were better understood, but nearly a decade on, it is arguably time for an objective re-evaluation of the revolutionary opportunities the technology can provide, armed with the knowledge gained over the last decade.

There are five distinct profiles for distributed manufacturing at this time. One involves low-level manufacturing outputs that are produced individually or in batches, generally using relatively low-cost technologies, where simple components are brought together after manufacturing to create a product outcome. The second is where more complex products are produced by individuals in a network, where intellectual property is shared, and the producer and consumer linked via a web service. The third profile has complex products that are designed professionally, but independent of the manufacturing service, and the products produced through a service bureau where high-end machines and materials are available for customers in communication with the designer through their business. The fourth profile is where individuals create the designs, and the communication with customers is through an online service bureau. The final approach is where individuals have their own mid-level machines and produce complex products that they sell directly to customers in person or online through their website. Considering these five approaches through the lens of changes to working practices and patterns for decentralised manufacturing, there are workforce development and networked location services required to exploit the opportunities they could provide. In addition, there will be difficult transition issues even where a shift to distributed manufacturing could arguably provide positive benefits for communities experiencing economic hardship, following localised industrial decline or collapse.

## Building Capacity and Capability

In a digitally connected community, whether remote or central to the main concentrations of populations in a country, new patterns of work are emerging. The rise in entrepreneurial programs in universities reflects a growing interest in graduates of working for themselves (Loy & Novak, 2019). Financial independence and flexible working hours are positives in this approach. Also, greater opportunities for entrepreneurs can support greater inclusivity. However, on the negative side, self-employment is accompanied by a lack of economic security, which can make it difficult for an individual to borrow money. From a societal point of view, there are longer-term concerns with the break-up of larger companies in favor of micro-businesses. The fragmentation of an industry can inhibit its growth, and there is a risk of deskilling as smaller companies are generally less able to invest in research and professional development than more established organisations.

In the context of distributed manufacturing, 3D printing build farms and online service bureaus have the potential to provide different ways of working that can bridge the divide between independent working and mass production. They have the potential to change the balance of power in manufacturing, with products designed differently, both enabled and constrained by digital fabrication technology (Gershenfeld, Gershenfeld & Cutcher-Gershenfeld, 2017). These products can be designed in short runs or as one-off products because of the ability to produce each part directly from digital data with no need for tooling. It allows products to be adapted in response to market feedback, and this theoretically gives the distributed manufacturer a commercial advantage. This is particularly pertinent in relation to high-value products, from medical devices to jewelry.

However, product designers will need to ensure they upskill in order to exploit the evolving process characteristics. For an individual or micro-business, this could be challenging. Community investment in supporting the upskilling of entrepreneurs for distributed manufacturing will be needed to create new ways of working in the future. Viewed in isolation, the impact of a structured plan to support the development of 3D printing build farms may not seem to be significant. However, it could provide the basis for new ways of thinking about the role of digital technology in enabling distributed working in different industries, as a bridge between entrepreneurship and Small and Medium Enterprises (SMEs). As sustainability issues become more significant, the introduction of a distributed working practice mentality could contribute to developing viable alternatives for a more sustainable future (Loy & Tatham, 2016).

Over the last two centuries, the division of labor and the growth of mechanisation and automation have contributed to an overall deskilling in the mass-manufacturing workforce. Instead of building the skills of the individual and valuing their contribution, and the collective development of society, capitalism generally has prioritised economic wealth over social capital. Inequality in pay and conditions over the last century has become extreme, as those with capital have exploited those without, creating conditions where labor is a commodity, irrespective of the impact on society as a whole. The makers in society have become disenfranchised and factory workers disempowered. However, problems in society are often viewed as disconnected from the deskilling of the workforce and the lack of self-worth that the commodification of labor produces. The ability of an individual to earn a living is seen as the measure of success, and the overall deskilling and alienating of society by this approach has been largely ignored. With a change in priorities, and appropriate societal support and investment, additive manufacturing and associated digital technologies could have the potential to provide new opportunities for those without control, through the democratisation of manufacturing.

## THE AUSTRALIAN EXAMPLE

Australia is a vast country; at just under 7.9 million square kilometers, it is 2 million kilometers smaller than the United States of America (USA) or China. However, Australia has vast deserts at its center, and its population is around 23 million, compared to over 303 million in the USA, and just under 1.4 billion in China. India's land size is less than half that of Australia, at just under 3.3 million square kilometers, yet its population is over 1.3 billion. In Australia, the population is concentrated along the Eastern seaboard with the three largest cities in this zone. However, there are other cities around the coastline of the country, and smaller towns in the deserts. Alice Springs is the most central city with approximately 30,000 people, and Darwin is the most northern, with 140,000 people. There is a concentration of people in two major cities: Melbourne, with just under 4 million people, and Sydney with just over 5 million, compared to a London population in 2019 of over 9 million.

Where the United Kingdom and America have large populations relative to their size, Australia does not. This means that the disposable income for the government for infrastructure spending is limited, yet the distances for infrastructure to span are vast. Over the last twenty years, the expansion of congestion in the major cities has outpaced the investment in infrastructure. According to Engineers Australia (2020), road users in the two major cities need to allow half as much time again for journeys compared to driving in free-flow traffic conditions, with over 90% of the cause attributed to traffic congestion. The cost of commuter travel in cities is high in terms of infrastructure maintenance and expansion costs, as well as the loss of time for workers commuting, and the impact on health and wellbeing for society.

For a country with the profile of Australia, investing in creating distributed work opportunities makes particular sense. For example, the country relies on immigration for population growth, but one of the criteria is that those arriving should live in regional and rural Australia, not the major cities. This is difficult to enforce as workers are forced to move to where jobs are available, which in Australia tends to be where there are large concentrations of population. The populations in rural and regional Australia have dropped significantly over the last ten years. However, the country is dependent on primary industry sectors, such as agriculture, to sustain the population overall (Wright & Bagshaw, 2019). This contradiction is an ongoing challenge and is common to many developed and developing countries.

In the Australian Smart Cities and Suburbs program (Australian Gov., 2019), projects have been successfully funded from regional and rural councils, such as Alice Springs, Bundaberg, Launceston, Ballarat and Cairns, demonstrating the Government commitment to the distributed Smart City approach rather than focused on the major cities. Geelong, Wollongong, Newcastle and Townsville have all been identified as supporting the Smart City initiative. The project work is diverse across the Smart Cities network. Nevertheless, the projects to-date tend to evidence a bottom-up approach to adoption, rather than a top-down one. There appears to be momentum building, but it tends to focus on individual project areas to support ideas enabled by digital technology, rather than as a precursor to a broader, more comprehensive change to the profile of regional and rural cities and towns.

In Australia, because of the infrastructure problems caused by the concentration of populations in a small number of major cities, notably Melbourne and Sydney, there needs to be a reframing of work and the movement of people to and from their workplace to reduce the load. There is a growing trend towards entrepreneurship in Australia, but as yet it remains concentrated in the cities. The recent push towards smart city integration of digital technology in urban planning allows for new ways of working. Digital communication technology allows independent designers and producers to reach their target market directly. Also, the cities themselves are changing, becoming more flexible.

In contrast, city layout over the last century had developed a clear and necessary demarcation between heavy industry and suburbia, the shift in the economy from heavy industry to service industries has broken down that demarcation. The rigidity of previous planning is no longer appropriate in cities where populations fluctuate and work is flexible, and frequently occurs at home. Businesses are more transient, and smaller manufacturing has moved increasingly off-shore as some larger manufacturers either shut down or withdraw from the market.

With a population of under 24 million, Australia can be considered an insufficient market for the investment of manufacturing facilities, and some of the current additive manufacturing supply chains available in Europe and the USA, such as recycling programs for used materials, are not made available in Australia. If this trend continues, Australia could become exclusively dependent on imports for its manufactured goods. Additive manufacturing provides an interesting alternative. Until recently, it was considered a niche making tool, with little prospect for production manufacturing. Irrespective if this is the case for the large manufacturers, for a country where manufacturing is gradually being withdrawn, it makes sense for Governments to invest in AM as a potential alternative. At this time, that investment is frequently focused on supporting existing manufacturers to adopt the technology to expand into overseas markets. However, it could be time for more significant investment in research into the viability of AM to build new frameworks for networked, distributed manufacturing. 3D printing build farms could contribute to providing new ways of making and working that could benefit communities in Australia, and maybe transferable to countries around the world.

## SOLUTIONS AND RECOMMENDATIONS

3D printing allows for new ways to manufacture and supply products. Currently, research in the field is dominated by engineering and medical applications. There has been interest in the role of 3D printing in democratisation on making, but this has been very much a bottom-up approach, where technology and innovation hubs are provided for individuals to build opportunities. There may be business mentoring available, and, in the example provided by Gershenfeld's Fablabs initiative (Gershenfeld, 2007), the facilities are networked to provide additional support. However, the emphasis is on a crowdsourcing type of approach, and recent evidence shows that such models may be unsustainable, for example, the Fablab chain TechShop declared bankruptcy in 2017, closing ten facilities across the USA (Kumparak, 2017).

The research this chapter draws from suggests there is a middle ground between the individual entrepreneur using 3D printing for their products, and existing manufacturers considering the integration of 3D printing into their business practice. This is a 3D printing build farm approach, where there is a top-down investment by councils and governments in infrastructure supporting the development of 3D printing build farms for communities, that enable micro-businesses over individual entrepreneurs to become established in communities. This is particularly relevant for communities in post-industrial cities and towns, and in the post COVID-19 context (Novak & Loy, 2020a). From this base, distributed working networks could be built to service the manufacturing needs of rural communities.

While 3D printing build farms are a new opportunity, they are not an isolated trend for smaller, distributed means of production. Microbreweries are a recent trend that has been a reaction against homogenised production of beer and other beverages, "reestablishing a sense of place in local communities" (Holtkamp et al., 2016), and particularly popular in the USA and Australia. Urban Agriculture has also infiltrated cities and towns in the form of community gardens and urban farms (Lohrberg et al., 2016), empowering people to grow fresh food for themselves and their community in small spaces between buildings, on rooftops and in parks. Craftspeople are also becoming more visible and distributed within communities, reclaiming abandoned industrial and retail spaces through programs such as Renew Newcastle (www.renewnewcastle.org) in Australia, with Newcastle once known as the "steel city" of Australia before processing largely moved off-shore, resulting in large areas of the city being abandoned as people left to find work elsewhere. Renew Newcastle has helped revitalise the city center, allowing artisans to set up studios and retail spaces rent-free in vacant buildings, bringing production directly to the consumer. 3D printing build farms offer the same opportunities for localised production, centralised like a microbrewery, or distributed as separate production nodes that are networked together, similar to a collection of artisans dispersed throughout the vacant spaces of a town or city.

However, there are also challenges for a future workforce utilising distributed build farms to manufacture products, much like any distributed means of production. Supplying the raw materials to feed production becomes more challenging when smaller amounts of material must be dispersed to a larger number of build farms, or individual machines making up a networked build farm, compared to supplying raw materials to a single centralised facility. 3D printing service bureaus with internal build farms may be better able to maintain supply, or offer lower prices through bulk purchase of materials, compared to a distributed networked build farm which must separate the supply of 3D printing materials. Reacting to sudden demand may be challenging from a material supply perspective. However, it may also be possible to accommodate demand by adding new printers into the build farm, drawing upon the flexibility of workers who are part of the gig economy.

Within more rural and remote regions, 3D printing build farms require more significant investment in infrastructure to support them, particularly around the supply of materials. As recycling technology, mainly related to recycling of 3D printing waste, lags behind the 3D printing technologies themselves, new capabilities are needed to allow isolated build farms to be more self-sustaining (Mohammed et al., 2017). It is foreseeable that a region could utilise its waste materials to create materials to be fed into their 3D printing build farm, gaining a unique identity just like a region known for a specific variety of wine or timber. A region may focus on a particular type of polymer as feedstock for printers, or a particular type of feedstock to suit its build farm needs, for example, filament or powder. It may also develop new materials that include local waste timber (Le Duigou et al., 2016), algae and other biomaterials (Liu et al., 2019) that characterise the region. Such developments require ongoing scientific research and are enabled by the ability to 3D print with an increasing variety of materials.

Furthermore, internet services must be reliable to support the networking of 3D printers, especially to efficiently transfer large 3D files for printing, and higher volumes of files. Within Australia, the National Broadband Network (NBN) has been the largest infrastructure project in Australian history and is the key infrastructure for accessing the Internet. However, there remains a disparity between access within major towns and cities and more regional locations which are yet to gain any NBN infrastructure (Gregory, 2020). As a result, regional areas may still rely on satellite or fixed wireless systems which lack speed, making any sort of digital communication or business challenging (Cradduck, 2016). In order for 3D printing build farms to service such an area, reliable and fast internet access is an essential part of the digital ecosystem, and governments must better address this challenge in order to support people to remain in such locations, rather than leave for larger towns and cities.

## FUTURE RESEARCH DIRECTIONS

*What happens as AI, robotics, virtual reality, digital biology, and sensors crash into 3D printing, blockchain, and global gigabit networks? How will these convergences transform today's legacy industries? What will happen to the way we raise our kids, govern our nations, and care for our planet? (Diamandis & Kotler, 2020, Intro.)*

It may be that experiences from Detroit, and other post-industrial communities will contribute to the development of smart city initiatives and communities beyond the current capitalist framework. It may be too, that digital technologies, such as 3D printing, are seen as integral to changing work patterns to enable greater flexibility and therefore the subject of more sociological, over technological, research. If so, research into the potential for 3D printing build farms in digital ecosystems to contribute to more flexible, and inclusive working conditions would help evaluate their viability. This can be researched within a macro versus micro theoretical framework, to ensure broad, sociological perspectives are researched, over short-term, localised ones. Currently, there is a lack of integrated technical, business and sociological research to explore this potential, and research into re-educating designers, engineers and educators themselves into the appropriate use of 3D printing is still in its infancy (Novak, 2019; Loy & Novak, 2019).

A distributed workforce that reduces commuting and subsequent pollution in cities would contribute to sustainability strategies. However, there are accompanying regulatory and monitoring systems issues that need to be addressed. On customer satisfaction and safety levels, distributed manufacturing sets up challenges for reliability and quality control. For 3D printers, there are multiple types of technologies with very different technical requirements, which will only increase in capability and complexity over time. Ensuring a sufficient level of technical support for distributed manufacturing will require an investment in training and support. Even with desktop printers, ensuring appropriate calibration and quality control calls for a controlled, systems approach. While many of the processes today require significant human involvement, from loading of materials, maintenance and repair, to the post-processing of completed parts (e.g. removing support material), what remains unclear is how long it will be before build farms become 'lights-out' facilities, capable of autonomous manufacturing with minimal need to employ humans. Build farms today may create new employment opportunities. However, it will be essential to plan for the future and understand how people can be supported in their local community by distributed manufacturing over the longer term.

Regulation also requires ongoing research, with all manufacturers subject to standards and environmental protection agency regulations. These regulations differ from one country to another. Companies are currently allowed to track their emissions and submit reports to organisations, such as the US Environmental Protection Agency (EPA). The agencies compare data from manufacturers of similar size and similar profile, to identify potential issues. If the networks of distributed manufacturing rapidly expanded, then there could be potential issues in terms of monitoring emissions in order to meet regulatory requirements. However, the capabilities of networked manufacturing organisations to embed sensor-based modelling and real-time monitoring into production systems have also increased. This needs to be researched, and new ways of monitoring distributed manufacturing developed. With the unusual development profile of 3D printing technology across sectors, rather than in a single industry, it is recommended that industrial conglomerates are established to research monitoring (D'Aveni, 2015). Similarly, where distributed manufacturing frameworks are being built, there needs to be a collaborative approach to researching and maintaining standards across the network.

Beyond these technical and social challenges, it is important to understand 3D printing build farms as an opportunity yet to be realised, rather than a certainty. While build farms have started to create new business opportunities within industries such as dentistry, the rapid pace of development of 3D printing technology makes predicting change difficult, as with any emergent technology. The slow adoption of additive processes within the broader manufacturing industry suggests that a new paradigm is needed to fully realise the potential of the technology, leapfrogging entrenched manufacturing processes, while responding to the needs of people to be financially and emotionally fulfilled.

*Shaping the fourth industrial revolution to ensure that it is empowering and human-centered, rather than diverse and dehumanising, is not a task for any single stakeholder or sector or for any region, industry or culture. The fundamental and global nature of this revolution means it will affect and be influenced by all countries, economies, sectors and people (Schwab, 2017, p.4).*

For 3D printing build farms to be effective, they will require a cooperative organisation of infrastructure by governments, manufacturers, entrepreneurs and policymakers. They will need to be part of an agenda for smart regions to complement current smart city schemes. Build farms could support people to live and work in any place of their choosing, rather than being forced to larger city centers with centralised employment options, reducing commuter pressures on transport systems. Advancing additive manufacturing beyond niche manufacturing applications and small entrepreneurial activities could integrate it as part of a more holistic working practice strategy for the twenty-first century. Research is needed to test this hypothesis for smart community development, alongside those of more conventional smart city schemes.

## CONCLUSION

The last decade has seen the maturing of digital technologies to a level of sophistication where they can support new ways of working anywhere. 3D printing for digital fabrication is one of those technologies. However, it is currently used to build incremental improvements to existing working practices, rather than disruptive, social change and revising the future of work. Nevertheless, there are contemporary environmental and societal imperatives that require more innovative thinking about the future of work, the relocation of populations – particularly outside major cities – and a dematerialisation of the economy. 3D printing build farms provide a starting point for considering how manufacturing and the workforce could be distributed and flexible. Research exploring alternative development pathways for 3D printing build farms could help map the implications of a more distributed production workforce enabled by digital communication technologies. These could help inform strategies for communities, councils and government in providing infrastructure to support working anywhere.

This chapter highlights where 3D printing and digital communication technologies could provide the basis for a paradigm shift in relationships between people, making and product use, through a higher community focus on establishing distributed manufacturing infrastructure. While 3D printing build farms are yet to be proven as a sustainable business case beyond niche commercial applications, the networking of 3D printers warrants targeted research in order to support a digitally-enabled, distributed workforce. Now is the time to be exploring the potential of 3D printing build farms to influence community development, through research that brings together supply chain experts, federal and local government departments, town planners, policymakers, manufacturers, entrepreneurs and academics. Expanding smart city initiatives to encompass distributed, digital manufacturing in wider communities could create new ways of thinking about the future of work, and working anywhere strategies, for both.

## REFERENCES

Anderson, C. (2012). *Makers: The Next Industrial Revolution*. Random House Business Books.

Australian Government, Department of Infrastructure, Transport, Regional Development and Communication. (2019). *Smart Cities Collaboration Platform*. Retrieved from https://www.infrastructure.gov.au/cities/smart-cities/collaboration-platform/

Baumers, M., Dickens, P., Tuck, C., & Hague, R. (2016). The cost of additive manufacturing: Machine productivity, economies of scale and technology-push. *Technological Forecasting and Social Change*, *102*, 193–201. doi:10.1016/j.techfore.2015.02.015

Bregman, R. (2017). *Utopia for Realists*. Bloomsbury.

Cradduck, L. (2016). Rolling out the future: The current status of the Australian NBN and its impact for property. *Proceedings of the 22nd Pacific Rim Real Estate Society (PRRES) Annual Conference.*

D'Aveni, R. (2015). *3D printing will revive conglomerates*. Retrieved from https://hbr.org/2015/05/3d-printing-will-revive-conglomerates

Davies, S. (2019). *Smilelove & SmileDirectClub discuss the benefit of 3D printing moulds for clear aligners.* Retrieved from https://www.tctmagazine.com/3d-printing-news/aligner-start-ups-show-their-teeth-smilelove-smiledirectclub/

Diamandis, P., & Kotler, S. (2020). *The Future is Faster Than you Think: How Converging Technologies Are Transforming Business, Industries, and Our Lives.* Free Press.

Diegel, O., Nordin, A., & Motte, D. (2019). *A practical guide for design for additive manufacturing*. Springer. doi:10.1007/978-981-13-8281-9

Engineers Australia. (2020). *Sydney and Melbourne the worst for traffic congestion.* Retrieved from https://www.engineersaustralia.org.au/News/sydney-and-melbourne-worst-traffic-congestion

Formlabs. (2017). *How a 3D printer farm can help your business*. Retrieved from https://formlabs.com/blog/3d-print-farm-business-benefits/

Forty, A. (1986). *Objects of Desire: design and society since 1750.* Thames & Hudson.

Gershenfeld, N. (2007). *Fab: The Coming Revolution on Your Desktop - from Personal Computer to Personal Fabrication*. Basic Books.

Gershenfeld, N., Gershenfeld, A., & Cutcher-Gershenfeld, J. (2017). *Designing Reality: How to survive and thrive in the third digital revolution*. Basic Books.

Gibson, I., Rosen, D., & Stucker, B. (2014). *Additive Manufacturing Technologies: 3D printing, rapid prototyping and direct digital manufacturing*. Springer.

Gramenz, J. (2020). *Holden brand to disappear by the end of 2020*. Retrieved from https://www.news.com.au/technology/innovation/motoring/holden-brand-to-disappear-by-the-end-of-2020/news-story/c81a5e2993f664fc62965ad349601d0e

Gregory, M. A. (2020). *Rural and remote Australia and telecommunications and digital services*. Retrieved from https://regionaldevelopment.org.au/remote-rural-australia-dudded-nbn/

Griffith, L. (2018). *IMTS 2018 to showcase latest trends in manufacturing automation and robotics*. Retrieved from https://www.tctmagazine.com/3d-printing-news/imts-showcase-latest-trends-manufacturing-automation/

Gushchin, A., Martynovich, V., & Torubarov, S. (2020). *Automatic print job scheduling and management over multiple 3D printers*. Paper presented at the 5th International Conference on Industrial Engineering (ICIE 2019), Cham. 10.1007/978-3-030-22063-1_51

Hamalainen, M., & Karjalainen, J. (2017). Social manufacturing: When the maker movement meets interfirm production networks. *Business Horizons*, *60*(6), 795–805. doi:10.1016/j.bushor.2017.07.007

Holtkamp, C., Shelton, T., Daly, G., Hiner, C. C., & Hagelman, R. R. III. (2016). Assessing Neolocalism in Microbreweries. *Papers in Applied Geography*, *2*(1), 66–78. doi:10.1080/23754931.2015.1114514

Hornborg, A. (2019). The money-energy-technology complex and ecological marxism: Rethinking the concept of "use-value" to extend our understanding of unequal exchange, Part 1. *Capitalism, Nature, Socialism*, *30*(3), 27–39. doi:10.1080/10455752.2018.1440614

Jackson, B. (2019). *Stryker allots share of $225.8M to develop 3D printing R&D in Ireland*. Retrieved from https://3dprintingindustry.com/news/stryker-allots-share-of-225-8m-to-develop-3d-printing-rd-in-ireland-156966/

Kellner, T. (2018). The devil is in the details: How GE found a way to bring 3D printing to mass production. *GE Reports*. Retrieved from https://www.ge.com/reports/devil-details-3d-printed-part-jet-engine-part-now/

Krywko, J. (2018). *3D printing farms: A glimpse into the future*. Retrieved from https://zortrax.com/blog/3d-printing-farms-a-glimpse-into-the-future/

Kumparak, G. (2017). *TechShop shuts down all US locations, declares bankruptcy*. Retrieved from https://techcrunch.com/2017/11/15/techshop-shuts-down-all-u-s-locations-declares-bankruptcy/

Laplume, A., Anzalone, C., & Pearce, M. (2016). Opensource, self-replication 3D printer factory for small-business manufacturing. *International Journal of Advanced Manufacturing Technology*, *85*(1), 633–642. doi:10.100700170-015-7970-9

Le Duigou, A., Castro, M., Bevan, R., & Martin, N. (2016). 3D printing of wood fibre biocomposites: From mechanical to actuation functionality. *Materials & Design*, *96*, 106–114. doi:10.1016/j.matdes.2016.02.018

Lipson, H., & Kurman, M. (2013). *Fabricated: The new world of 3D printing, the promise and peril of a machine that can make (almost) anything*. John Wiley and Sons.

Liu, J., Sun, L., Xu, W., Wang, Q., Yu, S., & Sun, J. (2019). Current advances and future perspectives of 3D printing natural-derived biopolymers. *Carbohydrate Polymers*, *207*, 297–316. doi:10.1016/j.carbpol.2018.11.077 PMID:30600012

Lohrberg, F., Lička, L., Scazzosi, L., & Timpe, A. (2016). *Urban Agriculture Europe*. Jovis.

Louis, M., Seymour, T., & Joyce, J. (2014). *3D opportunity in the Department of Defense: Additive manufacturing fires up*. Deloitte University Press.

Loy, J. (2015). The future for design education: Preparing the design workforce for additive manufacturing. *International Journal of Rapid Manufacturing*, *5*(2), 199–212. doi:10.1504/IJRAPIDM.2015.073577

Loy, J., & Novak, J. I. (2019). The Future of Product Design Education Industry 4.0. In A. Raman & M. Rathakrishnan (Eds.), *Redesigning Higher Education Initiatives for Industry 4.0* (pp. 164–182). IGI Global. doi:10.4018/978-1-5225-7832-1.ch010

Loy, J., & Tatham, P. (2016). Redesigning Production Systems. In S. S. Muthu & M. M. Savalani (Eds.), *Handbook of Sustainability in Additive Manufacturing* (pp. 145–168). Springer. doi:10.1007/978-981-10-0549-7_7

Lozova, L. (2016). *Bringing the Ultimaker 3 to market with bridge manufacturing*. Retrieved from https://ultimaker.com/learn/bringing-the-ultimaker-3-to-market-with-bridge-manufacturing

MANUFACTUR3D. (2019). *Markforged unveils print farm – an affordable solution to scale metal and carbon fiber 3D printing production*. Retrieved from https://manufactur3dmag.com/markforged-unveils-print-farm-an-affordable-solution-to-scale-metal-and-carbon-fiber-3d-printing-production/

Mavri, M. (2015). Redesigning a production chain based on 3D printing technology. *Knowledge and Process Management*, *22*(3), 141–147. doi:10.1002/kpm.1466

Mohammed, M. I., Mohan, M. D., Johnson, M. D., Badwal, P. S., McLean, D., & Gibson, I. (2017). A low carbon footprint approach to the reconstitution of plastics into 3D-printer filament for enhanced waste reduction. In *DesTech 2016: Proceedings of the International Conference on Design and Technology,* (pp. 234-241). Dubai, UAE: Knowledge E.

Novak, J. I. (2019). Re-educating the Educators: Collaborative 3D Printing Education. In I. M. Santos, N. Ali, & S. Areepattamannil (Eds.), *Interdisciplinary and International Perspectives on 3D Printing in Education* (pp. 28–49). IGI Global. doi:10.4018/978-1-5225-7018-9.ch002

Novak, J. I., & Loy, J. (2020a). A critical review of initial 3D printed products responding to COVID-19 health and supply chain challenges. *Emerald Open Research, 2*(24).

Novak, J. I., & Loy, J. (2020b). Moving 3D printing beyond the desktop within higher education: Towards a service bureau approach. In M. S. Khine & N. Ali (Eds.), *Integrating 3D Printing into Teaching and Learning: Practitioners' Perspectives* (pp. 206–227). Brill.

Palmer, T. (2018). *3 major manufacturing changes loom*. Production Machining.

Peels, J. (2018). *3D Hubs killing off its community? 3D printing company commits suicide for no reason*. Retrieved from https://3dprint.com/224758/3dhubs-killing-off-its-community-3d-printing-company-commits-suicide-for-no-reason/

Průša, J. (2018). *Three hundred 3D printers in one room: A quick look to our printing farm*. Retrieved from https://blog.prusaprinters.org/a-quick-look-to-our-printing-farm/

Ransikarbum, K., Ha, S., Ma, J., & Kim, N. (2017). Multi-objective optimisation analysis for part-to-printer assignment in a network of 3D fused deposition modelling. *Journal of Manufacturing Systems, 43*, 35–46. doi:10.1016/j.jmsy.2017.02.012

Ross, A. (2016). *The Industries of The Future*. Simon & Schuster.

Schwab, K. (2017). *The Fourth Industrial Revolution*. Crown Business.

Skawiński, P., & Siemiński, P. (2017). The 3D printer farm – function and technology requirements and didactic use. *Mechanik, 90*(8-9), 796–800. doi:10.17814/mechanik.2017.8-9.117

Staak, S. (2018). *Ford: Reinventing efficient manufacturing using 3D printing*. Retrieved from https://ultimaker.com/learn/ford-reinventing-efficient-manufacturing-using-3d-printing

Vries, S. (2017). *Volkswagen Autoeuropa: Maximising production efficiency with 3D printed tools, jigs and fixtures*. Retrieved from https://ultimaker.com/learn/volswagen-autoerupoa-maximizing-production-efficiency-with-3d-printed

Weber, P. (2013). The rise and fall of Detroit: A timeline. *The Week*. Retrieved from https://theweek.com/articles/461968/rise-fall-detroit-timeline

Wohlers. (2019). *Wohlers report: 3D printing and additive manufacturing, State of the Industry*. https://wohlersassociates.com/2019report.htm

Wright, S., & Bagshaw, E. (2019). *As cities grow, parts of regional Australia disappear and get angry*. Retrieved from https://www.smh.com.au/politics/federal/as-cities-grow-parts-of-regional-australia-disappear-and-get-angry-20190829-p52m26.html

## ADDITIONAL READING

Bryan, V. C., Musgrove, A. T., & Powers, J. R. (2017). *Handbook of Research on Human Development in the Digital Age*. IGI Global.

Gore, A. (2013). *The Future: Six Drivers for Global Change*. WH Allen.

Hajkowicz, S. (2015). *Megatrends: Seven Patterns of Change Shaping our Future*. CSIRO. doi:10.1071/9781486301416

Hawken, P. (2018). *Drawdown: The Most Comprehensive Plan Ever Proposed to Reverse Global Warming*. Penguin.

Johnston, L. (2015). *Digital Handmade: Craftsmanship in the new industrial revolution*. Thames and Hudson.

## KEY TERMS AND DEFINITIONS

**3D Printing:** 3D printing, also called additive manufacturing, refers to fabrication technologies that build parts in layers based on a 3D computer model.

**3D Printing Build Farm:** A networked collection of similar 3D printers controlled through a central system.

**Distributed Workforce:** Geographically dispersed employees that work collectively utilising online systems and software.

**Gig Economy:** Flexible, temporary and freelance employment offered through an online platform.

**Mass Production:** Manufacturing of large quantities of standardised parts or products.

# Compilation of References

Aabø, S., Audunson, R., & Vårheim, A. (2010). How do public libraries function as meeting places? *Library & Information Science Research*, *32*(1), 16–26. doi:10.1016/j.lisr.2009.07.008

Aceros, J. C., Pols, J., & Domènech, M. (2015). Where is grandma? Home telecare, good aging and the domestication of later life. *Technological Forecasting and Social Change*, *93*, 102–111. doi:10.1016/j.techfore.2014.01.016

Adams, L., & Oldfield, K. (2012). Opening up work: The views of disabled people and people with long-term health conditions. *IFF Research.* https://www.equalityhumanrights.com/sites/default/files/research_report_77_opening_up_work.pdf

Adler, N., & Gunderson, A. (2008). International dimensions of organizational behavior (5th ed.). Mason: South-Western College Publishing, International Thomson Publishing.

Aged Community Services Australia. (2015). *The aged care workforce in Australia: position paper.* Retrieved from https://www.acs.asn.au/wcm/documents/ACS%20Website/Resources/Publications%20Submissions/ACSA%20Submissions%20Documents/ACSA%20Workforce%20White%20Paper%20-%20July%202014.pdf

AIG. (2012). *Working smarter: flexible work and telework, Report of the Australian Industry Group.* http://ict-industry-reports.com.au/wp-content/uploads/sites/4/2013/09/2012-Telework-Working-Smarter-AIGroup-Nov-2012.pdf

Alexopoulos, A. N., & Buckley, F. (2013). What trust matters when: The temporal value of professional and personal trust for effective knowledge transfer. *Group & Organization Management*, *38*(3), 361–391. doi:10.1177/1059601113488939

Ali, M., Schur, L., & Blanck, P. (2011). What types of jobs do people with disabilities want? *Journal of Occupational Rehabilitation*, *21*(2), 199–210. doi:10.100710926-010-9266-0 PMID:20924777

Allen, T., Golden, T., & Shockley, K. (2015). How Effective Is Telecommuting? *Assessing the Status of Our Scientific Findings Psychological Science in the Public Interest, 16*(2). https://journals.sagepub.com/stoken/rbtfl/EnhOwEhELZ4aI/ful

Allen, D. K., Brown, A., Karanasios, S., & Norman, A. (2013). How should technology-mediated organizational change be explained? A comparison of the contributions of critical realism and activity theory. *Management Information Systems Quarterly*, *37*(3), 835–854. doi:10.25300/MISQ/2013/37.3.08

Allen, D., Karanasios, S., & Slavova, M. (2011). Working with activity theory: Context, technology, and information behavior. *Journal of the American Society for Information Science and Technology*, *62*(4), 776–788. doi:10.1002/asi.21441

Allen, T. D., Johnson, R. C., Kiburz, K. M., & Shockley, K. M. (2013). Work–family conflict and flexible work arrangements: Deconstructing flexibility. *Personnel Psychology*, *66*(2), 345–376. doi:10.1111/peps.12012

An, M. (2019, August 9). Vietnamese workers are more productive with flexible working hours. *Hanoi Times*. Retrieved from http://hanoitimes.vn/vietnamese-workers-are-more-productive-with-flexible-working-hours-45588.html

Analytics Insight. (2020). *Top Robotics Investments and Funding in January 2020.* Retrieved from https://www.analyticsinsight.net/top-10-robotics-investment-funding-january-2020/

Anderson, J., & Douma, F. (2009). *Telework for Workers with Disabilities Pilot Projects Synthesis Report (under sub-contract to CESSI for the Office of Disability Employment Policy, U.S. Department of Labor)*. Minneapolis, MN. Online resource, accessed December 29, 2019, from https://www.dol.gov/odep/research/TeleworkSynthesisReport.pdf

Anderson, C. (2012). *Makers: The Next Industrial Revolution*. Random House Business Books.

Andersson, M., & Larsson, J. P. (2016). Local entrepreneurship clusters in cities. *Journal of Economic Geography*, *16*(1), 39–66. doi:10.1093/jeg/lbu049

Anell, K., & Hartmann, D. (2007). *Flexible Work Arrangement in Asia, what companies are doing, why they are doing it and what lies ahead.* A Report Prepared for the Members of the Global Workforce Roundtable, Boston College Center for Work & Family.

Angeloni, S. (2013). Integrated Disability Management: An interdisciplinary and holistic approach. *SAGE Open*, *3*(4), 1–15. doi:10.1177/2158244013510303

Arendt, H. (1958). *The Human Condition*. University of Chicago Press.

Argyle, M. (1992). *The Social Psychology of Everyday Life*. Routledge.

Argyris, C. (1967). *Personality and Organization: The Conflict between System and Individual.* Harper Collins.

Armfield, N. R., Edirippulige, S. K., Bradford, N., & Smith, A. C. (2014). Telemedicine — is the cart being put before the horse? *The Medical Journal of Australia*, *200*(9), 530–533. doi:10.5694/mja13.11101 PMID:24835716

Arnoldi, E., Bosua, R., Cooper, V., Greenfield, C., & Ch'ng, H. (2018). *Coworking and an Outer urban community: What can we learn from a grassroots community coworking hub?* Analysis and Policy Observatory.

Ashman, H., Brailsford, T., Cristea, A. I., Sheng, Q. Z., Stewart, C., Toms, E. G., & Wade, V. (2014). The ethical and social implications of personalization technologies for e-learning. *Management & Information*, *51*(6), 819–832. doi:10.1016/j.im.2014.04.003

Ashton, K. (2015). *How to Fly a Horse: The Secret History of Creation, Invention and Discovery*. Windmill Books.

Asia Research. (2018). *The push for flexible working in Asia*. Retrieved from https://asia-research.net/push-flexible-working-asia/

Ask a Lawyer on Call. (2020). *Ask a Lawyer*. Retrieved from https://www.askalawyeroncall.com

Asmawi, A., & Othman, N. (2018). Barriers to Flexible Work Arrangements (FWA) in Malaysian Knowledge-based Industries. *2018 IEEE International Conference on Industrial Engineering and Engineering Management (IEEM)*. 10.1109/IEEM.2018.8607349

Aston, J., & Cornett, B. (2016, July 12). Michael Page staff in ski scandal. *The Australian Financial Review*, 35.

Augustin, S. (2014). Designing for collaboration and collaborating for design. *Journal of Interior Design*, *39*(1), ix–xviii. doi:10.1111/joid.12020

Australian Bureau of Statistics 4430.0. (2018). *Disability, Ageing and Carers, Australia: Summary of Findings, 2018)*. https://www.abs.gov.au/ausstats/abs@.nsf/Lookup/4430.0main+features12018

Australian Bureau of Statistics. (2016). *4364.0.55.001 - National Health Survey: First Results, 2014-15*. Retrieved from http://www.abs.gov.au/ausstats/abs@.nsf/Lookup/by%20Subject/4364.0.55.001~2014-15~Main%20Features~Diabetes%20mellitus~12

Australian Bureau of Statistics. (2020). *Population clock*. Retrieved from http://www.abs.gov.au/ausstats/abs%40.nsf/94713ad445ff1425ca25682000192af2/1647509ef7e25faaca2568a900154b63?OpenDocument

Australian Government Australian Institute of Health and Welfare. (2016). *Chronic disease comorbidity*. Retrieved from http://www.aihw.gov.au/chronic-diseases/comorbidity/

Australian Government, Department of Infrastructure, Transport, Regional Development and Communication. (2019). *Smart Cities Collaboration Platform*. Retrieved from https://www.infrastructure.gov.au/cities/smart-cities/collaboration-platform/

Australian Human Rights Commission. (2016) *Willing to Work National Inquiry into Employment Discrimination Against Older Australians and Australians with Disability*. https://www.humanrights.gov.au/sites/default/files/document/publication/WTW_2016_Full_Report_AHRC_ac.pdf

Australian Institute of Health and Welfare (AIHW). (2019). *People with disability in Australia.* https://www.aihw.gov.au/reports/disability/people-with-disability-in-australia

Australian Institute of Health and Welfare. (2018). *Australia's health 2018.* Retrieved from Canberra https://www.aihw.gov.au/reports/australias-health/australias-health-2018/contents/table-of-contents

Australian Institute of Health and Welfare. (2019). *Health expenditure Australia 2017–18.* Retrieved from https://www.aihw.gov.au/reports/health-welfare-expenditure/health-expenditure-australia-2017-18/contents/data-visualisation

Avdikos, V., & Kalogeresis, A. (2017). Socio-economic profile and working conditions of freelancers in coworking spaces and work collectives: Evidence from the design sector in Greece. *Area*, *49*(1), 35–42. doi:10.1111/area.12279

Avent, R. (2016, September 19). A world without work is coming – it could be utopia or it could be hell. *The Guardian*. Retrieved from https://www.theguardian.com/commentisfree/2016/sep/19/world-without-work-utopia-hell-human-labour-obsolete

Badham, Clegg, & Wall. (2000). Sociotechnical Theory. In *Handbook of Ergonomics*. New York: John Wiley.

Bailey, D. E., & Kurland, N. B. (2002). A review of telework research: Findings, new direction and lessons for the study of modern work. *Journal of Organizational Behavior*, *23*(4), 383–400. doi:10.1002/job.144

Baker, P. M. A., Bricout, J. C., Moon, N. W., Coughlan, B., & Pater, J. (2013). Communities of participation: A comparison of disability and aging identified groups on Facebook and LinkedIn. *Telematics and Informatics*, *30*(1), 22–34. doi:10.1016/j.tele.2012.03.004

Baker, P. M., Linden, M. A., LaForce, S. S., Rutledge, J., & Goughnour, K. P. (2018). Barriers to employment participation of individuals with disabilities: Addressing the impact of employer (mis) perception and policy. *The American Behavioral Scientist*, *62*(5), 657–675. doi:10.1177/0002764218768868

Baker, P., & Moon, N. (2008, Fall). Wireless Technologies and Accessibility for People With Disabilities: Findings from A Policy Research Instrument. *Journal of Assistive Technologies*, *20*(3). PMID:18939655

Baldwin, R., Chenoweth, L., & dela Rama, M. (2015). Residential Aged Care Policy in Australia– Are We Learning from Evidence? *Australian Journal of Public Administration*, *74*(2), 128–141. doi:10.1111/1467-8500.12131

Barnes, C. (2012). Rethinking Disability, Work and Welfare. *Sociology Compass*, *6*(6), 472–484. doi:10.1111/j.1751-9020.2012.00464.x

Bashshur, R. L., & Reardon, T. G. (2014). Commentary on "Critical Appraisal of Published Systematic Reviews Assessing the Cost-Effectiveness of Telemedicine Studies". *Telemedicine Journal and e-Health*, *20*(9), 883–884. doi:10.1089/tmj.2014.9980 PMID:25184946

Bauer, W., & Vocke, X. (2019). Work in the Age of Artificial Intelligence – Challenges and Potentials for the Design of New Forms of Human-Machine Interaction. *International Conference on Applied Human Factors and Ergonomics*, 493-501.

Baumers, M., Dickens, P., Tuck, C., & Hague, R. (2016). The cost of additive manufacturing: Machine productivity, economies of scale and technology-push. *Technological Forecasting and Social Change*, *102*, 193–201. doi:10.1016/j.techfore.2015.02.015

Bavelas, J. (1978). *Personality: Current Theory and Research.* Brooks/Cole.

Bayrak, T. (2012). IT support for Telecommuting Workforce. *Telematics and Informatics*, *29*(3), 286–293. doi:10.1016/j.tele.2011.10.002

Beauregard, Basile, & Canonico. (2019). *Telework: outcomes and facilitators for employees.* Academic Press.

Bélanger, F., Watson-Manheim, M. B., & Swan, B. R. (2012). A multi-level socio-technical systems telecommuting framework. *Behaviour & Information Technology*, *32*(12), 1257–1279. doi:10.1080/0144929X.2012.705894

Bentley, K., & Yoong, P. (2000). Knowledge work and telework: An exploratory study. *Internet Research*, *10*(4), 346–356. doi:10.1108/10662240010342658

Bentley, T. A., Teo, S. T. T., McLeod, L., Tan, F., Bosua, R., & Gloet, M. (2016). 'The role of organizational support in teleworker wellbeing: A socio-technical systems approach'. *Applied Ergonomics*, *52*, 207–215. doi:10.1016/j.apergo.2015.07.019 PMID:26360212

Bentley, T., McLeod, L., Bosua, R., Gloet, M., Teo, S., Rasmussen, E., & Tan, F. (2013). *The Future of Work Program: The Trans-Tasman Telework Survey New Zealand Work Research Institute AUT and IBES (Institute for a Broadband Enabled Society).* The University of Melbourne.

Berger, P., & Luckmann, T. (1967). *The Social Construction of Reality.* Penguin.

Bergmo, T. (2009). Can economic evaluation in telemedicine be trusted? A systematic review of the literature. *Cost Effectiveness and Resource Allocation*, *7*(1), 18. doi:10.1186/1478-7547-7-18 PMID:19852828

Berrell, M. (1994). The nature of work: An introduction. In F. Crowther, B. Caldwell, J. Chapman, G. Lakomski, & D. Ogilvie (Eds.), *The Workplace in Education: Australian Perspectives. Yearbook of the Australian Council for Educational Administration, 1.* Edward Arnold.

Berrell, M. (2017). The Social Relations of Anywhere Working: Major Themes and Meanings. In Y. Blount & M. Gloet (Eds.), *Anywhere Working and the New Era of Telecommuting.* ICI Global. doi:10.4018/978-1-5225-2328-4.ch002

Berrell, M., & Macpherson, R. (1995). Educational sociology and educational administration: Problems with paradigms, epistemology, research, and theory. *Journal of Educational Administration and Foundations*, *10*(1), 9–32.

Bilandzic, M., & Forth, M. (2017). Designing hubs for connected learning: Social, Spatial and technological insights from Coworking, Hackerspaces and Meetup groups. In L. Carvalho, P. Goodyear, & M. de Laat (Eds.), *Place-Based Spaces for Networked Learning, Routledge* (pp. 191–206). United Kingdon.

Bilandzic, M., & Foth, M. (2013). Libraries as coworking spaces: Understanding user motivations and perceived barriers to social learning. *Library Hi Tech*, *31*(2), 254–273. doi:10.1108/07378831311329040

Bilevičiūtė, E., & Bilevičienė, T. (2010). Telework organization model as method of development of disabled persons' employment quality. *Perspectives of Innovations, Economics and Business*, *2*(5), 71–74. doi:10.15208/pieb.2010.53

Bishop, C. (2006). *Pattern Recognition and Machine Learning*. Springer.

BlackStone Discovery. (2020). *BlackStone Discovery Home Page*. Retrieved from https://www.blackstonediscovery.com/about/

Blauner, R. (1964). *Alienation and Freedom: The Factory Worker and His Industry. Chicago*. University of Chicago Press.

Blok, M. M., Groenesteijn, L., Schelvis, R., & Vink, P. (2012). New ways of working: Does flexibility in time and location of work change work behavior and affect business outcomes? *Work (Reading, Mass.)*, *41*, 5075–5080. doi:10.3233/WOR-2012-0800-5075 PMID:22317507

Blount, Y. (2015). Pondering the Fault Lines of Anywhere Working (Telework, Telecommuting): A Literature Review. *Foundations and Trends® in Information Systems, 1*(3), 163-276.

Blount, Y. (2015). Pondering the Fault Lines of Anywhere Working (Telework, Telecommuting): A Literature Review. *Foundations and Trends® in Information Systems, 1*(3), 163-276. doi:10.1561/2900000001

Blount, Y., & Gloet, M. (2015). *Adoption of ICT Enabled Telehealth Services in the Australian Context: Implications of Technology Use for Telehealth Workers*. Paper presented at the Hawaii International Conference on System Sciences HICSS-48, Kauai, HI.

Blount, Y. (2011). Employee management and service provision: A conceptual framework. *Information Technology & People*, *24*(2), 134–157. doi:10.1108/09593841111137331

Blount, Y. (2015). *Telework: Not Business as Usual. In Business Technologies in Contemporary Organizations: Adoption, Assimilation, and Institutionalization.* IGI Global.

Bluestone, B., & Harrison, B. (1982). *The Deindustrialization of America: Plant Closings, Community Abandonment, and the Dismantling of Basic Industry*. Basic Books.

Boden, M.A. (1977). Social implications of intelligent machines. *Radio and Electronic Engineer*, *47*(8.9), 393-399.

Boden, M. A. (1984). Impacts of artificial intelligence. *Futures*, *16*(1), 60–70. doi:10.1016/0016-3287(84)90007-7

Bosch-Sijtsema, P. M., & Sivunen, A. (2013). Professional virtual worlds supporting computer-mediated communication, collaboration, and learning in geographically distributed contexts. *IEEE Transactions on Professional Communication*, *56*(2), 160–175. doi:10.1109/TPC.2012.2237256

Bosua, R., Kurnia, S., Gloet, M., & Mendoza, A. (2017). Telework Impact on Productivity and Wellbeing: an Australian Study. In J. Choudrie, S. Kurnia, & P. Tastsou (Eds.), *Social lnclusion and Usability of ICT-enabled Services*. Taylor and Francis Group. doi:10.4324/9781315677316-10

Boxall, P., Purcell, J., & Wright, P. (Eds.). (2008). *The Oxford Handbook on Human Resource Management*. Oxford University Press.

Boyer, R. H. (2016). Achieving one-planet living through transitions in social practice: a case study of Dancing Rabbit Ecovillage. *Sustainability: Science, Practice and Policy, 12*(1), 47-59.

Bregman, R. (2017). *Utopia for Realists*. Bloomsbury.

Brenner, N., & Keil, R. (2014). From Global Cities to Globalized Urbanization. *Glocalism: Journal Of Culture, Politics And Innovation*, 3. www.glocalismjournal.net

Breure, A., & van Meel, J. (2003). Airport offices: Facilitating nomadic workers. *Facilities*, *21*(7/8), 175–179. doi:10.1108/02632770310489918

Brownson, K. (2004). The benefits of a work-at-home program. *The Health Care Manager*, *23*(2), 141–144. doi:10.1097/00126450-200404000-00007 PMID:15192994

Brynjolfsson, E., & McAfee, A. (2011). *Race Against the Machine: How the Digital Revolution Is Accelerating Innovation, Driving Productivity, and Irreversibly Transforming Employment and The Economy*. Research Brief, MIT Center for Digital Business. Retrieved from http://ebusiness.mit.edu/research/Briefs/Brynjolfsson_McAfee_Race_Against_the_Machine.pdf

Buksh, B., & Davidson, J. (2013). Digital Work Hubs-An Activation Framework for South East Queensland. *The Digital Work Hub Project, Regional Development Australia.* Available at: digitalworkhub.com.au

Burgess, P. M. (1994). *Lone eagles.* Center for the New West Points West Advisory.

Burrell, G., & Morgan, G. (2005). *Sociological Paradigms and Organizational Analysis: Elements of the Sociology of Corporate Life*. Ashgate.

Business Council of Australia. (2011). *Lifting the Quality of Teaching and Learning in Higher Education*. BCA.

Business Council of Australia. (2016). *Being Work Ready, A guide to what employers want.* BCA.

Business Council of Australia. (2017). *A Sustainable Higher Education System.* BCA.

Butcher, T. (2013). Coworking: locating community at work. *Annual Australia New Zealand Academy of Management (ANZAM) Conference*.

Capdevila, I. (2013). *Knowledge Dynamics in Localized Communities: Coworking Spaces as Microclusters*. Available at SSRN: https://ssrn.com/abstract=2414121

Cappelli, P., & Keller, J. R. (2013). Classifying work in the new economy. *Academy of Management Review*, *38*(4), 575–596. doi:10.5465/amr.2011.0302

Capterra. (2020). Retrieved from https://blog.capterra.com/free-legal-advice-5-easy-to-use-sites-that-are-actually-free/

Carati, C., & Margelis, G. (2013). *Towards a National Strategy for Telehealth in Australia 2013-2018*. Retrieved from http://aths.org.au/wp-content/uploads/2013/05/TelehealthStrategy.pdf

Carey, M.A., Asbury, J. & Tolich, M.B. (n.d.). *Focus Group Research*. Taylor & Francis Group.

Channel News Asia (CNA). (2020). Virus breaks the mold for telework in office-bound Japan. *CNA International Edition*. Retrieved from https://www.channelnewsasia.com/news/asia/coronavirus-covid-19-japan-work-from-home-12592548

Cherns, A. (1986). Principles of socio-technical design revisited. *Human Relations*, *40*(3), 153–161. doi:10.1177/001872678704000303

Chiang, J., & Lundgren, A. (2017). *What is the Evolution of Flexible Work in Corporations and What are the Key Trends?* Available from: https://digitalcommons.illr.cornell.edu/student/168

Chomik, R., & MacLennan, M. (2014). *Aged Care in Australia: Part I-Policy, demand and funding, CEPAR research brief 2014/01*. Academic Press.

Churchman, C. (1967). Wicked Problems. *Management Science*, *14*(4), B-141–B-146.

Çimen, T. (2008). *Teknolojik gelişmelerin sonucunda değişen üretim ilişkilerinin, ofis yapılarına etkisi ve ofis mekanları* (Unpublished master's dissertation). Istanbul Technical University, Istanbul.

Clark, S., & Holdsworth, L. (2017). *Flexibility in the Workplace: Implications of flexible work arrangements for individuals, teams, and organizations*. Alliance Manchester Business School, University of Manchester, for the Advisory, Conciliation and Arbitration Service UK. www.acas.org.uk

Clegg, C. (2000). Socio-technical Principles for System Design. *Applied Ergonomics*, *31*(5), 463–477. doi:10.1016/S0003-6870(00)00009-0 PMID:11059460

Cole, R. J., Bild, A., & Olivre, A. (2012). The changing context of knowledge-based work: Consequences for comfort, satisfaction and productivity. *Intelligent Buildings International*, *4*(3), 182–196. doi:10.1080/17508975.2012.695950

Collier, D. (2016). *Inclusion of people with disabilities in the workplace: Best practices for HR professionals*. Retrieved 19 December 2019 from Cornell University, ILR School site: https://digitalcommons.ilr.cornell.edu/student/142

Colliers International. (2019). *The Flexible Workspace Outlook Report: APAC*. Colliers International. Retrieved from http://flexiblespace.colliers.com/

Commission of the European Communities (CEC). (2006). *Adult learning: It is never too late to learn*. Access to European Union Law. Retrieved from https://eur-lex.europa.eu/legal-content/EN/ALL/?uri=CELEX:52006DC0614

Connelly, F. M., & Clandinin, D. J. (1990). Stories of experience and narrative inquiry. *Educational Researcher, 19*(5), 2–14. doi:10.3102/0013189X019005002

Cornish, S. D. (2014). *Living in Australia's rural areas will cut your life short*. Retrieved from http://www.news.com.au/lifestyle/health/living-in-australias-rural-areas-will-cut-your-life-short/story-fneuzlbd-1226947018877

Cradduck, L. (2016). Rolling out the future: The current status of the Australian NBN and its impact for property. *Proceedings of the 22nd Pacific Rim Real Estate Society (PRRES) Annual Conference.*

Creswell, J. W. (2007). *Qualitative inquiry and research design: choosing among five approaches*. Sage.

Creswell, J. W., Hanson, W. E., Clark Plano, V. L., & Morales, A. (2007). Qualitative research designs: Selection and implementation. *The Counseling Psychologist, 35*(2), 236–264. doi:10.1177/0011000006287390

Crowther, F., Caldwell, B., Chapman, J., Lakomski, G., & Ogilvie, D. (Eds.). (1994). *The Workplace in Education, Australian Perspectives, 1*. Edward Arnold.

Curaoğlu, F., & Demirbaş, D. (2017). From coworking places to new education places. *The Design Journal, 20*(sup1), S4765-S4767.

D'Aveni, R. (2015). *3D printing will revive conglomerates*. Retrieved from https://hbr.org/2015/05/3d-printing-will-revive-conglomerates

Dahrendorf, R. (1959). *Class and Class Conflict in Industrial Society*. Stanford University Press.

Davenport, T., & Pearlson, K. (1998). Two Cheers for the Virtual Office. *Sloan Management Review, 39*(4), 51–65.

Davies, S. (2019). *Smilelove & SmileDirectClub discuss the benefit of 3D printing moulds for clear aligners*. Retrieved from https://www.tctmagazine.com/3d-printing-news/aligner-start-ups-show-their-teeth-smilelove-smiledirectclub/

Davison, E., & Cotton, S. (2010). *Connection Disparities: The Importance of Broadband Connections in Understanding Today's Digital Divide. In Overcoming Digital Divides: Constructing an Equitable and Competitive Information Society*. IGI Global.

de Grazia, S. (1962). *Of Time, Work and Leisure*. Krauss Reprint Co.

Deaux, K., & Snyder, M. (Eds.). (2012). *The Oxford Handbook of Personality and Social Psychology*. Oxford University Press. doi:10.1093/oxfordhb/9780195398991.001.0001

Demerouti, E., Derks, D., Lieke, L., & Bakker, A. B. (2014). New ways of working: Impact on working conditions, work–family balance, and wellbeing. In *The impact of ICT on quality of working life* (pp. 123–141). Springer Netherlands. doi:10.1007/978-94-017-8854-0_8

Department of Education and Science (DES). (2000). *Learning for Life: Paper on Adult Education*. Dublin: Stationery Office.

Department of Education, Employment and Workplace Relations (DEEWR). (2012). Employability Skills Framework, Stage 1. Canberra: DEEWR.

Department of Environment, Land, Water and Planning. (2017). *Metropolitan Partnerships: Western Region.* Victoria State Government. www.delwp.vic.gov.au

Department of Health and Ageing. (2012). *Living longer. Living better: Aged Care Reform Package April 2012*. Author.

Department of Health. (2019). *Home care packages - reform*. Retrieved from https://agedcare.health.gov.au/aged-care-reform/home-care/home-care-packages-reform

Department of Health. (2019). *Overweight and Obesity*. Retrieved from https://www1.health.gov.au/internet/main/publishing.nsf/Content/Overweight-and-Obesity

Department of Sustainability, Environment, Water, Population and Communities (DES). (2011). Sustainable Australia - Sustainable Communities: A sustainable population strategy for Australia, Canberra.

Dewa, C. S., & Lin, E. (2000). Chronic physical illness, psychiatric disorder and disability in the workplace. *Social Science & Medicine*, *51*(1), 41–50. doi:10.1016/S0277-9536(99)00431-1 PMID:10817467

Diamandis, P., & Kotler, S. (2020). *The Future is Faster Than you Think: How Converging Technologies Are Transforming Business, Industries, and Our Lives*. Free Press.

Diegel, O., Nordin, A., & Motte, D. (2019). *A practical guide for design for additive manufacturing*. Springer. doi:10.1007/978-981-13-8281-9

Disability Discrimination Act (DDA). (1992). https://www.humanrights.gov.au/sites/default/files/GPGB_disability_discrimination.pdf

Disability Works Australia, Ltd. (n.d.). http://www.dwa.org.au/whatisadisability.htm

Disability Works Australia. (2015). http://www.dwa.org.au/whatisadisability.htm

Donnelly, N., & Proctor-Thomson, S. B. (2015). Disrupted work: Home-based teleworking (HbTW) in the aftermath of a natural disaster. *New Technology, Work and Employment*, *30*(1), 47–61. doi:10.1111/ntwe.12040

Downs, A. (1999). Some realities about sprawl and urban decline. *Housing Policy Debate*, *10*(4), 955–974. doi:10.1080/10511482.1999.9521356

Duffy, F. (1997). *The New Office*. Conron Octapus.

Dunbar, R. (2016). Do online social media cut through the constraints that limit the size of offline social networks? *Royal Society Open Science*. Retrieved from http://rsos.royalsocietypublishing.org/content/3/1/150292

Duplantie, J., Fortin, J.-P., Gagnon, M.-P., & Landry, R. (2007). Telehealth and the recruitment and retention of physicians in rural and remote regions: A Delphi study. *Canadian Journal of Rural Medicine*, *12*, 30. PMID:17229362

Durkheim, E. (1964). *The Rules of Sociological Method*. The Free Press.

Economics, D. A. (2011). *Next Generation Telework: A Literature Review*. Department of Broadband, Communications, and the Digital Economy. Retrieved from https://melbourneinstitute.unimelb.edu.au/assets/documents/hilda-bibliography/other-publications/2011/Next_Generation_Telework-A_Literature_Review-July_2011.pdf

Edirippulige, S., Brooks, P., Carati, C., Wade, V. A., Smith, A. C., Wickramasinghe, S., & Armfield, N. R. (2018). It's important, but not important enough: eHealth as a curriculum priority in medical education in Australia. *Journal of Telemedicine and Telecare*, *24*(10), 697–702. doi:10.1177/1357633X18793282 PMID:30343657

Effrat, A. (1976). Book Review, *Sociology, A Multiple Paradigm Science* by George Ritzer. *American Journal of Sociology*, *81*(6), 1512–1514. doi:10.1086/226243

Eldridge, J. (1971). *The Sociology of Industrial Life*. Nelson.

Eleanor, P., & Oughton, J. (2007). The Affective Domain: Undiscovered Country. *The College Quarterly*, *10*(4), 1–7.

Engeström, Y. (2009). The future of Activity Theory: A rough draft. In Learning and Expanding with Activity Theory. New York, NY: Cambridge. doi:10.1017/CBO9780511809989.020

Engeström, Y. (2000). Activity theory as a framework for analyzing and redesigning work. *Ergonomics*, *43*(7), 960–974. doi:10.1080/001401300409143 PMID:10929830

Engineers Australia. (2020). *Sydney and Melbourne the worst for traffic congestion*. Retrieved from https://www.engineersaustralia.org.au/News/sydney-and-melbourne-worst-traffic-congestion

Erdener, H.E. (1996). Büro binalarında yeni kullanım yöntemleri. *Yapı*, (181), 77-83.

Erdoğan, S. (2012). *Yeni emek sistemleri: ev-ofis sistemi üzerine bir inceleme* (Unpublished master's dissertation). Ankara University, Ankara.

Ergin, E. (2012). *Hazır ofislerin iç mekân tasarım yaklaşımları* (Unpublished master's dissertation). Cukurova University, Adana.

Everymind. (2020). Retrieved from https://everymind.org.au/need-help/self-care

Fair Work Act 2009 No. 28, 2009 as amended.

Fay, M. J., & Kline, S. L. (2012). The influence of informal communication on organizational identification and commitment in the context of high-intensity telecommuting. *The Southern Communication Journal*, *77*(1), 61–76. doi:10.1080/1041794x.2011.582921

Fear, J. (2011). *Polluted time Blurring the boundaries between work and life*. The Australia Institute.

Felstead, A., Jewson, N., Phizacklea, A., & Walters, S. (2002). Opportunities to work at home in the context of work-life balance. *Human Resource Management Journal*, *12*(1), 54–76. doi:10.1111/j.1748-8583.2002.tb00057.x

Felstead, A., Jewson, N., & Walters, S. (2005). The shifting locations of work: New statistical evidence on the spaces and places of employment. *Work, Employment and Society*, *19*(2), 415–431. doi:10.1177/0950017005053186

Feros Care. (2015). *Feros Care - Annual Report 2014-2015*. Retrieved from https://www.feroscare.com.au/about/annual-reports/

Feros Care. (2016). *Feros Care: Celebrating Aging Vision and Mission Statement*. Retrieved from https://www.feroscare.com.au/about/mission-statement/

Ferreira, A. I., Martinez, L. F., Cooper, C., & Gui, D. M. (2015). LMX as a negative predictor of presenteeism climate: A cross-cultural study in the financial and health sectors. *Journal of Organizational Effectiveness: People and Performance*, *2*(3), 282–302. doi:10.1108/JOEPP-02-2015-0005

Fiorentino, S. (2019). Different typologies of 'coworking spaces' and the contemporary dynamics of local economic development in Rome. *European Planning Studies*, *27*(9), 1768–1790. doi:10.1080/09654313.2019.1620697

Florida, R. (2002). *The Rise of the Creative Class—and How It Is Transforming Leisure, Community and Everyday Life*. New York: Basic Books.

Florida, R. (2017). *The New Urban Crisis*. Basic Books.

Fonner, K. L., & Stache, L. C. (2012). All in a day's work, at home: Teleworkers' management of micro role transitions and the work–home boundary. *New Technology, Work and Employment*, *27*(3), 242–257. doi:10.1111/j.1468-005X.2012.00290.x

Formlabs. (2017). *How a 3D printer farm can help your business*. Retrieved from https://formlabs.com/blog/3d-print-farm-business-benefits/

Forty, A. (1986). *Objects of Desire: design and society since 1750*. Thames & Hudson.

Foster, H., Towers, B., Whittaker, J., Handmer, J., & Lowe, T. (2013). Peri-urban Melbourne in 2021: Changes and Implications for the Victorian Emergency Management Sector. *Australian Journal of Emergency Management*, *28*, 6–12.

Freek, L., Stevenson, D., Leser, M., Horecký, I. J., Kaserer, B., & Mattersberger, M. (2019). *Long Term Care 2030.* https://www.ecreas.eu/uimg/ecreasportal/b80760_att-report-ean-ltc-2030-digital.pdf

Freeland, G. (2019). *If Home Is Where The Heart Is, Work Is Where The WiFi Is.* Retrieved 20 November 2019, from https://www.forbes.com/sites/grantfreeland/2019/11/18/if-home-is-where-the-heart-is-work-is-where-the-wifi-is/#533e54659024

Gagnon, M.-P., Paré, G., Pollender, H., Duplantie, J., Côté, J., Fortin, J.-P., Labadie, R., Duplàa, E., Thifault, M.-C., Courcy, F., McGinn, C. A., Ly, B. A., Trépanier, A., & Malo, F.-B. (2011). Supporting work practices through telehealth: Impact on nurses in peripheral regions. *BMC Health Services Research, 11*(1), 27–35. doi:10.1186/1472-6963-11-27 PMID:21294882

Gajendran, R., & Harrison, D. (2007). The Good, the Bad, and the Unknown about Teleworking: Meta-Analysis of Psychological Mediators and Individual Consequences. *The Journal of Applied Psychology, 92*(6), 1524–1541. doi:10.1037/0021-9010.92.6.1524 PMID:18020794

Gandini, A. (2015). The rise of coworking spaces: A literature review. *Ephemera, 15*(1), 193.

Gardiner, H. (1983). *Frames of Mind: The Theory of Multiple Intelligences.* Basic Books.

Garner, C., Forbes, P., Sheldon, H., Shoesmith, D., & Ternouth, P. (2016). *Working Anywhere, A Winning Formula for Good Work?* The Work Foundation (Lancaster University), The Work Foundation Alliance Limited. Retrieved from http://www.theworkfoundation.com/Reports/398/Working-Anywhere

Garrett, L. E., Spreitzer, G. M., & Bacevice, P. (2014). Co-constructing a sense of community at work: the emergence of community in coworking spaces. Academy of Management Proceedings, 1, 14004. doi:10.5465/ambpp.2014.139

Garrett, R., & Danziger, J. (2007). Which Telework? Defining and Testing a Taxonomy of Technology-Mediated Work at a Distance. *Social Science Computer Review, 25*(1), 27–47. doi:10.1177/0894439306293819

Gedera, D. S. P. (2016). 4: The Application of Activity Theory in Identify Contradictions in a University Blended Learning Course. In *Activity Theory in Education* (pp. 53–60). Sense Publishers.

George, V. (2017). A new approach to disability in the workplace. *Pursuit.* Accessed on 1 December 2019, from: https://pursuit.unimelb.edu.au/articles/a-new-approach-to-disability-in-the-workplace

Gershenfeld, N. (2007). *Fab: The Coming Revolution on Your Desktop - from Personal Computer to Personal Fabrication.* Basic Books.

Gershenfeld, N., Gershenfeld, A., & Cutcher-Gershenfeld, J. (2017). *Designing Reality: How to survive and thrive in the third digital revolution.* Basic Books.

Gerstner, L. (2002). *Who Says Elephants Can't Dance? Leading a Great Enterprise through Dramatic Change.* Harper Business.

Gibson, I., Rosen, D., & Stucker, B. (2014). *Additive Manufacturing Technologies: 3D printing, rapid prototyping and direct digital manufacturing*. Springer.

Gill, T. J. (2006). Workplace continuity: How risk and technology will affect facilities strategy. *Journal of Facilities Management*, *4*(2), 110–125. doi:10.1108/14725960610651205

GlobalWorkplaceAnalytics. (2019). *Latest Telecommuting/Mobile Work/Remote Work Statistics*. Retrieved 15 January 2020, from https://globalworkplaceanalytics.com/telecommuting-statistics

Gloet, M., & Berrell, M. (2003). The dual paradigm nature of knowledge management: Implications for achieving quality outcomes in human resource management. *Journal of Knowledge Management*, *7*(1), 78–89. doi:10.1108/13673270310463635

Golden, L. (2009). A Brief History of Long Work Time and the Contemporary Sources of Overwork. *Journal of Business Ethics*, *84*(2), 217–227. doi:10.100710551-008-9698-z

Golden, T. D. (2009). Applying technology to work: Toward a better understanding of telework. *Organizational Management Journal*, *6*(4), 241–250. doi:10.1057/omj.2009.33

Goleman, D. (2005). *Emotional Intelligence: Why It Can Matter More Than IQ*. Bantam Books.

Goleman, D. (2008). *Working with Emotional Intelligence*. Bantam Books.

Gorz, A. (n.d.). *Farewell to the Working Class: An Essay on Post-industrial Society*. London: Pluto Press.

Gramenz, J. (2020). *Holden brand to disappear by the end of 2020*. Retrieved from https://www.news.com.au/technology/innovation/motoring/holden-brand-to-disappear-by-the-end-of-2020/news-story/c81a5e2993f664fc62965ad349601d0e

Gregory, M. A. (2020). *Rural and remote Australia and telecommunications and digital services*. Retrieved from https://regionaldevelopment.org.au/remote-rural-australia-dudded-nbn/

Griffith, L. (2018). *IMTS 2018 to showcase latest trends in manufacturing automation and robotics*. Retrieved from https://www.tctmagazine.com/3d-printing-news/imts-showcase-latest-trends-manufacturing-automation/

Gushchin, A., Martynovich, V., & Torubarov, S. (2020). *Automatic print job scheduling and management over multiple 3D printers*. Paper presented at the 5th International Conference on Industrial Engineering (ICIE 2019), Cham. 10.1007/978-3-030-22063-1_51

Habermas, J. (1971). *Knowledge and Human Interests*. Beacon Hill.

Haddon, L., & Silverstone, R. (1994). Telework and the Changing Relationship of Home and Work. In R. Mansell (Ed.), Management of Information and Communication Technologies: Emerging Patterns of Control (pp. 234-247). London: Aslib.

Haddon, L., & Lewis, S. (1994). The experience of teleworking: An annotated review. *International Journal of Human Resource Management*, *5*(1), 193–223. doi:10.1080/09585199400000010

Hager, P. (2001). Lifelong Learning and the Contribution of Informal Learning. In D. Aspin, J. Chapman, M. Hatton, & Y. Sawano (Eds.), *International Handbook of Lifelong Learning. Springer International Handbooks of Education* (Vol. 6). Springer. doi:10.1007/978-94-010-0916-4_5

Hall, E. (1976). *Beyond culture*. Anchor-Doubleday.

Hall, E. (1992). The silent language in overseas business. In H. Lane & J. Di Steffano (Eds.), *International management behavior*. PWS-Kent.

Hamalainen, M., & Karjalainen, J. (2017). Social manufacturing: When the maker movement meets interfirm production networks. *Business Horizons*, *60*(6), 795–805. doi:10.1016/j.bushor.2017.07.007

Hammond, C. (2004). Impacts of lifelong learning upon emotional resilience, psychological and mental health: Fieldwork evidence. *Oxford Review of Education*, *30*(4), 551–568. doi:10.1080/0305498042000303008

Handy, S., & Mokhtarian, P. (1996). The Future of Telecommuting. *Futures*, *28*(3), 227–240. doi:10.1016/0016-3287(96)00003-1

Hansen, L. (2016). *Humans need not apply: How robotic accelerator technology are challenging our ideas of work and innovation* (Masters' thesis). Copenhagen Business School.

Harvard Health Publishing, Harvard Medical School. (2017). *Dr. Google: The top 10 health searches in 2017*. Retrieved from https://www.health.harvard.edu/blog/google-top-10-health-searches-2017-2018022113300

Hauser, M. (2019). *Guiding Principles For Coworking Interior Design*. Available at https://www.globalworkspace.org/blog/guiding-principles-for-coworking-interior-design/

Hayes. (2017). *2017 Gender Diversity Report*. Retrieved from https://www.hays.com.au/gender-diversity/HAYS_1832068

Hayes. (2019). *Flexibility a hot topic that shows no signs of cooling down in Malaysia*. Retrieved from https://www.hays.com.my/press-releases/HAYS_118017

Hegewisch, A. (2009). Flexible working policies: a comparative review. *Institute for Women's Policy Research, Equality and Human Rights Commission 2009*.

Hemp, P. (2004). Presenteeism: At work-but out of it. *Harvard Business Review*, *82*(10), 49–58. PMID:15559575

Henderson, J., Willis, E., Xiao, L., Toffoli, L., & Verrall, C. (2016). Nurses' perceptions of the impact of the aged care reform on services for residents in multi-purpose services and residential aged care facilities in rural Australia. *Australasian Journal on Ageing*, *35*(4), E18–E23. doi:10.1111/ajag.12343 PMID:27334723

Henson, B. (Ed.). (1997). Remote Working: marvelous, perilous, or both. *Staff Notes Monthly*. Retrieved from https://www.ucar.edu/communications/staffnotes/9704/telecommuting.html

Hickson, D., & Pugh, D. (1995). *Management worldwide: The impact of societal culture on organizations around the globe*. Penguin.

Hill, J., Ferris, M., & Martinson, V. (2003). Does it matter where you work? A comparison of how three work venues (traditional office, virtual office, and home office) influences aspects of work and personal/family life. *Journal of Vocational Behavior*, *63*(2), 220–241. doi:10.1016/S0001-8791(03)00042-3

Hirschi, A. (2018). The Fourth Industrial Revolution: Issues and Implications for Career Research and Practice. *Career Development Quarterly*, *66*, 192–204.

Hislop, D., & Axtell, C. (2009). To infinity and beyond? Workspace and the multi-location worker. *NTWE*, *24*, 60–75.

Hislop, D., Axtell, C., Collins, A., Daniels, K., Glover, J., & Niven, K. (2015). Variability in the use of mobile ICTs by homeworkers and its consequences for boundary and social isolation. *Information and Organization*, *25*(4), 222–232. doi:10.1016/j.infoandorg.2015.10.001

Hofstede, G. (1994). *Cultures and organizations: Software of the mind - intercultural cooperation and its importance for survival*. Harper-Collins.

Hofstede, G. (2011). Dimensionalizing Cultures: The Hofstede Model in Context. *Online Readings in Psychology and Culture*, *2*(1). Advance online publication. doi:10.9707/2307-0919.1014

Holtkamp, C., Shelton, T., Daly, G., Hiner, C. C., & Hagelman, R. R. III. (2016). Assessing Neolocalism in Microbreweries. *Papers in Applied Geography*, *2*(1), 66–78. doi:10.1080/23754931.2015.1114514

Hornborg, A. (2019). The money-energy-technology complex and ecological marxism: Rethinking the concept of "use-value" to extend our understanding of unequal exchange, Part 1. *Capitalism, Nature, Socialism*, *30*(3), 27–39. doi:10.1080/10455752.2018.1440614

Horwitz, F. M., Bravington, D., & Silvis, U. (2006). The promise of virtual teams: Identifying key factors in effectiveness and failure. *Journal of European Industrial Training*, *30*(6), 472–494. doi:10.1108/03090590610688843

ILO & OECD. (2019). *New job opportunities in an ageing society Paper prepared for the 1st Meeting of the G20 Employment Working Group*. Retrieved from https://www.oecd.org/g20/summits/osaka/ILO-OECD-G20-Paper-1-3-New-job-opportunities-in-an-ageing-society.pdf

Inkpen, A., & Beamish, P. (1997). Knowledge, bargaining power, and the instability of international joint ventures. *Academy of Management Review*, *22*(1), 177–202. doi:10.5465/amr.1997.9707180263

Ishikura, Y. (2019, August 11). Flexible work style - can it be sustainable? *The Japan Times*. Retrieved from https://www.japantimes.co.jp/opinion/2019/08/11/commentary/japan-commentary/flexible-work-style-can-sustainable/

Jackson, B. (2019). *Stryker allots share of $225.8M to develop 3D printing R&D in Ireland.* Retrieved from https://3dprintingindustry.com/news/stryker-allots-share-of-225-8m-to-develop-3d-printing-rd-in-ireland-156966/

Jackson, P., & van der Wielen, J. (2002). *Teleworking: International Perspectives.* Routledge. doi:10.4324/9780203053089

Jamal, A. C. (2018). Coworking spaces in mid-sized cities: A partner in downtown economic development. *Environment and Planning A. Economy and Space, 50*, 773–788.

Jang-Jaccard, J., Nepal, S., Alem, L., & Li, J. (2014). Barriers for Delivering Telehealth in Rural Australia: A Review Based on Australian Trials and Studies. *Telemedicine Journal and e-Health, 20*(5), 496–504. doi:10.1089/tmj.2013.0189 PMID:24801522

Jarrahi, M. H. (2018). Artificial intelligence and the future of work: Human-AI symbiosis in organizational decision making. *Business Horizons, 61*(4), 577–586. doi:10.1016/j.bushor.2018.03.007

Jarvis, P. (2009). Lifelong Learning and Globalization: Towards a Structural Comparative Model. In R. Cowen & A. Kazamias (Eds.), *International Handbook of Comparative Education, Springer International Handbooks of Education, 22.* Springer.

Jenkins, C., & Sherman, B. (1979). *The collapse of work.* Eyre Methuen.

Johns, G. (2010). Presenteeism in the workplace: A review and research agenda. *Journal of Organizational Behavior, 31*(4), 519–542. doi:10.1002/job.630

Johnson, R. W. (2011). Phased Retirement and Workplace Flexibility for Older Adults: Opportunities and Challenges. *The Annals of the American Academy of Political and Social Science, 638*(1), 68–85. doi:10.1177/0002716211413542

Johns, T., & Gratton, L. (2013). The third wave of virtual work. *Harvard Business Review, 91*(1), 66–73.

Johns, T., & Gratton, L. (2013). The Third Wave of Virtual Work. *Harvard Business Review, 91*(1/2), 66–73.

Jones, D., Sundsted, T., & Bacigalupo, T. (2009). *I'm Outta Here: How Coworking is Making the Office Obsolete.* Austin: Not an MBA Press.

Kang, S. Y. (2016). The ICT Technology for Geriatric Diseases Healthcare. In J. K. Kim & N. Joukov (Eds.), *Information Science and Applications (ICISA) 2016* (pp. 1495–1500). Springer Singapore. doi:10.1007/978-981-10-0557-2_144

Kaplan, J. (2016). *Humans Need Not Apply: A Guide to Wealth and Work in the Age of Artificial Intelligence.* Yale University Press.

Kelliher, C., & Richardson, J. (2019). *Work, Working and Work Relationships in a Changing World* (1st ed.). Routledge.

Kellner, T. (2018). The devil is in the details: How GE found a way to bring 3D printing to mass production. *GE Reports*. Retrieved from https://www.ge.com/reports/devil-details-3d-printed-part-jet-engine-part-now/

Khadka, J., Lang, C., Ratcliffe, J., Corlis, M., Wesselingh, S., Whitehead, C., & Inacio, M. (2019). Trends in the utilization of aged care services in Australia, 2008–2016. *BMC Geriatrics*, *19*(1), 213. doi:10.118612877-019-1209-9 PMID:31387533

Khidhir, S. (2018, November 4). Looking at flexible work arrangements. *The Asian Post*. Retrieved from https://www.google.com/search?q=Looking+at+flexible+work+arrangements%2C+The+Asian+Post.&rlz=1C1AZAA_enAU744NZ745&oq=Looking+at+flexible+work+arrangements%2C+The+Asian+Post.&aqs=chrome.69i57j33.1536j0j8&sourceid=chrome&ie=UTF-8

Kiesel, L. R., Dezelar, S., & Lightfoot, E. (2019). Equity in social work employment: Opportunity and challenge for social workers with disabilities in the United States. *Disability & Society*, *34*(9-10), 1399–1418. Advance online publication. doi:10.1080/09687599.2018.1561354

King, D., Mavromaras, K., He, B., Healy, J., Macaitis, K., Moskos, M., & Zhang, W. (2013). *The aged care workforce 2012 final report*. Department of Health and Ageing.

Kingma, S. F. (2016). The constitution of 'third workspaces' in between the home and the corporate office. *NTWE*, *31*, 176–193.

Kış, E. (2009). *Geleneksel ve sanal ofislerde iş doyumu: Bir alan araştırması* (Unpublished master's dissertation). Gazi University, Ankara.

Klitmøller, A., & Lauring, J. (2013). When global virtual teams share knowledge: Media richness, cultural difference and language commonality. *Journal of World Business*, *48*(3), 398–406. doi:10.1016/j.jwb.2012.07.023

Kluckhohn, C. (1962). Universal categories of culture. In S. Tax (Ed.), Anthropology Today: Selections (pp. 304-20). Chicago: University of Chicago Press.

Kluckhohn, F., & Strodtbeck, F. (1961). *Variations in value orientations*. Row Peterson.

Knight, F. (2017). *Bridging the Gap: Melbourne's Coworking Culture*. https://kfcontent.blob.core.windows.net/research/1100/documents/en/melcowork1702-4438.pdf

Koh, J., Kim, Y. G., & Kim, Y. G. (2003). Sense of virtual community: A conceptual framework and empirical validation. *International Journal of Electronic Commerce*, *8*(2), 75–94. doi:10.1080/10864415.2003.11044295

Kojo, I., & Nenonen, S. (2014). User experience in an academic coworking place: The case of Aalto university's design factory. *Proceedings of the CIB Facilities Management Conference*, 21-23.

Kojo, I., & Nenonen, S. (2016). Typologies for coworking spaces in Finland–what and how? *Facilities*, *34*(5/6), 302–313. doi:10.1108/F-08-2014-0066

Kojo, I., & Nenonen, S. (2017). Evolution of coworking places: Drivers and possibilities. *Intelligent Buildings International*, *9*(3), 164–175. doi:10.1080/17508975.2014.987640

Kostas, M., Knight, G., Isherwood, L., Crettenden, A., Flavel, J., Karmel, T., . . . Wei, Z. (2017). *2016 National Aged Care Workforce Census and Survey – The Aged Care Workforce 2016*. Retrieved from https://www.gen-agedcaredata.gov.au/Resources/Reports-and-publications/2017/March/The-aged-care-workforce,-2016

Krause, I. (2019). Coworking Spaces: Windows to the Future of Work? *Foresight and STI Governance*, *13*(2), 52–60. doi:10.17323/2500-2597.2019.2.52.60

Kroeber, A., & Kluckhohn, C. (1963). *A critical review of concepts and definitions*. Vintage.

Krywko, J. (2018). *3D printing farms: A glimpse into the future*. Retrieved from https://zortrax.com/blog/3d-printing-farms-a-glimpse-into-the-future/

Kuhn, T. (1970). *The Structure of Scientific Revolutions*. University of Chicago Press.

Kulkarni, M., Boehm, S. A., & Basu, S. (2016). Workplace inclusion of persons with a disability: Comparison of Indian and German multinationals. *Equality, Diversity and Inclusion*, *35*(7/8), 397–414. doi:10.1108/EDI-08-2016-0066

Kumparak, G. (2017). *TechShop shuts down all US locations, declares bankruptcy*. Retrieved from https://techcrunch.com/2017/11/15/techshop-shuts-down-all-u-s-locations-declares-bankruptcy/

Kurkland, N. B., & Bailey, D. E. (1999). The advantages and challenges of working here, there anywhere, and anytime. *Organizational Dynamics*, *28*(2), 53–68. doi:10.1016/S0090-2616(00)80016-9

Kuuti, K. (1996). Activity Theory as a potential framework for human computer interaction research. In B. Nardi (Ed.), Context and consciousness: Activity Theory and human computer interaction, (pp. 17-44). Cambridge, MA: MIS Press.

Kwiatkowski, A., & Buczynski, B. (2014). *Coworking: Building community as a space catalyst*. Cohere, LLC.

Lafferty, G. (2000). Telework in Australia: Findings from a National Survey in selected industries. *Australian Bulletin of Labour*, *26*(3), 236–252.

Lake, A. (2013). *Smart Flexibility: Moving Smart & Flexible Working from Theory to Practice*. Routledge.

Lamb, R., & Kling, R. (2003). Reconceptualizing Users as Social Actors in Information Systems Research. *Management Information Systems Quarterly*, *27*(2), 197–235. doi:10.2307/30036529

Lam, P. L., & Shiu, A. (2010). Economic growth, telecommunications development, and productivity growth of the telecommunications sector: Evidence around the world. *Telecommunications Policy*, *34*(4), 186–199. doi:10.1016/j.telpol.2009.12.001

Laplume, A., Anzalone, C., & Pearce, M. (2016). Opensource, self-replication 3D printer factory for small-business manufacturing. *International Journal of Advanced Manufacturing Technology*, *85*(1), 633–642. doi:10.100700170-015-7970-9

LawGeex. (2020). *LawGeex Home Page.* Retrieved from www.lawgeex.com

Lawpath. (2020). *Lawpath Home Page.* Retrieved from https://lawpath.com.au/

Le Duigou, A., Castro, M., Bevan, R., & Martin, N. (2016). 3D printing of wood fibre biocomposites: From mechanical to actuation functionality. *Materials & Design*, *96*, 106–114. doi:10.1016/j.matdes.2016.02.018

Leclercq-Vandelannoitte, A., & Henri Isaac, H. (2016). The new office: How coworking changes the work concept. *The Journal of Business Strategy*, *37*(6), 3–9. doi:10.1108/JBS-10-2015-0105

Lee, S., Trimi, S., & Kim, C. (2013). The impact of cultural differences on technology adoption. *Journal of World Business*, *48*(1), 20–29. doi:10.1016/j.jwb.2012.06.003

Lee, S.-Y., & Hong, J. H. (2011). Does Family-Friendly Policy Matter? Testing Its Impact on Turnover and Performance. *Public Administration Review*, *71*(6), 870–879. doi:10.1111/j.1540-6210.2011.02416.x

Levi-Strauss, C. (1969). *The Scope of Anthropology*. Jonathan Cape.

Levi-Strauss, C. (1979). *Structural Anthropology*. Penguin.

Liang, T.-P., Huang, C.-W., Yeh, Y.-I., & Lin, B. (2007). Adoption of mobile technology in business: A fit-viability model. *Industrial Management & Data Systems*, *107*(8), 1154–1169. doi:10.1108/02635570710822796

Lima, J. (2020, January 27). Why You Should Invest in Machine Learning. *Data Economy*. Retrieved from https://data-economy.com/why-you-should-invest-in-machine-learning/

Lin, C. (2012). Communication Technology and Social Change. In C. Lin & D. Atkin (Eds.), Communication Technology and Social Change: Theory and Implications (pp. 3-15). New York: Routledge.

Lipson, H., & Kurman, M. (2013). *Fabricated: The new world of 3D printing, the promise and peril of a machine that can make (almost) anything*. John Wiley and Sons.

Liu, J., Sun, L., Xu, W., Wang, Q., Yu, S., & Sun, J. (2019). Current advances and future perspectives of 3D printing natural-derived biopolymers. *Carbohydrate Polymers*, *207*, 297–316. doi:10.1016/j.carbpol.2018.11.077 PMID:30600012

Lohrberg, F., Lička, L., Scazzosi, L., & Timpe, A. (2016). *Urban Agriculture Europe*. Jovis.

Lopes, H., Lagoa, S., & Calapez, T. (2014). Work autonomy, work pressure, and job satisfaction: An analysis of European Union countries. *Economic and Labour Relations Review*, *25*(2), 306–326. doi:10.1177/1035304614533868

Louis, M., Seymour, T., & Joyce, J. (2014). *3D opportunity in the Department of Defense: Additive manufacturing fires up*. Deloitte University Press.

Lowe, M., Whitzman, C., Badland, H., Davern, M., Hes, D., Aye, L., Butterworth, I., & Giles-Corti, B. (2013). *Liveable, Helthy, Sustainable: What are the key indicators for Melbourne Neighbourhoods? Research Paper 1, Place, Health and Liveability Research Program, University of Melbourne*. http://mccaugheycentre.unimelb.edu.au/research/health_and_liveability

Loy, J. (2015). The future for design education: Preparing the design workforce for additive manufacturing. *International Journal of Rapid Manufacturing*, *5*(2), 199–212. doi:10.1504/IJRAPIDM.2015.073577

Loy, J., & Novak, J. I. (2019). The Future of Product Design Education Industry 4.0. In A. Raman & M. Rathakrishnan (Eds.), *Redesigning Higher Education Initiatives for Industry 4.0* (pp. 164–182). IGI Global. doi:10.4018/978-1-5225-7832-1.ch010

Loy, J., & Tatham, P. (2016). Redesigning Production Systems. In S. S. Muthu & M. M. Savalani (Eds.), *Handbook of Sustainability in Additive Manufacturing* (pp. 145–168). Springer. doi:10.1007/978-981-10-0549-7_7

Lozova, L. (2016). *Bringing the Ultimaker 3 to market with bridge manufacturing*. Retrieved from https://ultimaker.com/learn/bringing-the-ultimaker-3-to-market-with-bridge-manufacturing

Lumley, R. M. (2014). A Coworking Project in the Campus Library: Supporting and Modelling Entrepreneurial Activity in the Academic Library. *New Review of Academic Librarianship*, *29*(1), 49–65. doi:10.1080/13614533.2013.850101

Lyotard, J.-F. (1986). *The post-modern condition: A report on knowledge*. Manchester University Press.

Mackenzie, N., & Knipe, S. (2006). Research dilemmas: Paradigms, methods, and methodology. *Issues in Educational Research*, *16*(2), 193–205.

Mahler, J. (2012). The Telework Divide: Managerial and Personnel Challenges of Telework. *Review of Public Personnel Administration*, *32*(4), 407–418. doi:10.1177/0734371X12458127

MANUFACTUR3D. (2019). *Markforged unveils print farm – an affordable solution to scale metal and carbon fiber 3D printing production*. Retrieved from https://manufactur3dmag.com/markforged-unveils-print-farm-an-affordable-solution-to-scale-metal-and-carbon-fiber-3d-printing-production/

Mariotti, I., Pacchi, C., & Di Vita, S. (2017). Coworking spaces in Milan: Location patterns and urban effects. *Journal of Urban Technology*, 1–20.

Marr, B. (2018, May 23). How AI and Machine Learning are Transforming Law Firms and the Legal Sector. *Forbes Magazine*. Retrieved from https://www.forbes.com/sites/bernardmarr/2018/05/23/how-ai-and-machine-learning-are-transforming-law-firms-and-the-legal-sector/#5116da832c38

Marr, B. (2019, July 15). The Future of Work: 5 Important Ways Jobs Will Change in the 4th Industrial Revolution. *Forbes Magazine*. Retrieved from https://www.forbes.com/sites/bernardmarr/2019/07/15/the-future-of-work-5-important-ways-jobs-will-change-in-the-4th-industrial-revolution/#7570158a54c7

Marx, K., & Engels, F. (2010). Collected Works (Vols. 1–50). Lawrence & Wishart.

Mason, C., & Brown, R. (2017). Looking Inside the Spiky bits: A critical review and conceptualization of entrepreneurial ecosystems. *Small Business Economics*, *49*(1), 11–30. doi:10.100711187-017-9865-7

Mavri, M. (2015). Redesigning a production chain based on 3D printing technology. *Knowledge and Process Management*, *22*(3), 141–147. doi:10.1002/kpm.1466

McKinney, S., Sieniek, M., & Godbole, V. (2020). International evaluation of an AI system for breast cancer screening. *Nature, 557*. Retrieved from https://www.nature.com/articles/s41586-019-1799-6

Meacham, H., Cavanagh, J., Shaw, A., & Bartram, T. (2017). HRM practices that support the employment and social inclusion of workers with an intellectual disability. *Personnel Review*, *46*(8), 1475–1492. doi:10.1108/PR-05-2016-0105

Mead, R. (1994). *International management: Cross cultural dimensions*. Blackwell.

Melián-González, S. (2019). The impact of digital technology on work. University Institute of Tourism and Sustainable Economic Development (TIDES), Las Palmas de Gran Canaria (Canary Islands): University of Las Palmas de Gran Canaria. doi:10.2139srn.3353258

Merkel, J. (2015). Coworking in the City. *Ephemera*, *15*(1), 121–139.

Merkel, J. (2015). Coworking in the city. *Ephemera*, *15*, 121–139.

Meshur, A., & Ulusoy, C. (2013). Attitudes of people with disabilities towards teleworking as an employment opportunity: IT modelling in terms of the Turkish case. *African Journal of Business Management*, *7*(4), 227–243.

Messenger, J. C. (2019). *Telework in the 21st Century: An Evolutionary Perspective: The ILO Future of Work Series*. ElgarOnline., doi:10.4337/9781789903751

Messenger, J., & Gschwind, L. (2016). Three generations of Telework: New ICTs and the (R) evolution from Home Office to Virtual Office. *NTWE*, *31*, 159–208.

Messenger, J., Llave, O., Gschwind, L., Boehmer, S., Vermeylen, G., & Wilkens, M. (2017). *Working anytime, anywhere: The effects on the world of work*. Publications Office of the European Union, Luxembourg, and the International Labour Office.

Miles, M. B., Huberman, A. M., & Saldana, J. (2014). Qualitative Data Analysis: A Methods Sourcebook (3rd ed.). Thousand Oaks, CA: SAGE Publications, Inc.

Miller, S., Glisson, W. B., Campbell, M., & Sittig, S. (2019). *Risk Analysis of Residual Protected Health Information of Android Telehealth Apps*. Academic Press.

Mills, C. W. (1973). The Meanings of Work throughout History. In F. Best (Ed.), The Future of Work (pp. 6-13). Englewood Cliffs: Prentice-Hall.

Mistry, H. (2012). Systematic review of studies of the cost-effectiveness of telemedicine and telecare. Changes in the economic evidence over twenty years. *Journal of Telemedicine and Telecare*, *18*(1), 1–6. doi:10.1258/jtt.2011.110505 PMID:22101609

Mistry, H., Garnvwa, H., & Oppong, R. (2014). Critical Appraisal of Published Systematic Reviews Assessing the Cost-Effectiveness of Telemedicine Studies. *Telemedicine Journal and e-Health*, *20*(7), 609–618. doi:10.1089/tmj.2013.0259 PMID:24820406

Mohammed, M. I., Mohan, M. D., Johnson, M. D., Badwal, P. S., McLean, D., & Gibson, I. (2017). A low carbon footprint approach to the reconstitution of plastics into 3D-printer filament for enhanced waste reduction. In *DesTech 2016: Proceedings of the International Conference on Design and Technology,* (pp. 234-241). Dubai, UAE: Knowledge E.

Mokhtarian, P. L., & Salomon, I. (1996). Modeling the choice of telecommuting: 2. A case of the preferred impossible alternative. *Environment & Planning A*, *28*(10), 1859–1876. doi:10.1068/a281859

Montreuil, S., & Lippel, K. (2003). Telework and occupational health: A Quebec empirical study and regulatory implications. *Safety Science*, *41*(4), 339–358. doi:10.1016/S0925-7535(02)00042-5

Moody, L., Saunders, J., Leber, M., Wójcik-Augustyniak, M., Szajczyk, M., & Rebernik, N. (2017). An exploratory study of barriers to inclusion in the European workplace. *Disability and Rehabilitation*, *39*(20), 2047–2054. doi:10.1080/09638288.2016.1217072 PMID:27665671

Moriset, B. (2013). Buildi308ng new places of the creative economy. The rise of coworking spaces. In 2nd *Geography of Innovation International Conference*. Utrecht University.

Moriset, B. (2013). *Building new places of the creative economy. The rise of coworking spaces*. Academic Press.

Moriset, B. (2011). Developing the Digital Economy in France's Rural Regions: A Critical Assessment of Telecenters. *NETCOM*, *25*(3-4), 249–272. doi:10.4000/netcom.175

Morley, S., Cromican, K., & Folan, P. (2015). An analysis of virtual team characteristics: A model for virtual project managers. *Journal of Technology Management & Innovation*, *10*(1).

Morozov, E. (2013). *To Save Everything, Click Here: The Folly of Technological Solutionism*. Public Affairs.

Mubin, O., Stevens, C., Shahid, S., Al Mahmud, A., & Dong, J.-J. (2013). A Review of the Applicability of Robots in Education. *Technology for Education and Learning*, *1*(1), 1–7. doi:10.2316/Journal.209.2013.1.209-0015

Mumford, E., & Beekman, G. J. (1994). *Tools for Change and Progress: A Socio-technical Approach to Business Process Re-engineering*. CSG Publications.

MyDoctor.com. (2020). *My Doctor*. Retrieved from https://www.mydr.com.au/

Myerson, J., Bichard, J. A., & Erlich, A. (2010). *New Demographics, New Workspace: Office Design for the Changing Workforce*. Gower Publishing Limited.

Myerson, J., & Ross, P. (2003). *The 21st century office*. Laurence King Publishing.

Neuman, W. L. (2014). *Social Research Methods: Qualitative and Quantitative Approaches* (7th ed.). Pearson.

Nicolaus, M. (1967). *Proletariat and the Middle Class in Marx: Hegelian Choreography and the Capitalist Dialectic. Studies on the Left.*

Nilles, J. (1976). *The Telecommunications-Transportation Tradeoff: Options for Tomorrow*. Wiley.

Nilles, J. M. (1975). Telecommunications and Organizational Decentralization. *Communications. IEEE Transactions on, 23*(10), 1142–1147. doi:10.1109/TCOM.1975.1092687

Nilles, J. M. (1998). *Managing Telework: Strategies for Managing the Virtual Workforce*. Wiley.

Novak, J. I., & Loy, J. (2020a). A critical review of initial 3D printed products responding to COVID-19 health and supply chain challenges. *Emerald Open Research, 2*(24).

Novak, J. I. (2019). Re-educating the Educators: Collaborative 3D Printing Education. In I. M. Santos, N. Ali, & S. Areepattamannil (Eds.), *Interdisciplinary and International Perspectives on 3D Printing in Education* (pp. 28–49). IGI Global. doi:10.4018/978-1-5225-7018-9.ch002

Novak, J. I., & Loy, J. (2020b). Moving 3D printing beyond the desktop within higher education: Towards a service bureau approach. In M. S. Khine & N. Ali (Eds.), *Integrating 3D Printing into Teaching and Learning: Practitioners' Perspectives* (pp. 206–227). Brill.

OECD. (2019). *Health at a Glance 2019*. OECD.

Oldenburg, R. (1999). *The Great Good Place: Cafés, Coffee Shops, Bookstores, Bars, Hair Salons, and Other Hangouts at the Heart of a Community*. Marlowe.

Olson-Buchanan, J. B., & Boswell, W. R. (2006). Blurring boundaries: Correlates of integration and segmentation between work and nonwork. *Journal of Vocational Behavior, 68*(3), 432–445. doi:10.1016/j.jvb.2005.10.006

Örs, N. (2001). ABD'de büronun dünü ve bugünü, National Building Museum'da 'On The Job: Design and The American Office' sergisi kataloğu çevirisi. *Arredamento Mimarlık*, (135), 90-95.

Osaki, T. (2020, March 22). For many in Japan, remote work during coronavirus outbreak is not an option. *The Japan Times*. Retrieved from https://www.japantimes.co.jp/news/2020/03/22/national/social-issues/coronavirus-remote-work-not-option-for-all/#.Xo-7msgzbZY

Osnowitz, D. (2016). *Freelancing expertise*. Cornell University Press. doi:10.7591/9780801460388

Österle, H., Fleisch, E., & Alt, R. (2011). *Business networking: shaping collaboration between enterprises*. Springer Science and Business Media.

Oygur, I., & McCoy, J. M. (2011). User: Inspiration or constraint? *Journal of Interior Design, 36*(3), 1–13. doi:10.1111/j.1939-1668.2011.01058.x

Pahl, R. (Ed.). (1988). *On Work, Historical, Comparative and Theoretical Approaches*. Basil Blackwell.

Palmer, A. (2019 January 2). The AI that learnt to hide data from its creators to CHEAT at tasks they gave it. *The Daily Mirror*. Australia. Retrieved from https://www.dailymail.co.uk/sciencetech/article-6545281/The-AI-learnt-hide-data-creators-CHEAT-tasks-gave-it.html

Palmer, T. (2018). *3 major manufacturing changes loom*. Production Machining.

Papageorgiou, A. (2016). *Living in Beta: hubs, collectives and the emergence of moral economies in Athens*. The Dynamics of Virtual Work, Working Paper Series (7). Accessed 1 November 2019: http://dynamicsofvirtualwork.com/wp-content/uploads/2015/08/working-paper-No-7.pdf

Parrino, L. (2015). Coworking: Assessing the role of proximity in knowledge exchange. *Knowledge Management Research and Practice, 13*(3), 261–271. doi:10.1057/kmrp.2013.47

Pauleen, D., Campbell, J., Harmer, B., & Intezari, A. (2015). Making Sense of Mobile Technology. *Sage Open, 5*(2).

Peels, J. (2018). *3D Hubs killing off its community? 3D printing company commits suicide for no reason*. Retrieved from https://3dprint.com/224758/3dhubs-killing-off-its-community-3d-printing-company-commits-suicide-for-no-reason/

Peeters, J., Mistiaen, P., & Franke, A. (2011). Costs and financial benefits of video communication in care at home: A systematic review. *Journal of Telemedicine and Telecare*, 17. PMID:22025744

Persolkelly. (2018). *2018 APEC Workforce Insights: Gig Economy; How free agents are redefining work*. Persolkelly. Retrieved from https://www.persolkelly.com/media/persolkelly/client/2018%20APAC%20Workforce%20Insights%20-%20Q1/PERSOLKELLY%202018%20APAC%20Workforce%20Insights%20-%20Gig%20Economy%20How%20Free%20Agents%20Are%20Redefining%20Work.pdf

Peters, P. B., & Oldenkamp, E. (2009b). Cultural Sources of Variance in Telework Adoption in Two Subsidiaries of and ICT-Multinational. *International Journal of Employment Studies, 17*(2), 66–101.

Peters, P., Den Dulk, L., & de Ruijter, J. (2010). May I work from home? View of the employment relationship reflected in line managers' telework attitudes in six financial-sector organizations. *Equality, Diversity and Inclusion, 29*(5), 517–531. doi:10.1108/02610151011052799

Phillipson, L., Low, L. F., & Dreyfus, S. (2019). Consumer-directed care for older Australians: Are resources identified on the Web adequate to support decisions about home-based care packages? *The Australian Journal of Social Issues, 54*(2), 135–156. doi:10.1002/ajs4.66

Piaggesi, D., Castelnovo, W., & Battistella, R. (2013). *ICT for Social Inclusion and Equal Opportunities. E-Government Implementation and Practice in Developing Countries: 147*. IGI Global.

Polisena, J., Coyle, D., Coyle, K., & McGill, S. (2009). Home telehealth for chronic disease management: A systematic review and an analysis of economic evaluations. *International Journal of Technology Assessment in Health Care*, *25*(03), 339–349. doi:10.1017/S0266462309990201 PMID:19619353

Polycom. (2019). *The Changing World of Work: A Global Survey*. Digital Whitepaper, Polycom. Retrieved from https://www.polycom.com/content/dam/polycom/common/documents/whitepapers/changing-needs-of-the-workplace-whitepaper-enus.pdf

Powell, A., & Craig, L. (2015). Gender differences in working at home and time use *patterns*: Evidence from Australia. *Work, Employment and Society*, *29*(4), 571–589. doi:10.1177/0950017014568140

Pratt, J. H. (1984). Home teleworking: A study of its pioneers. *Technological Forecasting and Social Change*, *25*(1), 1–14. doi:10.1016/0040-1625(84)90076-3

Productivity Commission. (2019). *Report on Government Services 2019*. Retrieved from https://www.pc.gov.au/research/ongoing/report-on-government-services/2019/community-services/aged-care-services

Průša, J. (2018). *Three hundred 3D printers in one room: A quick look to our printing farm*. Retrieved from https://blog.prusaprinters.org/a-quick-look-to-our-printing-farm/

PwC. (2015). *Weighing the cost of obesity: A case for action. Retrieved from Recker, J. (2013). Scientific research in information systems: a beginner's guide*. Springer Berlin Heidelberg.

Raghuram, S., Wiesenfeld, B., & Garud, P. (2003). Technology enabled work: The role of self-efficacy in determining telecommuter adjustment and structuring behavior. *Journal of Vocational Behavior*, *63*(2), 180–189. doi:10.1016/S0001-8791(03)00040-X

Rana, R., Hume, M., Reilly, J., & Soar, J. (2015). *wHealth - Transforming Telehealth Services*. Academic Press.

Randolph, D. S. (2004). Predicting the effect of disability on employment status and income. *Work (Reading, Mass.)*, *23*(3), 257–266. PMID:15579934

Ransikarbum, K., Ha, S., Ma, J., & Kim, N. (2017). Multi-objective optimisation analysis for part-to-printer assignment in a network of 3D fused deposition modelling. *Journal of Manufacturing Systems*, *43*, 35–46. doi:10.1016/j.jmsy.2017.02.012

Ravasi, D., & Schultz, M. (2006). Responding to organizational identity threats: Exploring the role of organizational culture. *Academy of Management Journal*, *49*(3), 433–458. doi:10.5465/amj.2006.21794663

Remøy, H., & Van der Voordt, T. J. M. (2014). Priorities in accommodating office user preferences: Impact on office users decision to stay or go. *Journal of Corporate Real Estate*, *16*(2), 140–154. doi:10.1108/JCRE-09-2013-0029

Reuschke, D., Kleinhans, R., Syrett, S., Van Ham, M., & Mason, C. (2019). Understanding entrepreneurship in residential neighbourhoods and communities of place. In C. Mason, D. Reuschke, S. Syrett, & M. van Ham (Eds.), *Entrepreneurship in Cities: Neighbourhoods, Households and Homes, 297 – 308*. Edward Elgar.

Riches, V. C., & Green, V. A. (2003). Social integration in the workplace for people with disabilities: An Australian perspective. *Journal of Vocational Rehabilitation*, *19*, 127–142.

Ritzer, G. (1975). *Sociology, a Multiple Paradigm Science*. Allyn & Bacon.

Rockwood, K. (2017, June). Rethinking the Workspaces and Build Movement. *Entrepreneur*.

Ross, A. (2016). *The Industries of The Future*. Simon & Schuster.

Royal Flying Doctor Service. (2016). *Royal Flying Doctor Service: History*. Retrieved from https://www.flyingdoctor.org.au/about-the-rfds/history/

Ruppel, C., Tworoger, L., & Tworoger, T. (2012). Telework: Identifying a Personal Dimension to Work-Related Socio-Technical Theory. *Advances in Business Research*, *3*(1), 12–24.

Ruth, S., & Chaudhry, I. (2008). Telework: A Productivity Paradox? *IEEE Internet Computing*, *12*(6), 87–90. doi:10.1109/MIC.2008.132

Sailer, K., Budgen, A., Lonsdale, N., Turner, A., & Penn, A. (2009). *Comparative studies of offices pre and post—how changing spatial configurations affect organizational behaviours. Royal Institute of Technology*. KTH.

Samson, D., & Daft, R. (2015). *Fundamentals of Management* (5th ed.). Cengage.

Sanoff, H. (2006). Multiple views of participatory design. *METU Journal of the Faculty of Architecture*, *23*(2), 131–143.

Schmidt, S., & Brinks, V. (2017). Open creative labs: Spatial settings at the intersection of communities and organizations. *Creativity and Innovation Management*, *26*(3), 291–299. doi:10.1111/caim.12220

Schmidt, S., Brinks, V., & Brinkhoff, S. (2014). Innovation and creativity labs in Berlin. *Zeitschrift für Wirtschaftsgeographie*, *58*(1), 232–247. doi:10.1515/zfw.2014.0016

Schneier, B. (2015). VW scandal could just be the beginning. *CNN Opinion*. Retrieved from https://edition.cnn.com/2015/09/28/opinions/schneier-vw-cheating-software/index.html

Schopfel, J., Roche, J., & Hubert, G. (2015). Coworking and innovation: New concepts for academic libraries and learning centres. *New Library World*, *116*(1/2), 67–78. doi:10.1108/NLW-06-2014-0072

Schwab, K. (2017). *The Fourth Industrial Revolution*. Crown Business.

SEO Digital Group. (2020). Retrieved from https://seodigitalgroup.com/best-legal-keywords/

Serrano, M. (Ed.). (2014). Between Flexibility and Security; The Rise of Non-standard Employment in Selected ASEAN Countries. ASEAN Services Employees Trade Unions Council (ASETUC), Ciujung No. 4.

Servos, M. (2019). *The Future of Work? Work of the Future! On how artiðcial intelligence, robotics and automation are transforming jobs and the economy in Europe*. European Commission. Retrieved from https://ec.europa.eu/epsc/sites/epsc/files/ai-report_online-version.pdf

Sharkey, A. (2016). Should we welcome robot teachers? *Ethics and Information Technology*, *18*(4), 283–297. doi:10.100710676-016-9387-z

Sheedy. C. (2019). Teaching Machines. In *In the Black*. Southbank: CPA Australia.

Sheppeard, A. (2014). GP waiting times can be double for rural patients. *Australian Rural Doctor.* Retrieved from http://www.ruraldr.com.au/news/gp-waiting-times-can-be-double-for-rural-patients

Simonite, T. (2018). When Bots teach themselves to cheat. *Wired* Business. Retrieved from https://www.wired.com/story/when-bots-teach-themselves-to-cheat/

Simovic, D. (2019). *The Ultimate List of Remote Work Statistics – 2020 Edition*. Retrieved 15 January 2020, 2019, from https://www.smallbizgenius.net/by-the-numbers/remote-work-statistics/

Singh, P., Paleti, R., Jenkins, S., & Bhat, C. R. (2013). On modeling telecommuting behavior: Option, choice, and frequency. *Transportation*, *40*(2), 373–396. doi:10.100711116-012-9429-2

Skawiński, P., & Siemiński, P. (2017). The 3D printer farm – function and technology requirements and didactic use. *Mechanik*, *90*(8-9), 796–800. doi:10.17814/mechanik.2017.8-9.117

Smith, A., & Anderson, J. (2014). *AI, Robotics, and the Future of Jobs*. Pew Research Center. Retrieved from https://www.pewresearch.org/internet/2014/08/06/future-of-jobs/

Smith, F. (2015). *PricewaterhouseCoopers' trusts' staff, makes all roles flexible*. Australian Financial Review, Fairfax Media.

Solovieva, T. I., & Walls, R. T. (2013). Implications of Workplace Accommodations for Persons with Disabilities. *Journal of Workplace Behavioral Health*, *28*(3), 192–211. doi:10.1080/15555240.2013.808079

Southern Cross University. (2014). *Telehealth Pilot Full Report. - Feros Care*. Retrieved from https://www.feroscare.com.au

Spinuzzi, C. (2012). Working alone together. *Journal of Business and Technical Communication*, *26*(4), 399–441. doi:10.1177/1050651912444070

Srinivasa Rao, A., & Vazquez, J. (2020). Identification of COVID-19 can be quicker through artificial intelligence framework using a mobile phone-based survey when cities and towns are under quarantine. *Infection Control and Hospital Epidemiology*, *41*(7), 826–830. doi:10.1017/ice.2020.61 PMID:32122430

Staak, S. (2018). *Ford: Reinventing efficient manufacturing using 3D printing*. Retrieved from https://ultimaker.com/learn/ford-reinventing-efficient-manufacturing-using-3d-printing

Stam, K., Sieben, I., Verbakel, E., & De Graaf, P. M. (2015). Employment status and subjective wellbeing: The role of the social norm to work. *Work, Employment and Society*, *29*, 1–25.

Standing, C., Gururajan, R., Standing, S., & Cripps, H. (2014). Making the Most of Virtual Expertise in Telemedicine and Telehealth Environment. *Journal of Organizational Computing and Electronic Commerce*, *24*(2-3), 138–156. doi:10.1080/10919392.2014.896714

Statista. (2020). *Flexible workspace in Asia Pacific - Statistics & Facts*. Statista Research Department. Retrieved from https://www.statista.com/topics/5411/flexible-workspace-in-asia-pacific/

Steiner, C. (2012). *Automate This: How Algorithms came to Rule our World*. Portfolio Penguin.

Strauss, A., & Corbin, J. (1998). *Basics of Qualitative Research Techniques and Procedures for Developing Grounded Theory* (2nd ed.). Sage Publications.

Suleman, F. (2016). Employability skills of higher education graduates: Little consensus on a much-discussed subject. *Procedia - Social and Behavioral Sciences*. *228*, 169-174.

Summit of the G7 science academies. (2019). *Artificial intelligence and society: Executive summary and recommendations*. Summit of the G7 science academies. Retrieved from https://www.leopoldina.org/uploads/tx_leopublication/AI_G7_2019_EN.pdf

Surman, T. (2013). Building social entrepreneurship through the power of coworking. *Innovations: Technology, Governance, Globalization*, *8*(3-4), 189–195. doi:10.1162/INOV_a_00195

Susskind, D. (2020). *A World Without Work: Technology, Automation and How We Should Respond*. Allen Lane.

Sykes, K. (2014). Coworking: A workplace paradigm shift. *Contract (New York, N.Y.)*, *55*(6), 140–145.

Taleb, N. (2007). *The Black Swan: The Impact of the Highly Improbable*. Penguin.

Tang, S. (2011). Foundational Paradigms in the Social Sciences. *Philosophy of the Social Sciences*, *41*(2), 211–249. doi:10.1177/0048393109355294

Taplett, F. B., Krentz, M., Garcia-Alonso, J., & Hoteit, L. (2019). *Flex-Work Programs That Actually Work*. Boston Consulting Group.

Taskin, L., & Edwards, P. (2007). The possibilities and limits of telework in a bureaucratic environment: Lessons from the public sector. *New Technology, Work and Employment*, *22*(3), 195–207. doi:10.1111/j.1468-005X.2007.00194.x

Tayeb, M. (1995). The competitive advantage of nations: The role of HRM and its socio-cultural context. *International Journal of Human Resource Management*, *6*(3), 588–606. doi:10.1080/09585199500000037

The Law Buddy. (2020). *The Law Buddy Home Page*. Retrieved from https://www.lawbuddy.com.au/

The Myer Foundation. (2002). *2020 A Vision for Aged Care in Australia*. Retrieved from http://myerfoundation.org.au/wp-content/uploads/2014/09/2020-A-Vision-for-Aged-Care-in-Australia.pdf

Third Age Matters. (2020). *Third Age Matters*. Retrieved from https://thirdagematters.com.au/need-more-information/resources/

Tilgher, A. (1930). Work: What is has meant to Men through the Ages. New York: Arno Press. (Original work published 1929)

Toffler, A., & Toffler, H. (1990). *Powershift, Knowledge, Wealth, and Violence at the Edge of the 21st Century*. Bantam Books.

Tomlinson, Z. (2018). 15 Medical Robots That Are Changing the World. *Interesting Engineering*. Retrieved from https://interestingengineering.com/15-medical-robots-that-are-changing-the-world

Topol, E. (2015). *The Patient Will See You Now: The Future of Medicine is in Your Hands*. Basic Books.

Triandis, H. (1983). Dimensions of cultural variations as parameters of organizational theories. *International Studies of Management & Organization*, *12*(4), 139–169. doi:10.1080/00208825.1982.11656354

Turetken, O., Jain, A., Quesenberry, B., & Ngwenyama, O. (2011). An Empirical Investigation of the Impact of Individual and Work Characteristics on Telecommuting Success. *Professional Communication, IEEE Transactions on*, *54*(1), 56–67. doi:10.1109/TPC.2010.2041387

Uda, T. (2013). *What is Coworking? A Theoretical Study on the Concept of Coworking*. Discussion Paper, Series A. 265:1-15.

Uhereczky, A. (2020). *Teleworking During The Coronavirus Outbreak - Could It Save Lives?* Retrieved 8 February 2020, from https://www.forbes.com/sites/agnesuhereczky/2020/02/06/teleworking-during-the-coronavirus-outbreak-could-it-save-lives/#76824d237bc2

Valenduc, G. (2019). New Forms of Work and Employment in the Digital Economy. In A. Serrano-Pascual & M. Jepson (Eds.), *The Deconstruction of Employment as a Political Question*. Palgrave Macmillan. doi:10.1007/978-3-319-93617-8_3 van Dyke, L. (2014). A Review of Telehealth Service Implementation Frameworks. *International Journal of Environmental Research and Public Health, 11*(2), 1279–1298. doi:10.3390/ijerph110201279 PMID:24464237

Van Meel, J., & Brinkø, R. (2014). Working apart together. *FMWorld*. http://www.fm-world.co.uk/

Vandelannoitte, A. L. (2015). Managing BYOD: How do organizations incorporate user-driven I.T. innovations? *Information Technology & People, 28*(1), 2–33. doi:10.1108/ITP-11-2012-0129

Veruggio, G., Operto, F., & Bekey, G. (2016). Roboethics: Social and Ethical Implications. In B. Siciliano & O. Khatib (Eds.), *Springer Handbook of Robotics*. Springer Handbooks. doi:10.1007/978-3-319-32552-1_80

Vithayathawornwong, S., Danko, S., & Tolbert, P. (2003). The role of the physical environment in supporting organizational creativity. *Journal of Interior Design, 29*(1-2), 1–16. doi:10.1111/j.1939-1668.2003.tb00381.x

Vries, S. (2017). *Volkswagen Autoeuropa: Maximising production efficiency with 3D printed tools, jigs and fixtures*. Retrieved from https://ultimaker.com/learn/volswagen-autoerupoa-maximizing-production-efficiency-with-3d-printed

Wade, V. A., Eliott, J. A., & Hiller, J. E. (2014). Clinician Acceptance is the Key Factor for Sustainable Telehealth Services. *Qualitative Health Research, 24*(5), 682–694. Advance online publication. doi:10.1177/1049732314528809 PMID:24685708

Wade, V., Karnon, J., Elshaug, A., & Hiller, J. (2010). A systematic review of economic analyses of telehealth services using real time video communication. *BMC Health Services Research, 10*(1), 233. doi:10.1186/1472-6963-10-233 PMID:20696073

Wagner, J., & Watch, D. (2017). *Innovation spaces: The new design of work*. Anne T. and Robert M. Bass Initiative on Innovation and Placemaking at Brookings.

Walsh, T. (2019). Virtual Team Success with the Power of Technology Advancements. In *Advances in the Technology of Managing People: Contemporary Issues in Business* (pp. 99–107). Emerald Publishing Limited. doi:10.1108/978-1-78973-073-920191009

Wang, B., & Loo, B. P. (2017). Hubs of Internet entrepreneurs: The emergence of coworking offices in Shanghai, China. *Journal of Urban Technology, 24*(3), 67–84. doi:10.1080/10630732.2017.1285124

Warner, M. (Ed.). (2013). *Managing across diverse cultures in East Asia: issues and challenges in a changing globalized world*. Routledge. doi:10.4324/9780203106952

Waters-Lynch, J.M., Potts, J., Butcher, T., Dodson, J. & Hurley, J. (2016). *Coworking: A Transdisciplinary Overview*. Available at SSRN 2712217 (2016).

Wattanapisit, A., Teo, C. H., Wattanapisit, S., Teoh, E., Woo, W. J., & Ng, C. J. (2020). Can mobile health apps replace GPs? A scoping review of comparisons between mobile apps and GP tasks. *BMC Medical Informatics and Decision Making*, *20*(1), 5. doi:10.118612911-019-1016-4 PMID:31906985

Waxman, L. (2006). The coffee shop: Social and physical factors influencing place attachment. *Journal of Interior Design*, *31*(3), 35–53. doi:10.1111/j.1939-1668.2006.tb00530.x

Weber, P. (2013). The rise and fall of Detroit: A timeline. *The Week*. Retrieved from https://theweek.com/articles/461968/rise-fall-detroit-timeline

Weber, M. (1947). *The Theory of Social and Economic Organization*. The Free Press.

Weijers, T., Meijer, R., & Spoelman, E. (1992). Telework remains 'made to measure': The large-scale introduction of telework in the Netherlands. *Futures*, *24*(10), 1048–1055. doi:10.1016/0016-3287(92)90136-4

Weijs-Perrée, M., van de Koevering, J., Appel-Meulenbroek, R., & Arentze, T. (2019). Analysing user preferences for coworking space characteristics. *Building Research and Information*, *47*(5), 534–548. doi:10.1080/09613218.2018.1463750

Weinert, C., Maier, C., & Laumer, S. (2015). Why are teleworkers stressed? An empirical analysis of the causes of telework-enabled stress. *Proceedings 12th International Conference on Wirtschaftsinformatik*. Retrieved from https://aisel.aisnet.org/wi2015/

Weinstein, R., Lopez, A., Joseph, B., Erps, K., Holcomb, M., Barker, G., & Krupinski, E. (2014). Telemedicine, Telehealth, and Mobile Health Applications That Work: Opportunities and Barriers. *The American Journal of Medicine*, *127*(3), 183–187. doi:10.1016/j.amjmed.2013.09.032 PMID:24384059

Wessels, C., Schippers, M. C., Stegmann, S., Bakker, A. B., van Baalen, P. J., & Proper, K. I. (2019). Fostering Flexibility in the New World of Work: A Model of Time-Spatial Job Crafting'. *Frontiers in Psychology*, *10*, 505. doi:10.3389/fpsyg.2019.00505 PMID:30941072

West, D. (2018). *The Future of Work: Robots, AI and Automation*. Brookings Institute Press.

Wevorce. (2020). *Wevorce Home Page*. Retrieved from https://www.wevorce.com/

Wheatley, D. (2012b). Work-life balance, travel-to-work, and the dual career household. *Personnel Review*, *41*(6), 813–831. doi:10.1108/00483481211263764

Wiberg, M., & Ljungberg, F. (2000). Exploring the vision of "anytime, anywhere" in the context of mobile work. In J. Malhotra (Ed.), *Knowledge Management and Business Innovation*. Ideas Group Publishing.

Wilkens, N. (2019). *Artificial Intelligence: A Comprehensive Guide to AI, Machine Learning, Internet of Things, Robotics, Deep Learning, Predictive Analytics, Neural Networks, Reinforcement Learning, and Our Future*. Amazon.com LLC. Retrieved from https://www.amazon.com/Artificial-Intelligence-Comprehensive-Predictive-Reinforcement-ebook/dp/B07QFL4HG3/ref=sr_1_12?keywords=artificial+intelligence%2C+machine+learning+and+robotics&qid=1575655795&sr=8-12

Wilmot, K., Boyle, T., Rickwood, P., & Sharpe, S. (2014). *The Potential for Smart Work Centres in Blacktown, Liverpool and Penrith. Report by the Institute for Sustainable Futures*. UTS.

Wohlers. (2019). *Wohlers report: 3D printing and additive manufacturing, State of the Industry*. https://wohlersassociates.com/2019report.htm

Wojcak, E., & Barath, M. (2017). National Culture and Application of Telework in Europe. *European Journal of Business Science and Technology*, *3*(1), 65–74. doi:10.11118/ejobsat.v3i1.79

Wong, W., & Saiu, K. (2019). Artificial Intelligence, Machine Learning, Automation, Robotics, Future of Work and Future of Humanity: A Review and Research Agenda. *Journal of Database Management*, *30*(1), 61–79. doi:10.4018/JDM.2019010104

Wooden, M., & Fok, Y.-K. (2013). *Working at home: Whatever happened to the revolution?* Retrieved from https://www.smh.com.au/technology/what-ever-happened-to-the-working-from-home-revolution-20150101-12gb1f.html

World Bank. (2019). World Development Report. In *The Changing Nature of Work*. World Bank Publications. Accessed 8 May: http://ebookcentral.proquest.com

World Health Organization (WHO). (2011). *International Classification of Functioning, Disability and Health*. ICF.

World Health Organization. (1986). *The Ottawa Charter for Health Promotion*. Retrieved from https://www.who.int/healthpromotion/conferences/previous/ottawa/en/index.html

Wrathall, J., & Berrell, M. (2017). Infusing Employability Skills in Teaching, Learning and Curriculum Development: An Event Management Perspective. In *THE-ICE IPoE Forum 2017*. William Angliss Institute.

Wright, S., & Bagshaw, E. (2019). *As cities grow, parts of regional Australia disappear and get angry*. Retrieved from https://www.smh.com.au/politics/federal/as-cities-grow-parts-of-regional-australia-disappear-and-get-angry-20190829-p52m26.html

Yang, Y., Kankanhalli, A., & Chandran, S. (2015). A stage model of information technology in healthcare. *Health and Technology*, *5*(1), 1–11. doi:10.100712553-015-0097-z

Yin, R. K. (2014). *Case Study Research: Design and Methods* (5th ed.). SAGE Publications.

Zenkteler, M., Darchen, S., Mateo-Babiano, I. & Baffour, B. (2019). Home-based work in cities: in search of an appropriate urban planning response. *Futures*. .futures.2019.102494 doi:10/1016/j

Zhu, P., & Mason, S. G. (2014). The impact of telecommuting on personal vehicle usage and environmental sustainability. *International Journal of Environmental Science and Technology*, *11*(8), 2185–2200. doi:10.100713762-014-0556-5

Zuboff, S. (1988). *In the Age of the Smart Machine: The Future of Work and Power*. Basic Books.

# About the Contributors

**Yvette Blount** is an Associate Professor at Macquarie University Business School and is a member of the Centre for Workforce Futures and the Optus Macquarie University Cyber Security Hub. Before her academic career, Dr. Blount worked in senior management and consulting roles relating to information systems in the banking and IT sectors. Dr. Blount's areas of expertise include anywhere working (telework, telecommuting), telehealth, cyber security governance, e-governance, the sharing economy, artificial intelligence effective utilisation of information and communication technology (ICT) including social media and utilisation of ICT in learning and teaching. Dr Blount's research program utilises multidisciplinary approaches to investigate how information systems are utilised to achieve organisational strategies and objectives. Dr Blount teaches information systems in the Master of Cybergovernance and Management including the subjects Blockchain for Competitive Advantage and Cyber governance, management, and ethics.

**Marianne Gloet** is a Research Associate in the Centre for Workplace Leadership at the University of Melbourne and an Associate Member of the Centre for Workforce Futures at Macquarie University. She is also a Lecturer in Business and Engineering at the University of Melbourne. Marianne has over 30 years of experience as an educator, researcher and senior academic manager in higher education institutions, including RMIT University (in Melbourne, Hong Kong and Kuala Lumpur), Higher Colleges of Technology, Abu Dhabi and the University of Melbourne. Marianne's PhD from The University of Melbourne examined the relationship between knowledge management and innovation performance in service sector organisations. Marianne consults widely for SMEs, as well as public and private sector organisations. She has lived and worked in Canada, the U.S., Malaysia, Singapore, the United Arab Emirates, Hong Kong and Vietnam. Along with Professor Danny Samson, Marianne co-authored Entrepreneurship and Innovation: Creating New Value (Oxford University Press, 2016) and Innovation: The New Imperative, a report on research conducted in conjunction with the Australian Institute of Management involving over 2,400 Australian managers.

* * *

**Emsie Arnoldi** coordinates the Entrepreneurial Edge Studio in the School of Media and Communication at Royal Melbourne Institute of Technology University (RMIT) in Melbourne, Australia. Her research interests include the future of work in a networked economy; resilience, expertise and shifting places and spaces of work, sustainable organizational and communication practices; the nexus between sustainable work practice and entrepreneurship; digitilization and the relationship between communication, health and wellbeing. She plays an active role in leading research, teaching, professional activities and policy development and has helped to establish RMIT as a Fair Trade organisation, highlighting her commitment to social responsibility and collaborative practice.

**Mike Berrell** is a Director of WADEmatheson Australia. Mike held professorial positions in universities in Australia and overseas. He was Professor of Work Organization at RMIT University and Professor of Management and Head of the Business School at James Cook University, both in Australia. Mike also served as Academic Director at the Higher Colleges of Technology in the United Arab Emirates. His research interests include Chinese business networks, international business, the influence of culture on the organization of work, international management and high performance organizations.

**Rachelle Bosua** received her PhD in 2008 from the University of Melbourne. She is an Asst. Professor at the Open University (OU) of The Netherlands and an Honorary Senior Fellow in Computing and Information Systems (CIS) School of the University of Melbourne. Her work at the Open University in the Information Science group focuses on a variety of aspects that relate to the adoption and use of IT in: regional SMEs, data-rich environments such as healthcare, startups. and scale-ups, work hubs, the Internet of Things and innovation and digitalsation. Her recent research concentrates on the multiple facets of individual privacy and the use of IT in the context of the European General Data Protection Regulation (GDPR). Rachelle is co-author of the 4th edition of the book: Knowledge Management in Organizations: a Critical Introduction (2018), Oxford University Press.

**Huch Ying Ch'ng** (PhD, International Communication, Macquarie University, 2008) has 20 years of research and teaching experience. She has researched across a diverse range of fields, e.g. on reporting of international news, music and identity of Malaysian youth, coworking hubs in Melbourne, and natural disaster emergency/ risk communication in Victoria. Her long-term research interests are in citizenship, culture, and the governance of identity. Her current research addresses representations of Australian migrants from East Asia, and issues of 'regional cultural literacy' for Australia in the Asia-Pacific region in the 21st century.

**Vanessa Cooper** is a Professor in Information Systems at RMIT University and co-leads the Digital Business, Work and Life research program within the Centre for People, Organisation and Work. Vanessa's research examines the impact of technology on organisations and complex contexts such as environmental sustainability, emergency management and the future of work. Vanessa's research has been published in leading academic journals and won multiple awards, including best paper awards at international conferences and from the Australian Computer Society.

**Cathy Greenfield** is Associate Professor of Communication, in the School of Media & Communication, RMIT University. Her research deals with the role of media in the government of populations, with journal articles across a range of topics such as populism, financialization, ecological sustainability, and political economic literacy, and most recently in How We Are Governed: Investigations of Communication, Media and Democracy (2014) and Media & the Government of Populations (2018). Current projects include: the Fact Check Research project with RMIT ABC Fact Check: and Talking Country, investigating use of media technologies to facilitate cross-cultural engagement between indigenous and non-Indigenous people.

**Jennifer Loy** is Professor of Additive Manufacturing Engineering at Deakin University in Geelong, Australia. Jennifer has a background in Industrial Design, with a specialisation in digital technologies. Her research interests are in design for additive manufacturing, with a particular focus on sustainability, and on design for health. Her work includes product design and development, workforce evolution and training and supply chain management.

**James Novak** is a research fellow in additive manufacturing (3D printing) at Deakin University, Australia. He has previously been a postdoctoral researcher in product design and design for additive manufacturing at the University of Technology Sydney, and a lecturer and course convener at Griffith University. James is an award-winning designer and researcher, winning the prestigious Dick Aubin Distinguished Paper Award at RAPID in 2015 for his 3D printed bicycle, which has also been exhibited around the world at venues including the Red Dot Design Museum in Germany. He is currently an Assistant Editor of the Computer-Aided Design and Applications Journal, and has previously been a guest writer for several 3D printing companies.

**Gabriele Taylor** is highly regarded expert practitioner within the aged and community sector and an early adopter of 'working anywhere'. During her two decades in the industry she has successfully delivered the exponential growth of national community services across multiple jurisdictions and states, has been instrumental in the achievement of an international award for excellence recognising the centralised operating model, and is a passionate driver of new models of care fit for purpose in the 21st century.

**Umut Tuğlu Karslı** is an Associate Professor and Head of the Department of Interior Architecture in the Faculty of Architecture at Istanbul University. Dr. Karslı is an architect and received her PhD from Mimar Sinan Fine Arts University in the field of Interior Architecture. She conducts interior architecture design studio courses and teaches spatial organization and sustainable design for both undergraduate and graduate students. Dr. Karslı is widely published in her area of expertise including interior architecture and sustainable design. Other research areas include user centered design, post-occupancy evaluation and adaptive reuse.

# Index

## D



## E



## F



## G



## H



## I



## L

## M



## N



## O



## P



## R



## S



## T



## W

www.ingramcontent.com/pod-product-compliance
Lightning Source LLC
LaVergne TN
LVHW081331300926
849161LV00008B/1942